P9-DDH-776

ORTHO'S COMPLETE GUIDE TO VEGETABLES

Created and Designed by
the Editorial Staff of Ortho Books

Author
Jacqueline Heriteau

Project Editor
Barbara Ferguson Stremple

ORTHO BOOKS

Publisher
Robert B. Loperena

Editorial Director
Christine L. Jordan

Editors
Robert J. Beckstrom
Michael D. Smith

Managing Editor
Sally W. Smith

Prepress Supervisor
Linda M. Bouchard

Sales & Marketing Manager
David C. José

Publisher's Assistant
Joni Christiansen

Graphics Coordinator
Sally J. French

Address inquiries to:
Meredith Corporation
Ortho Books
1716 Locust Street
Des Moines, IA 50309

Copyright © 1997 Monsanto Company

Some text, photography, and artwork copyright © 1997 Meredith Corporation

1	2	3	4	5	6	
97	98	99	2000	01		Softcover

1	2	3	4	5	6	
97	98	99	2000	01		Hardcover

ISBN 0-89721-514-9 Softcover
ISBN 0-89721-517-3 Hardcover
Library of Congress Catalog Card Number 96-67631

Editorial Coordinator
Cass Dempsey

Recipe Consultant
Barbara Moller

Recipe Copyeditor
Lynne Piade

Copyeditor
Elizabeth von Radics

Illustrator
Pamela J. Manley

Proofreader
Alice Mace Nakanishi

Indexer
Frances Bowles

Thanks to
Deborah Cowder
David Van Ness

Separations by
Color Tech Corp.

Printed in the USA by
Banta Book Group

Photographers
Names of photographers are followed by the page numbers on which their work appears.

All American Selections: 297B

Liz Ball: Photo/Nats: 78L

Gay Bumgarner: 90–91, 103

Karen Bussolini: 182–183, 206–207, 253B

Karen Bussolini/Positive Images: 47

Christi Carter: 58, 111, 116B, 150, 152, 189, 193, 216, 218, 219, 242, 252, 276, 299

Walter Chandoha 1996: 7, 8, 10, 22, 50, 93, 215

Wendy W. Cortesi: 77

Crandall & Crandall: 4–5, 33, 37T, 43T, 60, 74, 78R, 88, 114, 130, 133, 134, 247, 285

Deborah Crowell: Photo/Nats: 3CT, 104–105

R. Todd Davis Photography, Inc.: 122T, 162, 174

Alan & Linda Detrick: 148, 173

Wally Eberhart: Photo/Nats: 40, 45, 108, 262

Elemental Images: 156B

Thomas E. Eltzroth: 116T, 122B, 176, 196, 239

Derek Fell: 3T, 6, 15, 21, 30–31, 37B, 63, 72, 84, 89, 112, 113, 120, 125T, 127, 129, 159, 161, 165, 167, 168, 184, 187, 198, 202, 210, 213, 214, 222, 225, 227, 230, 232L, 232R, 236, 243, 245, 249, 251, 253T, 256, 265, 267, 279, 280, 282, 293, 301, 304

David Goldberg: 39, 92

Nelson Groffman: 248

Harry Haralambou/Positive Images: 67T, 274–275

Margaret Hensel/Positive Images: 234

Saxon Holt: 1, 11, 43B, 46, 53, 70, 82, 95

Jerry Howard/Positive Images: 9, 28, 34, 35, 52B, 67B, 87, 141, 147, 154, 194, 240–241, 302

Don Johnston: Photo/Nats: 56–57, 96

Dency Kane: 137, 158, 191, 209, 246, 260–261, 283, 288–289

D.J. Lambrecht: 3CB, 138–139

Susan M. Lammers: 25

Michael Landis: 19, 26, 55, 66T, 66B, 76, 224

Robert E. Lyons: Photo/Nats: 79, 205

Ivan Massar/Positive Images: 52T

Ortho Photo Library: 14, 24, 29, 54, 68, 106, 118, 144, 146, 257, 266, 286

Pam Peirce: 64T, 64B, 151, 156T, 211, 233, 270, 295, 297T

William Reasons: 296

Ann Reilly: Photo/Nats: 244, 284

Cheryl R. Richter: 220–221

Susan A. Roth: 20, 124, 142, 180, 200, 255, 258, 268, 272, 287

Richard Shiell: 121, 126, 164, 170, 177, 179, 290, 292

Pam Spaulding/Positive Images: 3B, 12–13, 228–229

Thompson & Morgan, Inc.: 264

Tom Tracy: 86

Virginia Twinam-Smith: Photo/Nats: 125B, 226

Lee Anne White/Positive Images: 16

CONTENTS

FLAVOR AND HEALTH

Tastier, more nutritious, handier—the freshly harvested vegetables from your own garden beat market vegetables in every aspect.

A beautiful garden, fabulous flavor, great nutrition, and the thrill of tremendous diversity at your command—this is your reward when you grow your own vegetables.

The flavor of just-picked produce is superior to any store-bought counterpart because it is so fresh. And fresh is better. An ear of just-harvested corn retains more nutrients than an ear that has been on a produce truck all night, or all week, busy converting its delicious fruit sugars to gluey starches. A fresh-picked, vine-ripened tomato has up to three times the vitamin C of a supermarket tomato, and the flavor is so rich and delicious it's hard to believe that the two are related.

A yard full of ambrosial vegetables encourages good nutrition. They are major sources of essential vitamins and minerals. As maturing vegetables approach the moment of best flavor, their vitamin and nutrient content also is peaking. Once vegetables are harvested, the enzymes that bring them to top flavor continue the process, and they begin to deteriorate. Eating the harvest at the peak of maturity means enjoying optimal nutritional content.

Vegetables and fruits are very high in fiber and generally low in calories. When they are irresistibly good, you will eat more of what is good for you.

Some harvested plants deteriorate more rapidly than others. In corn the change begins sooner and progresses more quickly than in apples or carrots. On the whole, root vegetables are stable over a longer period—something to keep in mind when deciding which vegetables to give garden space and which to buy at the market.

You will never be bored growing your own vegetables. Money cannot buy the diversity available to the gardener. Garden catalogs lure the chef with seeds of exotic plants that astonish the palate and delight the family. Harvest lemon cucumbers, golden pearl tomatoes, and other heirloom vegetables and fruits our forebears nurtured. Grow wondrously perfumed 'Galia' melons from Israel and pungent tat-soi greens. Harvest head lettuce and squash no bigger than your palm. Try for 600-pound pumpkins. Be tempted by white eggplant, purple and orange peppers, red potatoes, yellow watermelons, or golden beets. Serve radicchio, arugula, real *haricots verts,* and true *petits pois* without concern for the price.

Flavor your food with herbs so fragrant and beautiful your vegetable garden rivals the flower beds—opal basil, bronze fennel, pepperbox poppies, minty lavender buds, scent-leaved geraniums, and ferny dill.

WHERE TO BEGIN?

If you start with the "core" garden described on page 105—plants for the salad bowl and a few extras—you master growing your own food in easy steps. As garden and gardener mature, the vegetable plot becomes more satisfying and easier to maintain. The first year or two there are challenges. There is a lot to learn, but the food garden's seasonal chores soon become routine, and the cycles that rule the garden are endlessly entertaining. Each season is different from the last. Mistakes happen and become great learning experiences. The sun, the sky, and the earth work with you to gloss over the small things that go wrong. And you can count on unexpected success: Some plants grow and produce far better than you hoped. It is something that happens every year—and one reason gardeners become so dedicated. This is a pastime with rewards on every level.

HEALTH FOOD

Fresh fruits and vegetables are full of vitamins and minerals. The fruits and vegetables listed below are in order of highest to lowest content. The National Garden Bureau is the source of this summary.

Vitamin A, an antioxidant and immune system booster, is found in yellow-orange and dark green fruits and vegetables, such as carrots, spinach, red and green bell peppers, butternut squash, romaine lettuce, parsley, loose-leaf lettuces, and zucchini.

Vitamin B_6 metabolizes protein and is found in spinach, beans, cauliflower, broccoli, bell peppers, parsley, zucchini, tomatoes, summer squash, romaine lettuce, beans, and eggplant.

Vitamin C, an antioxidant said to strengthen the immune system and considered protection against cancer and cardiovascular disease, is present in red and green bell peppers, parsley, cauliflower, broccoli, cabbage, romaine lettuce, brussels sprouts, spinach, tomatoes, watermelon, and snap beans.

Vitamin E is an important antioxidant found in legumes such as peas, beans, and lentils, and some leafy greens.

Calcium, for strong bones and maintaining the pH balance of the blood, is found in parsley, broccoli, loose-leaf lettuces, snap beans, and cauliflower.

Iron, which carries oxygen to the cells, is found in parsley, spinach, butterhead lettuces, loose-leaf lettuces, garden peas, broccoli, snap beans, and tomatoes.

Magnesium, essential to the nervous system, is found in spinach, beet greens, broccoli, parsley, summer squash, cucumbers, snap beans, loose-leaf lettuces, tomatoes, and bell peppers.

Manganese, which metabolizes proteins and fats, is found in beans, peas, and lentils.

Potassium, which helps maintain fluid levels in the cells, is found in spinach, romaine lettuce, parsley, zucchini, radishes, loose-leaf lettuces, cauliflower, winter and summer squash, tomatoes, cucumbers, eggplant, snap beans, bell peppers, carrots, and broccoli.

Selenium, an antioxidant that protects the cells and strengthens immunity, is found in corn, legumes, and most vegetables grown in good soil.

Zinc, for DNA synthesis, cell division, growth, and healing, is found in spinach, parsley, romaine lettuce, summer squash, loose-leaf lettuces, and beans.

The time spent properly preparing the soil pays off in tasty, problem-free vegetables.

its late-winter slant to midsummer overhead high. Time will make clear to you which energy-hungry plants take poorly to the shade of a neighbor's suddenly huge hollyhocks and which plants benefit from the shade of a nearby evergreen. The unexpected presence of microclimates can fool you, but you can learn to take advantage of the potential they offer. The chapter starting on page 13 explains how to evaluate the light and choose the perfect site for your garden.

Learn to Prepare the Soil

The only plant sure to grow in poor, untilled soil is a weed. The chapter starting on page 31 describes several ways to prepare the soil for a vegetable garden. Good soil is essential. Double-digging and mixing in well-rotted manure was once considered the only way to properly prepare soil. Double-digging is hard work, but it is a first-rate approach to starting a garden. Now there are other acceptable ways to begin. One popular method is creating a raised bed. This, too, takes some work, but the yields are very rewarding.

Whatever approach you choose to starting your garden, the good news is that once you take the trouble to get the soil in top condition, you will have more vegetables and fewer problems. Healthy plants are less susceptible to pests and diseases. Sowing seeds in properly prepared soil with the rich, clean earth smell in your nostrils and a little sun on your back is a joy—and the harvests are spectacular.

Ins and Outs of Watering

The chapter beginning on page 31 also describes watering techniques. To thrive, food plants need constant moisture. A thick mulch and a network of soaker hoses saves hours of wasteful overhead watering.

A SEASONAL OVERVIEW

Growing leafy greens, vegetables, and herbs for the salad bar and the grill, and a few extras for winter storage, is easier than maintaining a flower bed of comparable size. Here is an overview of the steps detailed in the following chapters.

Study Light and Site

To yield luscious crops of vegetables and sweet fruits, plants need lots of sunlight. After the first few seasons, you come to know just how the sun moves around the landscape from

When you first install the garden, devise a practical system for watering. You also need to allow for the fact that your annual trip to the mountains or the shore invariably coincides with the hottest, driest week in the garden.

Planting the Garden

The chapter entitled Seeds and Seasons, starting on page 57, takes you from seed catalogs and garden centers to harvesting and storing produce. First, use catalogs to familiarize yourself with the way the various vegetables perform. Without that knowledge, you cannot make an efficient planting plan. Each garden year begins with a love/hate investigation of the seed catalogs that arrive in December and January—love, because what they offer is irresistibly presented; hate, because no planting plan ever seems big enough to accommodate the appetite the catalogs inspire. Indulge all of your whims, and the garden will run away with your life.

When you choose seeds, you need to know if they can be sown in the open garden, or if they must be set out as seedlings. The farther north you are, the shorter the growing season. In frost-belt gardens, most vegetables need a jump on the season to mature before fall. Sow these seeds indoors in sunny windows or under grow lights and set them out as soon as the soil warms; or buy vegetable seedlings from garden centers.

To stake or not to stake? The answer affects your choice of seeds and cultivars. Do you want to put in the time and effort for vegetables that need staking? Peas, shell beans, and tomatoes are among the popular vegetables that are healthier and more productive given some support. With tomatoes, you can choose the laissez-faire approach by setting out many plants and letting them

sprawl. It may not be tidy, but it works fairly well. Aesthetics have a role in your decision, too.

Extending the Seasons

Extend your harvest with early-bird planting in spring and by providing fall and winter protection for late crops. The chapter beginning on page 57 teaches head-start tricks and techniques for lengthening the growing season, from cold frames and hotbeds to grow lights and plant protectors.

The Seeds and Seasons chapter also delves into the mysteries of

Watering can be done by hand, as here, or with a variety of time-saving tools and systems.

Protecting plants even slightly from cold weather can extend your gardening season from weeks earlier in the spring to weeks later in the fall.

harvesting—what must be harvested at once, and what can stay in the row until you have more time. The need to keep midseason crops such as snap beans harvested as they mature can conflict with vacation plans. Once some plants start to produce, they must be harvested or they stop producing. Zucchini and snap beans have a way of "coming in" (peaking in productivity) just when the beach beckons. The coincidence of crop readiness and vacation time is something you need to consider when devising your planting plan.

Preserving surplus produce can be a wonderfully satisfying experience. But as you study the seed catalogs, be sure to consider just how many tomatoes and snap beans you really want to harvest and freeze, can, or dry.

Help!

The chapter beginning on page 91 offers solutions to the most common challenges a gardener encounters—particularly weeds and pests. For extra-tough problems, find help at the cooperative extension office at the local state university. Some states now have a central phone number for specialists at the county level. But chatting with a neighbor who grows a great vegetable garden is often the best source of information. Garden centers and nurseries also have professionals who understand the local soil and what it needs to be productive. They know the climate and the microclimates likely to occur in your area.

Take all advice for consideration—and with a grain of salt. Let your garden do some of the talking.

Growth is never routine. No two seasons are exactly alike, and the plants rarely replicate past performances. A gardener's best friend is a thoughtful garden log kept faithfully year after year.

PLAN FOR SUCCESS

Start small. This is so important it is the philosophy upon which the organization of this book is based. Be successful with a small, core garden (beginning on page 105). Learn what you are doing and how light, site, watering, and climate affect your garden. Then expand by gradually adding one or two of the vegetables from each of the groups discussed in the "vegetable chapters" (beginning on page 139). Any experienced gardener will tell you that a well-cared-for small garden yields more produce and gives far more satisfaction than a big garden for which you have neither the time nor the energy. Learning first to handle a small garden equips you to handle a large garden later with ease and confidence.

GIVING BACK TO THE LAND

Contribute to the ecological cycle that sustains your garden by giving back to the soil as much as you take from it. One way to do this is to compost and return to the soil all the wholesome organic debris the yard produces—finished food plants, fallen leaves, wood ashes, weeds, and grass clippings. The chapter, Soil and Water, pages 38 to 40, shows how easy this is to do. Composting allows you to take part in the magical cycle of the seasons from sowing, cultivating, harvesting, storing, and, finally, to replenishing.

Growing your own food is a special kind of pleasure. The flavor is

fantastic; the nutrition is tops. But even more rewarding is the satisfaction you feel as you amble out at dusk to gather fruits, vegetables, and herbs that you planned for, planted, and nurtured from vulnerable seedling to sturdy maturity. Bringing a food garden into being binds us to earlier ways and people and imparts a grand sense of wholeness with the earth.

Nothing improves garden soil quite as much as incorporating compost. Compost loosens sticky soil, helps sandy soil hold water, provides plant nutrients over a sustained period, and generally improves all soils.

LIGHT AND SITE

Good design makes a garden easier to care for as well as more attractive. This beautiful vegetable garden is on the estate of English garden writer Rosemary Verey. Paved paths avoid muddy feet and help avoid weeding. The tidy beds make working there a pleasure. And, as one would expect of Verey's garden, the color and texture harmonies lend beauty to the whole.

Success with vegetables depends on a few basic rules. This chapter answers questions about where to locate the garden and how to prepare the soil for planting. When the site is right and the soil is in good condition, seeds sprout quickly, transplanted seedlings take hold readily, and the plants survive bad weather. A well-thought-out, well-prepared garden produces more and needs a lot less care than a garden planted without a plan. Stocky plants that are growing sturdily have rich green foliage and produce bountiful harvests. And a healthy garden survives the occasional attack by pests or disease.

Decide first how big the garden is going to be. As the previous chapter emphasized, it is smart to start small. Depending on the site, you can enlarge the garden as you become successful and find that you want to devote more time and space to growing vegetables. Size and layout are decisions you make as you look over the property and choose the site. Realistically consider how much time you can devote to the garden. How much produce do you really want to grow? And how much sunny space do you have?

A really big garden is 50 by 100 feet. It provides plenty of core-garden vegetables, herbs, melons, strawberries, asparagus, artichokes, and rhubarb for six people, with considerable produce left over for freezing and storing. A garden 40 by 60 feet is still big and provides amply for a family of four, with some extra for freezing.

The largest size recommended for a first vegetable garden is 25 by 25 feet—625 square feet overall. With careful planning it can keep four people supplied with loads of salad makings, herbs, vegetables, and some special treats, such as bok choy and strawberries.

But a raised bed 5 feet by 5 feet with just tomatoes, peppers, parsley, basil, and lettuce is also a fine way to get started. The happiest approach is to start small and expand a bit each year.

WHERE TO PLACE THE GARDEN

Food plants grow in almost any space, almost anywhere there is lots of sun. Plant vegetables in the patch of soil by the kitchen door, in a raised bed, or with annuals in a flower bed. Grow vegetables and fruits in big planters, tubs, or window boxes on the roof, patio,

or balcony. Grow a movable feast—cucumbers twining the mailbox one year, climbing a drainage pipe the next. Compensate for poor soil, lack of water, and too much water by growing plants in containers. Small cultivars of fruit trees and vegetables developed for limited spaces flourish in pails, planters, pots, and even shipping crates. Move the containers to take advantage of changing light or just for the fun of altering the view.

Finding the Light

What you absolutely must have for a thriving food garden is lots of sunlight. In looking over potential sites, light is the first consideration. Only a mushroom grows in the dark. Second to light is the need for proper drainage. Only swamp plants thrive in wet soil. Ample light and good drainage are not simply recommendations—they are a must for success.

All leafy green plants make their own food in a process that uses light and chlorophyll, the substance that makes plants green. The process is called photosynthesis, and light is the energy that allows it to take place. Plants grow for some time in less light than they need, but at the expense of food stored in their tissues. Lack of light causes weak growth and spindly plants.

Most food plants need full sunlight, which means a daily dose of at least six hours of direct sun—eight is better in northern gardens. In warm regions a garden plot whose sun exposure is primarily in the cooler hours of early- and mid-morning is more desirable than a site that bakes under high heat later in the day. Such direct late-afternoon sun adds to the heat built up during the day. In very hot regions, it may be necessary to provide some screening in the afternoon for certain plants.

This urban garden is on the shady side of the house. The gardener has determined by trial and error just how far to extend the garden along the north side of the house.

To every rule, of course, there are exceptions. Some of the herbs, basil for instance, can do with a little less-direct light. The chapter entitled Herbs for the Chef (starting on page 139) suggests others. Leafy lettuces, snap beans, broccoli, and cabbage can endure more shade than tomatoes, corn, cucumbers, melons, and potatoes and other root crops.

The selection of a site in a big suburban or country landscape is a matter of aesthetics. Where there are no obstructions, there is direct sun. Where sun-loving flowers and shrubs—roses, hollyhocks, mums, and yarrow—are thriving, food plants also prosper.

But when you garden in a small urban yard, or on a patio, deck, or balcony, finding the spot with the most access to direct light takes more thought. You can count on summer sun being high overhead at midday. But early and late in the day when it is lower on the horizon, light may be blocked by shade trees, shrubs, or walls. In the first and last growing weeks of the season—early spring and late summer or early fall—the position of the sun is low and can be blocked anytime of day by hedges, low walls, and evergreens.

Though six or more hours of direct sun is the general rule, you will find vegetables thriving in what at first glance seems much less. They are basking in reflected light. Reflected light can greatly increase the potential of an area that

You can have a container vegetable garden anyplace. If you do not have good soil or enough light, grow your vegetables in containers alongside a driveway, or on a balcony or a windowsill.

A sloping site has advantages even over level ground. Although it took some effort to put in, this terraced garden is charming and convenient to garden.

seems too shaded for food plants. The usual sources of reflected light are white and pale-colored walls and expanses of glass and water. You can create reflected light by whitewashing a wall or fence.

Finding the Site

How the food garden looks from the patio, porch, or your favorite upstairs window is significant. You must enjoy the garden, if only for practical reasons. If you enjoy your garden, you pay attention to it and it thrives. If the site is ugly, it is easy to neglect, and it suffers and just gets uglier. Position your food plants as carefully as you do your flowers. Be sure they enhance the landscape. A big rectangle of vegetables in the middle of the backyard is not necessarily gorgeous, but there are ways to lay it out that make it attractive.

Here are some practical considerations when choosing a site.

■ Look for ground that is relatively level, because it is easier to work. Gentle slopes are good because the soil drains well. Also, where there are strong drying winds, or cold winds that add to the chill factor, a gentle slope away from the wind may be the ideal site. In the north, farmers plant the fruit trees and the kitchen garden on a sun-warmed south-facing slope.

▮ Soil erodes on steep slopes, but a steep slope is advantageous if it is terraced. Be wary of low spots at the bottom of a steep slope—water may collect and stay. Cold air and frost also settle in depressions early and late in the growing season and can damage frost-tender plants. A low spot is not the choice site for early-early seedlings, nor for heat-loving plants.

▮ Breezy areas can improve pollination and keep insects from settling. Airless corners are bad. In pockets of dead air, pests and diseases thrive.

▮ Do not plant near big ornamental perennials, tree roots, or large shrubs. They rob the soil of moisture and nutrients and cut down on air flow.

▮ Locate the vegetable garden within reach of the water supply.

▮ If you live in a wooded area, put as much distance as you can between your food plants and the hunger pangs of furry critters.

▮ If your landscape has hot and cold spots, choose cold-season and warm-season plants suited to each. These are discussed on page 65.

Checking the Drainage

Drainage is important because, like us, roots need oxygen. The fine, hairlike threads growing from a plant's roots draw carbon, hydrogen, and oxygen from the soil. In soggy soil, oxygen is not available and the plants literally drown.

When choosing a garden site, study the levels of the yard. Ideally, the land should drop away from the house at the rate of about 4 inches every 10 feet. On flatter grades, water may stand; on steeper grades, it may run off precipitously. A little regrading can do wonders for your views of the landscape. Major regrading work requires professional equipment, but a shovel and a strong back can solve most of the problems likely to be present in the average home landscape.

In new housing developments, the preparatory earth-moving often leaves depressions that turn to wet pockets in rainy weather. Regular flooding from poorly contoured terrain, yours or a neighbor's, can make soil soggy. The presence of moss is a clue that there is inadequate drainage, even when the problem is not otherwise obvious.

Spots that remain wet only at certain times of year—with spring thaw, for instance, and after big storms—need help. When water stands for more than an hour or two, and the ground remains soft and soggy long after a storm, plants may have problems. Digging a drainage trench and lining it with gravel is one solution. If the wet spot is lower than the level of the surrounding land, the problem may disappear if you raise the level of the vegetable bed to the height of the grade. Installing a raised bed also improves drainage.

Resolve wet spots created by runoff from your own property, or a neighbor's, by building a berm that reroutes the water coming into the garden area. A berm is a low, grassy mound that acts as a barrier. The berm heads the water in another direction so you can fill the wet spot and improve the soil with sand and humus before you plant.

Drain large swampy areas by creating a trench wide enough to accept clay or composition drainage tiles. Slant the trench so the water runs downhill to a storm sewer, creek, dry well, or some other suitable low point, but never direct drainage onto someone else's property. Fill the trench with gravel and top that with leaves if you want it to look more natural. But do not fill the trench with soil or sand.

TYPES OF GARDENS

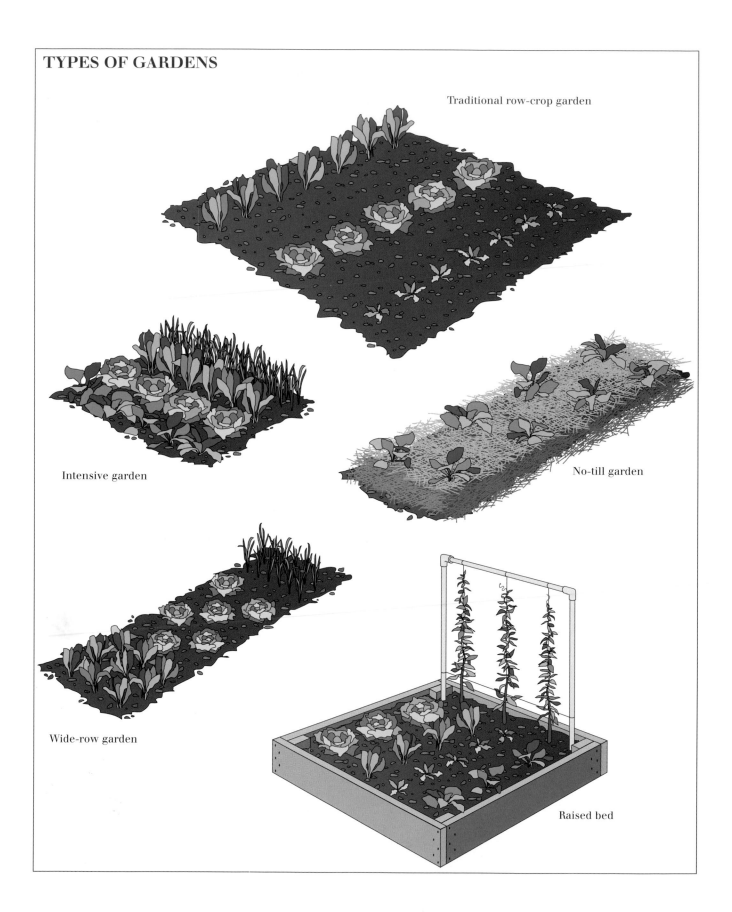

Traditional row-crop garden

Intensive garden

No-till garden

Wide-row garden

Raised bed

WHAT TYPE OF GARDEN?

Once you have a site in mind, you must decide what the garden should look like. Close your eyes and visualize the garden of your dreams. The image has to give you real pleasure. Do you picture a trim and tidy Victorian row garden with scarecrows to fend off the birds? A plot with wide rows and wild combinations of vegetables, herbs, fruits, and flowers? Garden beds for food plants can take any form. You can have container gardens, vertical gardens, or in-ground, island, or raised beds.

There are as many approaches to laying out and preparing a food garden as there are gardeners. But keep in mind that the crops reflect the condition of the soil. Lay out the beds so that you do not pack the earth by stomping around where the plants are growing. Create beds you can reach from both sides. A vegetable row worked from both sides can be twice as wide as a bed accessible from only one side.

Traditional Row-Crop Garden

The traditional layout for a food garden is a rectangle divided by parallel rows of planting beds with wide paths between them. The term for this design is *row-crop gardening*. There is a satisfying, unpretentious beauty in a well-kept, well-ordered vegetable plot laid out this way.

Intensive Garden

You can maximize the productivity of the garden using intensive-gardening techniques. Three ways to garden intensively are spacing plants closely together, intercropping, and succession cropping.

Single-row gardens have a lot of room to work around the plants—but a lot of room for weeds to grow, too. This type of garden evolved at a time when weeds were controlled by cultivating with a horse or tractor.

Intercropping makes the most use of limited space by planting several crops in the same bed. In this garden, the scallions are being harvested now. Parsley will be snipped for a few more weeks, when it will be crowded to the side by the lettuce. As the lettuce is harvested, the parsley will expand to fill the gaps. The plants outside the bed are boxwood, which will be an enclosing border next year.

An intensive garden is possible in part because, with a few exceptions (among them strawberries, asparagus, artichokes, and most herbs), the food plants are annuals. You sow the seeds, harvest the plants, and finally rip out the roots, often leaving space and time for one or two more crops in the same season.

Intercropping Intercropping pairs, or couples, fast- with slow-growing crops in the same row. As the first crop matures and is harvested, space becomes available for the second crop which is beginning to fill out. The combinations of vegetables are almost infinite; any small, fast-growing vegetable can be intercropped with almost any slow-growing larger one.

One pair that go well together are radishes and carrots: The radishes are ready in three to four weeks, just as the carrots begin to fill out. The carrots remain in the row 90 days before they're ready to pull. Sow lettuce among rows of almost any larger plant, beans for instance. As the final lettuces are harvested, the beans begin to take over the space. Pair onion sets with any long-standing plant, and pull for use as green onions to make way for the later crop.

Succession Planting In this approach the soil is never without a crop. As soon as one crop, or a portion of a crop, is harvested, another is sown. For instance, as you harvest radishes planted in early spring, sow the empty spaces with squash or beans. Follow the peas you plant in early spring with spinach, a quick cool-season crop. A typical succession begins with radishes and lettuce, then snap beans, and finally winter carrots.

In another form of succession planting, sow seeds in small successive waves planned to produce a season-long harvest of a single type of vegetable. You plant the second batch before you harvest the first, and the third before you harvest the second. Follow a small March sowing of cold-hardy lettuce with a second set of lettuce seeds as space opens up from harvesting the first crop. Sow yet another group of seeds as the second crop finishes. For a small family, this is a wise approach. One long row of lettuces maturing all at the same time is more than most families can consume.

No-Till Garden

The late garden author Ruth Stout had another way of preparing a permanent bed. Her aim was a no-till garden with year-round mulch. Stout avoided cultivating the soil. One of her systems is to cover the garden area with a layer of compost 3 to 4 inches deep. Sow the seeds on top and mulch lightly. The nutrients in the compost seep down into the soil beneath, and the plant roots and earthworms work the soil and improve it. Mulch the plants as they grow to replenish the compost.

Another no-till approach is to put the compost beneath the soil. Make a compost pile 3 to 4 feet high and 4 to 5 feet square on top of the sod. Strip the soil all around the pile to make a path 2 feet wide and 2 to 4 inches deep. Throw the soil from the path on top of the compost bed to make a layer 2 to 4 inches deep. Wait a few weeks for the heat in the compost pile to subside, then plant in the soil on top. The roots grow right into the compost, and if ever you have had something green sprout on a compost pile, you know it thrives.

Wide-Row Garden

Much in favor now is the wide-row garden, designed more for beauty than practicality. This type of garden is laid out so the planting rows are twice as wide as the paths between them. The bed can be rectangular with parallel planting rows and paths, or it can be laid out in curves. Curved paths seem to disappear in the rows of corn, tomatoes, or sunflowers. Paved with bricks, flagstones, gravel, wood pavers, or whatever suits the landscape, the path lends the wide-row vegetable patch the charm of an ornamental garden.

If you let your imagination run wild, you will come up with all kinds of adaptations. For instance, the path can appear to end in a trellised arch supporting grape vines, gourds, or baby pumpkins. Along the way add a birdbath—or a little in-ground fountain to keep the air moist and fresh. Whatever fantasy dictates is fine as long as it contributes to the success of the plants.

Wide-row planting relies on close plant spacing for its abundant harvests. Sow the seeds closely so that mature foliage shades the earth. In effect, you are sowing a living mulch to cool the soil, preserve water, and rob weeds of sunlight. Whereas the row-crop garden uses about 30 percent of the garden for crops, wide-row planting with intensive cropping uses about 70 to 80 percent. To implement this design, seeds are spaced more closely than seed packets or the vegetable chapters suggest. Sow the seeds in conventional rows, in a triangular or staggered pattern, or in swirls or circles, grouped to create contrast in colors, textures, and forms.

Creasy's Wide-Row Garden

The grand master of the flowering food garden is California author and landscape designer Rosalind Creasy. Her books, *The Complete Book of Edible Landscaping* and *Cooking for the Garden,* are best-sellers. Creasy plants in wide rows, and with unbridled imagination has shown us that food plants make practical companions for flowering annuals. She proves that a food garden can be extravagant fun. She planted her first food garden in her front yard in Sunnyvale, California. She made it so beautiful and exciting that, instead of complaining, her neighbors copied her. She now creates a new theme garden every year. Knowing what she dares to do will inspire you.

In honor of the United States Centennial, for example, Creasy designed her garden with a U.S., Mexican, and South American theme. It celebrated the arrival of Columbus to the New World with new-world plants. On either side of a deep blue arbor shading the front walk, there were chiles, beans, corn, tomatoes, and squash growing with dahlias, cosmos, salvias, nasturtiums, morning glories, Peruvian lilies, bougainvillea, and cannas.

Her first purchase for the next year's garden was a child's tea set, one of the props for an *Alice in Wonderland* vegetable and flower garden. She included a white rosebush with red roses grafted onto it. Her daughter-in-law made soft sculptures for the garden—the Queen of Hearts and a playing card with a painted face.

FOOD AND FLOWER COMBINATIONS

Here are some delightful food and flower combinations inspired by gardener Rosalind Creasy.

■ Bush beans backed by tall red zinnias, ruby chard, and coreopsis.

■ Eggplant and purple alyssum, purple basil, and lavender petunias.

■ Carrots interplanted with low-spreading 'Gem' series marigolds.

■ Mix different lettuce colors and interplant them with Iceland poppies; back them with white stock or orange and yellow calendulas.

■ Sweet bell peppers with small, yellow marigolds.

■ White Swiss chard with red and orange cosmos and red Swiss chard, fronted by nasturtiums, or 'Thumbelina' or 'Peter Pan' dwarf zinnias.

■ Summer squash with tall marigolds and blue salvia—white petunias in front.

■ Tomatoes backed by tall cleome, hollyhocks in salmon, pink, and white—and in front, red geraniums and multiflora petunias to match.

Although you may not be ready to go this far with garden design, a real vegetable patch does not have to be a sea of green. Just a few well-placed, brilliantly colored annual flowers and flowering herbs can make it exciting and beautiful. Plunk the flowers up front where they make the greatest show.

Start in the Flower Beds   There is another way to combine flowers and food plants. You can try your hand at food gardening by planting a few vegetables in your flower beds. Edge perennials with tiny wild strawberries—their crinkled foliage and bright berries are delightful, and the tiny, grainy fruit is delicious. All the herbs you need will thrive in a sunny flowering

Some vegetables are beautiful enough to be grown as ornamentals. These flowering garlic chives are attractive in this flower bed, and still available to be snipped for a salad.

border. Most of the herbs are perennials, and many have colorful foliage—blue borage, tricolor sage, and silver-green lavender, for instance. In late summer the mints put up fuzzy flower heads that add the marvelous dimension of fragrance to bouquets. A window box filled with bright red or hot pink geraniums is beautifully set off with the addition of a few herbs.

Leafy vegetables such as fennel and bold, handsome, red-stemmed chard can set off many of the perennial flowers. But think twice before crowding these and other vegetables next to trees and shrubs that can block the sun. The fast-

growing annual vegetables (which make up the bulk of a food garden) need sustained moisture, sunlight, and nutrients. They do not compete well with the roots of trees and shrubs. They are safest combined with annual flowers. Some small cultivars of cherry tomatoes look great anywhere and even produce fruit when hanging from baskets in a container garden. Peppers look wonderful with everything—both the chunky sweet 'Bell' types and the hot chiles that color so beautifully in late summer and early fall.

Raised Bed

A raised bed is the organic gardener's ideal: optimum soil, intensive cropping, and abundant harvests. What's important is not how the beds are laid out or designed, but how they are built. Any permanent garden, large or small, can be set up using the raised-bed technique. The method is just as popular for flower gardens as it is for food gardens. Among the advantages of this type of bed is that the soil dries out and warms more quickly in early spring, which allows you to plant sooner—a desirable feature especially in the frost belt. The crops usually are planted in wide-row fashion (see page 22).

First remove the sod and double-dig the subsoil (see page 48). Next pile on a growing medium that raises the level 4 to 15 inches above the original ground level; 4 inches if the original soil and drainage are good, more if they are not. The material you add can be high-quality topsoil or compost. Topsoil from a nursery must be weed free and purchased from a source that backs its claims. Bad soil is no bargain— it's a disaster. Less expensive is a homemade artificial soil mix suited to container gardens. A suitable growing medium can be put to-

gether from any of the recipes on page 36.

Raised beds are laid out as islands, narrow enough so you can reach the center from either side without stepping onto the soil.

When the soil is prepared, flatten the top of the bed, making it slightly concave so the rain will not run off. If the bed is freestanding, mulch the sides. If the bed is framed, however, it looks better, is easier to work, and less soil is lost to erosion. The frame can be an elaborate stone wall or constructed of simple concrete block, 2×2 lumber, or railroad ties. All are effective and reasonably attractive. Avoid new railroad ties treated with fresh creosote, which is not good for the soil. Red cedar and pressure-treated wood make the most long-lasting frames. If you use pressure-treated wood, discard the sawdust, do not use the scraps for firewood, and wear gloves and a mask when working with it. Although pressure-treated wood is bad for you, it will not harm the soil. A framed bed topped by a sill wide enough to sit on makes gardening more leisurely.

Kitchen Garden

Before the age of supermarkets, when many fruits and vegetables came fresh from the yard, the garden was just a short distance from the farmhouse, and the paths were wide enough to accommodate a small tractor. Flowers were impractical, so the garden was filled almost exclusively with produce for the kitchen. Hence the name *kitchen garden*. In the northeastern United States, *kitchen garden* still refers to any garden where vegetables are grown.

Urbanized and used to buying our produce from a grocer, we use the term *kitchen garden* to describe a patch of edibles, mostly herbs

and salad makings, growing by the kitchen door. It is one of life's simple pleasures to dash down the steps to pick a few sprigs of parsley or some baby cucumbers for the salad bowl.

The herbs most often grown in today's kitchen garden are a dozen or so that add to the chef's repertoire. These are low growing and look good with flowers, if you choose to combine the two. There is no standard size; you can fit a kitchen garden into an existing flower bed, a window box, or a patio planter.

Three of the most versatile herbs—parsley, summer sage, and

This kitchen garden gives easy access to chives or greens for salads, just outside the kitchen door.

thyme—make pretty little clumps that complement any planting; they can even serve as edging. The fresh green of the basils, large or small, is beautiful in a mixed-flower border, as is the big, colorful 'Purple Ruffles' basil. Mint smells marvelous as you brush against it or crush it underfoot, and it is making its way into American recipes through interest in Middle Eastern cuisine. Watching with anticipation as the seeds sprout in the window box and spinach, arugula, 'Easter

Many vegetables, including tomatoes, can be grown on a trellis or fence to save space.

Egg' radishes, and bright hot peppers mature in the yard is satisfying to both the gardener and the chef in you.

Small-Space Garden

If space is limited, solving the problem takes only your imagination. With sun, moisture, and 8 to 18 inches of prepared soil, any plant will grow. Start by selecting plants that are especially compact or that can be trellised. Add to this approach intercropping and successive planting and you double and triple your harvests from even a very small space.

Vertical Garden   Where there is little space to grow out, grow *up*. Many vegetables and some fruits grow just as well vertically as horizontally. Some grow better. Squash, eggplant, cucumbers, some strawberry cultivars, pole beans, and especially the beautiful scarlet runner bean—all climb fences. There are 150 square feet of climbing room on the surface of a 5-foot by 30-foot fence. Tomatoes do well tied to a sunny lattice. Espaliered fruit trees look very handsome (and ripen earlier) against warm masonry walls.

Dwarf and Miniature Cultivars
Where space is limited, you can also make your harvests more varied by planting a lot of dwarf and miniature cultivars instead of a few standard sizes. Dwarf vegetables, such as miniature lettuces, do well in 4- to 6-inch-deep flats or pots. Smaller tomato plants thrive in just 12 inches of well-drained soil, and the container can be a pail, a plastic-lined bushel basket, or even a sturdy garbage bag.

Small root vegetables grow almost anywhere. Harvest the pretty, gourmet 'Little Ball' beets when they are 1½ inches around. 'Planet' is a round, space-saving carrot just

VERTICAL GARDEN ON WHEELS

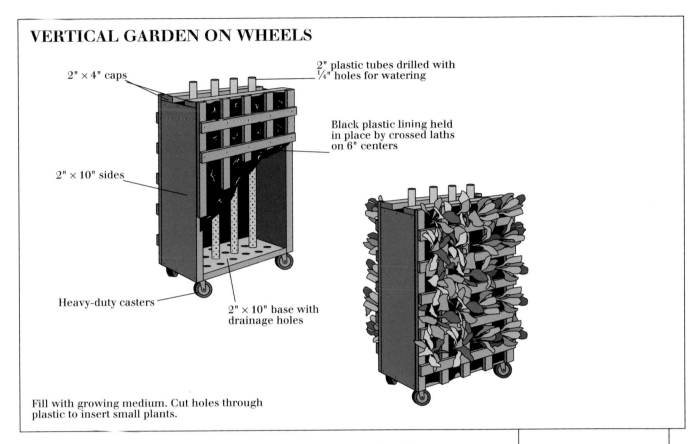

2" × 4" caps

2" plastic tubes drilled with ¼" holes for watering

Black plastic lining held in place by crossed laths on 6" centers

2" × 10" sides

Heavy-duty casters

2" × 10" base with drainage holes

Fill with growing medium. Cut holes through plastic to insert small plants.

a few inches long. A 3- to 4-foot circle of sun is all the miniature melons require. Baby watermelons and red and yellow grapefruit-sized cantaloupes such as 'Minnesota Midget' ripen early and are very sweet. 'Minicole' cabbages prosper in a 10-square-inch space. Some small zucchini and butternut squash plants need just 4 feet of space to flourish. Tiny pumpkins, miniature eggplants, 'Burpee's Tumbler Hybrid' tomato, and the miniature patty pan squash 'Peter Pan' are a few of the many cultivars that produce from hanging baskets.

Dwarf and semidwarf cultivars of apples, pears, and other fruits are perfect for small gardens and are so successful that many are now being used in commercial orchards. They are easy to both maintain and harvest.

Community Garden

If your landscape does not offer enough sunny space for vegetables, borrow an idea from the Victorians. In the late 1800s and early 1900s, townsfolk rented garden spaces beyond the city limits. Here they built gazebos, brought picnic lunches, and made Sunday gardening a family outing. That principle has been recaptured as the modern community garden.

A community garden is a great social project for neighborhoods. Many have been established in vacant city lots. An already functioning community garden has garden plots and water sources to offer. The vegetable beds in most community gardens are practical row-crop installations, intensely cropped.

If you find yourself organizing a community garden, be sure that

Community gardens make it possible to have a vegetable garden even if you live in an apartment or condominium.

everyone involved knows that to be successful you have to follow healthy garden practices. Be sure there is a reliable water source before you get started. And get as much information as possible from the organizers of already established community gardens in the area.

Container Garden

Where there is plenty of light but no soil, grow food plants in containers. Plants thrive in pots on rooftops, balconies, decks, paved driveways, and other nontraditional locations. The plants that do well in limited spaces are the same ones that thrive in containers. 'Salad

Bush' cucumber grows beautifully in a pot. Baby lettuces such as 'Mini Green' fit easily in window boxes.

The critical factors for successful container gardening are sufficient sun and soil deep enough to sustain moisture and accommodate roots. Otherwise, containers can be any size and made from just about any material. The shallower the container, however, the more often you need to water and fertilize. A 4-foot by 8-inch by 12-inch planter on a balcony in midsummer needs water at least once a day, twice a day if it is windy as well as hot. A dwarf apple tree growing on the same balcony in a tub 20 inches deep by 16 inches square needs watering only once or twice a week.

Planters, tubs, and pots suitable for vegetables and some fruits come in all shapes and sizes. Be sure that any container you choose allows for drainage. Without proper drainage, excess water is trapped at the bottom of the container, causing roots to rot because of lack of oxygen. Self-watering, double-walled containers that solve this problem are available at garden centers.

Wood planters are attractive, and if you are handy with a hammer they are not difficult to construct. Redwood is a lasting and naturally beautiful material for planters. Although it is expensive, tubs and planters made of redwood remain in fine condition for years. Planters of inexpensive wood or plywood often rot in one or two seasons; the combination of damp soil, frequent watering, and everyday weather takes its toll.

Plastic containers work well and are becoming more attractive as manufacturers imitate more-traditional materials. They are ideal for balconies and roofs because they are lightweight and durable, and the soil inside does not dry out as quickly as soil in clay pots. Clay containers are porous, which allows for beneficial air exchange, but this also allows them to dry out quickly, and they are easily chipped, broken, and discolored. But so long as they have drainage holes, both clay and plastic planters make fine containers for vegetable and fruit plants.

It is unnecessary to cover drainage holes with gravel or shards of pots. The drainage is not improved and the gravel blocks the holes. A layer of paper towel or newspaper over the holes effectively prevents soil from washing out. But if the container is very deep and you wish to save on soil, fill the bottom with gravel, rocks, or even foam packing "peanuts." When a container rests on a rooftop, use foam peanuts for lightweight fill, and be sure the pot is raised 2 to 3 inches above the surface. A wet or very heavy planter can damage a roof.

Synthetic growing media are ideal for containers because they are lightweight. Heavy planters can cause structural damage to rooftops, balconies, decks, and patios. If you mix your own growing medium, you can control the weight, fertility, moisture retention, and quality of drainage. Recipes for first-rate soil mixes are offered on page 36.

Perennials growing in planters are more susceptible to heat, cold, and drought than plants growing in the open garden. In Zones 6 and 7 and colder regions, perennial food plants such as asparagus and artichokes need containers at least 14 to 16 inches square, or the soil may freeze. In colder zones, increase the size.

These strawberry planters make perfect containers for some lettuces and a few herbs.

SOIL AND WATER

Soil is the foundation of a good garden. The time spent understanding and improving it will pay off handsomely as vegetables thrive. Here, new raised beds are being formed for a fall crop.

Go out to your garden site and gather a handful of dirt. Inhale its aroma, crumble it between your fingers, and let it sift away in the breeze. Gather another handful and rub it away between your palms. This is the foundation upon which your garden is built, the reservoir for the garden's lifeblood—water— and the medium in which nutrients are dissolved. It is your new partner in a great adventure. Learn to know it, understand it, and enjoy it.

Good garden soil resembles chocolate cake—it is moist, crumbly, soft, and dark. How closely your soil approaches this ideal depends on several things, most of which are under your control but which take some time and effort on your part. Some of the part that is *not* under your control is the soil texture—that is, the size of the particles that make up its mineral component. The finer these particles, the more water and the less air the soil will hold. If these particles are large, the soil won't hold much water but will be very well aerated; if small, it will retain lots of water but will be poorly aerated.

In addition to minerals, the components of soil are air, water, and organic material. This last element is the one that you can control most easily. In general, the best thing you can do for your soil—and the plants it supports and feeds—is to feed it organic material. This can be compost, manure, leaf mold, or many other forms. All organic material decomposes in the soil— with the help of bacteria, fungi, earthworms, and other soil life— into the dark, rich material that resembles chocolate cake. This is what gives good soil its look and feel, and what makes it good soil.

SOIL BASICS

Soil is not a static entity like a rock; the soil in your yard is more like a pond—a living ecosystem. Plant growth uses up elements that soil does not replace. It cannot replace them because a vegetable garden is a highly intensive growing area and uses up resources faster than an environment in the wild.

Soil was created by the weathering of rocks and by billions of generations of organisms absorbing plant and animal residues and decomposing them. Their action on dead animals, trees, and other plant materials releases nitrogen and other elements to make soil minerals available to plants. This cycle breaks down plant and animal remnants to create fertile, fibrous, moisture-retentive compost. Nature's way of replenishing the soil is to recycle all its waste. The organisms reduce the organic material which, in turn, restores the soil and readies it for a new season of growth.

Soil Structure

The way the particles of soil combine—its structure—determines how well the soil holds water and nutrients and how well roots can move through it.

When gardening books instruct you to plant in "good garden loam," they are describing soil composed of about equal parts sand, silt, clay, and humus—the composition of good soil structure. The structure of soil is as important to success as soil fertility. Very fertile soil with very poor structure, such as heavy clay soil, locks up nutrients so that plants cannot use them.

ELEMENTS OF SOIL

Sand   Small loose grains of rock, often quartz.

Silt   Sedimentary material usually found near streams, rivers, or lakes and composed of particles larger than clay and smaller than sand.

Clay   Very fine-grained particles, thick and moldable when wet.

Loam   Mix of sand, silt, clay, and organic matter. Loam is the best soil for gardening—what everyone hopes to find in the backyard.

Organic matter   Plant or animal residues in various stages of decomposition.

Humus   Well-decomposed plant matter, dark brown or black, improves fertility and water-holding capacity of soil.

Compost   Decaying organic matter, including plant and animal material, used to improve soil structure and fertility. Similar to humus. *Composting* refers to the decomposition process in which garden and animal waste breaks down into compost. Gardeners sometimes confuse compost with mulch.

Mulch   Any material, from living plants to sheets of plastic, used as a cover for soil. Mulch inhibits weeds, retains moisture, and protects roots from cold and heat. When the mulch is an organic material, it also serves to replenish the organic content of the soil.

Soil amendment   Anything added to change the composition of the soil. This includes sand, manure, compost, or chemical fertilizers.

SOIL COMPOSITION

Texture   The individual particles of sand, silt, and clay in a particular soil. These are the inorganic ingredients of soil.

Structure   The way the soil holds together given the amount of sand, silt, clay, and organic material present. Structure governs the soil's capacity to absorb and retain moisture, as well as the ability of tender roots to move through the soil.

pH reaction   (Potential of hydrogen) measures the relative acidity or alkalinity of soil. The pH level determines whether nutrients are available to the plants.

Fertility   The amount of nutrients in the soil needed for sturdy plant growth. As stated, nutrient availability is affected by pH levels.

Microorganisms   Tiny living organisms whose life cycles transform the organic matter in soil, making nutrients available to plant roots.

Sand This is an essential element of soil because the hard irregular surfaces of the tiny grains create pockets that hold air and allow water to seep into and down through the soil. But there can be too much of a good thing. When soil has too much sand and not enough organic matter, water runs right through it, depriving the plants of water and the nutrients dissolved in it.

Silt Somewhere in size between sand and clay, silt is a smooth, dark material most often associated with waterways. Silty soil is less common than sandy and clay soil.

Clay Described as superfine particles of nutrient-rich earth, the extremely small particles of clay cling together, locking out air and water when there is not enough sand and organic matter to keep them apart. Because roots "drink" their food supply, compacted clay soil leaves plants not only dry but starving. When wet, soil with a high clay content turns gummy and is impossible to work. Dry, it bakes hard as bricks.

Compost Organic matter, living organisms, and animal residues in states of decomposition make up compost. This spongelike decomposed organic material absorbs and stores moisture and provides surfaces where nutrients are held in reserve in the soil. Compost helps increase and improve air circulation. Earthworms abound, working and loosening the soil. Compost makes soil soft, crumbly, and very easy for young roots to expand into. Soil with a high compost content warms quickly in spring and is easy to work.

To keep garden soil healthy, work compost into the soil at the beginning of each growing cycle. An organic mulch decomposes

(composts) on the underside during the growing season, replenishing the soil, so topping the vegetable bed with mulch is also beneficial.

Testing Soil Structure

To gauge soil composition, pick up a handful of damp soil and, with two hands, pack it as though you are making a snowball. If the clay content is high, the ball packs hard and will not crumble readily under light pressure. It is likely to cake. Sandy soil or soil with too much humus or compost will not pack and falls

This is an example of "good garden loam." In addition to a balance of different mineral particle sizes, it also contains a high percentage of organic matter.

In areas that have a lot of summer rain, gardeners often add lime each year as they turn over the soil, to reduce its acidity. Warm rain leaches calcium from the soil, leaving it acid.

apart. The forest floor is one of the few places where soil is likely to have too much humus. Soil with good structure forms a ball with just a little pressure and crumbles readily. If this describes your soil, you are in luck. All you have to do is replenish the compost annually.

It is most likely that your soil needs improving. Most soil requires the addition of organic material. Your own compost is great, but if you do not have any, you can purchase soil conditioner at a local nursery. Spread the material over the soil 2 to 4 inches deep and dig it in to a depth of 6 to 8 inches.

You can also lay raw (uncomposted) organic material directly on the garden. Sawdust, shredded leaves blown out by a leaf vacuum, or the autumn blanket of leaves all act as a great mulch. But as microorganisms turn this stuff into crumbly compost, they use up nutrients in the soil, notably nitrogen. The soil then becomes temporarily deficient in elements essential to the growth of plants. Fertilize more often, with a high-nitrogen fertilizer, if you use this type of uncomposted mulch.

Improving Clay Soil Soil that contains a lot of clay compacts as the topsoil gets worn away with use. Hard clay stops water from draining, and tender roots cannot penetrate it. Break up the compacted soil. Add liberal qualities of compost and sharp, or builder's, sand. Do not use sand from salt shores nor the very fine sand that combines with clay to make cement. Dust on and dig in gypsum at the ratio of 50 pounds for every 1,000 square feet of soil. Repeat every year.

Improving Light-Textured Soil Heavy applications of compost or humus bind together silty and sandy soil, enhancing the soil structure and water-holding capacity.

Soil pH
The pH reaction of soil determines whether it is acid or "sour," alkaline or "sweet," or neutral, which is right in the middle. The pH scale ranges from 1.0 to 14.0 with pH 7.0 as the neutral point. Soil registering below pH 7.0 is classified as increasingly acid, and soil registering above pH 7.0 is classified as increasingly alkaline.

The fine, hairlike roots of a plant absorb dissolved trace minerals and elements that the plant requires for growth. If the nutrient solution is too acid or too alkaline,

certain minerals will not dissolve and the roots cannot absorb them. As a generalization, the elements required for the growth of food plants are most available when the pH of the soil solution is slightly acid, between 6.0 and 6.8. Among the exceptions are potatoes and blueberries, which require soil with a higher acid content.

Most soil in the U.S. is between pH 6.0 and 7.0, except where limestone deposits are plentiful—this soil tends to be alkaline and has a much higher pH. A garden that produces crop after crop often becomes increasingly acid. It's a good idea to keep track by testing your soil annually. In the acid range, iron becomes more available. But as acidity increases, many elements become less available, and some, such as aluminum, become available in quantities toxic to plants.

Acid Soil Applications of lime raises the pH, reducing the soil acidity, or "sweetening" the soil. Where lawns benefit from applications of lime every few years, the chances are good that the food garden will also profit. If the soil tests below pH 5.5, spread finely ground limestone or hydrated lime. Lime is most effective when it is mixed into the soil rather that dusted on and watered in. Do not apply it when you apply a chemical fertilizer; add lime at another time. To raise the pH significantly, apply small doses once or twice a year and retest a few weeks after each application.

Wood ashes from the fireplace also raise pH (lower the acidity) and are a bad choice for mulch when the soil already has a high pH. Ashes from deciduous trees are more beneficial than ashes from conifers. Ashes also supply

TESTING PH

The cooperative extension office at the local state university can provide sound advice about soil pH and will test your soil for a modest fee. The report usually includes other valuable information including lead content.

For a reliable do-it-yourself soil-testing kit sold by Cornell University, write for the "Standard Kit pH 5.0 to 7.2": Cornell Nutrient Analysis Laboratories, 804 Radfield Hall, Cornell University, Ithaca, NY 14853.

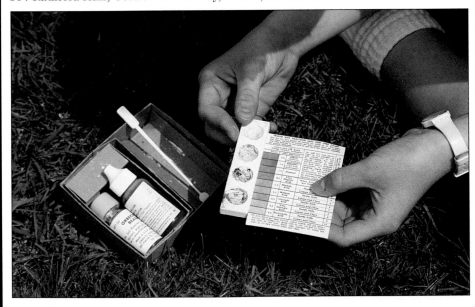

STERILE GROWING MIX COMPONENTS

Perlite   A white and glasslike volcanic ash derived from silica. Crushed and heated, it expands to 20 times its original volume. It sustains moisture and provides good air circulation around plant roots.

Peat moss   The dried organic residue of swamp plants. It sustains moisture and releases nutrients slowly.

Vermiculite   A very light micalike mineral that expands under heat to up to 20 times its thickness. It stores moisture and nutrients and releases them slowly.

Polymers   Granules of gel-like substances that hold many times their weight in water and release it to the growing medium as the medium dries.

SOIL MIXES

Most commercial planting or potting mixes work fine for vegetables, but are expensive in large quantities. If you'd like to make your own, mix thoroughly:

9 cubic feet coarse sand (not builder's sand or beach sand)
9 cubic feet peat moss
9 cubic feet ground bark or composted sawdust
5 pounds 5–10–5 fertilizer
5 pounds ground limestone

The ingredients consolidate, making a little less than 1 cubic yard of potting mix.

To make the mix lightweight for easy moving, substitute perlite for the coarse sand.

potassium, one of the essential nutrients. But remember, if a little is good, a lot is not necessarily better.

Alkaline Soil   If the soil of the vegetable garden tests above pH 6.8, apply water-soluble sulfur or iron. Sulfur is tricky: The rate and manner in which you spread it is best determined by a county extension agent or an expert at a local garden center. The treatment is not lasting, and you must repeat it every 8 to 12 months. Adding an acidic mulch such as peat moss, composted sawdust or bark, leaves, pine needles, or cottonseed meal has a slow but lasting effect on lowering the pH.

Soil for Containers

The success of a food garden growing in containers depends on fertile soil and sustained moisture. Every year the soil in baskets and small planters must be amended with organic matter or replaced with fresh soil. The perennials described in the chapter beginning on page 289 can overwinter in big tubs and planters, but they need an annual topdressing of 2 to 3 inches of compost or fresh soil. Scratch it into the surface along with fertilizer in late winter.

For container gardens, sterilized, commercially prepared soilless mixes are best. These are composed of peat moss and vermiculite, wood products and coarse sand, or other combinations of organic and mineral elements. To drain well, container soil needs to be much more porous than regular garden soil. The best mixes include components that drain well but hold a lot of water.

Enough commercial mix to fill a raised bed or many large planters can be costly. Without much trouble, you can make a mix of your own. Small containers dry out very quickly in summer heat and in high wind. Add water-holding gels to mixes destined for baskets and pots. These starch-based superabsorbent gels help keep the growing medium moist. They are sold in grains and in sticks and can hold 200 to 5,300 times their own weight in water. *Caution:* Mix the grains into the soil very thoroughly, or they will clump together into globs that look and feel like jellyfish.

Even with gel additives, many containers require daily watering in hot weather.

COVER CROPS

A cover crop is a fast-growing crop that you dig or rototill back into the soil three to four weeks before the planting season begins. If the cover crop begins to go to seed, dig it in immediately—do not wait for the planting season. Decomposing in the soil, this crop replenishes the organic content, improves soil structure, adds nutrients, increases microbial activity, and helps break up compacted areas.

Planting a cover crop after the harvest season or anytime the garden will lie fallow for a couple of months keeps the soil in top condition. In addition to replenishing the soil, a cover crop protects an empty garden from erosion by wind or rain. Even weeds turned under add valuable humus and nutrients to

Top: To thoroughly combine large amounts of soil mix, spread the components on a hard surface. Using a square-nose shovel, turn the pile twice, scattering each shovelful over the entire pile. Bottom: Legume cover crops, such as the ladino clover shown here, add nitrogen to the soil as well as their organic content.

the soil—so long as they have not developed seed.

The best cover crops are plants that naturally fix nitrogen in their roots as they grow. Plowing these plants into the soil boosts nitrogen content as it improves the soil structure. Legume plants are some of the best nitrogen fixers.

When to Plant Cover Crops

For the soil to benefit most from their nitrogen-fixing capacity, plow under legume cover crops before they form flowers. Clover is one of the most useful spring and summer cover crops. Plant red, white, and yellow clover in spring or summer. Plant ladino clover in early spring or early fall. Crimson clover is a spring or fall cover crop. Plant soybeans in spring or summer, hairy vetch in late summer or fall, and alfalfa in spring.

Among the more commonly used nonlegume cover crops is annual ryegrass, which you plant in spring. Plant buckwheat, oats, rape, and Sudan grass in spring or summer. In late summer or fall, plant annual winter rye and allow it to overwinter, then till it under four or five weeks before spring planting.

COMPOSTING

Compost is a crumbly, black, soil-like substance produced by the decomposition of organic material. In compost-enhanced soil, plants develop large, healthy root systems that see them through stressful periods. Compost-amended and mulched soil resists erosion and is rich in the organisms that keep it productive. Compost-rich soil tends to warm more quickly after winter and is easy to work early in the season.

The best and least costly source of abundant compost is made from yard and kitchen waste. When certain elements are piled together in more or less the right proportions, and the pile is kept damp, compost results. Decomposing material gives off heat from the microbial action. If you turn the pile now and then, the heat and air is more evenly distributed and the compost develops more rapidly. Warm weather speeds decomposition, but hot weather can cook the microorganisms and stop the process.

Composting Materials

In addition to air, moisture, and warmth, the essential ingredients in compost are dried organic materials, nitrogen-rich fresh greens,

---

GOOD COVER CROPS

Nitrogen-Fixing Plants	Fast-Growing Grasses
Alfalfa	Barley
Fava beans	Buckwheat
Various clovers	Field bromegrass
Cowpeas	Millet
Lupines	Mustard
Field peas	Oats
Soybeans	Rye
Vetch	Ryegrass
	Sudan grass

PROPORTIONS OF THE MAIN INGREDIENTS IN COMPOST

3 parts dry leaves (carbon)
3 parts fresh grass clippings (nitrogen)

or

6 parts dry leaves (carbon)
3 parts kitchen scraps (nitrogen)
3 parts fresh grass clippings (nitrogen)

or

2 parts dry leaves (carbon)
2 parts straw or wood shavings (carbon)
1 part manure (nitrogen)
1 part fresh grass clippings (nitrogen)
1 part fresh garden weeds or harvested plants (nitrogen)
1 part kitchen scraps (nitrogen)

or

3 parts dry leaves (carbon)
1 part fresh garden weeds or harvested plants (nitrogen)
1 part fresh grass clippings (nitrogen)
1 part kitchen scraps (nitrogen)

soil organisms, and patience. Dried leaves, grass clippings, weeds, garden waste, and fruit and vegetable parings are the most common composting materials; but any organic material can be composted—from sawdust to seaweed to cow manure. Do not include plants that have been destroyed by herbicides, nor waste from meat-eating animals. Omit poison oak and poison ivy, black walnut and eucalyptus leaves, and insect-infested or diseased plant materials.

Adding Fertilizer

Fertilizer aids the composting process and enriches the finished product. For every bushel of shredded waste, add a cup each of 5-10-5 slow-release fertilizer, gypsum, and limestone. With compost destined for acid-loving plants such as azaleas, use an acid-type fertilizer and omit the lime.

Composting Methods

If you simply heap leaves and grass on the ground, they compost in 12 to 36 months, depending on the climate. It happens faster in Florida than in northern Vermont, because organic material breaks down most quickly in damp, warm weather.

Layered in a traditional free-standing compost pile about 3 feet square by 3 feet high, the elements turn to compost sooner. Make the top concave to catch the rain; and if the weather turns cold, cover it with a tarp to keep in the heat—the sign that the process is working. Mix the pile with a pitchfork every three to four days to aerate the mass, and keep it damp. In warm weather it will produce finished compost in three to four months; less if the weather is hot. A free-standing compost pile is rather messy, so gardeners usually screen the pile with plants or a vine or hide it behind a tree or shed.

A compost bin is not necessarily easier, but it is tidier and better suited to a small garden or a city yard. Catalogs offer a variety of compost bins. One of the simplest is a bottomless, green plastic rectangle that you can just plunk down anywhere and start loading. It has vents on the top and bottom to keep the pile aerated, and a stir stick so you can mix it easily. (Stirring it up is more fun than turning it with a pitchfork.) In a warm climate, moistened and aerated often, a bin produces finished compost in four to eight weeks.

This homemade compost bin has three parts: Compost is assembled in one bin, "works" on breaking down in another, and is finished and used from the third bin.

Lawn clippings, shown on these potatoes, are an excellent, high-nitrogen mulch. To keep them from matting and smelling bad, spread the clippings from each mowing less than an inch deep. This allows them to dry without rotting.

The ultimate and most expensive composting method is a waterproof tumbler that is rotated at least once daily. Some types you must turn by hand, others run on electricity or solar power. They produce finished compost in three to six weeks.

Using Compost

As soon as the organic waste becomes brown, fibrous goo, which is its half-finished state, you can apply it to the garden 2 to 3 inches deep. It is especially beneficial in fall, when it can continue to release its nutrients all winter. Finished compost is dark and resembles soil.

Mix it into the existing garden soil or use it as mulch, spreading it over the soil 2 or 3 inches deep.

MULCHES

Mulch is any material applied to the soil as a protective covering. Its job is to keep down weeds, protect roots from temperature extremes, and retain moisture. Mulching not only benefits the soil and the roots, but saves you time and water.

Apply mulch right after you plant the garden. An early-spring mulch serves to insulate the cool soil from the warming weather and often slows the bolting of cool-weather plants such as lettuce. In the South and warm regions of the West, apply mulches before high heat to insulate the roots.

In areas that get only light frost in the winter, apply mulch before frost is expected, to protect crops left to overwinter in the ground.

Where soil freezes hard, place a winter mulch on perennials after the ground has frozen. This usually occurs after the second hard frost. By insulating the ground, the mulch keeps it frozen through cycles of warmth and freezing cold that damage plants later in the season. Materials suitable for winter mulching are pine boughs, marsh and salt hay, and straw. Apply the winter mulch in a layer thin enough so you can see through to the plant and soil. Remove the mulch when the first signs of new growth appear.

Organic Mulch

Mulches composed of materials that once were living are organic mulches. Over the course of the growing season, an organic mulch adds compost to the soil. Tilled back into the soil at the end of the season, or before planting the following season, an organic mulch conditions and restores the nutrient content of the soil.

Probably the most valuable mulch for a vegetable garden is compost. Most environments offer "found" materials that make fine mulch once they are composted—ground leaves, weeds that have not gone to seed, rotted sawdust, or grassy seaweed. Nitrogen-rich grass clippings, shredded newspaper, decaying straw, rotted hay, and pine needles may be applied as mulch without composting. Vary the type of organic material you use for mulching to vary the nutrients added, and check the soil pH annually.

Garden centers sell organic mulches by the bag, the bale, and the truckload. Peat moss is used as a mulch, but it tends to dry out, cake, and resist the penetration of rain; rewetting it is also tedious. Better and more attractive choices are cocoa hulls, pine needles, and finely shredded bark. Avoid the coarser mulches used on beds of ornamental plants, such as large wood chips. They look great but they do not decompose by the end of the season, and that makes it difficult to till the soil.

Do not overdo organic mulches. Applied more than 3 inches deep, many mulches cause root rot, stem rot, and suffocation. A fine mulch such as sawdust or cocoa hulls must be no more than 2 inches deep. It is very important to keep these mulches about 3 inches from the stems of plants or newly seeded areas. As the season advances, replenish the mulch to maintain the original depth. Apply straw, recommended as a winter mulch, 6 to 12 inches deep and 3 inches back from stems or seed beds.

Living Mulch

Plants set very close together grow into a living mulch. This is a great way to mulch closely spaced widerow gardens. The leaves form an overhead canopy thick enough to shade the soil and reduce the amount of moisture lost through evaporation.

Manufactured Plastic Mulch

Black plastic film is a popular synthetic mulch, but it is being challenged by thin, loosely woven fabrics called geotextiles, which keep down weeds but let air and water pass through to the soil. Geotextiles are sold in rolls 23 feet wide by 24, 50, or 100 feet long. Larger sizes are available from garden centers by special order.

Installation is the same whether you use plastic or geotextiles. Before seeding or planting, lay the material over the ground and weight the edges. Cut slits or *x*'s in the material where you want to place plants or seeds. These materials are not particularly attractive but can be hidden under a decorative mulch such as pine bark chips.

FERTILIZER BASICS

Vegetables must have fertile soil to succeed—to grow their fastest to maximize production before the season ends. Soil with plenty of the necessary nutrients produces the greatest harvests.

The basic elements essential to good plant growth are nitrogen, phosphorus, and potassium. These are the main ingredients of most fertilizers. There are other elements necessary for plant growth, but they are needed in far smaller quantities and often are already present in the soil. Many fertilizers contain these "micronutrients."

NPK Ratios

Any fertilizer you purchase has three numbers prominently displayed on the package label. They tell you the NPK ratio in that product. The *N* stands for nitrogen, the *P* stands for phosphorous, and the *K* stands for potassium. The numbers tell you the percentage of each of these in that particular fertilizer. The higher the number, the higher the concentration of fertilizer and the less you need to apply. A label with *10-10-10* indicates a fertilizer containing 10 percent nitrogen, 10 percent phosphorous, and 10 percent potassium. This is a "complete" fertilizer because it contains all three of the basic nutrients. Some fertilizers used for specific purposes may not include one or two of the nutrients, which is indicated with a *0*. An all-nitrogen fertilizer with *15-0-0* on the label is considered an "incomplete" fertilizer although it has legitimate uses.

Organic and Inorganic Fertilizers

Organic fertilizers originate from animal or vegetable by-products. Among the most effective organic fertilizers are dehydrated manures of various animals, including chickens, cows, and crickets. Meal from organic sources produces bonemeal, bloodmeal, cottonseed meal, alfalfa meal, and crabmeal. Most organic fertilizers also improve the soil when their mass is incorporated into the garden. They're usually inexpensive but are bulky to handle and store, and their nutrients may be released at unpredictable rates.

Inorganic fertilizers are composed of mineral compounds such as potassium nitrate, ammonium nitrate, and ammonium phosphate. They are a great source of nutrients for plants, but they also run through and beyond the reach of the roots more quickly than organic fertilizers. Inorganic fertilizers are potent and can burn plants, especially sensitive seedlings, so follow label directions. Always water immediately after applying dry inorganic fertilizers.

THE NPK ELEMENTS

Nitrogen (N)   Use for stem and leaf production and rich green foliage color. Signs indicating a shortage include small, yellowing lower leaves, light green foliage, and inadequate growth. Choose a fertilizer with a higher ratio of nitrogen, such as 10-5-5.

Phosphorus (P)   Use for root growth and flower and fruit production. Signs of a shortage are stunted growth and dark green or red lower leaves. Apply 5-10-5.

Potassium (K)   Use for flower and fruit production, strong stems, and disease resistance. Visible signs of a shortage include weak stems and susceptibility to disease. Apply a fertilizer with a higher ratio of potassium, such as 5-10-10.

Dry and Liquid Fertilizers

Dry fertilizers are applied to the soil and watered so their nutrients will travel to the roots. They tend to last longer in the soil than liquid fertilizers.

Liquid fertilizers are used most often for foliar feeding—applying directly to the leaves. They are sold as a concentrated liquid or as soluble crystals which you dilute in water before applying. They provide a quick picker-upper if you follow the instructions carefully.

"Compost tea" and "manure tea" are types of homemade liquid fertilizer. Compost or manure is steeped in water, strained through cloth, and applied to the foliage or to the roots.

Slow-Release Fertilizers

Slow-release fertilizers are just what the name implies: The nutrients are absorbed into the soil slowly, so there is a long-lasting effect. Apply these fertilizers early

Dry fertilizer can be applied directly from the box or bag. The pellets are soluble and must be watered into the soil. Liquid fertilizer must be diluted in water before application. Both types are effective; choose the one that is most convenient for you.

Slow-release fertilizers "leak" dissolved nutrients into the soil at a controlled rate, over several months. They are more expensive than either dry or liquid fertilizers, but more convenient. They must be in close contact with moist soil to work, so are dug into the top inch or so of soil.

FERTILIZER TERMS

Fertilizer   Anything that provides nutrients for growing plants.
Foliar feeding   To spray liquid fertilizer on plant foliage.
Side-dress   To scratch fertilizer into the soil around the plants.
Soil conditioner   Material that improves the soil structure—may or may not provide nutrients.
Top-dress   To apply fertilizer over the surface of the planting bed.

FERTILIZER TIPS

▮ Follow label instructions exactly.

▮ Be careful: Overfertilizing burns plants, whether you use too much manure or too much inorganic fertilizer.

▮ Follow every application of dry fertilizer with a thorough soaking to get the nutrients down to the roots.

▮ When fertilizing heavy feeders, such as those in the cabbage family, apply half the recommended amount before planting, and side-dress with the remainder after the plants are well established.

▮ Check the timing for applying fertilizer to each vegetable. The first application is crucial with many crops, because early vigorous new growth is beneficial.

▮ Give less nitrogen to plants growing in partial shade than to the same plants that are in full sun.

▮ Increase the amount of fertilizer when plants are crowded, intercropped, or succession cropped.

and they'll last the season. Soil microorganisms slowly discharge the nutrients into the soil.

Most organic fertilizers can be categorized as slow-release, so some gardeners assume that all fertilizers labeled "organic" are slow-release. But organics are sometimes quick fixes: Dissolved seaweed or fish emulsion as well as compost tea or manure tea make nutrients available immediately.

Inorganic slow-release fertilizers are available in formulations that release ingredients over a three- to four-month period or over an eight- to twelve-month period. Some of these are synthetics which are only slightly soluble in water and therefore release their nutrients slowly; others are fertilizers coated with a polymer that inhibits the release of the nutrients. Many commercially prepared fertilizers contain a mix of quick- and slow-release ingredients.

APPLYING FERTILIZER

As you prepare the planting bed for its first crop, broadcast a slow-release fertilizer over the topsoil when you apply the soil conditioners. Work it all into the soil 4 to 6 inches deep. To calculate the amount of fertilizer to apply per square foot or length of row, follow the label directions.

Annual Applications

In subsequent years even a well-prepared vegetable bed needs an application of fertilizer before the growing season begins. Dust the ground with a slow-release complete fertilizer, such as 10-6-4. Check with a local garden center for the best combination for your area. The fertilizer should be high in nitrogen because food plants, which include lots of foliage, use up nitrogen rapidly. There is usually plenty of phosphorus and potassium in the dry West. In areas with high rainfall, these elements may get leached out of the soil.

Midseason Side Dressings

If you are intercropping or growing a succession of crops in the same row, apply a side dressing of fertilizer in the middle of the season. Use a quick-release fertilizer and scratch it into the soil on both sides of the plants, 6 to 8 inches away. Water the area thoroughly after the application. The vegetable chapters, beginning on page 105, suggest rates of application for individual vegetables and fruits.

Quick Fertilizer Fixes

The fertilizers discussed so far feed plant roots. It is a good idea to give the garden an occasional picker-upper by feeding the foliage with a liquid fertilizer. The plants take up the nutrients through leaf pores. Foliar feedings can be made every

three to four weeks during periods of peak growth. This is especially helpful to fast-growing vegetables. The easiest to apply are fertilizers designed to be mixed in a jar that attaches to the end of a hose. The container siphons the correct dilution out of the spray tip. Follow label directions and do not use more than recommended. Water just enough to wet the surface of the leaves.

Fertilizing Container Plants

Vegetables growing in containers require more fertilizer than those in the open garden. The limited amount of soil in a container dries out quickly in sun and wind and requires heavy watering. The constant flow of water leeches nutrients from the soil which must be replaced to keep the plant growing vigorously. Each time you water leafy vegetables, dilute and mix in

FERTILIZER AMOUNTS

The following chart shows how the amount of fertilizer to be applied decreases as the percentage of nitrogen increases. Assume that 5-10-10 fertilizer recommendations call for 3 to 4 pounds per 100 square feet.

NPK Formula	Pounds per 100 square feet
5-10-10	3.5
6-20-10	2.8
8-24-8	2.0
10-10-8	1.7
16-16-16	1.0

an application of 10-10-10 fertilizer, one-quarter to one-half strength. For root vegetables and fruiting plants such as eggplant, use diluted 10-20-10.

PREPARING THE GARDEN BED

You can prepare the soil for the garden anytime of year, but fall is the best time in most regions. The fallow months of winter allow time for the soil amendments, microorganisms, and the wind and rain to transform the soil before the growing season begins. If you dig the bed in the fall, plant a cover crop such as clover in the late summer and rototill it into the ground before it goes to seed. Or plant a cold-resistant cover crop such as rye and turn it under in spring, three to four weeks before you plan to plant. In regions with very cold winters, turn under cover crops before the ground freezes. In warmer climates turn them under in late fall, or grow them over the winter and turn under in spring.

What follows is nursery professional Andre Viette's recipe for preparing a bed. This is a raised bed, which he feels produces the best crops, no matter what garden design you are planning.

1. Outline the bed with markers or a long garden hose. If the bed is to be a traditional row-crop garden, make sure the angles are square

These beds are being laid out with string and stakes. For curved beds, use a garden hose to mark the borders, or draw a line by dribbling lime from your hand.

TOOLS OF THE TRADE

Every gardener needs a modest array of tools. To start, a shovel, hoe, and something to deliver water to the site is about all you absolutely must have. Sooner or later you will accumulate a collection limited only by your enthusiasm. Tools make the job easier and save wear and tear on your body.

High-quality tools are worth the investment because they work well and last for years. Clean tools after each use to prevent rust, and sharpen seasonally. The following is a list of the basic garden tools.

File, sharpening stone, or diamond file   To keep tools clean and sharp.

Garden rake   For breaking up large clumps of soil and raking the soil surface level and smooth.

Hoe   For weeding, cultivating, and opening seed furrows.

Round-edged shovel   For digging large holes.

Scissors or pruning shears   For harvesting.

Spading fork   For double-digging and digging root crops such as potatoes.

Sprayer   To apply fungicides and insecticides.

Trowel and garden claw   For transplanting and scratching in side applications of dry fertilizer.

Water sources   Garden hose, watering can, and soaker hose or sprinkler system.

Wheelbarrow or child's wagon   For carrying transplants, tools, and other items to the garden and for transporting garden debris to the compost site.

This collection of gardening tools includes several kinds of shovels, spading forks, and spades.

DOUBLE-DIGGING

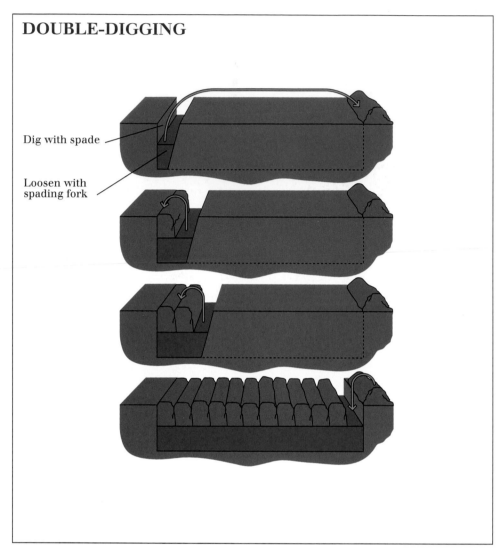

Dig with spade

Loosen with spading fork

and exact. If it is to be a decorative wide-row bed, or a decorative garden with flowers and vegetables, shape it with lazy s's and gentle sweeping curves. Strip away the sod and double-dig the area.

2. Next get rid of any weeds by watering the bed, then treating the existing weeds with a weed-killing herbicide such as Roundup®. Repeat the process in 10 days. Wait another 10 days before continuing.

3. Raise the bed by importing enough topsoil to bring up the level to between 4 and 15 inches above ground. Find first-rate soil that is weed free. Or add your own soil

mix, prepared according to the recipes on page 36.

4. Now improve the soil with additives, determined by the pH reaction of the soil. Optimum soil pH for the widest range of vegetables is slightly acid, in the 5.5 to 6.5 range. If your soil is above pH 6.5, apply water-soluble sulfur or iron. If the soil is below pH 5.5, spread finely ground limestone or hydrated lime. Ask a local garden center or nursery for product recommendations and apply the materials at the prescribed rates.

5. Spread on fertilizer according to label directions. For a bed being

prepared in fall for spring planting, choose 8- or 12-month slow-release formulations. The 12-month formulation will take the garden through the summer.

6. For clay soil, spread gypsum at the ratio of 50 pounds per 1,000 square feet. If the soil is very heavy clay, use 100 pounds per 1,000 square feet.

7. Apply phosphorous, which is essential for hearty root growth. The ratio for all soil is 50 pounds per 1,000 square feet. There are two preferred sources: superphosphate, now being marketed as triple superphosphate, and rock phosphate, which releases its nutrients very slowly.

8. Cover the bed with 2 to 4 inches of suitable organic material. Use decomposed bark, compost, leaf mold (partially decomposed leaves), sphagnum peat moss, black peat humus (composted peat), decomposed animal manure, composted sewage sludge (which is dry and relatively odorless), or a combination of any of these. Seaweed is wonderful where it is available.

9. Use a rotary tiller to churn it all into the soil. Just hang on while the tiller pulls ahead, tearing up and turning under the sod and soil. Even a small tiller is a major investment. Owning one is not necessary, because garden centers and hardware stores rent rotary tillers at reasonable rates. The easiest to operate are tillers with large wheels. The best have heat-treated carbon steel blades and rear tines. If the soil is heavy and hard to dig, rent the largest tiller you can find. The weight and power make the job easier.

10. When you are ready to sow the seeds, rake the bed smooth and discard any rocks, sticks, clods, or other debris.

WATERING THE GARDEN

Monitoring the garden's need for water all season long is essential if the plants are to grow unchecked. It is easy to understand why when you visualize soil as a reservoir in which nutrients are dissolved. A plant that goes dry also begins to starve.

As soon as a plant shows signs of wilt, the roots already have suffered some damage. If you water right away, the plant recovers and the roots mend quickly. But plant growth slows a bit even with the slightest wilting. If plants stay wilted over a period of time, the damage is more extreme. Recovery is slow and new growth even slower. With food plants this can mean the difference between a good harvest and no harvest at all.

Watering Seeds and Seedlings

The most essential time to water is right after you sow seeds or plant seedlings. Without moisture, seeds will not germinate. And a transplant plunked down into dry soil

CRITICAL PERIODS FOR WATERING
Lack of water checks the growth of vegetables, and they do not easily recover. Make sure the following vegetables receive all the water they need during these critical periods.

Vegetable	Critical Period
Asparagus	Fern formation
Broccoli	Head development
Cabbage	Head development
Carrot	Root enlargement
Cauliflower	Head development
Corn	Ear silk and tassel development
Cucumber	Flowering and fruit development
Eggplant	Flowering and fruit development
Lettuce	Head development
Lima bean	Pollination and pod development
Melon	Flowering and fruit development
Onion	Bulb enlargement

Water new trans-plants and seedlings with a delicate spray to avoid bat-tering them into the soil or washing them out.

droops very quickly, even if it is attached to a moist rootball. The surrounding dry soil wicks the water away from the rootball. Without a thorough watering right after planting, the seedling wilts immediately and dies in a few hours.

For that important first watering after planting, use a sprinkler run at a speed that lays down 1 to 2 inches in 5 to 12 hours. That is the equivalent of a gentle rain. A coffee tin under the sprinkler will help you calculate the rate at which the equipment deposits water. Clay soil needs to be watered half as often

as sandy soil but for a longer period in order to penetrate deeply.

If you worked a lot of compost into the soil as you prepared the bed, the moisture from the first watering should be enough to keep the plants growing for a day or two, depending on the weather. If there is no rain, you may need to water the seeds or plants daily.

Watering Established Plants

An established vegetable garden needs ½ to 1 inch of water every three or four days each week, depending on whether the soil is sandy or heavy, whether the air is dry or moist, and whether there is wind. This said, keep in mind that watering guidelines are just that—guidelines. Climate, weather, time of year, exposure, location, and especially soil affect the rate at which water disappears. Humus-filled soil absorbs water five times as fast as heavy clay soil. Mulched soil looses less moisture than soil that is bare to the sun and wind. If you are unsure whether the garden needs watering, poke a fingertip down into the soil. If it is bone dry, you should have watered a few days ago. If it is cool and dry, it is time to water. If the soil is moist 3 or 4 inches down, watering can wait.

Watering mature crops is most beneficial when it is deep; the roots grow farther down into the soil. After a good watering, soil needs to dry out a little before it is watered again. If the soil never has a chance to dry out, it gets soggy and the root growth is shallow. Watering for longer than necessary will not harm the garden, but it is wasteful. The extra water drains away, taking nutrients with it. To know if you have watered long enough, dig a hole to see how far down moisture has penetrated. If the soil is moist a foot or more down, you can turn off the water.

The best time to water an established garden is in early morning before the sun reaches the plants. Especially in hot, dry climates, watering during sunny hours is wasteful because the water evaporates almost as quickly as you lay it down. But when temperatures are running very high and plants are drooping, watering during the day can be helpful. Watering lowers leaf temperatures and stress and cools the garden environment.

Evening is not as good a time to water as morning. The foliage gets wet from the dew anyway, and the plants lose less water to evaporation, but plants that are habitually soaked during periods of steamy hot nights may become susceptible to diseases.

Surviving a Heat Wave

Healthy plants growing sturdily in well-prepared soil can go without water for a time. But when the thermometer hits 100° F, or the wind is high and hot, you may need to water daily.

During prolonged dry spells, plants have defense systems that throw them into semidormancy. You need to be sure to water thoroughly so the roots grow deeply. This also means allowing the soil to dry out between waterings. It is easy to get carried away when watering in high heat and drought. There are many regions in the U.S. that get little or no rain in summer. Reinforcing a plant's inherent strengths allows it to develop into a vigorous, problem-resistant specimen.

Watering Container Plants

For container-grown plants, watering is a constant necessity. If you find this burdensome, investigate the types of self-watering planters and pots described on page 55 or set up an automatic watering system.

When watering container plants, pour on water until it begins to drain from the bottom—and remember to include a light application of fertilizer every time. You are washing nutrients out of the container even as you water them in.

If there are saucers under the pots, be sure to pour out any residual water. This standing water keeps the bottom few inches of soil from draining completely, and deep roots may be killed from soggy soil and lack of oxygen.

Top: To some people, hand watering is a joy and a time to get close to their plants. Be sure you water thoroughly, however. It's easy to think you are through when only the top half-inch is wet. Dig into the soil to see how deeply the water has penetrated. Bottom: A reciprocating sprinkler head like this one dispenses water slowly, allowing the soil to absorb it without runoff.

Types of Watering Equipment

The best choice of watering equipment depends on the design and size of the garden. When the garden is small, watering with a hose in early morning is a pleasure. You have time to philosophize over sprouting seeds and rejoice in the almost measurable growth of young vegetables. But most gardeners soon tire of hand-watering. The solution is to use sprinklers or soaker hoses or establish an automatic watering system on a timer.

Sprinklers　Garden centers offer a large variety of moderately priced hose-end sprinklers. There are rotating-head sprinklers, square or round chambers that shoot jets of water in various patterns, the oscillating-arm type that project a steady stream back and forth, and the spike variety that squirt large and small drops in an arc or circle. The best are usually the simplest, because nothing can break or fail to do what it is supposed to do.

A system of in-ground sprinkler heads that pop up and water a predetermined area at the command of an electric timer is the easy way out (and also the most expensive). Plastic pipes conduct the water to the heads. If you are planning to rototill, do not put sprinkler heads within the garden area. Install them around the garden perimeter, and design the system so the watering patterns overlap slightly.

Soaker Hoses　Soaker hoses are designed to leak evenly along their length. When the water seeps into the ground from a soaker hose covered with 2 to 3 inches of mulch, you need 30 to 50 percent less water. Governed by a timer programmed to water one hour daily at a moderate rate, soaker hoses keep plants luxuriant and growing unchecked.

There are two common types of soaker hoses, both inexpensive. The simplest allows water to seep through tiny pores. Snake the hose through the garden and pin in place with plastic pegs designed

Drip emitter systems deliver water to individual plants. Many types of emitters are available, delivering water at different rates.

for that purpose. Or make your own pegs from U-shaped pieces of wire coat hanger. The coils of the hose can be looped 10 to 12 inches apart. A soaker hose is sold coiled and it wants to stay coiled; a few hours stretched out in hot midsummer sun makes it easier to arrange in an established garden. A soaker hose system is easiest to position *before* planting—place the coils exactly where the plants need them, before growth starts in spring and the annuals are planted.

The other type is a flat hose that shoots fine jets of water from pin-sized holes. This type can be set hole-side down so the water seeps into the soil, or it can be faced upward and allowed to shoot water into the air. In that position with the water pressure raised, this type

of soaker hose sprays a large area, so it can be used for overhead watering as well.

Soaker hoses are made of a variety of materials—nylon, vinyl, polyester, polyethylene, or recycled tires. The lengths are joined to couplings of various designs so you can create a network that covers the garden from one water source. Designing and installing the system is tedious but well worth the effort, because, once established, it stays in place. The hardest part is adjusting the water pressure so it drips at the front end and still has pressure enough to drip at the far end too. Once it is installed, check under the mulch on your daily rounds of the garden to make sure the system is working well.

Drip Emitter Systems In this type of system, water flows through a filter and a pressure regulator into a network of small-diameter pipes studded with emitters. The emitters, which deliver water drop by drop, may be positioned so they water one or more plants. Water moves through the soil to a distance of about 1 foot from the emitter. The systems can clog and need to be checked occasionally. They usually are controlled by a timer.

A drip emitter system is custom-designed to meet the needs of each plant in the garden. Do-it-yourself kits are available. You or the retailer do the designing. When buying a system, you submit a scale drawing of the garden, showing the planned plantings, the topography of the area to be watered, and other specifics. The system is equipped with recommended spacing for the emitters, and all the pipes and equipment needed to install it.

Drip emitter systems are easy to adapt to container gardens and, coupled with a timer, save you a lot of time.

Slow-Flow Emitters Drip emitters are being replaced by slow-flow emitters, which apply the water a bit faster and with less evaporation. Slow-flow emitters are used extensively in the West, usually with organic mulch or geotextiles, occasionally with black plastic.

Furrow Irrigation In dry regions, very large gardens planned for row-crop growing often are watered via a network of shallow, narrow furrows which are flooded by hoses or slow-flow emitters as needed. The furrows are dug the length of the planting rows, 5 or 6 inches from the plants and to a depth calculated to bring the water to the root systems. The furrows must angle slightly downhill

Furrow irrigation might be the most ancient type of irrigation system. A series of ditches or furrows are dug beside the plants and each one is filled with water for an hour or so. In home vegetable gardens, the water source is usually a garden hose laid at one end of the furrow.

to enable the water to flow to the end of the row; but an angle that is too steep deprives the upper part of the row of its share of water. The space left for paths must be wide enough to accommodate both the furrows and the gardener.

Self-Watering Planters Watering container plants is a constant necessity. If you find this burdensome, investigate the many types of double-bottomed planters and pots. Developed for indoor plants—and expensive—they do allow you to leave town. The water reservoir built into these containers carries the plants for several days, and even weeks, depending on the weather and the size of the planter.

SEEDS AND SEASONS

Planting seeds may be the most magical act in gardening. You plant a tiny, dry flake, and a few days later a living plant emerges—green, growing, and rich with promise.

Once you have chosen a site, planned the garden, and prepared the soil, it's time to look at the many vegetables available. Start by perusing the catalogs for the myriad possibilities you can consider.

If you are new to vegetable gardening, try to restrain yourself. It's easy to get carried away by all the wonderful vegetables you can grow and end up ordering more than you have the room for, or the time to tend. It's much more satisfying to plant too little and grow it well than to plant too much and not be able to care for it properly.

But if you can't have it all, how do you decide what to grow? For starters, select vegetables that you can't buy locally but would like to eat. If you like salads, grow a selection of salad greens that often aren't available in grocery stores, such as mâche, endive, or mustard greens. Select unusual varieties of ordinary vegetables, such as extra-flavorful tropical melons, blue corn for making corn meal, or white tomatoes. As you browse through seed catalogs, you will discover many strange and wonderful new vegetables.

Another criterion for making selections for your garden is to choose vegetables that are far superior fresh from the garden than when bought from a market. Garden peas, for example, begin converting sugar to starch as soon as they are picked. Peas cooked within an hour of picking are so sweet they hardly need cooking at all. Grocery store peas, however, are at least a day old and possibly much older than that. Much of their sugar has become starch, decreasing the flavor and making the peas tough and starchy. Corn, like peas, is sweeter right after picking.

Tomatoes, strawberries, and other tender vegetables are usually picked for market before they are

Seed catalogs are one of the best bargains in gardening. They are often free, at least if you make a purchase, and contain a wealth of information about the varieties they contain. The best place to locate seed catalogs is in the winter issues of gardening magazines, where the seed companies advertise their catalogs.

fully ripe because they become too soft and fragile to travel well. They are allowed to ripen en route to market, but at the price of flavor. Tomatoes picked from the vine when fully ripe are far sweeter and more flavorful than tomatoes picked a little green.

There are many other reasons to select certain vegetables. Some are fun to grow, such as giant pumpkins or sunflowers. And some are good selections for children, such as strawberries or peas, which children love to pick and eat right in the garden. Choose the vegetables that will give you the most satisfaction, but remember to use a touch of restraint.

CATALOGS

Take out the garden catalogs you have stashed away and stack them by an easy chair. Have a seat, relax, and, with this book in your lap, open to the vegetable chapters, be-

ginning on page 105. Leaf through the catalogs and make lots of shopping lists. This is the fun part and you should thoroughly enjoy yourself. The real challenge comes once your final list is made and you must then cut it in half to fit everything into your garden space.

Many companies mail their catalogs for free; others charge a modest fee which may be credited against your first order. The books land on your doorstep late December through mid-February, offering everything you could ever want in the way of seeds, bulbs, and gardening equipment.

Large Catalogs

The big mail-order companies often have the latest pest- and disease-free hybrids. They stay on top of the trends and have a little of everything. Although their selections are among the largest, they are not always fine-tuned to the needs of specific regions and climates.

Small Catalogs

The less glossy catalogs mailed by mom-and-pop companies generally reflect someone's particular passion. Look to the small catalogs for gourmet and novelty items, exotic vegetables, superb flavor, and unusual, imported, and heirloom cultivars. Specialty catalogs, for instance, may offer seeds of European or South American vegetables not available in local supermarkets.

Regional Catalogs

Look to regional catalogs for seeds that germinate and mature reliably in your area. This is especially important if you garden in high-risk climates such as the arid Southwest, the cool, wet Northwest, or in cold New England. Cultivars that originate in your region should do well in your garden. The small mail-order sources are in business because their customers always come back for more.

GARDEN CENTERS

Garden centers stock racks of name-brand seeds, but their major asset is their supply of seedlings. Early in the season and later when it is time to set out summer and early-fall crops, garden centers offer seedlings ready to beat the time clock.

Seeds Versus Seedlings

Sowing a pack of seeds is less work than transplanting dozens of seedlings. And it is the best method in regions where the climate allows the crop time to mature from seed. But setting out seedling transplants saves a lot of growing time. If the growing season is too short to mature two successive crops from seed, it may mature two crops set out as transplants. In the North, only the tiniest and earliest tomatoes started in the garden as

seeds have time to ripen a full crop before frost. In warmer regions cool-weather vegetables, such as broccoli, set out as seed may bolt in heat before harvest.

Many gardeners enjoy growing their own seedlings, especially in early winter while waiting for the garden to warm up. The chart on page 75 lists the vegetables most often set out as transplants and tells how soon before planting time seeds should be sown indoors. Few

---

PLANT NOMENCLATURE

The only accurate names for plants are the Latin botanical names. They are listed first by genus, then species, as in *Lycopersicon esculentum*, the correct name for tomato. Further names include the variety or the cultivar, if there is one. Most people use common names, which are usually dependable for vegetables but not for most ornamental plants; often many names exist for the same plant, and common names vary from region to region.

The *genus* is a subgroup of more closely related plants within a plant *family*.

The *species* is a subgroup of the genus and groups plants with even more similar characteristics.

The *variety* is a variation of a species found in the wild.

A *cultivar* is a "cultivated variety"—a variation of a species selected and developed by plant specialists.

A *hybrid* is a cross between two species, usually created by plant specialists. When two selected hybrids are crossed, the result is an F1 hybrid. The cost of pollination, which is done by hand, explains the higher price of the F1 hybrid seed.

ABOUT SEEDLINGS

Growing in the garden, seedlings suffer a little stress—enough to slow growth a bit and make sturdy plants. It takes a while for them to become as lush-looking as seedlings from a greenhouse. But plants fresh out of the greenhouse are sometimes overgrown and tender from their special treatment. They may need some time to get established and toughen up once you plant them in the garden.

Some neighborhood nurseries and garden centers grow their own seedlings. Some will even start seeds you bring in and then sell you the seedlings. But they tend more and more to sell seedlings purchased from wholesale growers. Seedlings from wholesalers are usually chosen for their quick germination, proven performance, shelf life, and visual appeal. The focus generally is not on grand old garden cultivars and taste treats. They offer a few of the tried-and-true favorites, but you will not find a lot of variety. If you did, the many small seed catalogs offering specialty herbs and vegetables would have gone out of business long ago.

This is 'Burpee's Big Boy' tomato, requiring a long growing season of warm weather. If your growing season is too short, purchase very large plants, perhaps in gallon cans or larger. Planted in your garden after the nights become warm, the tomato will continue to bear throughout the growing season.

gardeners set out seedlings of root crops. Spring radishes take only three to four weeks to sprout and mature, and turnips or carrots have time to mature from seed almost everywhere. Root crops have taproots, and these do not transplant well. But tomatoes and peppers are another story—everyone wants both early.

Tomatoes are one of the most popular warm-weather crops that cannot be sown outdoors until the temperature approaches 70° F. Some gardeners plant tomato seeds and seedlings. The tiny, very flavorful 'Sweet 100 Hybrid' tomatoes begin to mature in 57 days, so there is time for a crop from seed in most areas. The big, juicy beefsteak tomatoes require 80 days to mature, so gardeners in most of the country install these as big container-grown plants already flowering and sometimes fruiting.

Buying Quality Seedlings

When selecting seedlings, make sure you get the best the garden center has to offer. Garden centers are likely to care well for their stock. But some of the bargain chains, supermarkets, and hardware stores that offer seedlings in spring are not set up for plants. Seedlings whose growth has been checked by lack of water, light, or air are off to a poor start.

Look for seedlings with crisp, dark green foliage. Avoid flats whose seedlings are yellowing at the base.

Look for sturdy, stocky growth. Avoid seedlings whose leaves are stretched out on weak stems. They may have been deprived of light and perhaps nutrients.

Look for seedlings whose soil is damp. If the soil in the flats is bone dry, even if the seedlings have not yet wilted, they are facing a check in development that shows up as delayed growth after you transplant.

Look for pests. Are there minute holes in the leaves? Are patches of the leaves sticky looking? Do dustlike motes dance up when you brush the foliage? If you bring home critters, they will buzz off to infest the rest of the garden.

CHOOSING CULTIVARS

Appeal and timing are the first considerations in choosing seeds—but give thought to the advantages of disease-resistant plants as you peruse the catalog offerings.

Catalogs offer an astounding quantity of cultivars of each vegetable and fruit. Every one of those

cultivars has characteristics someone considered especially desirable. Flavor, appearance, use, ease
of cooking, and resistance to disease are some of the attributes described. The growers talk up their
strong points. Some are noted as
exceptional for making pies or
jams, or for freezing, preserving, or
canning; others are said to be ideal
for grilling or stir-frying, or for use
in Asian, Italian, or other ethnic
recipes. Think about how you plan
to use your harvest and make
choices accordingly.

Days to Maturity

As a generalization, you can expect
cultivars of the same vegetable to
be ready for harvesting in somewhat the same time frame. You can
begin picking 'Italian Summer'
spinach in 40 days and the Dutch
spinach called 'Wolter' in 37 days—
not much difference.

When the difference between
days to maturity is surprisingly
large, ask yourself why. Sometimes
there is a good reason. For instance, the Dutch radish cultivar
called 'Redball' matures in 24
days, whereas the hybrid Japanese
radish called 'Daikon Omny' requires 55 days. The difference is
that 'Redball' is a little spring
radish, and 'Daikon Omny' is a
long, large, late-winter radish that
matures from seeds planted in
late summer or early autumn.

Early, Midseason, and Late Cultivars

Some popular vegetable cultivars
are classed as early, midseason,
or late, and there can be significant
differences in days to maturity.
Often the early cultivars are smaller, but size is not everything, especially with tomatoes.

The little 'Peacevine' cherry
tomato grows on a small, 2- to 3-
foot vine and is ready in 50 days.

DAYS TO MATURITY

"Days to maturity" is the time from planting a seed to picking the
harvest. This can range from 26 days for radishes to five months for
sweet potatoes. This information is listed in catalog descriptions
and on seed packets, and with it you know whether your climate
has a long enough growing season for the crop to mature from seed
sown in the open garden.

By studying the days to maturity for different types of seeds, you
can use the same patch of soil to yield three crops in one season.
Do this by combining simultaneous sowings of small, quick-to-
mature vegetables such as radishes with taller, slow-to-mature
species such as brussels sprouts. Harvest the fast growers out of the
row as the slower ones start to take up space. You can also plant
mid- and late-season cultivars where fast-maturing early crops
have been harvested.

Though it is many times larger
than a cherry tomato, the early-
maturing cultivar called 'Early
Girl', a delicious, standard-sized
tomato, takes only two days longer
to be ready for picking.

The Japanese mid- or main-
season cultivar called 'Pink Odoriko' needs a full 76 days to mature.
The paste tomatoes are smaller
than 'Early Girl', but some take 100
days, whereas 'Big Boy', a huge,
dense tomato, is ready to pick in
78 days.

Early Often cultivars noted as
"early" and "late" withstand cold
weather in spring and at the end of
the summer more easily than those
labeled "midseason."

Early cultivars of fast-growing
crops are especially interesting
if you live in a cool climate and are
planning succession cropping to
maximize the harvest from a small
garden. Sown or set out early,
when the soil and the weather are
changeable, they mature quickly,
leaving behind plant material ready
for composting and a row ready for
a second round of plants.

Not all crops are conveniently
labeled "early," "midseason," or
"late." Often you must figure that
out for yourself. Early cultivars of

slow-growing crops, such as the little 'Scoop 11 Hybrid' cantaloupe, are not necessarily labeled "early," but they ripen in 68 to 70 days compared with 'Ambrosia Hybrid', which matures in 86 days. The earlier, smaller fruit has time to mature in the short season of the cool upper tier of the country.

Early, or fast-maturing, seed offerings are just what you want for a crop to succeed the early-spring plantings of peas, radishes, and lettuce. The 'Early Bird Hybrid' eggplant that matures in 50 days can follow a crop of lettuce, whereas 'Rosa Bianca', a beautiful, lavender Italian heirloom eggplant, will not make it before cool weather, because it needs a full three weeks more to mature, 75 days altogether.

Midseason   Midseason cultivars mature between the early cultivars and the late cultivars. They stay a fairly long time in the garden and have excellent flavor, but may be somewhat smaller than the late cultivars of the same plant. A valuable attribute of midseason cultivars is their capacity to stand up to hot weather better than those noted as either early or late.

Late   The cultivars labeled "late" withstand frost at the end of the growing cycle. Those that mature over a long season, such as the late tomatoes, often have especially rich flavor. Often late cultivars stand up to intense summer heat.

Pest- and Disease-Resistant Seeds

Each plant has natural defenses that protect it from disease. Plants may react to attack by sealing off infected areas to prevent the problem from spreading. They also have some fascinating chemical defenses that may be called into play when an attack occurs. There is even evidence that when one plant in a group suffers attack, or becomes weakened and susceptible to attack, others will rev up their defense systems to prepare for the onslaught. Scientists will continue to develop genetically altered cultivars. For now, the first line of defense against disease is to choose healthy specimens.

More resistant cultivars are being developed now that growers are dispensing with chemical blitzes to solve garden problems. Planting resistant seeds is easier and healthier than spraying for disease. Disease resistance is noted in the literature. If nothing is said, assume that there is no special resistance—there may be no need for it.

Because gardeners grow tomatoes more than any other food plant, a lot of work has gone into producing disease-resistant tomato plants. In the catalogs you will encounter tomato cultivars accompanied by strings of initials representing resistance to specific diseases (see page 131). *Big Beef VFFNTA*, for example, indicates resistance to verticillium, fusarium wilt 1 and 2, nematodes, tobacco mosaic, and anthracnose.

More often, disease resistance is noted in catalog text. For instance, descriptions of peas often include comments such as "very resistant to pea enation mosaic and powdery mildew" (pea enation is a virus that spoils the pods). This is a cue for you to ask the local extension agent whether pea enation and powdery mildew are prevalent in your area. The question to ask the agent is: "Are peas susceptible to any diseases or problems in this area?"

All-America Selections

All-America Selections (AAS) is a nonprofit organization that tests and evaluates seeds of new cultivars submitted by growers. The seeds of 20 new plants for the home garden are tested every year at universities, botanical gardens, and other professional horticultural facilities in the United States and Canada. You can see their choices at more than 200 AAS public gardens. The All-America Selection award goes to plants that show pest and disease resistance, give superior performance and yield in the home garden, and have a special appeal as well as better flavor, texture, efficiency, and nutritional value. Those designated as Gold Medal Winners represent a breakthrough in plant breeding, and you can expect truly wonderful results.

Heirloom Cultivars

Because market produce travels far and must last on the shelf, growers have developed extra-tough cultivars that are easy to harvest, uniform in size, and withstand shipping. These attributes are sometimes won at the cost of flavor. Many wonderful old cultivars have been lost, but some of the great heirloom fruits and vegetables are being collected and the seed saved and made available. The present interest in preserving our planet's biodiversity has attracted funding for the preservation of such treasures.

Although there are great expectations for today's hybrids and the

Heirloom vegetables are those that were developed long ago. Many are rare and available only from collectors and specialty seed houses, but some are still popular. This is the kitchen garden at the Governor's Palace, in Colonial Williamsburg, where the types of vegetables grown might also have been grown here before the Revolution.

Kale, one of the hardiest vegetables, tolerates some frost. It is shown here the morning after a hard frost, and again a couple of weeks later, growing strong.

genetically engineered plants of tomorrow, there is a cornucopia of flavor available right now from heirloom cultivars. Many of these plants were ignored because they do not do well as mass-produced farm products. Many have lesser commercial appeal because they bruise easily, are not uniform in color or shape, or ripen over a longer period. Some have been

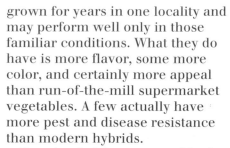

grown for years in one locality and may perform well only in those familiar conditions. What they do have is more flavor, some more color, and certainly more appeal than run-of-the-mill supermarket vegetables. A few actually have more pest and disease resistance than modern hybrids.

Growing heirloom vegetables has a special appeal for the romantic, the history buff, or the gardener who expects more from the garden than just food. These plants come to us from the days of this country's earliest settlers. They make a connection with people who planted the same seeds generations and generations ago. Heirloom seeds are turning up in more and more commercial catalogs. A National Seed Storage Laboratory is maintained by the federal government in Fort Collins, Colorado, as part of an effort to maintain genetic diversity.

PLANTING SEASONS

The traditional planting season for the open garden begins in the cool, wet weather of early spring. Depending on the vegetable, the harvest begins three weeks to three months later. In this vast country, "early spring" is a way of saying "cool weather with frequent rains to come," and it can happen from January to May, depending on the part of the country.

Frost Dates

The cooperative extension office or even a local nursery can tell you the frost dates for your area. In spring this is the approximate date of the last spring frost; in fall it is the approximate date of the first fall frost. These dates are an average over the years for a given area and serve as guidelines when planting seeds and seedlings.

VEGETABLE HARDINESS

Cool-Season Crops
The following plants tolerate some frost and air temperatures between 55° to 70° F.

Asparagus
Beet
Broccoli
Brussels sprouts
Cabbage
Collard
Kale
Kohlrabi
Lettuce
Onion
Parsnip
Peas
Radish
Spinach
Turnip
Turnip greens

Semicool-Season Crops
The following vegetables tolerate some cold but no frost at maturity.

Artichoke
Carrot
Cauliflower
Endive
White potato

Warm-Season Crops
The following crops are readily damaged by frost and are best adapted to 65° to 80° F. They rot in cold soil.

Beans
Cantaloupe
Chard
Corn
Cucumber
Muskmelon
Pepper
Potato
Pumpkin
Squash
Sweet corn
Tomato

Hot-Weather Crops
Planted when temperatures are between 65° and 80° F, these plants require a long growing season and do well in temperatures above 80° F.

Lima beans
Shell beans
Eggplant
Okra
Peanuts
Sweet potato
Watermelon

When to Plant

Plant vegetables in batches, according to their weather preference. There are cool-season crops, warm-season crops, and hot-weather crops. The cool-season crops are the seeds you can sow before the last frost date in spring. Plant warm-season crops later in spring when the soil has warmed a bit, and plant hot-weather crops last of all.

A variety of vegetables have adapted to every climate on the globe, from the short summers of the arctic to the year-round growing seasons of the southern states and subtropical regions. But most vegetables are seed-sown annuals that evolved where the early part of the growing season is cool and rainy. This is springtime, and seed packets for most vegetables suggest planting sometime in spring.

Just *when* in the calendar year spring occurs varies according to geographic location. In Anchorage, Alaska, this is in June, but to the south in San Jose, California, "early spring" arrives in late January. In fact, the planting season in San Jose is almost all year around. For most of the country, the planting seasons are somewhat more distinct.

Early Spring In warm regions, early spring and late winter overlap. In the North this is "when the ground dries enough to be worked" and "when the frost is out of the ground." During these cool few weeks, some frost-resistant cool-season plants can be started suc-

Top: In early spring, start plants in protected settings. This greenhouse made from a drink cooler grows seeds to transplant size. Bottom: A home-made row cover protects transplants.

are sown at this time, including head lettuces, spinach and other leafy greens, parsnips, and carrots.

Late Spring   When the night chill is gone and days begin to head toward 80° F, late spring has arrived. Now it is safe to set out warm-season crops such as tomatoes, peppers and squash, as well as the hot-weather crops such as watermelons and sweet potatoes.

Midsummer   In the cool northern tier, make successive sowings of snap beans, broccoli, cabbage, carrots, lettuces, and parsnips for early-fall harvesting. Where summer is too hot for sowing seeds outdoors, start them indoors or in a cold frame with some protection from heat and drying winds. In very hot regions, winter is usually mild, and sowing for the second season is delayed until the heat lets up and there is hope of rain.

Late Summer, Early Fall   In the South, sow winter crops of hardy vegetables such as beets, broccoli, and spinach.

Winter   In mild climates pull kale, carrots, and other root vegetables all winter. Almost everywhere parsnips, which taste better after a frost, can overwinter and be harvested as an early-spring crop. In mild regions plant peas in October for extra-early spring picking. Several of the cover crops listed on page 38 grow over the winter.

Perennials
Unlike the majority of vegetables, which are annuals, perennials must survive the year around. For these plants, winter weather is significant. Be sure to choose perennials that are hardy in your region. Before you order artichokes or any of the other perennials beginning on page 289, make sure they can survive the winter.

cessfully in the open garden: peas, onion sets, fast-growing radishes, and early leaf lettuces. In the cool North, gardeners force the season by planting under hot caps and plastic tents, cheating the cold as best they can.

Spring   This is the long, moderately warm period after the last frost and before the first real heat. Most of the cool-season vegetables

Top: Artichokes are perennial. They can be grown as perennials only in areas with mild winters, but are sometimes grown as annuals in other places.
Bottom: The microclimate on the south side of this white wall is hotter and brighter than elsewhere in the garden, good for starting spring transplants and for ripening tomatoes in the summer.

In early spring garden centers offer a handful of perennial fruits and vegetables as young container plants. In mid- to late summer in the South and mid-Atlantic states, container-grown perennials are available, because these regions can count on another two or three months of growing weather before winter sets in. As a rule, nurseries offer only those perennials that do well locally and can survive the winter. But it does not hurt to ask questions before purchasing a perennial.

Microclimates

The growing season is governed by prevailing temperatures and weather, but there are microclimates in your garden as well, places that are warmer or cooler than the rest of the yard. Here you can grow plants that may not usually succeed in your climate. Vegetables warmed by a south-facing wall withstand more cold than the same plants on a north-facing slope. Walls, corners, windows or other reflective surfaces that bounce the sun back at the garden, the shelter provided by a large tree or a bank of evergreen shrubs—all these can raise surrounding temperatures in any season. Planting below an overhanging roof protects plants from freezing temperatures in areas with only occasional winter frost.

HEAD START ON PLANTING

Another way to circumvent the limitations of climate and temperature is to extend the season at either end by starting seeds early. You can plant them indoors, or outside in a cold frame, a hotbed, or the open garden under hot caps or plastic tenting of various types.

If you can provide a cool room with grow lights or a bank of sunny windows, seeds grow very well indoors. They may not look like nursery seedlings, unless you have greenhouse conditions, but they will thrive and give you a head start on the season.

Start seeds indoors as little as three weeks before planting outside, or as much as three months early. As a rule, sow fast-growing cultivars four to six weeks before planting time, and slow-growing cultivars six to eight weeks ahead. The seedlings should be crowding their containers when planting time arrives. The chart on page 75 gives the time needed from seeding to transplant size for vegetables started early.

Two weeks after the last frost, it generally is safe to transplant to the open garden seedlings started indoors. The outside daytime temperature should have reached at least 55° F. Many annuals will not start growing until the ground warms up. Transplanting too early just means they will not begin to grow until the temperature rises.

Garden centers and catalogs sell peat pots, expandable peat wafers, and plastic containers and flats, all designed for starting seeds. The

The best location for growing seedlings is one with bright light or full sun, but moderate temperatures (under 75° F). A well-ventilated greenhouse window or home greenhouse is ideal.

flats without individual planting pockets are the easiest in which to plant. The flats with pockets are the easiest from which to transplant.

You can start seeds in almost any large, shallow container, from a milk jug to a cardboard egg carton. Be sure to cut a drainage hole or two. The two major impediments to home-grown seedlings are damping-off fungus and yellowing of the lower leaves, both encouraged by excessive moisture. The best medium for starting seeds indoors is a sterilized soilless growing medium. Any commercial mix labeled "sterile" that includes perlite, sphagnum peat moss, vermiculite, polymers, and nutrients is suitable.

You can make your own soilless medium, following the recipes given on page 36.

Temperatures for Indoor Germination

The answer to "Will it germinate?" is yes—if you keep it where the temperature is right day and night. Most seed packets list temperature requirements for germination. The best sprouting temperature for warm-season vegetables is 68° to 80° F day and night. Moisten with water that is room-temperature, not cold.

Once the seedlings are well established, they need a cooler environment. If the seeds have not germinated in 20 days, start over again with a fresh batch. The 20-day rule does not apply to seeds of lavender and a few other herbs. Read labels! If the seeds require an extra-long time to germinate, the packets will specify that.

Warmth and sustained moisture are essential to the development of seedlings. A seed comes packed with one or a pair of primitive leaves, the cotyledons, which are the first pair that open toward the top of the spindly stem. If all goes well, a pair of "true" leaves will follow, indicating that the seedling is developing roots and is on its way. If the cotyledon dries out during germination, the seed dies. To keep the growth of seedlings unchecked, loosely tent the growing medium with clear plastic to hold in moisture. Poke a few air holes in the plastic.

Sowing Seed in Peat Pots

A few herbs and vegetables do not transplant well, notably dill and the cucumber group. These fail if their roots are disturbed. They transplant more successfully when started in individual peat pots that can go right into the planting hole with the plant inside. Peat pots are also a good choice for larger seeds.

One type of "pot" is a compressed peat pellet, a coarse wafer of crushed peat moss with nutrients added. Some types are enclosed in a mesh that eventually disintegrates. When water is added, the pellets swell into small cylinders of peat about 2 inches across and seven times the original height. The following steps outline the procedures for starting seeds in peat pellets.

1. To prepare the pellets for planting, arrange them side by side in a large pan. Add enough warm water to cover the pellets, adding more water as needed until they are fully expanded.

2. When the pellets have reached their full size, use a pencil point to make one to three shallow planting holes in the top of each pellet (one when the seed is large, three when using smaller seeds), spaced as far apart as possible. Poke the seeds into the planting holes about ¼ inch, then press lightly with your thumb to cover the holes. Label each set of seeds.

3. Tent the containers with plastic that has several small holes for air exchange. Keep the pellets in a well-lighted area but out of direct sunlight. As soon as the seeds germinate, poke more holes in the plastic tent to increase ventilation and prevent overheating.

4. When the pellets begin to turn a lighter brown and dry out, add warm water to the container. Remember that at this stage they must stay moist but not soaking wet. After germination, reduce watering slightly, but do not let the seedlings dry out.

5. When the seedlings show their second set of true leaves, remove the tent and reduce watering. Place the containers in a south-facing window where they receive at least six hours of direct sunlight a day. At this stage seedlings do best in temperatures of 60° to 70° F during the day, dropping about 10° F at night. Turn the container daily to keep the stems growing straight. Plants are heliotropic, which means they bend toward the light.

6. As the seedlings begin to crowd each other, use scissors to thin them to one per pot, snipping off the weak ones. If you pull out the extras, you may unintentionally pull up the one you want to keep, because the roots are tangled.

7. Three to four weeks after the seeds have germinated, begin applying diluted liquid fertilizer.

8. When the roots begin to grow through the bottoms of the pots, it's time to transplant. See Transplanting Into the Garden on page 74.

Also available are peat containers shaped like 2-inch pots. You fill these with sterile growing medium and plant and care for the seeds as just described.

Sowing Seeds in Flats

Flats are large, shallow containers that hold many seeds, usually in rows. Provide the flats with drainage holes and a drip tray so you can water them from the bottom.

1. Soak the growing medium in a bucket several times until it is thoroughly wet. When you are ready to

Kits such as this one can be purchased to start seeds. This one provides individual containers in a tray to collect water, and a clear plastic cover to preserve moisture and heat. Don't put any container with a clear cover in direct sun or the plants will overheat.

PLANTING DEPTHS FOR SEEDS

Vegetable	Approximate Depth	Vegetable	Approximate Depth
Artichoke	Divisions	Kohlrabi	½"–1"
Arugula	¼"	Lettuce	¼"
Asparagus	Roots, 10"	Mâche	¼"
Bean	1"–1½"	Muskmelon	½"
Beet	½"	Mustard greens	½"
Broccoli	½"–1"	Okra	¼"
Brussels sprouts	½"–1"	Onion	Sets, 1"–2"
Cabbage	½"–1"	Parsnip	½"
Carrot	½"	Peanuts	1"–2"
Cauliflower	½"–1"	Peas	2"
Celeriac	¼"	Pepper	¼"
Celtuce	½"	Potato	2"–3" eyes
Chard	½"	Pumpkin	1½"–2"
Chayote	4"–5"	Radicchio	¼"–½"
Collards	¼"	Radish	½"
Corn	1"–2"	Rhubarb	Divisions
Cress	¼"	Rutabaga	½"
Cucumber	1"	Sorrel	⅛"
Dandelion	½"	Spinach	½"
Eggplant	¼"–½"	Squash	1½"–2"
Endive	¼"–½"	Strawberry	Plants, ground level
Escarole	¼"–½"	Sunflower	1"
Fennel, Florence	¼"	Sweet potato	Plants
Garlic	Bulb, 1"	Tomatillo	½"
Gourd	1½"–2"	Tomato	½"
Jerusalem artichoke	Tubers, 4"	Turnip	¼"–½"
Kale	½"	Watermelon	½"

sow seeds, soak the medium once more with warm water. Allow it to drain thoroughly, then fill the flats to within ¼ inch of the top.

2. Plant each type of seed according to the chart above. A pencil works well to poke planting holes in the medium. Seeds should be at least ⅛ inch apart.

If the seed is very fine, mix it with sand before sowing. Press very fine seed gently onto the growing medium. Cover slightly larger seed with a sprinkling of vermiculite or the growing medium. Label the flats.

3. Mist the top of each flat with warm water and follow the instructions for growing seeds in peat pellets, starting with step 3 on the previous page.

Transplanting Seedlings Indoors

Many gardeners move flat-grown seedlings to 2- or 4-inch pots and "grow them out" before planting in the garden. It is more work, but the seedlings grow bigger and stronger. Most gardeners reserve the effort for prize tomatoes. After you transplant, water the seedlings as before, but discontinue fertilizing until two or three new sets of leaves begin to unfold. At this point the root system is beginning to grow again and you can resume fertilizing. Provide very bright natural light, or grow the seedlings under continuous overhead artificial light.

Growing Seedlings Under Lights

Seedlings grow dark green and sturdy in any cool indoor spot under artificial light. Many types of fixtures are available for growing plants indoors. A simple light source is a 3½- to 4-foot cool-white or warm-white fluorescent bulb, or a combination of the two. Fluorescent bulbs sold as "grow lamps" cost more, and the experts say nothing has proved they do more.

The handiest growing frames mount the lights on adjustable legs so they can be raised or lowered according to the needs of the plants. Because fluorescent bulbs are most efficient their first year, with their intensity diminishing as time passes, replace the bulbs every few years.

For the first few weeks after transplanting seedlings, use fluorescent tubes, or grow lights, set about 3 inches above the seedlings. Fluorescent plant lights can be left on 24 hours a day at this stage. As the seedlings grow, raise the light to 4 to 6 inches overhead. Once the seedlings show strong growth, reduce the exposure to 14 to 16 hours a day.

Seeds germinate under grow lights if you maintain the required temperature both day and night. Two 40-watt fluorescent tubes set 5 to 6 inches above the seeds trays provide enough light and warmth for germination and early growth. Use plastic sheeting such as the type from a dry cleaner to create a makeshift growth chamber if a cool room makes warmth hard to sustain on a 24-hour basis.

OUTDOOR PROTECTION

Cold frames and hotbeds are invaluable for starting seeds early and preparing indoor-grown seedlings for outdoors (see Hardening Off Seedlings on page 74). They are especially useful in cold regions where frost lingers and the soil

This cold frame is made from old windows. It must be vented during the day to keep from overheating. Cold frames and hot beds (heated cold frames) are used to start vegetables early in short-season areas. After the early vegetables are planted out in the garden, many gardeners fill the cold frame with heat-loving plants such as cucumbers for an early summer harvest.

warms up late in the spring. In hot climates they provide a controlled environment for starting perennials and fall crops during the heat of summer. Where winters are mild, you can grow salad greens all through the cool months in a cold frame or hotbed. Try arugula, the early leaf lettuces, radishes, mâche, endive chives, and other cool-season greens.

Cold Frame

A cold frame is a passive solar collector. The basic form is a box without a bottom, roofed over with glass or clear plastic. The glass is set at a 45-degree angle toward the south so it warms up quickly, snow slides off easily, and water does not sit on the cover. The heat absorbed during the day keeps the interior relatively warm at night.

Some cold frames are permanent installations; others are portable. Permanent frames are set several inches into the earth and usually have a foundation. Portable frames sit on the ground. They offer less protection from the cold, but there are compensations: A portable cold frame can be moved around in the garden and used to extend the season for fall crops and, in mild regions, to protect winter crops.

Ready-made cold frames are sold as kits that are ready to assemble. You can make your own by setting pressure-treated boards into the earth and topping the frame with an old storm window or glass door. Heavy-duty plastic sheeting mounted on a hinged frame works, too. To maximize the amount of light that reaches the plants, paint the interior white or silver.

Because the cold frame heats up in direct sunlight, keep the top partially open during the day and close it at night. A thermometer is an essential part of the equipment, because on a hot day with the frame closed the interior can reach 100° F. You can buy cold frames equipped with solar-powered openers triggered by high temperatures.

Hotbed

A hotbed is a cold frame with a heat source inside. It has to be sunk into the ground at least 12 inches to allow space for an underground heating cable. Because it is heated, you can start seedlings in a hotbed earlier in the season. When horses and buggies were rapid transport, hotbeds were heated by the composting of an underground layer of raw horse manure.

Hot Caps and Other Toppers

Hot caps are passive solar collectors for individual plants. They are variations on the old-time plant "cloche," a bell-shaped jar set over a plant. Cloches were used extensively to speed and protect the growth of prize plants. They let in the light and keep out the cold and wind. As

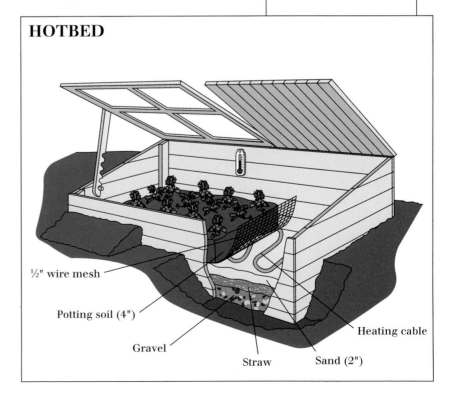

HOTBED

½" wire mesh

Potting soil (4")

Gravel

Straw

Sand (2")

Heating cable

Plastic milk jugs with the bottoms cut off protect individual plants in cool spring weather. Leave the cap on during colder days and remove it for ventilation during warmer days.

sorb the sun's heat during the day and release it slowly at night. The water keeps the temperature more stable while allowing sunlight to pass through easily. The makers claim it can protect plants to 20° F.

In the frosty upper tier of the country and in Europe, truck farms provide extra-early garden produce by starting the plants under elongated fiberglass tunnels. Sometimes the plants grow to maturity inside these little greenhouses. The tunnels are offered in mail-order catalogs.

TRANSPLANTING INTO THE GARDEN

When the seedlings have at least two sets of true leaves, you can transplant them into the garden. As mentioned, you may prefer to transplant them into bigger containers and grow them into larger specimens before placing them in the garden, especially if the weather is too cold or wet. When you are ready to plant them outdoors, be sure the forecast is for fair weather.

Hardening Off Seedlings

Hardening off is a method of toughening up seedlings started indoors so they can survive outside. Do this by gradually getting them used to the extremes of outdoor temperatures. If you have a cold frame or hotbed (see page 73), put them inside for about a week, leaving the top open for longer and longer stretches. Otherwise, place the seedlings in a warm spot but out of direct sunlight for three or four days. Then place them in a spot with direct morning sun for another three or four days. Be sure to keep them watered—they dry out quickly. After this period of acclimation, they are ready to go into the ground.

the sun goes down and the evening cools, the heat stored in the dark soil beneath the hot cap or cloche releases slowly, creating a greenhouse effect that promotes growth.

A number of modern toppers are available, some made of waxed paper, others of plastic. The dome heats up quickly under hot sun, so it is important to monitor or remove the hot caps when the sun is high. A bottomless plastic milk jug without the cap yields similar results. See Winter Protection on page 79.

A popular and rather more elaborate invention for insulating plants is the Wall-O-Water® (see photo on page 79). The hollow plastic walls hold three gallons of water that ab-

Seedlings in Peat Pellets Before transplanting seedlings growing in peat pellets, soak the bottoms of the pellet, then pull apart the bottom third of the pellet, leaving the top intact.

Seedlings in Peat Pots When you plant the seedlings, pot and all, remove the bottom of the pot just as you would a peat pellet. You must also tear off any top edges of the pot just below the soil line before pressing it into the planting hole. Bury the pot completely. If a peat-pot edge protrudes from the soil, it will wick moisture away from the rootball.

Seedlings in Flats You can free seedlings that have become intertwined in a flat by cleanly slicing them apart with a sharp knife. Some gardeners prefer to grasp the rootball with their fingers and gently pull the seedling away from the others, keeping as many of the roots intact as possible.

Seedlings in Pockets To transplant seedlings growing in pockets in a flat, use your thumbs to push up the bottom of the pocket and gently lift out each rootball, one at a time.

Planting the Seedlings

Dig the planting holes and pour a little water containing fertilizer into each. Loosen roots if they are binding the rootball. Set each seedling upright in its planting hole and press soil around it. Try not to push the plant down into the soil or you end up burying it too deeply and compacting the rootball in the process. When it is properly set, the top of the rootball is just at the soil surface. Water the plant and, when the water has drained, add a little more earth to the planting hole if the soil sinks. Press the soil in around the stem of the seedling.

TRANSPLANT TIMETABLE

Vegetable	Weeks to Transplant Size
Artichoke	4–6
Asparagus	Set out 2–3-year-old roots
Broccoli	5–7
Brussels sprouts	4–6
Cabbage	5–7
Cabbage, Chinese	4–6
Cauliflower	5–7
Celeriac	10–12
Celtuce	4–6
Chives	6–8
Collards	4–6
Cucumber	4
Eggplant	6–9
Endive	4–6
Kale	4–6
Kohlrabi	4–6
Lettuce	3–5
Mâche	3–5
Muskmelon	3–4
Okra	4–6
Onion, seed	12
Pepper	6–8
Rhubarb	1-year-old crown matures in second season
Spinach	6–8
Squash	3–4
Tomatillo	6
Tomato	5–7

Young seedlings need attention. If a night frost threatens, cover them with newspaper, coffee cans, or thin plastic sheeting. If daytime frosts are a concern, protect the seedlings with hot caps or plastic tenting (see Outdoor Protection on page 72). Be sure to leave air vents, as the heat buildup at noon can be considerable. Do not let the seedlings dry out. If they wilt, water them gently, making sure to wet the foliage. Wind can be as devastating to a seedling as heat and sun. If threatened, arrange a makeshift wind screen of burlap, lattice, or old sheets. In cold regions keep a roll of geotextile handy. You can tent it over tender plants if low temperatures are expected.

DIRECT SEEDING

Sowing seeds outdoors in most regions of the U.S. begins in late winter or early spring with the hardiest seeds—peas, radishes, onions sets, hardy lettuces, and the cool-season vegetables. The vegetable chapters (beginning on page 105) give specific planting times for each of the vegetables listed.

Seed-Sowing Techniques

Before planting, rake smooth the prepared soil (see page 49) where you plan to sow the seeds. Plant the seeds using the planting-depth information on page 71. The following are three common techniques for sowing seeds.

Broadcasting   To broadcast seeds, sprinkle them thinly over the entire planting area. Seeds that are quite fine and produce small plants, such as lettuce, carrots, and radishes, are often sown this way. After sowing, lightly press the seeds into the soil, which should be damp enough to hold them against a breeze. Or sift a little soil or compost over the seeds and tamp gently but firmly with your hands, a rake, or a square-ended hoe.

Hills   To plant in hills, mound the soil and sow the seeds in groups of three to five, equidistant from each other. This is the traditional approach for sprawling plants, such as cucumbers and winter squash, whose vines are trained away from the hill. Seeds also are sown in hills when the intention is to thin the group later to just one sturdy plant. Corn is usually planted in hills. For melons, enrich the soil with an extra shovelful of compost; then mound.

Drills   Drills are the same as rows, and plants are seeded in a straight line. Dribble the seeds, usually at spaced intervals, along a shallow furrow made by dragging the edge of a hoe along the planting line. This is the way seeds of fairly large plants such as peas and beans are sown in the traditional garden.

Row planting allows individual plants maximum breathing room, which encourages their health and productivity. It is the best method for upright bushy plants that need good air circulation, such as tomatoes and zucchini. Parallel rows are ideal when growing plants that need trellis or string supports, such as peas, and for sprawling plants. Make a tent, or an inverted V-shaped support, and grow the climbers up both sides.

Sowing the Seeds

A lot of gardeners get nervous when it comes to deciding how

A hill is a planting method in which several seeds are sown in a small area. As these pumpkins develop, their vines will grow outward from the center, covering an increasing area. The hill method is often used for vining crops, and also for corn, which pollinates better if grown in tight quarters.

deep to plant a seed. Most seeds germinate and turn into plants no matter what you do. Unless you bury them very deeply, or let the seedlings dry out after they have germinated, most seeds pop up despite any miscalculations.

If the seed packet has no specific instructions regarding depth, and the chart on page 71 is not handy, just remember: Sow the seeds at a depth that is about three times the seed's diameter, not its length. A good system is to make the planting hole, or furrow, twice the depth at which the seed is to be planted. Then, after the seed is placed in the ground, half-fill the furrow with soil or finely pulverized compost. As the seedlings grow, wind and the water eventually fill the furrows with soil, and the plants have a deeper, firmer

footing than if they had been planted closer to the surface.

With your planting plan at hand, measure off the planting rows and the paths and mark the measurements with rocks or sticks. To make a straight row, tie string between two stakes at either end of the planting row.

The next move is to dig a planting furrow or drill. Position the tip of a pointed or square-ended hoe under the string at the depth you intend to plant the seeds. Then drag the tool the length of the row. When you reach the far end, turn and walk back up the row, dropping seeds into the furrow at the distances specified. A board or a strip of cardboard marked with notches at measured distances takes the guesswork out of spacing. But your eye does a

A drill, or row, is probably the most common way to sow seeds. In wide beds, sow several drills side by side. Use the corner of a hoe to make a drill for larger seeds. For small seeds, such as carrots or radishes, press the corner of a board into the soil. Drop the seeds into the drill individually, or dribble them from the corner of the seed packet.

pretty good job, too. Now go back along the row in the opposite direction, drawing the earth back over the seeds. Come back one more time, gently but firmly tamping the soil over the seeds to establish contact with the soil.

When all the seeds have been planted in the row, jab a long stick through the seed packet and press the stick into the earth at the end of the row. You think you will remember what is planted where, but you probably will not. Plus, there is satisfaction is the gesture—a sense of completeness. Mark the date in your garden calendar or on your planting plan so you know when to expect seedlings—and a crop. This also lets you plan when to harvest this crop and plant the next one.

When you've finished planting for the day, spray the rows with water. Use a gentle stream that won't wash away the seeds. In the days ahead, keep the bed evenly moist until the seeds sprout and show second and third pairs of leaves.

Thin plants without mercy as they become crowded. Some seedlings are delicious, especially young lettuces and beet greens. Harvest half-grown onion sets as scallions.

PLANT SUPPORTS

Many vegetables need staking or support to grow straight and make the most efficient use of space. Some food plants, such as tomatoes, bear just too much fruit to stay upright without help. Others are natural-born climbers, such as the vining peas and pole beans. Sun reaches all parts of a staked pole bean, and air circulation is enhanced, keeping the plant healthy. In windy locations, tall plants often benefit from some form of support.

Plants most often staked include peas, pole beans, tomatoes, cucumbers, squash, and melons. The first place to look for support for food plants is a fence, preferable a wire fence through which air circulates

"Pole" beans can be grown on poles, strings, fences, brush, or many other supports. In the photo on the left, scarlet runner beans are growing on a beautifully woven string fence. Beans in the right photo are growing on a "teepee" of poles.

readily. Failing that, the easy way to support a plant is with a single stake off to one side of the main stem and secured with ties in several places. These are eventually hidden by leaves.

Start staking when the plant is young so it grows up straight. Set the stake or stakes a few inches from the stem—not against it. Invest in attractive, sturdy bamboo canes or wooden stakes, preferably of redwood or cedar, which are reliably strong and last for several years. Metal and wire stakes are solid, but they heat up and can harm new growth and the tendrils plants use to climb. Single poles and angled poles joined at the top to form a teepee are suitable for high climbers such as pole beans. Embed the stakes deep into the ground so they hold up against wind and rain.

Use green wool, raffia, cotton string, plastic tape, or twist ties to draw flopping branches upright one by one and tie them to the stake. A soft tie is essential. Wire cuts into the stems, severely damaging the plant. Cut a generous length and attach the tie to the stake first, then loop it around the stem of the plant. If the plant branches widely, as tomatoes do, tie up large branches as well as the central stem and, if necessary, add more stakes.

WINTER PROTECTION

When the first severe cold threatens, it seems there are always pepper plants loaded with bright fruit, and magnificent tomatoes ripening on the vine. These late crops can be saved.

Hot caps and other covers that allow early planting in cool regions also lengthen the season as winter approaches. A transparent or semi-transparent wind-proof covering can save plants from early frostbite as well as from drying winds. A cover helps the plant continue to grow by holding the daytime

This commercially available plant protector depends on the heat-holding ability of water. The plastic tubes are filled with water, which absorbs heat during the day and radiates it to the plants inside at night.

warmth of the sun and releasing it at night when the air cools. And it preserves the warmth that remains in the soil almost until hard frosts. In the Northeast it is said that if you can get the tomato plants through the September 5 chill, they will keep producing through Indian summer, traditionally in October.

In addition to domes and cloches made of plastic, glass, and waxed paper, garden centers offer a vast array of frost guards. Light-as-air geotextiles allow the plants to breathe while protecting them from frost. Fabric protectors need to be weighted down with boards, rocks, or bricks so they don't blow away.

The arching row tunnels of clear fiberglass do a great job of saving row plantings of late carrots and late lettuce. A row tunnel can keep a late crop of arugula, mâche, and other mesclun cultivars growing well into late fall. They are offered in all sizes, including some large enough to shelter mature tomato plants. Commercial row tunnels protect crops from temperatures as low as 25° F.

One of the most effective products for insulating plants is the Wall-O-Water® (see pages 74 and 79). Bottomless plastic milk jugs with the caps off also offer effective protection. You can shelter plants with tents of newspapers, plastic, or sheets. If the frost promises to be hard, add a low-wattage bulb under the covering. Black or clear plastic, which is sold in rolls for mulching, laid on the soil increases the temperature of the ground beneath 5° to 15° F on sunny days.

An old trick once relied upon by Florida orchardists to save the orange groves is to turn a sprinkler on trees threatened by frost. Leaves and buds do not freeze, but the water freezes and the ice shell actually keeps the temperature at 32° F and protects the plant from lower air temperatures. This works because plants freeze at lower temperatures than water.

Winter mulch is used in regions bordering the frost belt. It keeps the soil warm and protects roots from light frosts. In areas with hard frosts where the soil freezes, mulch keeps the ground frozen until warm weather has come to stay. Without it the ground thaws, then freezes again, heaving the roots and damaging them. For both these purposes, any organic mulch can be used, including evergreen branches, dried leaves, hay, straw, or shredded newspaper. Apply mulch about 3 inches deep, close to the main stem but not touching it. In cold regions, remove winter mulch gradually in spring as new growth appears. For more on mulching, see page 40.

SEASONS OF HARVEST

A few crops are ready for harvest in three to four weeks from the time you sow the seeds. Radishes and the peppery salad green called curly cress are ready in a couple of weeks. But more often, harvest from seed takes 7 to 12 weeks or more to mature.

The Harvest Timetable opposite is helpful when you are laying out your planting plan. The indicated days to harvest are approximations, since individual cultivars vary widely in performance, depending on size, variety, region, climate, and many other variables. Seed packets have more-precise information about the variety inside, but this chart will help you plan.

When to Wait

How do you know when a plant is ready to be harvested? Baby snap beans, just 4 or 5 inches long, are absolutely delicious, although it

HARVEST TIMETABLE

Vegetable	Approximate Days to Harvest	Vegetable	Approximate Days to Harvest
Artichoke	1 year	Escarole	55–90
Arugula	43–60	Fennel, Florence	65–100
Asparagus	1–2 years from mature roots	Garlic	90 from bulbs
		Gourd	100–120
Bean—shell cultivars		Jerusalem artichoke	90–100 tubers
chickpea/garbanzo	105	Kale	45–65
cowpea	65–80	Kohlrabi	40–60
fava	80–90	Lettuce	45–60
lima bush	60–80	Mâche	45–80
lima pole	85–90	Muskmelon	60–94
scarlet runner	60–70	Mustard	48–64
Bean—snap cultivars		Okra	48–64
snap bush	50–60	Onion	95–120
snap pole	60–65	Parsnips	100–120
Yard-long bean/		Peanuts	110–145
asparagus bean	65–80	Peas	65–85
Beet	53–80	Pepper	45–90 transplants
Black-eyed pea/cowpea	65–80	Potato	90–120–140
Broccoli	60–80 transplants	Pumpkin	
Brussels sprouts	75–95 transplants	giant	110–120
Cabbage	50–95 transplants	miniatures and small	85–105
Cabbage, Chinese		standard	90–115
loose-leaf	47–55	Radicchio	60–110
head	45–85 transplants	Radish	
Carrot		spring	22–28
miniatures	52–60	winter	45–70
short	55–75	Rhubarb	1-year-old crown matures second season
standard	60–100		
Cauliflower	55–65 transplants	Rutabaga	80–95
Celeriac	90–120 transplants	Shallot	110–150
Celtuce	90	Sorrel	100
Chard	55–60	Spinach	40–65
Chayote	Perennial	Malabar	70
Chives	80–90	New Zealand	70–80
Collards	70–75 transplants	Squash	
Corn	60–105	summer	45–60
Popcorn	90–110	winter	85–120
Cress		Sunflower	68–110
curly	12	Sweet potato	90–125
upland/winter	50	Tomatillo	90–100 transplants
Cucumber	55–65	Tomato	
Dandelion	70–95	giants	73–90 transplants
Eggplant		main season	65–100 transplants
miniature	50–60	paste/plum	63–90 transplants
standard	75–95 transplants	patio/cherry types	50–80 transplants
Endive	45–100	Turnip, standard	45–82
		Watermelon	80–100

81

Radishes are tasty from the time they are big enough to eat until they reach maturity, a few weeks later. If left too long, especially in hot weather, they become woody and pungent.

Root crops are different—they wait for you. Winter carrots left in the row until close to frost time, such as the last sowings of late-season carrots, have a rich, sweet flavor not present in young carrots nor those planted for spring harvest. Parsnips are in a class of their own: They are crisp and sweet and taste best dug after the first frost. In New England, they stay in the ground all winter and are delicious harvested in spring. Turnips, however, grow bitter as they get older. Spring radishes that are not picked become coarse and overly hot. Daikon and other late radishes can stay in their rows longer without losing flavor.

When to Use at Once

Most vegetables taste best eaten immediately after they have been harvested. The vegetable that most rapidly converts its sugars to starch is corn. There was a time when true aficionados of corn would start the water boiling before they picked the ears and then run all the way from the corn row back to the stove, shucking as they went. We now have corn cultivars that convert their sugars more slowly. But it is still a fact that vegetables that stand at 70° F—room temperature—over a 24-hour period lose up to 50 percent of their vitamin C. When they are refrigerated at 43° F, the loss is about 10 percent over a 10-day period. So, if you harvest before you can use the crops, get them into the refrigerator as quickly as possible. (This is true only for fully ripe produce. If you pick vegetables early, they ripen best at room temperature out of direct sunlight.)

When certain vegetables get into full production, they must be harvested regularly. In a day or two, the delicious little 6-inch cucumbers and zucchini become

takes a lot of them to make a suitable serving. There is a day when closely watched pea pods begin to show the swelling of young peas inside and you have gourmet *petits pois*. Like many other vegetables, they go from too young to just perfect to past perfect in a few days.

Some vegetables taste best when picked slightly overripe, but the moment of perfection is fleeting. A fully ripe sun-warmed tomato just off the vine may be too soft to travel well, but it tastes like heaven when dressed with a touch of extravirgin olive oil and shreds of basil. A day or two later, it is too soft to cut without mashing.

big, coarse vegetables full of seeds. Lettuce bolts, especially as summer approaches. If you neglect to pick the perfect little peas, they are no better than frozen peas. Worse, the plants stop producing. A plant that is putting its energies into maturing huge vegetables is not working at producing little new vegetables. Picking garden produce is akin to deadheading flowers—if you want the crops to keep coming, you have to keep them picked, and the earlier the better.

One of the profound pleasures a food garden offers is the daily walk along the rows to see what is happening where, what wonderful things are ready now, and what will be ready tomorrow. Keeping a log of the momentous events, the first harvests of peas in spring or the first salads from your own lettuce, is very helpful when planning next year's garden.

STORING THE HARVEST

Though it is true that you must keep the garden picked once harvests start coming in, it does not necessarily follow that you must eat immediately everything you pick. For the ultimate in flavor, yes—but garden produce harvested at its peak is good preserved one way or another. You can put things by very casually, but if you take canning and preserving seriously, choose seeds of cultivars recommended as good keepers or for preserving.

Preparing Produce for Keeping

Any food will certainly deteriorate if it is kept longer than its natural life, and that may be anytime from an hour or two to many months. Foods are subject to attack by their own enzymes as well as by microorganisms. Every method of food storage has been designed to

---

TIMETABLE FOR HARVESTING
Some mature crops hold their flavor—others do not. The following is an overview of the best times to harvest.

Can't-Wait Crops
Beans
Corn
Cucumbers
Peas

Crops That Can Wait a Few Days
Broccoli
Cabbage
Lettuce and other salad
  greens
Radishes
Summer squash
Tomatoes
Zucchini

Crops That Can Wait a Few Weeks
Beets and other root
  vegetables
Carrots
Kale
Leeks
Most herbs
Pumpkins
Winter squash

---

minimize spoilage or to avoid it entirely. (There are some effective methods used industrially that are neither possible nor practical for home use.)

Probably the oldest means of preserving food is by drying it, and this is still a popular and effective method. Many foods last a long time if they have been brined or salted, sugared, smoked, potted, canned, bottled, frozen, or treated with chemical preservatives. Some methods are superior to others. If the primary hope of preserving foodstuffs is to seal out the destructive microorganisms, the most effective and widespread methods are bottling and canning. Although this is certainly true for the home gardener and cook, freezing is an excellent alternative for home food preservation. For home processing of vegetables, it is actually to be preferred. Most vegetables are so low in acid that they must be processed for long periods to ensure their safety. Statistics show that most outbreaks of deadly botulism (food poisoning) are the result of improper home canning.

Some garden vegetables, such as these 'Green Arrow' peas, are best if they are blanched and frozen as soon as they are picked. As you harvest peas, pick all those that are ready, and freeze the excess as you are preparing dinner. It will take just moments if you have the equipment on hand, and results in delicious garden produce well into the winter.

Home canning is most success–fully accomplished in preserving fruits, jams and jellies, chutneys, sauces, and catsups with high sugar and vinegar concentrations. Perhaps it is best to reserve it for these purposes. Even though food can be canned free of bacteria, if it is stored for too long a time, other changes may make it unpalatable. It is best—and safest—to use home-preserved food within the recommended time periods.

When you plan to preserve vegetables, it is important to harvest the best, most unblemished produce and process it as quickly as possible. Whatever method of preservation you choose, clean the vegetables meticulously, then proceed with the steps recommended in the following sections.

Freezing

The organisms that cause spoilage in foods are slowed and their processes finally stopped when the temperature is lowered enough. Although commercial freezing methods are far faster and superior to home freezers, if you take the proper steps in preparing it, the food you freeze will maintain the same nutritive values it had when fresh. Set the freezer to maintain a temperature of 0° F (–18° C). The length of time food can be kept frozen depends on the kind of food. There is no rule of thumb; it varies from a few days to many months. The key to success is in correct preparation and packaging before the food is put into the freezer.

When freezing vegetables, use only very fresh, very young produce. Theoretically, all your crops may be frozen, but not all are best kept this way. Generally, vegetables that you normally cook freeze well. Those with a high water content that are usually eaten raw do not; carrots, celery, and bell peppers, for example, lose their crispness. Handled quickly and with care, ears of corn, baby beans, and young peas are still superb after freezing—and it is easy to do.

To prepare vegetables, wash, trim, and cut them up as you would for cooking, and then blanch them. Blanching is an important step; it destroys the enzymes that encourage deterioration and helps maintain color, flavor, and vitamins. Most vegetables need from two to four minutes of blanching. There are two methods for blanching vegetables: steam blanching and immersion in boiling water. Steam blanching preserves water-soluble vitamins and minerals much better than immersion in boiling water, and so is preferable.

To steam-blanch vegetables, bring 1 inch of water to boil in a large saucepan, place the prepared vegetables in a steaming basket above the water, and cover the pan tightly. When they are adequately steamed, remove the basket. They will air-dry almost instantly. Package them in freezer containers or heavy plastic bags, sealing them as airtight as possible.

Frozen vegetables will cook more rapidly than fresh ones because they were previously blanched. Most will be best cooked in a small amount of lightly salted water while they are still frozen. Frozen corn on the cob, however, is an exception—it is best thawed first. Most frozen vegetables keep well for 9 to 12 months.

Canning and Preserving

Canning is the most complicated and time consuming of the home food preservation methods. Canning and preserving require big kettles, canning jars, rings and lids, and other specialized equipment. Low-acid foods such as corn, peas, and beans must be processed in canning-sized pressure cookers. Sealed jars of jams and preserves, such as tomato purée, are sterilized in what is called a boiling-water bath—processed in a large canning kettle with boiling water to a depth of 2 to 4 inches over the tops of the canning jars.

Home canning is not highly recommended for the average vegetable gardener. There is potential for contamination in underprocessed foods, and one must weigh the risks inherent in such an undertaking. Given the relative ease and speed with which homegrown vegetables can be prepared and frozen, and the quality of the finished product, it is not surprising that most contemporary gardeners and cooks opt for this method of food preservation.

Drying Vegetables

Vegetables can also be preserved by drying or dehydrating. This particularly suits households in which soups and stews and backpacking are a way of life. Herbs and pithy vegetables such as carrots, corn, peas, and beans dry readily in a dehydrator. Drying preserves strawberries as well. In recent years dried tomatoes have seen more frequent usage, showing up in salads, pasta sauces, soups, and other appetizing concoctions. After drying, either in the oven or in sunlight, they may be stored as they are or in jars covered with fruity olive oil. It is very satisfying for a cook to have access to the intensely fresh flavor of home-dried herbs and vegetables when the plants are out of season. Properly packaged and stored, dried vegetables keep well for long periods of time and are a welcome adjunct to any pantry.

Dehydrator   If you become deeply committed to drying produce, buy a home dehydrator fitted with drying racks. You will be spared the competition with animals, birds, flies, and assorted buzzing insects that you have to contend with when drying foods on

bring in the screen if mist or rain threatens.

When drying thick produce, such as carrots, cut them in ¼-inch slices before spreading them on screens. After two or three days in direct sunlight, the food should be two thirds dry. Move the screens to a shady place to finish drying. If bad weather threatens, finish the drying process in the oven.

Oven Drying You can oven-dry produce in fairly large batches. For sliced vegetables, set the temperature to 160° F. If the oven is electric, prop open the door ½ inch. If the oven is gas heated, prop open the door ⅛ inch. Expect 4 to 12 hours for oven drying, depending on the thickness of the vegetable slices.

To ensure even drying, fill the oven with no more than 4 to 6 pounds of produce. You may stack trays so long as there are at least 3 inches of air space between the racks. Rotate the trays three or four times during the drying period.

Store dried foods in airtight, screw-top containers. Check for any spoilage the first few days; remove spoiled pieces and redry the remaining food. Dried food stored in a cool, dark place keeps for about a year.

Another popular use of dried vegetables is to make vegetable powders. Dehydrated onion, garlic, carrots, celery, spinach, and green and red bell peppers make wonderful powders for use in stews, fresh pasta sauces, gravies or soups, or to sprinkle on hot popcorn. Place the dried vegetables in a food processor or blender and reduce to a powder. Store as you would any dried vegetable. The powders can be stored individually, or mixed together to make a vegetable medley. They add a richness and depth of flavor that is otherwise difficult to achieve.

Many types of food dehydrators are available commercially. Some provide a frame and racks to spread out produce conveniently. Others include heat sources and fans to circulate air.

outdoor screens. Foods dried in a dehydrator are cleaner and more appetizing. Many simple machines are available; they are not costly, use little energy, and are very easy to use.

Sun Drying In hot, arid regions, the sun dries produce quickly. In the south of France, farmers still dry figs and grapes on corrugated and tiled roofs. The heat generated from the roofing material hastens the drying process.

You can improvise drying screens by stretching nylon window screening or clean cheesecloth over oven racks, or use framed window or door screens. Place the elevated screens in direct sunlight in an airy outdoor corner. Don't forget to

Drying Herbs

Herbs are among the easiest crops to dry, because the foliage and seeds are fairly dry already. Herbs should be picked in late summer, early in the morning when the oils in the leaves are at their peak.

The simplest method for drying herbs is to air-dry them. Gather the herbs in bunches and tie them snugly with twine. Hang them in a cool, dark spot that has adequate ventilation. They may be woven into wreaths and their beauty enjoyed as they dry. It is also possible to dry them in a microwave oven, taking care to not burn them or make them overbrittle.

When the herbs have dried sufficiently, place them on a tray, one bunch at a time, and gently stroke the leaves from the stems. Gather the bits into small jars with screw-on lids, close tightly, and store in a cool, dark place. They also may be stored in the freezer if wrapped well or packed with a minimum of air into small jars. They will keep well for months this way.

NUTRITION

As a society we are becoming more nutrition conscious, but our diets are still less than ideal. Sugars and white flours contain "empty" calories and carbohydrates; fatty foods are high in calories and fats. These foods lack the vitamins, minerals, and roughage that the body needs. By including more fruits and freshly harvested vegetables in our daily diets, we provide our bodies with the essential minerals and trace elements needed for strong muscles and bones. Vegetables provide sufficient roughage to stimulate intestinal movement and aid digestion.

Our food consists of a variety of substances that supply the body with energy—fat, protein, carbohy-

drates—as well as substances that provide for a good metabolism—water and roughage, vitamins, minerals, and trace elements. Fats, carbohydrates, and protein are generally found in only small amounts in vegetables (there are a few exceptions), but vegetables distinguish themselves primarily through their generous contributions of roughage, vitamins, and minerals. These nutritional elements prevent many health problems and help the body resist disease. Vitamins A, B, C, and D are especially important.

To preserve as many vitamins and minerals as possible, harvest vegetables in the afternoon of a sunny day (unless it is so hot that the vegetables are wilting). The

Herbs are most commonly stored by drying. Drying them can be as simple as hanging a bundle in the kitchen for a few days. To preserve their fresh flavor, which is different from their flavor when dried, freeze the herbs.

light a plant receives affects the vitamin C content. Studies show that a good crop still on the vine loses vitamin C in darkness or reduced light but regains what is lost when reexposed to strong light.

Some simple kitchen practices can make the difference between optimizing and undermining the nutrition content of your produce. Tuberous vegetables store nutrients in and just underneath their skins. Do not scrape off the skin of carrots and new potatoes: It is especially high in vitamins and minerals. Use the dark green outer leaves of lettuce and cabbage, and wait until you are ready to cook before chopping or dicing. Steam, rather than boil, vegetables whenever possible. Water leaches out valuable water-soluble nutrients; boiling can destroy more than two thirds of the B and C vitamins as well as potassium, iron, and other minerals. Others are lost down the sink when you pour off the cooking water.

Because it is so nutritionally rich, never throw out the water in which you have cooked vegetables. Store it in a closed jar in the refrigerator or freezer. You can cook other vegetables in it, and before long you will have a stock flavorful enough to make soup. Use it for the water called for in stocks or gravies.

COLLECTING AND STORING SEEDS

When you collect seeds from the best, most vigorous producers in the garden, you create your own family of heirloom plants to pass out and hand down. Collecting seeds is now a hobby, not an economy measure. But during the early days of colonization in America, the only way to obtain seeds for the kitchen garden was to collect them from mature plants at the end of the growing season. New cultivars could be obtained only from friends and

For the maximum vitamin C content, harvest vegetables in the afternoon. Preserve vitamins by eating vegetables raw or cooking them quickly in the minimum amount of water, then using the water in soups or stews.

relatives. The trials were exciting, and the outcome eagerly awaited.

Collecting seeds from the herb garden is a sensory pleasure. But because many of the popular herbs are perennials, it is easier to multiply herb plants by dividing the root systems. Biennials, such as parsley and its relative the carrot, set seed only the second season. Let the carrot plants die back for winter, then grow and bloom in the spring of the second season. Watch for seed formation, and collect.

The seeds of hybrids generally are not worth collecting. Hybrids produce seeds whose characteristics may resemble one of either of the parent plants crossed to create the hybrid. They do not reliably reproduce the qualities that attracted you to the hybrid.

Seeds of open-pollinated (nonhybrid) flowers usually grow "true" and resemble the parents. Tomatoes, lettuce, and peas are self-pollinating and require no special attention:

Just gather the seeds when they ripen. Members of the cucurbit family will cross with each other, resulting in such offspring as melons with the flavor of cucumber or squash. These seeds are not assets.

When to Collect

Harvest seeds after they have fully ripened. Mature seeds are shriveled and darkened. At this stage they often tumble out before you can get to them. One solution is to place a paper bag over the seed head as the seeds begin to mature. When they are really ripe, a good shake tumbles them into the bag.

Allow seeds to dry indoors on screens for several days. Store them in airtight containers in a cool, dry place with temperatures between 35° and 50° F.

Saving seeds is more than just interesting. It is a way of connecting with the ways and wisdom of our forebears and imparts a sense of wholeness.

Seeds that are borne in large fruit, such as peppers and squash, can be simply removed when you open the fruit. If the seeds are wet, as they are in ripe tomatoes, let some of the seeds and juice sit in a bowl for a couple of days. The juice will ferment and lose its mucilaginous nature, making the seeds easy to separate. Dry the seeds before storing or planting.

WEEDS, PESTS, AND PROBLEMS

This is a tomato hornworm (see page 99), a large and bright-colored caterpillar. The white things on its back are the eggs of a wasp. When the eggs hatch, the emerging larvae will parasitize the hornworm, killing it. If you find a hornworm with eggs like this, let it be. Nature is handling your problem for you.

Weeds, pests, and diseases are unsettling, especially when your beautiful vegetable garden is being destroyed. How much nibbling can the garden stand? When should it be left alone? When should you spray? These questions are tough to answer, especially if damage is occurring right before your eyes. The best defense is a well-prepared garden, soil in top condition, and healthy garden practices.

Garden plants evolved in the wild along with the insects and disease organisms that plague them, so they have developed defenses against these pests. Most of the defenses are chemical. Many of the compounds that give plants their flavor or character are created by the plant as a defense against some sort of pest. The aromatic compounds for which we value herbs, for example, are natural insecticides. The sulfur compounds that give radishes and mustard greens their pungency repel some insects.

Strong plants are more able to make these compounds than weak plants. For this reason, vegetables that are well established and healthy fight off pests and diseases better than weak or sick plants. This is so true that many pests recognize weak plants and are drawn to them, just as a wolf will pick the weakest caribou in the herd to attack.

After keeping your plants healthy, the best way to prevent pest and disease problems is to select varieties that are naturally resistant to them. Most herbs, for example, grow with little or no attention on your part and are seldom bothered by pests or diseases. Also, some vegetable varieties have been bred to have natural resistance to specific problems. Some corn cultivars, for example, have ears that are so tightly wrapped in the husk that corn earworms can't penetrate them. Some tomato varieties are resistant to a range of diseases.

If you know that a particular pest is an ongoing and serious problem in your area, avoid the plant that hosts it. For example, if asparagus beetles attack your asparagus every year and you are tired of fighting them, pull out your asparagus and buy it from the store. Plant strawberries or rhubarb instead.

The easiest way to deal with problems is to avoid the problem in the first place. By careful plant selection and keeping the plants strong, you will have few problems with pests and diseases. Weeds, however, need other techniques.

WEEDS

A weed is any plant growing where you do not want it. Weeds are not always ugly, and many, such as purslane, dandelion greens, and lamb's-quarters, are edible. But weeds rob vegetables of space,

water, and nutrients. One weed often produces hundreds and hundreds of seeds; in a newly established garden, these can haunt you for a long time.

Suppose you fill a raised bed with a sterile soilless growing medium. Will weeds appear? Yes. Grass and other weeds that go to seed in the neighborhood blow in, birds flying over drop them, furry animals carry them, and they arrive on your own shoes. A few wind-wafted dandelion seed heads can transform a lawn.

One of the best deterrents to weeds is keeping the perimeter of the garden and the rest of the yard mowed, and cutting down patches of wild grasses and flowers before they go to seed. Even so, soil will have its complement of weed seeds. The grass clippings, manure, hay, and other organic materials you mix into the soil usually have their share of weed seeds. Turning the sod and working the land brings up

Hand-weeding is the only way to get rid of weeds in tight quarters, such as in this radish row. It is slow and laborious, however. Prevent weeds with a mulch, if possible.

hordes of seeds, some that were dormant for years.

Annoying as they can be, weeds that grow from seeds are not as noxious as quackgrass (*Agropyron repens*) which spreads from creeping roots as well as from seed. Even if you do not have it now, it can appear just about anytime. Quackgrass roots grow 5 feet into fertile ground. Be sure to completely remove the roots, because every node can send up a new plant.

Preventing Weeds

Once weeds get started, they are tough to eradicate. Remove existing weeds before they go to seed, and the weed population will decline and eventually fade away. The most critical period is the first few weeks after the ground begins to warm. This is generally right after you have planted the first vegetable seeds. Hoe the weeds weekly during this period of rapid growth. Hoeing is a breeze when the weeds are less than 1 inch high. Chop them off just under the soil surface as you move down the garden row. Small weeds are easy to pull by hand if the garden is not too large.

Firmly rooted weeds are easier to pull after a rain or a thorough watering. If the weeds ever get to be 2 to 3 feet high, use a hoe to chop them from their roots, then cover the stubs with 2 to 3 inches of mulch to rot them out. Do not pull big weeds from dry soil, especially during a drought. Chop them off at the soil line. The upheaval of the soil can cause moisture loss and disturb nearby vegetables. Dandelions are an exception: They have a long taproot that you must remove or the plant grows back.

Recycle weeds that have not gone to seed by adding them to the compost pile. Fresh greens are essential to the composting mix. Never compost poison oak or poison ivy.

Tilling Weeds Wide paths among the planting rows can be tilled instead of mulched to keep down the weeds. Manufacturers offer many types of small garden tillers. Do not rototill if quackgrass is present—you will only make the problem worse.

Chemicals Herbicides are definitely not recommended for use on or around food plants approaching harvest time. Try to prevent weeds before you prepare the soil. Spray with a systemic herbicide such as Roundup®, which enters the plant's system and kills it. The active ingredient is glyphosate, which breaks down quickly and is gone from the soil in just a few days. Never apply it when food crops are present.

Mulch A barrier placed on the planting rows keeps weeds from sprouting. Mulch with black plastic, sheets of geotextile material, five

Mulching is the best way to control weeds. A mulch, such as this one of leaf mold, prevents weeds at the same time as it improves the soil, feeds the plants, and conserves water in the soil.

or six layers of newspaper, or a thick layer of well-rotted compost. Newspaper rots into the ground in about three months. If you choose a geotextile product, use one that has a close weave. To keep the garden attractive, cover unsightly fabric or plastic barriers with sterile compost. One of the advantages of putting organic materials through the composting process before using them as mulch is that composting destroys most seeds.

In a mature garden, closely spaced plants shade the soil and prevent germination. Plants that do germinate do not thrive in the heavy shade.

A ground cover planted in the paths among the vegetable rows is a beautiful form of living mulch. In a large row-crop garden, use living mulch as a cover crop that can be rototilled back into the garden as green manure: Those paths become the plant rows the following season. As a permanent cover for paths, plant lawn grass cut low to prevent the development of seed.

DISEASES AND PESTS

Good garden practices are the first line of defense against pests and disease. Find out which problems are prevalent locally and look for seeds resistant to those. Garden centers can alert you to pests and offer remedies against them. Members of local community gardens, hosts on garden talk shows, authors of garden Q&A columns, and the county extension agent are eager to share information about local conditions. But the person who is likely to know most is the neighbor whose garden you envy.

Rotate Crops

Because many diseases are soil-borne, it is important to rotate crops annually. If a soilborne disease attacks a crop, it is very difficult to eradicate if you keep planting the same crop in that spot. The answer is to plant a different crop that is not susceptible to the disease. Without a host, the disease dies out. The same type of plant growing in the same place year after year (monocropping) also depletes the soil of the minerals and nutrients demanded by that particular plant, and the area becomes more susceptible to pests whose food source is that plant. Well fed, they multiply.

The rotation rule applies to all the members of a plant family, not just to individual plants. The brassicas (cabbage, cauliflower, and their relatives) and the cucurbits (cucumber, gourds, and their relatives) are especially vulnerable. They should never be replanted in the same space in successive years. The vegetable chapters (beginning on page 105) provide more information about the relationships among members of the various families.

Allow Breathing Room

Where diseases are known to be a problem, avoid close planting, which results in poor air circulation. Aphids often spread certain viruses. If you control them, you

---

PLANTS TO ROTATE

Annual crop rotation helps keep a garden healthy. Avoid following a crop with a member of the same plant family. Below are six plant families that benefit from crop rotation.

Cabbage or cole family Broccoli, brussels sprouts, cabbage, cauliflower, Chinese cabbage, collards, kale, kohlrabi, radishes, and turnips.

Carrot family Carrots, coriander, dill, fennel, parsley, and parsnips.

Cucumber family Cucumbers, gourds, melons, pumpkins, squash, and watermelons.

Legumes Beans and peas.

Onion family Onions and garlic.

Tomato family Eggplant, peppers, potatoes, and tomatoes.

avoid having to control any diseases they carry. Do not plant in airless corners. Use fencing that allows some air flow.

Mulch Wisely

Mulch is wonderfully beneficial, but it can be overdone. Remember to keep mulch less than 3 inches deep and 3 inches away from plant stems and the edges of seeded rows.

Water and Fertilize in Moderation

Plants in the garden are not meant to be as lush as a florist's arrangement. Seedlings fresh from a nursery have been pushed with daily watering and generous fertilization. They are tender from constant watering, fertilizing, and regulated temperatures. But continuing the practices that made them lush results in crowded, weak plants susceptible to pests and disease.

Through 60 years of maintaining extensive gardens of every sort, from vegetables to herbs and roses, the U.S. National Arboretum in the Washington, D.C., area found that plants stressed by their environment are stronger and more successful than overly coddled plants. A little stress activates defensive processes and slows growth enough to make very sturdy organisms.

Yes, a lot of fertilizer can make plants lush, but pushing growth does not result in better plants. Overfertilizing adds to pollutive levels of nitrogen and other chemicals in rivers and streams. Plants cannot take up more than they can use, so the excess runs off in the water you apply to the garden.

Follow the rules for watering: Allow the soil to dry out a little between waterings. Constantly wet environments are breeding grounds for all pests and diseases. The fungal diseases are spread by water and thrive in wet conditions. If you en-

counter fungus, water only in the early morning; the leaves will dry with the rising sun. Watering in the afternoon or evening leaves plants wet for prolonged periods. Adopt a more open planting design to keep air circulating among the plants. Control every outbreak of aphids. Keep the weeds down.

Clean Up in the Fall

When harvests are complete, remove the plants to the compost pile as soon as possible. Burn infected plants or dispose of them with the trash. Because excess debris can provide overwintering habitats for pests and diseases, clean up fallen leaves as well. Everything healthy belongs in the compost pile.

Garden hygiene is basic to good garden health, just as hygiene is essential to the health of your body. Clean up weeds and trash in the fall. Compost healthy plants and destroy diseased plants.

Stay Calm

Do not panic if plants are imperfect. Wilted leaves, cracked or discolored skin, or yellowed stems may simply be the result of natural stresses experienced during a season of growth. If the symptom becomes a real problem, or occurs with frequency, and you cannot identify or treat it, have it analyzed by a nursery professional or county extension agent. Apply the remedies recommended.

Once you have identified a disease, get the diseased material out of the environment. Do not compost it or throw it elsewhere in the garden. Bag it and send it off with the trash. Do not replant in the same spot a crop that showed infection, and do not plant any of its relatives there. Wash your hands after handling infected material.

Keep a garden log. The knowledge you collect over the years is your most effective weapon. Study the garden and record when certain conditions occur, which plants exhibit the symptoms, and what methods reduce the problem. This builds a personal management program into everyday gardening and keeps you and the garden healthy and productive.

INTEGRATED PEST MANAGEMENT: IPM

Integrated pest management is a scientific and commercial approach to handling pests. By "pests" horticulturists mean unwanted creatures, vegetation, and diseases. The methods chosen to handle pests take into account the entire ecosystem—the whole environment in which the problem occurs—so they will have the least disruptive impact.

The first and most important step in IPM is to grow the garden well. The good garden practices described on the previous pages result in plants that have few pests and that survive the pests they do encounter. Chemical controls are used as a last resort when a problem gets out of hand, and are used sparingly and correctly.

Your garden pests are somebody's dinner. This dragonfly, along with hundreds of other insects, birds, bats, lizards, frogs, and other creatures, dine on insects. Encourage a diversity of animals and insects in your garden to take advantage of nature's balancing act.

BENEFICIAL INSECTS

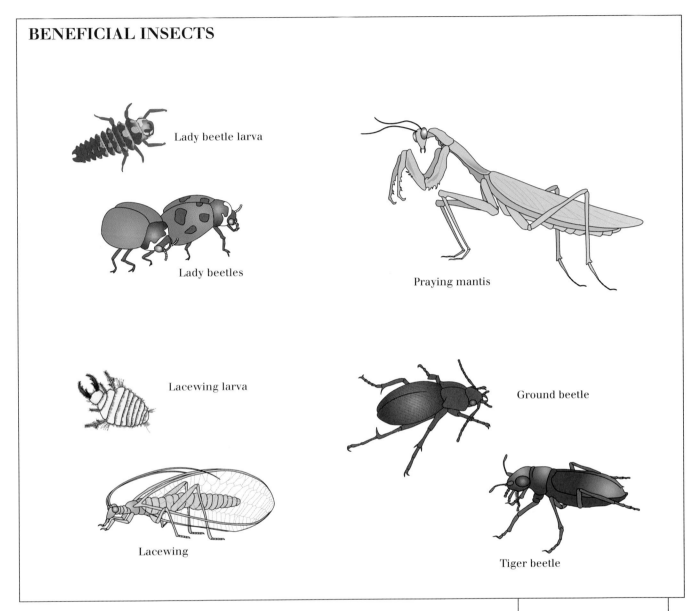

Lady beetle larva

Lady beetles

Praying mantis

Lacewing larva

Ground beetle

Lacewing

Tiger beetle

You must be willing to lose a little to hungry visitors. Butterflies and their larvae, as well as birds, are a natural part of a garden's ecosystem. And not all insects are bad. Most wasps are parasitic and destroy countless whiteflies, aphids, and some caterpillars. Yellow jackets are predators that feed flies and caterpillars to their young. Lady beetles (ladybugs) eat aphids, mealybugs, and spider mites. There are beneficial beetles, flies that attack corn borers and cutworms, and midges

ATTRACTING BENEFICIAL INSECTS
The insects that are beneficial to a garden are especially drawn to the following flowers.
Alyssum
Coriander
Parsley flowers
'Sensation' cosmos
'Summer pastels' yarrow
Sunflowers
White lace flowers

PLANTS THAT REPEL INSECTS

Using plants to repel certain pests is a common organic-gardening practice. The results are not always reliable, but there are enough successes to keep gardeners working at it. Deter the following insects by planting the flowers or vegetables noted.

Aphids   Garlic and nasturtiums.

Asparagus beetles   Tomatoes.

Beetles   Nasturtiums; and radishes near beans, cucumbers, eggplant, squash, and tomatoes.

Colorado potato beetles   Marigolds.

Mexican bean beetles   Potatoes near beans.

Mites   Radishes near beans, cucumbers, eggplant, squash, and tomatoes.

Nematodes   Marigolds.

that devour aphids. Others insects generally considered beneficial are dragonflies, lacewings, spiders, and predatory mites.

Many catalogs sell beneficial insects. Buy the insects that meet your garden's need. Release them as soon as you receive the package and then expect a time lapse between their release and their impact on your nemeses; it takes them a while to get established. The only thing that keeps a beneficial insect in a garden is a handy food supply. If they wipe out the source of the problem, they will move on. Wish them luck, and hope they multiply and hang around the neighborhood.

To find out more about insects and diseases, see *The Ortho Problem Solver*, available at most garden centers. If the problems persist, contact the local cooperative extension office. The professionals there can suggest the least toxic, most effective controls. Ask about the most vulnerable stages of pest development, and use your heavy weapons when they have most impact on the pests and the least impact on the beneficial insects.

Aphids

Aphids are those little, six-legged green bugs that cluster on the tips of spring's first rosebuds. They love the brassicas, broccoli, cauliflower, brussels sprouts, cabbage, and kale. They stunt and distort growth and spread many diseases. And not all of them are green: Some species are red, brown, gray, or black.

Control   Knock aphids off plants with a strong spray of water. Repeat if they return. If they persist, try a soap-based insecticide or products that contain diazinon, malathion, or pyrethrin.

Beetles

There are many kinds of beetles. Some are beneficial, such as the ladybug, which feasts on garden pests. Others are harmless, and some are very destructive. One of the worst is the cucumber beetle (*Diabrotica*).

Control   If the infestation is minor, pick off beetles by hand. Row covers and other physical barriers can keep beetles away. If the population gets large, you will probably end up using a chemical control designed specifically for food plants. Insecticides containing diazinon, rotenone, methoxychlor, or Sevin® control many of the destructive beetles. Do not use any of these when the vegetable flowers are open—the chemical kills beneficial bees.

Aphid

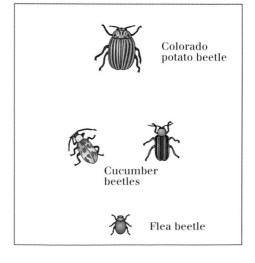
Colorado potato beetle

Cucumber beetles

 Flea beetle

Bugs

Bug has become a general term for insects. But to a botanist, a bug is a bug—one of a set of specific insects that are harmful pests. Among the worst is the stinkbug, which heads for carrots, lettuce, and okra. Other bugs attack peppers, squash, and pumpkins.

Control If there are just a few, pick the bugs off the plants by hand. Products containing Sevin® insecticide or methoxychlor work best, along with pyrethrin or malathion. These are most effective when the bugs are in an early stage of development.

Caterpillars and Worms

Butterflies and moths develop from larvae, which we know as caterpillars and worms. They come in a variety of sizes and color combinations. Some have spines or hairs, and others are smooth. They are all born with a yen to gorge. When there are enough of them, you can almost hear the chewing. A crowd of caterpillars can devour a promising young garden row in a day. The first time you lay your eyes on a cabbage looper or a tomato hornworm is a moment not easily forgotten.

Control One of the best ways to get rid of a minor infestation is to pick off the critters by hand. Good luck with the tomato hornworm. It will not bite, but boy is it ugly! An alternative is to spray with a biological control such as *Bacillus thuringiensis*, or try diazinon, malathion, pyrethrin, rotenone, or Sevin® insecticide.

Corn Earworms/ Tomato Fruitworms

These are the same worm. When it attacks corn, it is called the corn earworm, and it makes a gooey mess. It does its worst during the

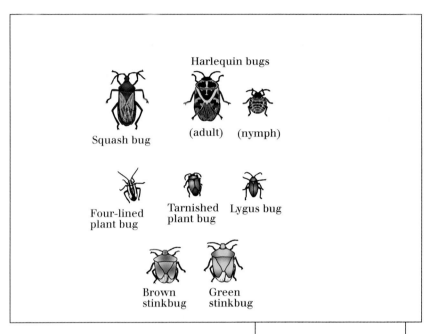

Harlequin bugs

Squash bug   (adult)   (nymph)

Four-lined plant bug   Tarnished plant bug   Lygus bug

Brown stinkbug   Green stinkbug

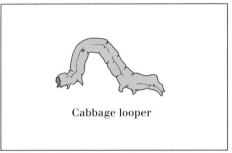

Cabbage looper

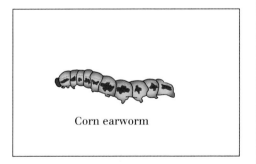

Corn earworm

silk stage. The eggs hatch on the corn silk, and the larvae chew their way right into the young ear, wrecking corn kernels and leaves. When it attacks tomatoes, it is called the tomato fruitworm. It eats the young fruit.

Control These creatures live through the winter in the soil as pupae. One solution is to dig up and turn over the soil in late fall in areas they have infested. It also helps if you plant corn early. Choose cultivars that have some resistance to this pest. You can also use floating row covers to protect the corn from the pests. Control at the feeding stage with Sevin® insecticide. Protect tomatoes with Sevin® when the fruit is no more than ½ inch in diameter.

Cutworms

The cutworm is another form of caterpillar. Its early-morning calling card is a tender new shoot cut off at the soil line as though by a sharp knife. During the day it lives just under the soil surface. At night it emerges to feed on the stems of young cabbage, peppers, beans, tomatoes, and corn.

Control A physical barrier is often the only solution. Make collars from cans or builder's paper and push one into the soil around each new plant. Cutworms do not like to climb. Or, before planting, treat the soil with a granular product containing diazinon or chlorpyrifos. Rototilling the garden as soon as the crops are gone exposes and kills cutworm eggs and pupae.

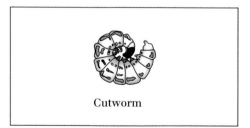
Cutworm

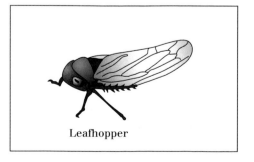
Leafhopper

Leafhoppers

The piercing, sucking feeding of these tiny wedge-shaped insects is very destructive to the foliage of beans, lettuce, potatoes, squash, and tomatoes in particular. They are fond of bean blossoms and spread disease wherever they go.

Control When the insects are young, they are deterred by reflective mulches such as aluminum foil. At later stages use sprays containing insecticidal soap, malathion, pyrethrin, rotenone, or Sevin® insecticide.

Leafminers

They are called "miners" because these insect larvae "mine" the tissue inside the leaves where they live. The loss of tissue weakens the plant and reduces the harvest. Some of the leafminer's favorite plants are melons, squash, cucumbers, peppers, and tomatoes.

Control The only effective control is to spray with a product containing malathion or diazinon.

Maggots: Onion, Radish, and Cabbage Root

In spring the flies appear and they lay their eggs near the base of the vegetables they eat. Their favorite targets are onions and radishes, but they are not fussy.

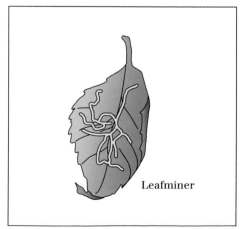
Leafminer

Control The mature flies may be prevented from laying their eggs if you place a fine-mesh wire cover over the seedling row. Diazinon or chlorpyrifos in a granular or dust form offers some control.

Mites

A mite is a tiny spider that looks like a speck. Indications include tiny webbing on the undersides of leaves and speckled leaf tops. Mites enjoy hot, dry, dusty conditions and can destroy an entire plant if not stopped.

Control Often you can eradicate the mite population simply by washing down the infested plants, especially under the leaves. Do this daily for a week. If the problem persists, spray beans, peas, broccoli, and brussels sprouts with malathion. Use diazinon or an insecticidal soap for melons and squash.

Slugs and Snails

Half-eaten leaves and slimy, silver trails on the earth are signs that you have one of the worst of all garden pests. Snails and slugs abound in lush, closely planted vegetables and are especially difficult to eradicate in cool, damp climates. They feed mostly at night and sleep it off during the day in cool, damp spots. They are voracious and can decimate a planting in just days. If you do not get rid of them, you will have a population explosion the next season.

Control You can pick them off by hand in the evening or early morning and toss them into a wide-mouthed can filled with soapy water. Or you can put out saucers filled with beer for them to climb into and drown. You can also spread diatomaceous earth around plants you want to protect; snails will not cross it. This is a very effective, organic, flourlike substance

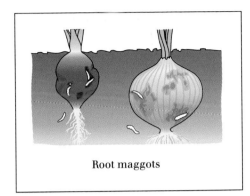

Root maggots

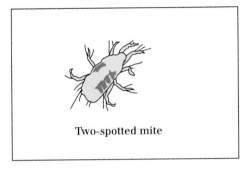

Two-spotted mite

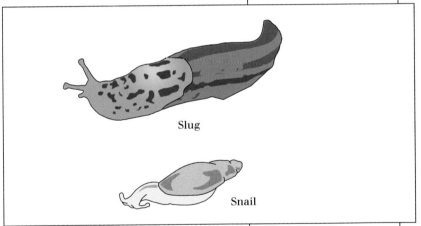

Slug

Snail

produced by grinding shells of primitive creatures. It loses its effectiveness when wet, however, and must be renewed.

You can also try tacking a copper-plated strip all around the garden or around each bed. Snails will not cross the copper. Be sure to pick out any snails already in the bed.

Bait containing metaldehyde, in powder, liquid, and pellets, is also effective. It kills the snails but must be reapplied every couple of weeks. The bait is very toxic to pets.

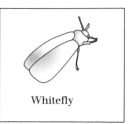

Whitefly

Whiteflies

Wedge-shaped adult whiteflies are just $\frac{1}{16}$ inch long. They look like fast-moving snowflakes or bits of dust when disturbed, but they soon settle right back where they were. The young are called nymphs, and they are the biggest problem. They look like flat, oval scales and come in white, black, brown, or pale green. They suck the juices from the undersides of leaves, leaving them pale and lifeless.

Control Apply products designated as safe for food crops, including diazinon, pyrethrin, or malathion, and follow label directions. Whiteflies cling to the undersides of leaves, so be sure to spray there most thoroughly. Insecticidal soap can control small infestations. For persistent infestations, new insecticides based on seeds of the neem tree, which grows primarily in India and Africa, appear to be effective.

Birds

Birds come to yards that provide shelter, water, and food. They repay your hospitality with song and a voracious appetite for garden pests—as well as people pests such as mosquitoes. In one afternoon a house wren consumes hundreds of insect eggs, grubs, and beetles. In 60 seconds, a Baltimore oriole can down 18 tent caterpillars. Chickadees live mostly on aphids in winter, and the swallow swallows more than 1,000 leafhoppers in half a day. As gardening allies, birds are spectacular and worth attracting and keeping.

Birds also love seeds. They love small seeds, which they seem able to spot from miles away, and big seeds, such as corn and peas. Their natural diet is berries and cherries, but they will pick at and spoil even larger fruit, such as tomatoes.

By meeting the needs of your flying allies at spots far away from the vegetable and fruit plants, you may be able to spare the garden. Set up a cat-proof birdbath in the front yard. Lure seed eaters such as sparrows, finches, grosbeaks, and bunting to the front yard with a well-stocked bird feeder near the birdbath. Or plant a few of the beautiful fruiting shrubs as far from the garden as you can get. Rugosa roses, viburnum, sweet elder, autumn olive (*Elaeagnus umbellata*), and firethorn—all are striking ornamentals that produce showy berries that birds enjoy. Deciduous hollies such as 'Sparkleberry', which covers itself with lipstick-red berries fall and winter, attract birds in the off-season.

Control If, in spite of your best efforts, seeds and seedlings are disappearing, use physical barriers to keep birds out. Cover planters with screens; tent netting over seeded rows. Netting can also save the strawberries, raspberries, peaches, and nectarines. Tie paper plates or bits of foil to tomato supports, and get the kids together to make an old-fashioned scarecrow.

Animals

As the garden fills with lush lettuce, bright berries, and crisp carrots, you may begin to see more of the local wildlife. Suburbs across the nation have their very own endearing, encroaching animal populations. Chemical blitzes are generally unacceptable, and not everyone has a vigilant dog, so the solution is a physical barrier. When the strawberries redden and the corn is high, haul out the netting.

Deer Beautiful and nervous, but often bold, deer will trample the vegetable garden and devour anything and everything from lettuce to rhododendron.

From late winter through summer into fall, spread Milorganite® over the soil where vegetables and herbs are growing. Replenish it after every rain. It is nutrient-rich compost and will benefit the soil. According to experiments at Cornell, this compostlike substance from Milwaukee keeps deer away except in late fall and winter when the air is too cold to carry the scent.

Where deer are common visitors, it is wise to cover ripening orchard crops with lightweight plastic netting. If the deer are eating only specific crops—strawberries, for instance—place sections of nylon netting over the spots the deer usually visit.

If all this fails to deter the deer, a 10-foot-high deer fence, angled outward, made of 4-inch woven wire will keep them out.

Moles, Voles, and Gophers   Burrowing rodents dig and live in underground runs, where they feed on roots. They are prevalent in suburban lawns. They are notoriously hard to trap, but can be flooded out with a high-pressure hose if you find the end of the run. Garden centers sell bait, smoke bombs, and traps that kill burrowing rodents. You can try digging a trench around the perimeter of the garden and lining it with fine chicken wire to keep them out.

Rabbits   Those cute little bunnies munch lettuce, beans, beet tops, peas, carrots—you name it. If the property is large, create a bramble for them some distance from the garden and plant a lawn in between. If they have everything they need at home, they may not risk crossing the lawn.

If that fails, circle the garden with a waist-high chicken-wire fence with a 1-inch or smaller mesh. Sink the wire 12 inches into the ground. The babies get through anything else.

Raccoons   Raccoons are funny, poised, lumbering animals that are clever enough to outfox most maneuvers of even seasoned farmers. They are smart enough to live in the city as well as the suburbs and country. Among their favorite tricks are pulling off young ears of corn and picking and discarding tomatoes.

Electric fencing is about the only way to keep raccoons out if they really want in. They climb conventional fencing. Some people have saved corn by taping each ear firmly to the stalk. A large dog with a loud bark may have some effect for a time, but a raccoon can lick its weight in dogs. If they do too much damage, cage the garden with chicken wire.

Cute as they may be, raccoons cause serious trouble in a vegetable garden. They are difficult to fence out. Catch them with a live trap or build a chicken-wire enclosure entirely over the plants you want to protect.

A PRODUCTIVE CORE GARDEN

The most popular vegetables to grow are those that are often eaten raw in salads: lettuce, tomatoes, cucumbers, onions. This chapter concentrates on these salad ingredients.

The ideal food garden produces all the fresh produce you can use and takes no more time than you are able to give it enjoyably. The core garden described here includes salad makings and a few of the vegetables most popular with home gardeners. A few hours a week should keep it in good condition. Once you have mastered a garden this size and you decide you want to do more, add one or two vegetables each year from the vegetable chapters that follow.

Each of the following chapters introduces a different food group. The vegetables are organized, and the chapters sequenced, to ease you into vegetable gardening. Most gardeners grow only a few of the vegetables in each group. Just about everyone grows tomatoes, lettuces, and a few herbs. You may want to substitute plants from other chapters for something listed here. When your garden includes your favorite vegetables and occupies all the space and time you enjoy giving it, stop expanding.

The salad bar group, or core garden, described here includes favorite home-garden vegetables—tomatoes, eggplant, peppers, greens, and a few others. With succession and intercropping, these will supply your salad bowl spring through fall. The harvest begins with radishes and cool-season salad greens and continues into Indian summer with cucumbers, heat-loving tomatoes, and peppers.

Plant the second season—late summer and early fall—with cool-weather greens and winter radishes. Where winters are mild, you can keep the crisper full all winter.

CUCUMBERS

Many catalogs organize cucumbers according to type—greenhouse, slicing, pickling. The labels also indicate whether the plants are bush, white- or black-spined, "burpless," and gynoecious.

Bush cucumbers are compact plants, ideal for containers.

White-spined cukes are more attractive than black-spined cultivars but are not better. The spines protrude from cucumber warts when the fruit is young and eventually disappear. White-spined cucumbers turn creamy white when old; black-spined cultivars turn yellowish orange.

Cucumbers cause some people to burp. "Burpless" cucumbers don't have this effect and can be eaten by sensitive people without causing any problems.

Gynoecious refers to cultivars that have almost all female flowers. These usually have higher yields and mature fruit sooner. On a regular cucumber plant, there are more male blossoms than fruiting female flowers. When the first blossoms fail to set fruit, it is because they are male. In a gynoecious plant, the first blossoms usually set fruit. Packets of gynoecious seeds include seeds for male pollinator plants, because without them there will be no fruit: A male plant is needed for every five to six female plants. Seeds of male plants are green, and the female seeds are beige.

All the cultivars listed in this section are monoecious (have both male and female flowers) unless otherwise noted.

GROWING CUCUMBERS

Disease resistance is an important consideration when buying cultivars of the cucurbit family, which includes melons, squashes, and gourds. Never plant a cucurbit in the same spot where another had grown the previous season: The plants will be healthier if you allow the land a year or two between cucurbits. Keep cucumbers planted as far as possible from cantaloupes and other melons.

Four to six plants of early cultivars and another half-dozen long-season and pickling cultivars should be ample. Cucumbers climb, given a support, and some cultivars produce better fruit that way. For planters and very small gardens, the midget, or bush, cultivars are the best choice. They can be grown on the ground, in tubs and boxes, or in hanging baskets.

'Lemon' cucumbers

Cucumbers grow on straggly vines that mature quickly in warm to hot weather, 55 to 65 days from seed to picking size.

Culture

Where the growing season is short, start seedlings indoors in individual peat pots about four weeks before the last frost. Cucumbers transplant poorly, so disturb the roots as little as possible when you transplant.

Cucumbers advertised as self-fertilizing set fruit without pollination and are seedless. To prevent cross-pollination with other cultivars, these are usually grown in greenhouses.

If the growing season is long, sow seeds in the garden once the soil is well warmed and air temperatures are 65° to 70° F. Before planting, dig in generous amounts of organic matter. For extra-large harvests, dig beds 24 inches deep, half-fill with compost, and top with soil fertilized with 5–10–10.

Sow the seeds 1 inch deep, three to five seeds per foot. Thin the seedlings to about 12 inches apart. When the soil runs dry, water deeply. Cucumber roots can go down 2 to 3 feet. In high heat the leaves may wilt at midday: The plants probably are fine, but check the soil a couple of inches down and water if it is dry.

The male flowers open first; then about a week later you'll see female flowers with baby cucumbers at their bases.

Harvesting

To keep production high, pick cucumbers as they reach 6 inches. Slicing cucumbers are ready when they are 6 to 7 inches long. Cut them off with shears or a sharp knife.

Harvest pickling cucumbers as they reach 1½ to 3 inches long for sweet pickles, 3 to 5 inches for dill pickles.

To store cucumbers, seal them in a vegetable bag immediately after picking and store in the crisper. They will be good for at least a week, and probably 10 days.

COOKING WITH CUCUMBERS

Cucumbers for the salad bowl are dark green and have smooth skin. There are long, thin cultivars, burpless types, seedless varieties, and even yellow cucumbers. Pickling cucumbers are smaller, have bumpy rinds, a lighter color, and often are streaked with white or yellow. The 1½-inch-long gherkins are grown to make the gourmet's *cornichons*, superstar pickles that cost a fortune when you purchase them. Picked very small, slicing cucumbers can be pickled, and pickling cucumbers can be sliced for the salad bowl, but it's not the best use for either. All make great relishes. Scored cucumber peel makes for prettier slices with more flavor and nutrients than if the peels are removed.

Slicing cucumbers are the crispy, crunchy, cool ingredient in summer salads. Picked young, they have very fine flesh and almost insignificant seeds. They're delicious eaten unadorned—unpeeled or half peeled—or sliced in salads or chopped in relishes. Cucumbers make an excellent cold soup. Seeded, chopped cucumbers are used in pasta sauces and in stir-fry vegetable dishes. Seeded, steamed, and dressed with a little olive oil, cucumbers make an interesting side dish. No proper British tea would be complete without the classic cucumber sandwich—thinly sliced bread, lightly buttered and layered with peeled slices of cucumber and a trace of salt.

NUTRITIONAL ELEMENTS

Cucumber with skin, ½ medium

Calories	8
Vitamin A	250 mg
Vitamin C	6 mg
Calcium	13 mg
Potassium	160 mg

CUCUMBER DISEASE RESISTANCE

A   Anthracnose
AL   Angular leaf spot
BW   Bacterial wilt
DM   Downy mildew
LS   Leaf spot
M   Mosaic
PM   Powdery mildew
S   Scab

'Suyo Long' cucumbers

Indian Cucumber Relish

2 medium cucumbers
1 teaspoon salt
1 medium onion, peeled, minced
1 teaspoon freshly ground cumin
½ cup plain yogurt

With a fork, score the skin of the cucumbers. Slice the cucumber in very thin rounds. Layer slices in a wide, shallow bowl, sprinkling a little salt on each layer. Cover and refrigerate for 24 hours.

Squeeze out cucumber juice and dry the slices between sheets of paper towel. Toss with the onion, cumin, and yogurt. Cover and chill.
Serves 6.

Shep Ogden's Cornichons

20 tiny cornichon cucumbers, rinsed
1 cup water
1 cup white vinegar
1 teaspoon salt
½ teaspoon sugar
2 cloves garlic, sliced
1 tablespoon fresh tarragon, minced

Place the cucumbers in a jar that has a lid. In a saucepan, bring the water to a full rolling boil with the vinegar, salt, and sugar. Add the garlic and tarragon. Boil 1 minute. Remove from heat and pour over cucumbers. Cover and let stand 12 hours. Keep refrigerated.
Makes 1 quart.

SELECTED CULTIVARS

Bush Cucumbers

Crispy Salad Hybrid 55 days, thin-skinned burpless slicing cucumber.

Salad Bush 58 days, bears slicing cucumbers 8 inches long, All-America Selection. (DM, LS, M, PM, S)

Pot Luck 58 days, early dwarf hybrid vine for limited space, 6½- to 7-inch dark green fruit, gynoecious, slicing type. (M, S)

Bush Champion 60 days, short, compact 2-foot vines, 10-inch fruit over a long season, suited to slicing or pickling.

Spacemaster 60 days, widely adapted dwarf plant, 7½-inch dark green slicing fruit. (M)

Pickling Cucumbers

Early Russian 50 days, heirloom, prolific variety, 3- to 5-inch fruit, good for short-season gardens.

Smart Pickle 50 days, 3- to 6-foot vines, flavorful pickling fruit 4 to 7 inches long, disease resistant.

Northern Pickling 50 days, F1 hybrid, short, space-saving vines, high yields for short-season gardens.

Lucky Strike 52 days, compact, gynoecious plant for cool areas, tolerant of most diseases.

Vert de Massy 53 days, fancy French cornichon type, tiny, excellent for pickling, salads, and snacks; greenhouse plant, adapts well outdoors.

Gherkin 54 days, 3- to 5-inch fruit, good for both pickling and slicing.

Saladin 55 days, European, gynoecious hybrid, semismooth, tender, nonbitter skin, 5-inch bright green fruit, also used for slicing. (BW, M, PM)

H-19 Little Leaf 55 to 62 days, compact vigorous vine, climbs trellis without ties, good for pickling or slicing. (A, AL, BW, DM, M, PM, S)

Slicing Cucumbers

Jazzer 48 days, F1 hybrid, early slicer, smooth, dark green skin, 8-inch fruit with fine flavor, sets fruit without pollinating insects. (DM, PM, S)

Superset 52 days, F1 hybrid, 8- to 9-inch fruit, reliable, good flavor, disease resistant. (A, AL, DM, M, PM, S)

Slicemaster 55 days, gynoecious hybrid, 8-inch fruit. (A, DM, LS, M, PM, S)

Burpee Hybrid II 55 days, gynoecious, straight 8-inch fruit. (DM, M)

Marketmore 86 56 days, Cornell University's small, easy-to-pick slicing cucumber for northern areas; 8-inch fruit over a long season. (DM, M, PM, S)

Marketmore 76 56 days, larger than 'Marketmore 86', not as easy to pick.

Suyo Long 61 days, Chinese, long fruit to 15 inches, burpless, grows well in hot weather. (PM)

Burpless 60 to 62 days, a more digestible type, may be pickled, 10- to 12-inch fruit, straight if grown on a support, some disease tolerance.

Straight Eight 63 days, slightly striped, straight, 8-inch fruit, All-America Selection.

Sweet Slice 63 days, burpless, 10- to 12-inch mild fruit, straight if trellis grown, All-America Selection. (A, DM, LS, M, PM, S)

Poinsett 76 63 days, Clemson University's widely adapted, early-to-midseason 7½-inch cucumber, highly recommended for hot climates. (A, DM, LS, PM, S)

Fanfare 63 days, semidwarf plant, high yield of fine fruit, high disease resistance, All-America Selection 1994.

Lemon 65 days, also called 'Apple'; oval-round, yellow skin, very good eating; productive, 3- to 6-foot vines, 3- to 4-inch fruit until frost, tolerates some drought.

Armenian 70 days, ribbed, light green, to 3 feet long, one of the best flavored.

Mideast Prolific 70 to 85 days, 3- to 5-foot vines, 6- to 8-inch fruit in successive sets, hardy in many climates.

NUTRITIONAL ELEMENTS
Eggplant, cooked, ½ cup

Calories	19
Vitamin C	3 mg
Calcium	11 mg
Potassium	214 mg

EGGPLANTS

The standard eggplant is a large egg- or pear-shaped fruit with satiny black-purple skin. These large-fruited eggplants are the most popular supermarket cultivars, but the home gardener is increasingly attracted by the smaller European types which mature sooner. The slender eggplants with dull skin are Asian cultivars. There are very long, thin types, as well as finger-sized, egg-sized, and walnut-sized cultivars. Colors range from lavender to black to satiny white. And there are eggplants that look like pumpkins or striped cherry tomatoes that are enchanting on the plate (if somewhat sour to the palate!). The most beautiful are the small rose lavender cultivars.

GROWING EGGPLANTS

Eggplant is a modest, handsome vine with pretty violet flowers resembling tomato blossoms. Like tomatoes, they love heat and are set out as transplants after the weather has warmed. Eggplant is a member of the potato-tomato family. To keep the garden healthy, do not plant any of these where any other family member grew the year before.

Three to four plants will satisfy your curiosity; in another year you can add more. Just for their beauty, try some of the novelty cultivars—the tiniest with finger-sized fruit and the rose lavender types. Cultivars with small to medium-sized fruit carried high on the plant are suited to containers. Where summers are cool, place containers in the reflected heat of a south-facing wall.

Culture

Plant seeds ¼ to ½ inch deep in peat pots six to nine weeks before the weather is expected to reach 70° F, nights as well as days.

Plant seedlings 18 inches apart in fertile, well-drained soil. If nights are cool, protect them with hot caps. The first and second months after planting, apply a side dressing of compost or fertilizer. Vines heavy with fruit may need staking.

Harvesting

Harvest small eggplants early and keep the vines picked to encourage productivity. The small and miniature eggplant cultivars are ready to harvest 50 to 60 days after planting; standard sizes are harvested 75 to 95 days after transplants are set out. Shiny fruits are ripe for harvest. Dull, they are past prime.

Cut the eggplant from the vine, leaving the stem on the fruit. If the seeds inside are brown, the best eating stage has passed.

Sealed in plastic wrap, eggplant will keep a few days in the crisper. For a winter supply, cook and freeze eggplant dishes such as ratatouille.

COOKING WITH EGGPLANTS

Eggplant—aubergine to the chef and the bistro set—is one of the great summer vegetables. The pulpy fruit has a unique flavor and texture—nutty, sweet, bitter, lemony—difficult to describe, as it takes on the flavor of the foods that accompany it. It may be steamed, sauced with a garlic dressing, and served as a salad. Thick slices of unpeeled eggplant are delicious brushed with garlicky olive oil and grilled. The flavor of the very small fruit may not equal that of standard sizes, but they are fine for stir-fries and kabobs.

Eggplant is also baked, breaded and fried, steamed, sautéed, stuffed, and combined with cheese, tomatoes, onions, garlic, herbs, and meats. In Turkey and the Middle East, eggplant is skewered and roasted with kabobs. In the Balkans it is roasted over charcoal until the skin is burned off, then peeled, mashed, and combined with grated onion, peeled and seeded tomatoes, roasted red peppers, garlic, and lemon juice to make "poor man's caviar." In Provence chunks of unpeeled eggplant are simmered with tomatoes, peppers, onions, zucchini, garlic, and herbs to make ratatouille. Eggplant Parmesan is a classic Italian dish, and the most famous dish of traditional Greek cuisine is lamb and eggplant moussaka.

Eggplant has a tendency to release water. Eliminate excess moisture by salting slices and leaving them to "weep" for an hour or two, then drain, rinse, and dry. Or stack the slices, cover with a heavily weighted plate, and let stand for a few hours until the moisture is pressed out. These complex maneuvers are not really necessary, however, when you are cooking with young, garden-fresh, high-quality eggplant.

Eggplant Salad

1 medium eggplant, stemmed, halved
½ cup diced celery
⅓ cup roasted red bell pepper strips
2 tablespoons chopped capers
⅓ cup olive oil
⅓ cup tarragon vinegar
1 clove garlic
2 tablespoons minced fresh parsley
1 sprig dill
1 teaspoon minced fresh oregano
Salt and freshly ground black pepper, to taste

Steam eggplant until barely tender (about 15 minutes). Cut into 1-inch cubes. Place the cubes in a large bowl with the celery, pepper strips, and capers. Blend together the oil, vinegar, garlic, parsley, dill, and oregano. Pour the dressing over the eggplant mixture, toss gently, cover, and refrigerate 24 hours or until chilled. Toss, season with salt and pepper, and serve cold.

Serves 6.

'Rosa Bianca' eggplant

SELECTED CULTIVARS

The "days to maturity" applies to transplants. Cultivars resistant to tobacco mosaic virus are marked *TM*.

Easter Egg 52 days, ornamental, egg-shaped white fruit, 2 to 3 inches around. (TM)

Little Fingers 60 days, clusters of little fruit, can be picked at 3 to 7 inches long, plants bear all season.

Bambino Baby 60 days, 12-inch genetically altered baby plant with rounded 1- to 1½-inch fruit, glossy purple skin.

Swallow 51 days, elongated fruit, 7 inches by 1¼ inches around, tender skin needs no peeling.

Dusky F1 56 days, very productive hybrid; thin, cylindrical, jet black fruit, harvest at 5 inches. (TM)

Ichiban 60 days, Asian-type hybrid, thin 12-inch fruit, productive 36-inch-high plants, purplish leaves.

Agora 68 days, does well almost anywhere; vigorous, upright plants, pear-shaped purple-black fruit over a long season.

Beauty Hybrid 69 days, round fruit with glossy black skin, resistant to fusarium wilt. (TM)

Vernal F1 70 days, French hybrid, 10-ounce fruit, shiny black skin and small seeds.

Black Beauty 70 to 80 days, very uniform, standard eggplant; about four large, round, purple fruit per 18-inch plant.

Rosa Bianca 75 days, teardrop-shaped fruit, delicate shades of rose lavender with pretty green tops.

Purple Blush 62 days, rounded 6-inch fruit, creamy white blushed lavender.

Japanese Pickling 80 to 90 days, productive plants, long, thin fruit is wavy and deep purple.

LETTUCE

Four outstanding lettuces are grown in the home garden, and they are pretty well interchangeable in salad recipes: the loose-leaf and butterheads, and the romaines and crispheads.

Loose-Leaf The leaf lettuces mature in 45 to 60 days and are the easiest to grow. They develop as loose bunches of leaves, frilled and crumpled, or deeply lobed. The color varies from light green to red

'Ichiban' eggplant

and maroon. The frilly types are the most attractive and are used to display cold cooked foods. They are sown as seed in early spring.

Butterhead Butterheads mature in 60 to 75 days. These are heading types whose leaves are loosely folded. Outer leaves may be green or brownish, inner leaves cream or butter colored. Butterhead types are not favored commercially because they bruise and tear easily, but that is not a problem in the home garden. Butterheads are grown from seeds or transplants.

Romaine Romaine, or cos, matures in 75 or more days. It is 8 to 9 inches high, upright, and cylindrical. The leaves are tightly folded, medium green on the outside and greenish white inside. The texture and flavor of the blanched interior leaves is sweeter than other types of lettuce. In cool regions, romaines are started indoors four to six weeks before planting season and then set out as transplants.

Crisphead Crispheads mature in 75 or more days. Supermarket iceberg lettuce belongs to this group with its tight, firm heads of crisp leaves. It's the least tolerant of heat and is quick to bolt (see page 192) Crisphead lettuce is usually grown from transplants.

GROWING LETTUCE

Lettuces need not grow in rigid rows. They are ideal crops for wide-row planting, intensive gardening, and intercropping. A few heads of leaf lettuce or romaine can be tucked into large planters or a corner of the flower bed. 'Salad Bowl' and 'Ruby' lettuce are beautiful with Iceland poppies. For very small gardens, the miniature, or baby, lettuces are the answer.

Spinach grows with several varieties of lettuce in a checkerboard pattern. Each of the squares of the checkerboard can be harvested and replanted at one time. This is a popular planting scheme used with several vegetables.

Lettuces are annuals that thrive in cool weather and bolt in heat. Seeds are sown in early spring and again in late summer for a fall crop. Sow leaf lettuces for an early crop, romaines for the late crops, and a few seeds of the others to harvest in between. If you plant the first lettuce seeds March 15, make another planting April 1, another April 15, and another April 30. Leaf and romaine lettuces stand up to heat longer than others if they are in partial shade by noon. Succession crops for fall harvest are sown beginning in midsummer. Shade the seedbeds if the temperature exceeds 80° F.

Culture
As soon as the soil can be worked, sow seeds ¼ inch deep, 6 to 8 inches apart or in rows. Or sprinkle thickly and evenly over the bed. Maintain soil moisture: Lettuce can't afford to dry out. Thin the seedlings repeatedly as they become crowded.

Harvesting
To harvest thinnings, clip off the leaves at the base, or just pull up the plant. You can harvest 2 to 4 outer leaves from maturing loose-leaf types and romaines. Later, cut off the heads at the soil line. Cut off butterheads and crispheads at the soil level. Crisphead cultivars are picked when the center is firm. Harvest all lettuces when they start to bolt: The farther this progresses, the more bitter the greens become.

Tender-leaved garden lettuces keep a few days in the refrigerator; rinse them just before using. Crisp romaine will stay in good condition for a week or so stored in a vegetable bag.

COOKING WITH LETTUCE

In Europe young lettuces are served braised in olive oil or butter, and as greens in soups. Baby sweet peas, or *petits pois,* steamed with lettuce is a favorite spring dish in France. Lettuces also are served wilted, and sautéed Chinese-style with mushrooms and onions. There are myriad combinations of fresh lettuces with vegetables or fruits or grains as the bases for delicious salads.

Mesclun salad mixes are colorful combinations of the leaves and thinnings of many garden greens. A typical mesclun mix includes red and green lettuces for color; crisp, curly, lacy greens for texture; and spicy greens for contrast. Whatever

'Oakleaf' lettuce

greens and herbs in the garden are ready to be thinned, snipped, picked, or harvested can be used in a mesclun—crisp and buttery lettuces and mâche, pungent cress, arugula, dandelion, blanched inner leaves of curly endive, radicchio, young beet and mustard greens, and chervil, borage, sorrel, and similar herbs. To have a mix of greens for mesclun, plant a variety of contrasting colors, textures, and flavors that will mature within the same six-week to two-month period.

Romaine Salad

1 head romaine lettuce
1 small butterhead lettuce, torn
½ cup finely minced fresh parsley
½ cup Roasted Garlic Oil
    (page 160)
¼ cup tarragon vinegar
¼ cup water
1 tablespoon minced fresh basil
Salt and freshly ground black
    pepper, to taste
12 pitted, sliced black olives,
    preferably Kalamatas
1 canned pimento, slivered
1 cup feta cheese, crumbled

Slice the romaine in narrow strips starting at the top. Heap into a large bowl and top with the torn butterhead lettuce and the parsley. Blend the oil, vinegar, and water with the basil, and season with salt and pepper. Pour over the salad and toss. Sprinkle the olives, pimento, and feta cheese over the salad. Chill. Toss again before serving.

Serves 6.

Leaf Lettuce and Apricot Salad

6 cups torn leaf lettuce or thinnings, well washed, drained
1 cup dried apricots, slivered
¼ cup light olive oil
3 tablespoons raspberry vinegar
1 tablespoon water
½ tablespoon honey
4 green onions trimmed to
    3 inches, chopped

Salt and freshly ground black
    pepper, to taste
1 tablespoon fresh lavender buds
    or tiny leaves of fresh thyme

Place the greens in a salad bowl and sprinkle with apricots. Whisk the oil into the vinegar, water, honey, and green onions. Pour the dressing over the lettuce and toss well. Season with salt and pepper. Sprinkle with lavender buds or thyme leaves and toss again before serving.

Serves 6.

SELECTED CULTIVARS

Loose-Leaf Lettuces

Salad Bowl 40 days, tender, crinkly, deeply lobed lime green leaves, broad clump, heat tolerant, slow to bolt, All-America Selection.

Red Sails 40 to 42 days, ruffled and fringed reddish bronze leaves, reddest of any leaf lettuce, slow to bolt, All-America Selection.

Oakleaf 40 to 49 days, medium-sized plants, thin, deeply lobed leaves, sweet flavor, heat tolerant.

Black-Seeded Simpson 44 days, moderately crinkled, light green, curled margins, fast growing, heat tolerant.

Green Ice 45 days, extra-crisp, wavy margins, glossy dark green leaves, one of the slowest to bolt.

Grand Rapids 45 days, frilled and crinkled light green leaves, good choice for early sowing, resists tip burn, slow to bolt.

Prizehead (Bronze Leaf) 45 to 48 days, vigorous, mild in flavor, tender, broad, lightly frilled bronze-tinted leaves, very heat tolerant.

Deer Tongue 45 to 80 days, triangular round-tipped leaves, heat

NUTRITIONAL ELEMENTS

Butterhead, 3½ ounces

Calories	14
Vitamin C	8 mg
Calcium	35 mg

Crisphead, 3½ ounces

Calories	13
Vitamin C	6 mg
Calcium	20 mg

Romaine, 3½ ounces

Calories	18
Vitamin C	18 mg
Calcium	68 mg

Top: 'Black-Seeded Simpson' lettuce
Bottom: 'Marvel of Four Seasons' lettuce

tolerant, slow to bolt; there is a 'Red Deer Tongue'.

Red Salad Bowl 50 to 60 days, attractive and delicious, deeply lobed, bronze red leaves, crisp, heat tolerant, high nutritional value.

Ruby 50 days, crinkled light green leaves, bright red markings, heat tolerant, All-America Selection.

Red Oakleaf 55 days, large head, oak-shaped leaves turn burgundy, excellent in Pacific Northwest, unappealing to slugs and snails, somewhat heat tolerant.

Lolla Rossa 55 days, frilly, large, green and red edges, mild taste, bolt resistant.

Butterheads

Buttercrunch 50 to 75 days, more vigorous than 'Bibb', thick, dark green leaves, firm head, heat tolerant, slow to bolt, a greenhouse grower favorite, All-America Selection.

Pirat 55 days, flavorful, medium-green leaves tipped with red.

Tom Thumb 65 days, heirloom miniature, tennis-ball-sized heads, crisp, sweet, ideal for containers and very small gardens.

Marvel of Four Seasons 65 days, showy, red-green, slightly crinkled leaves, crimson edges, withstands early summer heat if shaded.

Bibb 75 days, small, loosely formed heads, flavorful leaves, good choice for the small garden.

Crispheads

Verano 58 days, Batavian type, crisp as romaine, shaped like butterhead, green-throated wavy leaves, withstands early-summer heat and late cold.

Summertime 68 days, medium heads, combination of 'Ithaca' and 'Salinas' cultivars, matures in summer heat, resists tip burn.

Ithaca 72 days, from Cornell University, mild, nonbolting, tipburn resistant in all seasons.

Romaines

Cosmo-Savoy Leaf 60 days, large heads, savoy leaf formation, heat tolerant.

Rouge d'Hiver 60 days, French heirloom, red romaine leaves, resists both heat and cold.

Little Gem 60 to 70 days, small conical heads, resists bolting, good for small gardens, plant late spring.

Parris Island Cos 70 days, slightly crinkled medium-green leaves, tight head, slow to bolt, resistant to tip burn.

Verte Maraîchère 75 days, sweet, smooth, crisp, uniform heads.

Romaine Dark Green 65 to 70 days, large, upright, thick, slightly crinkled dark green leaves.

ONIONS, GREEN ONIONS, SCALLIONS, EGYPTIAN ONIONS

Onions take a lot of space and rarely are grown in small gardens. In cool weather they put up round, hollow stems and when the weather turns warm, they form bulbs below or above ground. There are many types of onion, but the best known is the big-bulbed cooking onion. Besides this, there are also the green onion, the tiny bunching onion, the scallion, and the Egyptian or top onion.

Standard Cooking Onions There are two cultivars of cooking onion: the short-day onions grown in the South, and the long-day onions most often grown in the North. In the South, plant short-day onions in the fall. They grow through winter, and the bulbs mature by mid-spring as days lengthen to 12 hours. Planted in the North in spring or summer, the bulbs of short-day onions stay small; use these for pickling or for cocktail onions.

Long-day onions form bulbs when day length approaches 14 to 16 hours. In the cool northern tier of the country, plant these as soon as the soil can be worked in spring. The bulbs swell and mature in summer when days are long. In the South, pull spring planted, long-day onions as green onions; they will not form proper bulbs.

Green Onions, Bunching Onions, and Scallions Any variety of standard onion may be pulled at the green-onion stage. The flavor is mild early in the season and becomes stronger as the season advances. The specific type called "bunching onion" is a perennial whose several tubular stems grow in a bunch throughout the season, with either small or no real bulbs at the base.

Scallion refers to several kinds of small onions, usually non-bunching types.

Egyptian Onions The Egyptian, or top, onion produces handsome clumps of hollow stems about 24 inches high, topped by clusters of mild-flavored red bulblets. A second cluster of bulblets often develops above the first. Even a small garden can accommodate a few Egyptian onions. They are mild and usually grown for pickling.

Season and dry onions for a couple of weeks in a warm, shady spot after harvest.

GROWING ONIONS

Catalogs and garden centers sell onion transplants, usually in bunches of 75. They also offer bulblets (small, dry onions) called "sets," and onion seeds. A packet of seeds plants a 50- to 60-foot row but takes more than 120 days to mature a crop. Sow seeds of cultivars not sold as transplants or sets, or to harvest green onions. Where the growing season is short, start seeds indoors 8 to 12 weeks before the outdoor planting date. Transplants, purchased or started indoors, produce mature bulbs in 65 days. Onion sets mature in 85 days.

Onion sets are generally available only for long-day onions and come in three colors—white, red, and brown. White sets are usually chosen for green onions, but the other two will produce acceptable green onions. Divide the sets into groups of bulbs smaller than a dime and larger than a dime. Use the larger sizes for green onions. They have a tendency to bolt and produce poor bulbs. Grow the smaller sizes into large onions for cooking or storage.

To grow green onions, sow seeds in the open garden. Commercial green onions are always from white cultivars. 'White Lisbon' is one of the best. The plants grow very quickly, and the bulb end stays white. Green onions also are grown from sets. Green onions from yellow sets are usually the variety 'Ebenezer', which can be pulled for green onions or left to form standard cooking onions.

Plant Egyptian onions in the fall. They are hardy enough to withstand winters in most regions. By early spring pull and use some as green or bunching onions. By midsummer bulblets begin to form at the tops of the stems. As the tops wilt and dry, the bulblets become ready for harvest.

Culture

All members of the onion family are notorious for their need for fertile soil. To get good results, dig the rows 8 inches deep and mix in 1 pound of manure per square foot and 4 to 5 pounds of 5-10-10 fertilizer per 100 square feet. Keep the supply of moisture steady, especially as days lengthen and the bulbs mature.

Space rows 1 to 2 feet apart. Sow seeds thickly and about ½ inch deep, mixed with radish seeds. The radish harvest is over long before the onions mature. Thin seedlings to 1 inch apart, and thin again in four weeks to allow each plant 4 inches all around. Plant onions sets, or transplants, about 4 inches apart. Plant onions sets pointed end up.

Harvesting

Harvest onions when half the tops in the row are bent or broken. Pull the onions and leave them in the sun until the tops wilt.

Cut off the tops 1½ inches above the bulb. Hang the bulbs for two weeks or more in an open-mesh bag in a dry, airy place to finish drying. Rub off any remaining dirt and loose skin, and store between 35° and 50° F.

COOKING WITH ONIONS

Members of the onion genus are rich in nutritious plant chemicals (phytochemicals) believed to protect the body from common health disorders. Onions appear frequently in recipes from all the world's cuisines. The big onions lose most of their pungency and become quite mellow after slow cooking. Sautéing sliced onion is the first step in most recipes for savory soups, casseroles, curries, and stir-fries. Onions, oven roasted alone or with other vegetables, are a delicious accompaniment to meats and fowl.

Raw onions flavor snacks and appetizers. Half a thinly sliced raw red onion adds color as well as sharp flavor to a salad for four. A handful of parsley minced with a slice of sweet onion or six green onions makes a great topping for sardine canapés. Slivered onion, or chopped green onion and minced parsley, enhance baked or grilled fish.

To avoid tears when peeling onions, chill them briefly in the refrigerator or peel them under running water. Rub salt or vinegar on your fingers to kill the onion odor. To skin a quantity of small onions, drop them into boiling water for 10 seconds, then place them in cold water. The skins will slip off easily.

Baz's Glazed Onions

Perfectly suited to any other dish—fish, fowl, or fine red meat—these down-to-earth onions are neither sweet nor sour.

6 medium yellow onions, peeled
1 tablespoon butter
4 tablespoons honey
2 teaspoons Dijon-style mustard
1 tablespoon red wine vinegar
½ teaspoon mild paprika
Pinch of ground cloves
½ teaspoon salt
Freshly ground black pepper,
   to taste
¼ cup water

Preheat the oven to 350° F. Cut a cross ½ inch deep in the top of each onion. Spread them open slightly. Combine the butter, honey, mustard, and vinegar in a small bowl and blend until smooth. Add the spices and mix well.

Place the onions close together in a small ovenproof dish. Pour the water around them and spoon about 2 teaspoons of the glaze over each one. Bake the onions for an hour, basting with the remaining sauce every 10 minutes.
Serves 4.

NUTRITIONAL ELEMENTS

Onion, chopped, 1 tablespoon

Calories	4
Vitamin C	1 mg
Calcium	3 mg

'Walla Walla' onion

SELECTED CULTIVARS

Standard or Cooking Onions
Long day (LD), Short day (SD)

Granex Hybrid PRR 90 days, variety used to produce the famous sweet Vidalia onion from Vidalia, Georgia. (SD)

Early Yellow Globe 100 days, medium-sized, firm white flesh, pungent flavor, a good keeper. (LD)

Sweet Sandwich 110 days, flat to globe-shaped yellow onion, very sweet, stores well. (LD)

Sweet Spanish Hybrid 110 days, huge globes with yellow skin and mild white flesh, keeps well. (LD)

Yellow Sweet Spanish 120 days, large yellow globes, sweet, mild, medium keeper, resistant to thrips. (LD)

Granex Yellow 170 days, large flat globes, yellow skin, white flesh, mild flavor, fair keeper. (SD)

Yellow Bermuda 185 days, large flat bulbs, soft, mild, does not keep long. (SD)

Walla Walla 300 days, flat globes with a mild flavor, usually planted in the summer and harvested the following summer. (LD)

Bunching Onions and Egyptian Onions

Beltsville Bunching 60 days, crisp, mild, winter hardy, withstands dry, hot weather.

White Spear 65 days, large bunching type, blue leaves.

Evergreen White Bunching 120 days, perennial in some climates, clusters of hardy, slow-to-bolt onions, planted in early spring or in the fall.

PEPPERS
Bell peppers, pimientos, and the chiles take second place only to tomatoes in the home garden. The flavor they bring is an integral part of American cuisine, and their brilliant colors make food look exciting. Several different types are available.

Sweet Bells Bell peppers grow on attractive plants 2 to 3 feet tall with pretty, pointed bright green leaves. Most cultivars mature sweet, blocky fruit, but some are tapered and a few are hot. Bell peppers set fruit when nights are above 60° and days below 90° F. Early cultivars are best for northern gardens and where the season is short.

Pimientos Pimientos are grown only in the hottest regions. Most that come onto the market are raised in the Caribbean. They are of two types: cheese (also called squash) and heart-shaped. The heart-shaped are the familiar ones sold at the market and the best tasting.

Chiles Most but not all chile peppers that are long, tapered, thin, cone-shaped, or round are hot. The color of a chile has nothing to do with its spiciness; most chiles are sold when red, but they can be green or yellow. When dried, chiles become chili powder or cayenne pepper and are the base for Tabasco and other hot sauces. More than 100 cultivars have been counted, and they cross-pollinate with ease. Many cultivars have more than one name and flavor. A chile that is mild when grown in the temperate climate of a California coastal valley becomes hot when grown in the arid conditions of New Mexico.

'Super Cayenne' peppers

GROWING PEPPERS

To produce a crop, chiles need higher temperatures than bell peppers do. In cool areas a black plastic mulch will keep the ground warmer and improve the yield of chiles. If the growing season is short, start seeds six to eight weeks before planting weather, set the seedlings out under hot caps, and mulch the soil around them to maintain moisture.

The peppers are attractive enough to be grown anywhere in the garden, and they thrive in containers. A half-dozen of each type, sweet and hot, will probably be enough. Once they start producing, they continue until nights turn cold. Tomatoes, potatoes, and peppers are all members of the tobacco family and should not be planted next to each other in the garden row. Do not grow sweet and hot peppers side by side; when they cross-pollinate, the flavors go off.

Culture

Most gardeners plant bell pepper seeds indoors six to eight weeks before the nighttime temperatures reach the mid-sixties. Seeds should be sown ¼ inch deep.

When the weather warms, set out transplants 6 to 10 inches apart. When the first blossoms open, give the plants a light application of

121

Top: 'Thai Hot'
peppers
Bottom:
'Hungarian Hot
Wax' pepper

fertilizer. The peppers require high
nutrition early in the season. They
will not set fruit if they have too
much water or fertilizer later. Transplants mature fruit in 45 to 90 days.

Harvesting

Peppers seem to protect themselves
from overloading the plant with
fruit: When a full quota of fruit is
under way, new blossoms drop.
When some of the peppers are harvested, the plant will again set
fruit—if conditions are right.

Sweet bell peppers have a short
growing season and many ripen
at once. They are usually picked
green once they are full-sized and
firm; if they ripen on the plant,
they will be sweeter and higher in
vitamin content. Chiles are picked
at full maturity. Use pruning shears
or a sharp knife to cut the peppers
from their stems, and leave a short
piece of stem on the fruit. Sealed
in a vegetable bag and stored in the
crisper, peppers keep for at least
a week and usually two.

To freeze for later use, stem, seed, quarter, and seal them in a freezer bag. Cooked, stuffed bell peppers freeze well and reheat beautifully.

For winter use, dry chiles. In Mexico, dried chiles are ground in a mortar for a supply of chili powder.

COOKING WITH PEPPERS

Northern gardeners are accustomed to the flavor of sweet bell peppers when they are still green. Where summer is hot and long, green peppers mellow in flavor and mature to red, yellow, orange, lilac, or purple.

Stemmed and seeded, sliced, chopped, or cut in slivers and strips, bell peppers are served with Swiss cheese and in crudités as appetizers. They are combined with onions, garlic, tomatoes, and herbs in salads, in sauces for pasta and fish, in omelets, and, with eggplant added, in vegetable medleys such as ratatouille. Roasted or grilled for 10 to 15 minutes, then peeled, they add color to a vegetable platter. Halved green bell peppers are excellent baked when stuffed with rice and tomato or meat sauce.

The sweetest of all peppers is the pimiento. In the market it is sometimes hard to distinguish from the red bell pepper. It is a deep, brilliant red, longer than most cultivars of sweet pepper, and pointed at the tip. Roasted and peeled, pimientos are used in hors d'oeuvres, in pasta and fish sauces with black olives, and with fennel, basil, and feta cheese in salads. Dried, pimientos become paprika, the vivid red spice prevalent in Hungarian cuisine.

Chile peppers grow either mild, pungent, or hot. With corn and tomatoes, they form the basis of Mexican cooking. Mexican *moles* (pronounced *MOW-lays*) are sauces made with chiles, ground seeds, and sometimes chocolate. Generally speaking, the green chiles are used fresh and the red are dried. Most frequently, the smaller and slimmer the chile, the hotter it is, and the larger, broader chiles tend to be somewhat milder. Chiles have an honored place in international cuisine, particularly in the dishes of India, Africa, Spain, Portugal, Indonesia, and Korea.

Capsaicin, the oil from chiles, can be very irritating; be careful to avoid touching your eyes. Remove the stems and the seeds and inner membranes which contain the highest concentrations of capsaicin. To roast or peel sweet or hot peppers, blister them under the broiler, then put them into a brown paper bag, twist closed, and let stand 15 minutes to steam and cool. Remove them one at a time and slip off the skins. Rinse under cool running water.

Bell Pepper and Tomato Salad

1 heart of romaine, sliced crosswise into ¾-inch strips
½ red bell pepper, slivered
½ yellow bell pepper, slivered
½ green bell pepper, slivered
1 large ripe red tomato, quartered
2 ripe yellow tomatoes, quartered
½ cup Roasted Garlic Oil (page 160)
¼ cup tarragon vinegar
¼ cup water
1 large clove garlic
Salt and freshly ground black pepper, to taste
1 tablespoon minced fresh basil
1 tablespoon minced fresh parsley
12 ripe black olives, sliced
1 cup grated Swiss cheese
1 medium red onion, sliced in thin rings

Place the romaine in a large salad bowl. Top with the peppers and

NUTRITIONAL ELEMENTS
Pepper, bell, 5 tablespoons
Calories 7
Vitamin A 400 mg
Vitamin C 43 mg
Calcium 3 mg

Chile, green, 2 ounces canned
Calories 14
Vitamin A 350 mg
Vitamin C 34 mg
Calcium 4 mg

Chile, green, 3 tablespoons, raw, chopped
Calories 19
Vitamin A 385 mg
Vitamin C 118 mg
Calcium 6 mg

Chile, red, 3 tablespoons, raw, chopped
Calories 45
Vitamin A 10,700 mg
Vitamin C 85 mg
Calcium 15 mg

Pimientos, 3½ ounces
Calories 27
Vitamin A 2,300 mg
Vitamin C 95 mg
Calcium 7

tomatoes. Blend the oil, vinegar, water, and garlic. Season with salt and pepper. Pour over the salad and toss. Top with basil, parsley, olives, and cheese and toss again. Garnish with the onion rings.
Serves 6.

Oven-Roasted Vegetables With Rosemary and Garlic

2 cups carrots, peeled,
2 cups eggplant, peeled
2 cups summer squash
2 cups red onion
2 cups red potatoes, parboiled about 5 to 6 minutes, quartered
2 cups fresh red or yellow bell pepper
⅓ cup fruity olive oil
2 tablespoons chopped garlic
2 tablespoons chopped fresh rosemary
Kosher salt and freshly ground black pepper, to taste
Sprigs of rosemary, for garnish

Cut vegetables in 1½-inch cubes, adding any other vegetables in season that look appealing. Toss with the olive oil, chopped garlic, and rosemary. Add salt and pepper to taste. Turn oven to highest setting and preheat 15 minutes. Place vegetables one layer deep on a baking sheet and oven-roast until almost done (about 20 minutes). Finish cooking under the broiler until edges are black and caramelized. Do not stir the vegetables while they are cooking. Remove from pan and serve at room temperature with bunches of rosemary for garnish.
Serves 6.

SELECTED CULTIVARS

Cultivars resistant to tobacco mosaic virus are marked *TM*.

Red Sweet Bell Peppers

Park's Early Thickset 45 days, productive plant, fruit measures 4½ by 3½ inches, matures to scarlet, good for home gardens. (TM)

Cadice 55 days, French, early, does well in cooler areas where peppers are marginal, good container plant.

Vanguard 59 days, medium-large, for North, thick-walled green-red fruit. (TM)

New Ace 62 days, 3- or 4-lobed 4-inch fruit quickly turns from green to red, for northern gardens.

Redskin Hybrid 65 days, medium-sized fruit, tolerates low light and cool temperatures, good in containers.

Cubanelle 68 days, popular, tapered Italian type, 6-inch frying pepper, matures from yellow-green to red.

Big Bertha 72 days, 2½-foot-tall hybrid, green to red fruit, very thick

'Vanguard' pepper

walls, largest bell pepper at 7 by 4 inches, excellent for stuffing, grows well in cool climates. (TM)

Bell Boy 75 days, 1½- to 2-foot-tall plants, medium-long, 4-lobed, bell-shaped, thick-walled fruit, matures from glossy green to deep red, All-America Selection. (TM)

Yolo Wonder 76 days, market type, vigorous 2-foot plants, 4-inch fruit, matures from dark green to red, good for home gardens. (TM)

Other Bell Peppers

Sweet Chocolate 58 days, University of New Hampshire hybrid, early fruiting, cold tolerant, color of milk chocolate when ripe.

Gypsy 60 days, two wedge-shaped fruit, 3 by 5½ inches, matures from light green to golden yellow to red, very tolerant of cool weather, All-America Selection. (TM)

Golden Summer 67 to 70 days, lime green fruit, 4½ by 3½ inches, golden at maturity. (TM)

Lilac Belle 68 days, blocky fruit matures from lavender to a rich lilac, then red, flavor like green pepper. (TM)

Sweet Banana 70 days, sweet yellow frying pepper, 1½ by 6 inches, red at maturity, excellent for home gardens.

Orange Belle 70 days, large, blocky fruit, matures from green to bright orange.

Orobelle 72 days, vigorous plants, sweet 4- to 4½-inch fruit, golden yellow at maturity. (TM)

Golden Cal Wonder 72 to 74 days, blocky 3½- to 3¾-inch fruit, well shaped, green turning yellow at maturity; there is a 'Red California Wonder'.

Top: 'Sweet Banana' peppers Bottom: 'Large Cherry' peppers

Purple Bell 75 days, blocky, 4-lobed 3½-inch square fruit, matures from green to purple to red.

Pimientos

Pimiento Perfection 75 days, heart-shaped, thick-walled, 2- by 3-inch pepper. (TM)

Pimiento Select 75 days, heart-shaped, smooth and thick-walled.

Chiles

Super Cayenne 60 days, very hot; long, slim 4-inch peppers turn from green to red, All-America Selection.

Thai Hot 64 to 68 days, one of the hottest; small, cone-shaped green-red fruit, very small plants; there is a 'Giant Thai Hot'.

Hungarian Hot Wax 65 days, very pungent, long-podded cultivar for canning and pickling, 5½-inch fruit tapers to a point, waxy yellow maturing to red.

Poblano 65 days, called "ancho" when dried, moderately hot, flavor-ful, heart-shaped, widely used in Mexican cooking.

Jalapa 65 days, hot, oval tapering to a blunt point, 2½ inches long, an improved jalapeño.

Italian White Wax 70 to 75 days, for pickling, 2- to 3-inch tapering fruit, snappy mild flavor when young, pungent when mature, pale yellow maturing to pale red.

Jalapeño 72 days, very hot, widely adapted, dark green becoming red, 3½ by 1½ inches, with a blunt point.

Super Cayenne Hybrid 72 days, very hot, ornamental container plant, 4-inch bright red pepper, use green or red, fresh or dried, All-American Selection.

Anaheim TMR 23 74 to 77 days, large-fruited cayenne, 6 to 8 inches long, flat, tapering to a point, one of the mildest chiles, green fruit matures red. (TM)

Serrano Chile 75 days, recommended for the Southwest, green then red, small 2¼- by ½-inch fruit, slim and club-shaped, walls thin, used for pickling and sauces, one of the hottest.

Santa Fe Grande 76 days, popular in the Southwest, 3½- by 1½-inch conical fruit tapering to a point, yellow maturing orange-red. (TM)

Large Cherry 78 days, medium green to red, heavy crops, fruit 1 by 1½ inches, good for pickling, hot.

Habanero 90 days, hotter than 'Jalapeño', fruit 1 by ½ inch, wrinkled, tapered to a point, very popular, turns from light green to orange.

Anaheim 90 days, mildly hot, dagger-shaped fruit, 8 inches long, changes from green and mild to red and hot, choice for roasting, frying, and stuffing.

'Golden Summer' peppers

RADISHES

Radishes are divided into two groups—spring and winter. The term *spring radish* is misleading. Spring radishes can be grown throughout the season in cooler areas and in all but the hottest months in warmer areas—that is both early spring and late summer into fall. In the South they grow well from fall through spring. They are cold-hardy root crops that bolt in heat. Sow seeds for the little, red or white thin-skinned spring radishes as soon as the ground can be worked. Harvest is in 22 to 28 days. The almost instant gratification makes these a fine project for children interested in gardening.

GROWING RADISHES

Spring radishes do well in light, sandy, well-fertilized soil. Keep the soil moist: They need to grow quickly or they will crack.

Winter radishes are big and pungent, and seeds packets contain about 15 seeds. Daikon and the other winter radishes are slower growing and keep longer than the little spring radishes. Where the weather is mild, they can overwinter in their rows. Usually, seeds are sown in midsummer for fall harvest in 45 to 70 days. Winter radishes bolt as soon as the heat comes, so they make poor spring crops. In mild regions some "all season" types are sown in fall for early-spring harvests and in late winter for spring harvest.

Sow radish seeds in containers or in the vegetable garden as a companion crop to slower plants that remain after the radish crop is harvested.

Culture

Sprinkle spring-radish seeds thickly over the soil and tamp them down with your hands. Water

'Cherry Belle' radishes

lightly. Sow seeds every 7 to 10 days until early summer, then start again in late summer.

Sow winter radishes in midsummer, timed so they reach maturity during the fall. Scatter seeds in a 3- or 4-inch-wide row. To reduce competition, thin seedlings to 1 to 2 inches apart soon after they emerge.

Harvesting

Bright red, peppery, and crisp as a cool morning, spring radishes are the first harvest to come in from seed. Pull spring radishes as soon as a rounded shoulder emerges from the soil. Mature radishes left in the ground another day or two become too peppery and coarse.

NUTRITIONAL ELEMENTS

Radishes, 10 small

Calories	17
Vitamin C	26 mg
Calcium	30 mg

Winter radishes can stay in the ground until frost.

Rinse the radishes in cold water, cut off the roots, and trim the leaves an inch above the tops. Cleaned radishes sealed in a vegetable bag can be stored in the crisper for four to five days.

COOKING WITH RADISHES

In France radishes are picked very young, chilled, and served with hors d'oeuvres or with bread and butter as a first course. Serve sliced or grated into salads, or with salty dips as appetizers. Blends of varicolored radishes, such as 'Easter Egg 11' and the bicolored long, slim French hybrid 'Flamboyant', are especially attractive as garnishes.

Winter radishes are big, usually white- or black-skinned, and used most often in Asian and German dishes. Shredded daikon is the classic Japanese accompaniment to sashimi. Steamed or sautéed with green onions, their flavor is like turnips.

Radish au Beurre

    36 to 60 young radishes
    Ice
    1 baguette French bread, heated
    Butter

Trim radish leaves, leaving about an inch of green, and remove the rootlets. Rinse thoroughly. Working from the root end to the top, make 4 or 5 thin slices just under the skin to create "flower petals." Crisp the radishes in a large bowl of water topped with ice. When the petals curl back, the radishes are ready. Drain and arrange on 6 plates. Enjoy the fresh radishes along with chunks of hot French bread and fresh butter.

Serves 6.

SELECTED CULTIVARS

Spring Radishes

Cherry Belle 22 days, cherry-sized, red with white flesh, All-America Selection.

French Breakfast 24 days, oblong, red with a white tip, pure white flesh.

Golden Radish 20 to 30 days, round, golden, mild flavor.

Plum Purple 24 days, a new color, can stay in ground longer than other types.

Snow Belle 26 days, round and smooth, white roots, mild flavor.

Easter Egg 11 28 days, oval, an assortment of colors—red, purple, pink, violet, and white.

Flamboyant 28 days, French breakfast type, long cylindrical roots, red in the shaft, white at the tip.

White Icicle 28 days, long, slim white roots, with a pungent but mild flavor.

Winter Radishes

Summer Cross 45 to 55 days, F1 daikon-type hybrid, giant white radish 6 to 14 inches long.

China Rose 52 to 70 days, heirloom variety, rose roots, white flesh, 6 inches long, hot.

Round Black Spanish 55 days, globe-shaped roots to 4 inches across, with black skin and crisp white flesh.

April Cross 60 days, Japanese daikon-type winter radish, to 18 inches long, mild flavor.

TOMATOES

Tomatoes come in a wide range of fruit and plant sizes, from currant-sized, to giant beefsteaks that can weigh 2 pounds. Most tomatoes are red, but there are pink, yellow, and orange varieties as well. There are red and yellow stuffing tomatoes, round tomatoes, flat-topped tomatoes, and pointed tomatoes. Some of the best tasting are the heirloom plants which have been preserved because of their superior flavor.

Tomatoes, like peppers, are warm-season plants, especially sensitive to low nighttime temperatures. In early spring when daytime temperatures are warm but nights fall below 55° F, many cultivars will not set fruit. In most regions they are set out as seedlings, sometimes so large they are beginning to set fruit. In summer you can expect blossom drop when days are above 90° F and nights above 76° F.

There is a tomato plant just right for every garden, greenhouse, balcony, patio, and pot. There are early, midseason, and late cultivars. The rule of thumb in choosing tomato cultivars to fit your climate is this: The shorter the growing season, the more you should limit your choices to the early and early-midseason cultivars.

Days to Maturity The number of days shown in the chart on page 81 refers to the time from setting out transplants to the first fruit. These are average figures intended only as guides. The actual number of days a plant needs to reach maturity depends on the cultivar, how soon you set out seedlings, how large the seedlings are, and of course the climate. That's why catalogs that serve local areas are so useful.

Determinate and Indeterminate Determinate plants grow to 3 feet, more or less, and ripen a big crop just about all at once. They get by without stakes. Indeterminate plants keep growing in every direction until stopped by the cold. They need staking or caging. Catalogs state whether the variety is determinate or indeterminate. Take this into consideration when choosing tomatoes. If you want plants in and out by a certain time to make room for other plants, choose determinate cultivars. If you want a few plants to bear over a long season, choose indeterminate.

Containers Tomatoes grow in almost any container that has room for the roots. Gardeners with unfavorable soils grow them in containers with a sterile growing medium.

'Supersteak Hybrid' tomatoes

'Golden Boy' tomato

doors, gradually expose the seedlings to more sunlight and outdoor temperatures.

Culture

The soil for tomatoes should be well drained and have an ample supply of nutrients, especially phosphorus. To prepare the soil, use plenty of organic matter and add 3 to 4 pounds of 5–10–10 fertilizer per 100 square feet. Water it in, and allow two weeks before planting.

Set transplants deep, with their lowest leaves just above soil level. Place leggy plants in the ground with the rootball horizontal. Roots form along the buried stem and enhance subsequent growth. If cold or wind are threats, use hot caps or other protection.

Space determinate (bush type) and ISI (compact bush type) tomatoes 24 inches apart. Staked indeterminate (vine type) tomatoes need to be 18 inches apart, and those that grow in cages need 2½ to 3 feet between plants. Indeterminate tomatoes grown on the ground need 4 feet between plants.

The first fertilizer application takes care of the plant until it sets fruit. Feed once a month while the fruit develops and stop when it starts to mature.

Tomatoes require uniform moisture after setting fruit; alternate wet and dry spells can bring on stunting and blossom-end rot. If plants are not setting fruit, stretch watering intervals to bring on tomato production. This puts the plant under a little stress, so be careful not to overdo it. When harvest time is near, cut back slightly on irrigation to get fruit that is flavorful but not watery.

Training Tomatoes can be grown on upright stakes and trellises, in wire cages, or on horizontal trellises or ladderlike frames set a foot

Dwarf plants suit 8-inch pots, and there are several cultivars that can be grown in hanging baskets. Giant plants will thrive even in 2-gallon containers of planting mix if you compensate for the limited root space with extra water and fertilizer. Always provide drainage.

GROWING TOMATOES

Tomato transplants are available at garden centers at the earliest planting time. To start your own transplants, place seeds ½ inch deep in peat pots five to seven weeks before the outdoor planting date. The last 10 days before planting out-

above ground level. All these keep fruit from contact with the soil and reduce damage from slugs, cracking, sunscald, and decay. In wet fall climates, the yield of usable tomatoes is nearly doubled if the fruit is on supports.

Although indeterminate tomatoes can be grown on the ground and produce more fruit than if grown on a support, the fruit is smaller and takes longer to ripen.

The low-growing, bushy cultivars are difficult to stake but may be held up by horizontal frames. Or allow the plants to sprawl but protect them underneath with mulch.

Grow tall cultivars on 6-foot stakes set 1 foot deep into the soil, or prune them to one stem and train on strings on a wood frame.

Pruning You can harvest more fruit over a longer period by allowing a branch to grow from the base to form a two-stemmed plant, and later removing the rest of the lower branches on both stems. For early fruit production and later sun protection, remove all branches on the lower 18 inches of the stem, then let the plant bush out with the branches supported by cages or tied to stakes.

Protection Plants set out early often require protection from low temperatures. If you use a wire cage, cover new plants with polyethylene film to raise the temperature inside the cage. A row of four or five plants can be covered with a 2-foot-high polyethylene row tent.

Tomato Problems

Here is a quick summary of some of the problems you might encounter when growing tomatoes. With the right procedures, you can probably avoid them.

All Vine and No Fruit If the plant does not produce flowers, the prob-lem is too much nitrogen and water in the early growth stages. Too much nitrogen stimulates vigorous vine growth but delays maturity. Dry the plants up a bit to try to induce flowering. If flowers are forming but are dropping off before they are able to set fruit, the problem is blossom drop.

Blossom Drop For a tomato grower, this can create great anxiety. The blossoms are out, but the big question is, Will they drop or set fruit? To find out takes about 50 hours—the minimum time required for pollen to germinate and the tube to grow down the pistil to the ovary. With nighttime temperatures below 55° F, germination and tube growth are so slow that blossoms drop off before they can be fertilized. As a rule, most early-maturing cultivars set fruit at lower temperatures than the main-season types.

Fruit set is also hampered by rain and prolonged humid conditions. Growers in cool, humid climates can increase fruit set by shaking the plant, or vibrating it with a battery-powered toothbrush, to release pollen for pollination. With stake-trained plants, just hit the top of the stakes for the same effect.

Blossom-End Rot Symptoms of this disease appear as a leathery scar or rot on the blossom end of fruit. It can occur at any stage of development and is usually caused by sudden changes in soil moisture, most serious when fast-growing plants are hit by a hot, dry spell. Lack of calcium is another cause.

Mulch with black plastic or an organic material to reduce fluctuations in soil moisture and temperature. Avoiding planting in poorly drained soil. Staked and heavily pruned tomatoes seem more susceptible to the problem than unpruned plants.

TOMATO DISEASE RESISTANCE

A	Anthracnose
F	Fusarium race 1
F1 & 2	Fusarium races 1 & 2
N	Root knot nematode
TM	Tobacco mosaic
V	Verticillium

NUTRITIONAL ELEMENTS
Tomato, medium, raw
Calories   33
Vitamin C   23 mg
Calcium   13 mg

Curled Leaves Wilt during a hot spell at midday is normal. Plants in containers show top-growth wilt, curled leaves, and droop when they need water. Once watered, they recover rapidly.

Leaf curl often occurs during and after a long wet period. Heavy pruning also seems to encourage leaf curl.

Poor Fruit Color In hot-summer areas, high temperatures can prevent the normal development of fruit color. The red pigment of the fruit does not form in temperatures above 86° F.

Both high temperatures and high light intensities stop the color from forming in fruit exposed to direct sun, and fruit may sunscald. Where high temperatures are the rule, choose cultivars with dense foliage.

Harvesting

Pick tomatoes just before using. A ripe tomato at peak flavor is fully colored on all sides—not greenish—and soft but firm.

Tomato flavor is much fuller at room temperature. If you need to store tomatoes, just put them on the counter out of direct sunlight. The refrigerator is too cold; flavor rapidly decreases and the fruit develops a mealy texture. Leave not-quite-ripe tomatoes (yellow-green on the underside in red cultivars) at room temperature to ripen fully. Check their progress: If the tomatoes go from firm-soft to mushy, they are mealy inside and best used for cooking. To peel, cover with boiling water for 10 seconds, immerse in ice water until cool, then remove the skin with a knife.

Harvested before the first frost, left unwashed, and wrapped individually in newspaper, most green tomatoes that show some white in the green keep for up to two to three months when stored at temperatures between 55° and 70° F. 'Longkeeper' ('Burpee's Long Keeper'), 'Golden Treasure', and other "storage tomatoes" planted late in the season are ready to harvest in 70 to 85 days and usually keep longer both on the vine and in storage.

Putting up tomato juice, tomato sauce, canned tomatoes, or tomato preserves is a great way to save a sudden glut of ripe tomatoes. Canning is a satisfying, safe process if you follow instructions carefully.

COOKING WITH TOMATOES

Vine-ripened tomatoes are reputed to provide 30 percent more vitamin C than those on supermarket shelves—but you do not need statistics to tell you how much better they taste. Home gardeners grow tomatoes more than any other food plant. No supermarket tomato can equal fruit freshly picked from the garden, still warm from the afternoon sun.

Tomatoes fit into the gourmet's diet in innumerable ways—sliced for antipasto, in salads, stuffed with tuna or crabmeat, and as a colorful bed for cold salmon, hard-cooked eggs, or shrimp. Tomatoes are also excellent stewed, scalloped, stuffed, baked, or sliced and glazed with wine and brown sugar. For grilling, skewer cherry tomatoes and cook them quickly over hot coals.

Green tomatoes are delicious sliced, dipped in batter and bread crumbs, and fried in hot oil. They make tangy relishes, such as piccalilli, and can be cooked into chutney or mincemeat for use in cookies, cakes, and pies. Add them to orange marmalade for tartness, or make a simple green-tomato jam. For many cooks the best dish of all is green-tomato pie, often compared to rhubarb or apple pie in flavor.

Tomatoes With Fresh Tomato Sauce

2 cups mâche or young spinach leaves
2 large, ripe yellow tomatoes
2 large, ripe red tomatoes
1 medium, ripe red tomato
3 tablespoons basil olive oil
2 tablespoons raspberry vinegar
1 tablespoon water
2 small cloves garlic
2 sprigs fresh oregano
7 large fresh basil leaves
Salt and freshly ground black pepper, to taste
6 spikes pink or lavender basil flowers and leaves

Arrange the mâche on a serving platter. Cut the large yellow and red tomatoes in ¼-inch-thick slices. Arrange them inside the ring of greens, alternating colors. In a blender or processor, purée the medium red tomato, oil, vinegar, water, garlic, oregano, and basil. Season with salt and pepper. Spoon the tomato mixture over the tomato slices, and garnish the center with herb florets.
Serves 4.

SELECTED CULTIVARS

Because America's favorite vegetable comes in so many types and varieties, this list is grouped into many types. The first group, Greenhouse Tomatoes, are the best selections for a greenhouse. The others should do well in any garden.

Greenhouse Tomatoes

Sierra 62 days, early variety, medium-sized 5- to 6-ounce fruit, disease resistant.

Boa 67 days, popular, medium to small tomato.

Greenhouse 656 VFFNT 75 days, medium-sized fruit.

Buffalo 72 days, large fruit, 9 to 10 ounces, on tall, vigorous vine.

Cherry Tomatoes

Peacevine Cherry 50 days, high vitamin C content, tresses of ¾-inch red fruit on 2- to 3-foot vines, produces continuously, needs trellising.

Toy Boy VFA 58 days, ½-inch fruit, plant three or four in a single 10-inch pot or hanging basket, indoors or out, with plenty of light, recommended for Florida.

'Roma' tomatoes

**'Yellow Pear'
tomatoes**

Sub-Arctic 59 days, for northern gardens, 2-ounce fruit on compact plants, prolific bearers.

Tiny Tim 60 days, ¾-inch scarlet fruit on 15-inch plant, two per 8-inch pot or hanging basket.

Red Robin 63 days, 1¼-inch fruit, recommended for baskets and pots.

Micro-Tom 63 days, tiny fruit, good flavor, fits a 4-inch pot, plant three to a hanging basket, ripens with less sun.

Small Fry VFNA 65 days, 1-inch cherry-type fruit in clusters on 30- to 40-inch vine, All-America Selection 1970.

Supersweet 100 VF 60 to 65 days, flavor of 1-inch 'Sweet 100' on big vines, disease resistant.

Sweet Million FNT 65 to 75 days, clusters of exceptionally flavored 1- to 1½-inch fruit continue all season.

Sweet Chelsea VF1 & 2 67 to 75 days, large cherry tomato, very high yield of 1¾-inch fruit, harvest August until frost.

Sweet 100 Plus 65 to 70 days, cascading clusters of tiny, delicious fruit, less sweet than 'Sweet 100', big vigorous vines bear until frost, prune to a single stem and stake or cage.

Patio 70 days, small vine, dwarf plant, good for containers and small gardens, recommended for Florida.

Tumblin' Tom 72 days, 1½-inch fruit, early, high yield from 1- to 2-foot plants, good for hanging basket or window box.

Sweetie 75 days, similar to 'Sweet 100', huge clusters of red cherry-sized fruit.

Sungold 60 to 65 days, Japanese F1 hybrid, ¾-inch golden orange fruit borne in long trusses.

Golden Pearl 67 days, heirloom, tiny golden yellow cherry tomatoes in grapelike clusters.

Currant Tomatoes

Spoon 65 days, tiny tomatoes, large vines.

Red Currant 65 to 75 days, wild red currant tomato of South America, charming in hanging baskets and window boxes, very productive; there is a 'Yellow Currant'.

Early Tomatoes (Small to Medium)

Early Girl VFF 52 days, disease resistant.

Prairie Fire 54 days, Northwest favorite, lush compact plants, 3- to 4-ounce fruit.

Early Girl 55 days, very early; fine, full flavor, produces 5-ounce fruit all season.

Santiam 58 days, popular in Northwest, 4- to 6-ounce fruit on high-yielding vines up to 30 inches tall.

Moskvitch 60 days, heirloom from Siberia, 4- to 6-ounce fruit with a rich flavor.

Quick Pick VFFNTA 60 days, high yield, for slicing or canning.

Better Girl VFN 62 days, meaty, crack-resistant fruit on medium, high-yielding vines.

Early Pick 62 days, similar to 'Big Early', fruit up to 8 ounces, disease tolerant, succeeds in West Coast.

Big Early 62 days, bright red solid fruit on large vines.

Bonny Best (John Baer) 66 to 82 days, fruit under 8 ounces, needs a wire cage, produces especially well in the North, recommended for Coast range.

Coldset 68 to 74 days, seedlings slightly frost tolerant, 4- to 6-ounce fruit, good for canning.

Better Bush VFF 68 days, 4-foot bush tomato, productive until frost, suited to larger containers and small gardens.

Heatwave VFHFA 68 days, heat tolerant, 7-ounce tomatoes mature even at 90° F and hotter, especially suited to Southeast and other warm areas.

Valley Girl 69 days, 7- to 8-ounce fruit, may not need staking, sets in heat or cold.

Enchantment VFFN 70 days, oval 3- to 4-ounce tasty fruit, good for salads or paste, productive all season, recommended for Florida.

Hawaiian VFNT 70 days, heat tolerant, 10-ounce delicious fruit, recommended for Georgia.

Ida Gold 59 days, University of Idaho cultivar, brilliant orange, extra-early, egg-shaped 2- to 3-ounce fruit produced over an extended period.

Husky Gold Hybrid 70 days, 5-inch or larger yellow fruit; mild, sweet flavor; suited to patio, tub, and small garden; tidy plant needs staking, AAS gold medal winner, recommended for Florida.

Main Season Tomatoes (Large or Clusters)

Whopper Improved VFFNT 65 days, early crop of large fruit continues until frost, improved disease resistance.

Carmello TMV 70 days, very productive French hybrid, large fruit, exceptional flavor.

Moreton Hybrid 70 days, medium-sized fruit, rich flavor.

Floramerica VFFA 70 days, huge yields, large scarlet fruit, adapted to wide range of growing conditions, All-America Selection 1978.

Better Boy VFN 70 to 82 days, 1-pound fruit, rugged, widely adapted, heavy crops.

Super Boy Hybrid 785 70 to 75 days, excellent for salsa.

Suncoast VFF 72 days, developed at University of Florida for home gardens, sweet 8-ounce fruit, vines need staking, fertilize heavily.

Ramapo VFA 72 days, developed by Rutgers University, medium to large fruit, strong, vigorous, sets well under adverse conditions.

Big Boy VTMBG 78 days, smooth, firm, thick-walled, very

large fruit up to 10 ounces, productive vine.

Big Girl 78 days, like 'Big Boy' with disease resistance. (F, V)

Celebrity VFFNTA 70 to 78 days (cool regions need 95 to 100 days), 7-ounce firm fruit, rugged, productive, All-America Selection 1984, recommended for Florida.

Marion FA 78 days, medium vines, one of the best home-garden steak cultivars, widely recommended, especially in hot climates.

Longkeeper 70 to 78 days, 6-ounce fruit on compact vines, pick when skins turn light gold, stores for up to three months.

Marglobe Improved 75 to 80 days, 6- to 7-ounce fruit, improvement over longtime favorite 'Marglobe Select', good for canning.

Pink Odoriko 76 days, Japanese hybrid, rose red color, vigorous plant, disease resistant.

Pink Girl 76 days, large 8-ounce fruit with pink skin, crack resistant, excellent flavor.

Burgess Stuffing Tomato 78 days, easily scooped out and stuffed, holds its shape.

Supersonic VF 79 days, large vines, reliable main cropper in northern areas, crack resistant.

Cal-Ace VFA 80 days, large, smooth fruit, vine sets heavily and needs staking.

Super Bush VFN 80 days, compact vines, no staking needed, excellent for small gardens.

Ace 55 VFN 80 days, large, more disease resistant than standard 'Ace' but fruit is not as smooth, especially adapted to California, popular in Oregon.

Homestead 80 days, large vines, sets under variety of conditions, including high temperatures.

Dad's Mug 85 to 95 days, blocky stuffing tomato, prolific bearer, flavorful pink-red fruit makes good tomato paste.

Taxi 64 to 70 days, lemon yellow with pinkish flesh, mild flavor.

Golden Delight 70 to 80 days, 4- to 6-ounce golden orange fruit, prolific.

Golden Boy F1 78 to 80 days, bright yellow-orange fruit with a mild flavor.

Azoychka 81 days, Russian heirloom tomato, 3-inch yellow fruit, good flavor, very productive.

Giant Tomatoes

Big Beef VFFNTA 73 to 75 days (cool regions need 80 to 85 days), earliest of the beefsteak type, high yield, All-America Selection 1994, recommended for Florida.

Pink Ponderosa 80 days, 2-pound fruit, old-timer, meaty and firm flesh, low in acid, grow in cage.

Supersteak Hybrid 80 days, modern version of beefsteak tomato, meaty fruit up to 2 pounds.

Beefmaster VFN 80 to 90 days, to 2 pounds, very good flavor, vigorous, prolific, recommended for Florida.

Oxheart 90 days, old-fashioned favorite, heart-shaped huge fruit, pink meaty flesh, almost seedless; there is a yellow 'Oxheart'.

Paste Tomatoes and Plum Tomatoes

Milano 63 days, Italian, very early plum type, high yield, full flavor, disease resistant.

Heinz 1350 VF 75 days, medium to large; uniform 6-ounce fruit on strong, compact vine, early, productive, popular.

La Rosa 75 to 78 days, 2¼-ounce plum-shaped fruit.

Roma VF 75 to 80 days, 2- to 3-inch meaty pear-shaped fruit.

San Remo 76 days, Italian, giant, meaty, ripens on a climbing vine, high yield, disease resistant.

Roma 76 days, meaty fruit, superior paste tomato, high yield.

Red Pear 78 days, pear-shaped fruit, less than 1 ounce; big, productive vines; there is a 'Yellow Pear'.

Yellow Bell 62 days, 2- to 3-inch yellow fruit, suited to paste cooking, or salads.

Yellow Pear 73 to 80 days, heirloom, pear-shaped 1-inch clear yellow fruit, mild flavor, medium to large plants need staking, very low acid and good for pickling.

Yellow Plum 78 days, 1-ounce fruit for yellow paste.

Other Tomatoes

Golden Queen 65 days, Amish heirloom, ¾-inch fruit, very good flavor, high midseason yield.

Evergreen 70 days, beefsteak-sized fruit, green and yellow when fully ripe.

Super Marmande 70 to 75, French heirloom, 6- to 8-ounce lobed fruit, exquisite tomato flavor, thrives in hot, dry climates.

Great White 75 days, big yellow-white fruit, mild flavor, viney, medium-tall plants.

Costoluto 78 days, Italian heirloom, ridged lobes, full flavor, heat-

'Green Zebra' tomatoes

loving tomato with high yield, good for paste.

Green Zebra 80 days, heirloom, salad-sized fruit, juicy green flesh overlaid with amber, sweet-tart flavor.

Old Flame 80 days, heirloom beefsteak, sunny yellow shot with rose, ripens late.

Cherokee Purple 80 days, Tennessee heirloom, Cherokee Indian origin, dusky rose purple fruit with brick red interior, delicious flavor, thin skin and soft flesh, home garden special.

HERBS FOR THE CHEF

An herb garden is a season-long delight that brings out the chef in just about anyone. It is visually satisfying and adds a delicious dimension to cooking, limited only by your imagination. With a healthy herb garden growing outside the kitchen door, a cook is compelled to experiment and create. Stepping out to harvest leaves and seeds for ingredients and fresh flowers for garnish is a pleasure indeed.

Both annual and perennial herbs thrive in well-drained soil with a pH between 6.5 and 7.0. Most need six to eight hours of direct sunlight and withstand midsummer drought.

Allow plants to become well established before picking herbs, or you end up with a stump after the first harvest. If there is a main stem, pinch this first to encourage branching, then pinch off side shoots as the plant develops. Unless you want seeds, remove flower heads: Developing seeds slows foliage production. The flowers make beautiful, aromatic bouquets and edible garnishes.

For the freshest flavor, pick herbs just before using and rinse leaves only if necessary: Water washes away the essential oils that carry the flavor.

As summer ends, allow seed-producers such as anise, dill, and fennel to bloom freely. Gather the seeds when the seed heads show signs of yellowing or browning, but before the seed heads are dry or the seeds are fully ripe. Once ripe, seeds drop and scatter quickly.

HARVESTING AND STORING HERBS

Harvest and dry culinary herbs early in the morning in late summer. When the dew is dried but the sun is not yet on the plants, the oils are at their peak. There are several methods for preserving herbs, and the simplest is air-drying. Tie bunches with twine and hang in a cool, dark spot until thoroughly dried. Or weave them into a wreath, hanging it out of direct sunlight and humidity. Enjoy as decor until the herbs dry completely, then use in the kitchen. You can also freeze or microwave many herbs to preserve them. For more information on keeping herbs, see page 83.

ANISE

Anise, or aniseed, is one of the licorice-flavored herbs. The soft ferny leaves, the dried flowers, and the seeds have been appreciated for centuries as flavoring for confections, wine, soups, and stews. Mexican cuisine as well as Indian and Mediterranean cooking employ anise. The Dutch enjoy hot, sweetened, anise-flavored milk drinks, and the French use it to flavor carrots. In America the leaves are used for garnishing and flavoring fruit and vegetable salads. They add a slight sweetness and a hint of licorice.

Dried anise seeds are small, pinkish beige, rather soft, and have a sharp, strong licorice flavor. Their form and taste are reminiscent of fennel seeds, but the larger fennel seeds have a milder flavor. Aniseed is used with discretion in curries, cakes, confectionery, certain cheeses, and breads like German *Anisbrot.* Aniseed also flavors Anisette, one of the sweetest liqueurs.

GROWING ANISE

Anise is a sprawling annual plant 18 to 24 inches tall, with deeply notched aromatic leaves and heavy heads of yellowish white flowers in umbrellalike clusters. The seeds begin to form two to three months after planting. A few plants tucked in among the flowers are sufficient. Anise is not an essential kitchen herb but it does have its uses. Because it has a taproot, anise does not transplant easily.

Anise grows well in containers, planters, or pots, at least 12 to 18 inches deep.

Culture
Plant in full sun and warm soil. Sow the seeds directly when temperatures reach a steady 70° F, or set out seedlings that were started indoors in individual peat pots.

Harvesting
Pick tender young leaves before the flowers appear, and use them fresh. Harvest seeds about a month after the flowers open. Snip clusters into paper bags and hang to dry in an airy, warm, dark place.

COOKING WITH ANISE

Sprinkle aniseed on cookies, panettone, apple and pear tarts, spice cake, and biscotti. Add to broth for fish stews, crab dishes, and meat casseroles; use in the pickling liquid for sweet pickles, and in the cooking water for carrots and beets.

Aniseed Tea
Aniseed tea is believed to be an excellent digestive which soothes the stomach after a meal.

1 teaspoon tea leaves
½ teaspoon ground aniseed

Place the tea and the aniseed in a mug. Pour boiling water over and allow to steep for 2 to 3 minutes. Strain and drink.

Serves 1.

Grammy's Anise Cookies
Mildly redolent of licorice, these cookies are popular with children. In fact, this is a wonderful recipe to make with children. Wash their hands and turn them loose to squish and squeeze—it's a very forgiving recipe!

    2 cups all-purpose flour
    1 cup sugar
    1 teaspoon ground aniseed
    1 cup butter or margarine

Preheat oven to 350° F. Dump the ingredients into a large mixing bowl and mix together until well blended. Form walnut-sized balls of dough and place 3 inches apart on an ungreased baking sheet. Use a small glass (or a child's palm) and flatten the cookie dough. Bake until golden (about 12 to 15 minutes). Cool on a rack.

Makes 2 dozen cookies.

SELECTED VARIETIES

General catalogs offer the species *Pimpinella anisum.*

BASIL

There are dozens of basil cultivars, and more appear in the garden catalogs every year. Finding your way through the choices is not easy, because their characteristics overlap. To generalize, there are standard sweet basils; sweet basils with exotic flavors; large-leaved sweet forms called lettuce-leaf basil or Italian basil; tasty but tiny bush basils, also called Greek or window-box basil, that look like topiaries; and gorgeous ornamental (and edible) purple-leaved basils.

In addition to the distinctive flavor of its leaves, basil also produces abundant and aromatic flower

'Thai' basil

spikes throughout the season and when basil bushes out in late summer. These make splendid fragrant additions to flower bouquets. Dry and use the highly perfumed basil cultivars in potpourri and dried flower arrangements.

GROWING BASIL

In all but Zones 9 and 10, grow basil as an annual. A standard-sized plant reaches 12 to 30 inches in the home garden. It is upright, well branched, vigorous, and easy to grow. Basil seeds may be started indoors five to six weeks before setting out in midspring.

Plant six green basils and six purple basils for their beauty in the garden and for bouquets. The tiny bush basils are ideal plants for window boxes, in pots indoors by sunny windows, or under grow lights. They look charming edging the garden.

Culture

Sow basil seeds in the garden after the soil has warmed and night temperatures are above 50° F. They need a sunny spot in well-drained soil amended with humus; soil can be rich, ordinary, or somewhat acid, so long as moisture is maintained. Thin the seedlings to 8 to 12 inches apart. Pinch out branch tips and flowers early and often to encourage leaf production. Or set out a few seedlings in midspring, then follow through with two or three successive sowings of seeds of other cultivars, beginning in late spring.

Frost turns basil to black mush, so protect thriving plants from early fall frosts with hot caps—they often last through Indian summer.

Harvesting

Pinch off tips for seasoning when the leaves still are young. For big harvests, such as when making pesto, wait until the flower spikes begin to form.

In midseason, cut the plants back by about half and dry or freeze the leaves, or make pesto and freeze it in freezer bags.

COOKING WITH BASIL

If you have space for only one herb, it is a toss-up whether to give it to parsley or basil. The debate may favor basil because parsley is always available at the market and stays fresh longer. Basil's light green, slightly puckered leaves release a strong flavor that combines the cool bite of mint (to which it is related), with hints of anise, clove, and thyme. If you choose to grow

'Purple Ruffles' basil

basil, you may select from a wide variety of plants, each with a particularly distinctive flavor.

Fresh, mince the leaf into salads and tomato dishes. Fresh or dried, add it to pasta dishes, sauces, salads, lamb, and fish. Make pesto, a famous Italian sauce comprising basil, garlic, olive oil, Parmesan cheese, and pine nuts. Chew fresh leaves to freshen the breath.

Classic Pesto Sauce
    2 cups loosely packed fresh basil
      leaves
    3 cloves garlic
    ½ cup extravirgin olive oil
    ½ cup pine nuts
    1 teaspoon salt
    ¼ teaspoon pepper
    ½ cup freshly grated Parmesan
      cheese

Place all the ingredients except the oil in a food processor or a blender. Then add the oil very slowly and blend until smooth.
Sauces 6 portions of pasta.

Basil Beer Bread
This quick, easy bread hasn't the fine texture of yeast bread but is hearty and satisfying. Leftover, it makes excellent toast to accompany a bowl of vegetable soup.

    3 cups self-rising flour
    2 tablespoons sugar
    ½ cup chopped fresh basil leaves
    1½ cups warm beer
    Melted butter, optional

Preheat oven to 350° F. Mix the flour and sugar in a large bowl. Stir in the basil, then the beer. Blend thoroughly, then pour into a well-oiled 9×5×3-inch loaf pan. Bake in the center of the oven about 50 minutes. Turn the loaf out of the pan and cool on a rack. If you like a softer crust, brush the top with melted butter while it is still warm.
Makes 1 loaf.

SELECTED CULTIVARS

Sweet Basil

These French basils are small-leaved, neatly shaped plants that have fine aroma and flavor. They make good pot plants.

Fino Verde Recommended as a classic pesto basil, fine dark green leaves, 12-inch plant.

Lettuce-Leaf Basil

Neapolitano Large, round luxuriant leaves, light green, sweet fragrance, mellow rich flavor.

Mammoth Basil (*Basilico monstruoso*) One of the best.

Crispum Very pungent form.

Sweet Genovese Also sold as 'Perfume Basil', long, pointed, glossy leaves, intense flavor, recommended for pesto sauce.

Exotic-Flavored Basil

Holy Basil Asian, valued for its bloom, small fuzzy leaves, lasting clove-lemon flavor, dries well.

Cinnamon Purplish leaves, aroma of cinnamon, deep violet-red veining on leaves, lavender flowers with deep violet bracts.

Thai Looks like cinnamon basil but paler; there is a Thai lemon basil that Japanese beetles are said to dislike.

Citriodora Grouped with lemon basil, small leaves, lemon scent, white flowers.

Licorice Basil More pronounced anise and lemon flavor, purple stems, large whorls of purple florets, leaves are narrow and light green at the base, and may be purple near the lavender-and-white flowers.

Anise Basil Fennel-scented, dark green mulberry-tinted leaves, rose-colored stalks, rose lavender flowers, rich aroma of anise; there is a 'Persian Anise' basil, 30 inches with aromatic purple foliage.

East Indian Basil (*Ocimum kilimandsharicum*) Perennial to 6 feet, aromatic, clove-scented foliage, pale yellow flowers.

Bush Basil

Spicy Globe Smallest basil, tiny, globe-shaped plant.

Basilico Finissimo Verde a Palla Tiny, Italian, globe-shaped bush basil; very small, thin leaves, very sweet fragrance and flavor.

Piccolo Verde Fine-leaved miniature, 12 inches tall; strong, sweet pungent flavor, leaves grow in tight clusters.

Purple Goddess Topiary-shaped basil, tiny purple leaves.

Purple Basil

Opal Purple leaves, green markings, pink-mauve flowers, nice ornamental, but a bland flavor.

Dark Opal Very little or no green; pale lavender on red stems, plant grows vigorously to 30 inches; fine, sweet, aniselike flavor.

Red Rubin European selection of 'Dark Opal', holds its color well.

Purple Ruffles Large, fringed, ruffled leaves; pinkish flowers, All-America Selection; 'Green Ruffles' is a green form.

BAY

Bay is a slow-growing, stately tree of modest height that flourishes in tropical and subtropical regions. Even when fresh, the 2- to 4-inch leaves are stiff. Until they are dried and added to a liquid, they yield little flavor. The tree bears insignificant yellow flowers in late spring, followed in early fall by black berries.

GROWING BAY

If yours is a frost-free climate and the garden a fair size, try a young bay in the yard. If the climate includes frost, plant the tree in a 14-inch tub and let it winter indoors in a cool, sunny room. The bay tree responds favorably to pruning and shearing.

Some strains are more aromatic than others, so before you invest, try a leaf or two of the plant you plan to buy in a fish broth or a stew.

Bay

Culture

If north of Zone 7, plant the tree in full sun; if you live very far South, plant it in partial sun. Bay prefers soil in the neutral range.

Harvesting

Bay leaves are sweeter after drying. They dry quickly on screens. Dried bay leaves are included in potpourri and dry perfumes.

COOKING WITH BAY

The sweet bay, or bay laurel, is one of the most important of all the flavoring herbs. Dried, the stiff evergreen leaves of this handsome tree add a hint of sweetness, a touch of mint, and an essence of perfume. Bay is indispensable to fine cuisine.

Bay leaf is one of the four herbs in the famous seasoning bouquet called fines herbes that flavors broths and court bouillons, meat stews, fish soups and chowders, tomato dishes, and salad dressings. In the cooking water for vegetables, a bay leaf is sometimes used as a substitute for salt. In Morocco, cooks line the couscous pot with bay leaves. In Latin America, bay flavors custards and puddings as well as savory dishes; and cooks in Zimbabwe add it to rice dishes and breakfast cereals. No Greek cook would prepare a hearty meal without the laurel leaves that formed the wreaths that were used to honor their heroes.

Bouquet Garni

  1 medium bay leaf
  1 small onion stuck with 4 whole
    cloves
  ¼ teaspoon dried thyme
  1 large sprig curly parsley

Tie into a small square of cheesecloth and add to broths, stew pots, stock pots, court bouillon for fish, and savory casseroles and soups.

Green Lentil Salad

  1 cup green or brown lentils,
    sorted and washed
  1 bay leaf
  1 onion, coarsely chopped
  Salt and pepper, to taste
  1 onion, finely chopped
  2 tablespoons vegetable oil
  2 tablespoons vinegar
  ¼ teaspoon dry mustard
  1 tablespoon chopped fresh
    parsley

Put the lentils into a saucepan with the bay leaf, the coarsely chopped onion, and the salt and pepper to taste. Cover with cold water. Bring to a boil, cover, and simmer gently until the lentils are just tender but not mushy (about 1 hour). Drain. Add the finely chopped onion to the hot lentils with the oil, vinegar, mustard, parsley, and additional salt and pepper, if necessary. Mix well and chill before serving.
  Serves 4.

SELECTED VARIETIES

A few garden catalogs offer the bay laurel species *Laurus nobilis.* Do not confuse this plant with the California bay or Oregon myrtle, *Umbellularia californica.*

BORAGE

The foliage of borage is a beautiful celadon green. The beauty of its flowers earn it a place in the cottage garden or a larger herb garden, and honeybees love it. The blossoms are borne in clusters.

GROWING BORAGE

Borage is a sprawling, fast-growing annual or biennial with succulent stems that reach 2 to 3 feet high and about 3 feet across. Borage may fade in high heat but often comes back when cool, wet weather arrives, and stays handsome into

Borage

COOKING WITH BORAGE

Tender young borage leaves impart the flavor of fresh cucumber to salads and wines. Add fresh, very young borage leaves to mesclun salad mixes, or use in pickling. Candy the leaves and float the flowers in drinks.

Young leaves are sometimes chopped with fresh chives, and are also used in the place of lettuce in sandwiches. The older leaves are too fuzzy to eat raw, but ½ cup in soup stock adds a refreshing cucumber flavor. Borage tea is made by steeping dried borage leaves, sometimes combined with hawthorn berries.

The pretty little blue or pink borage flowers are edible and make attractive garnishes. Float in lemonade, iced tea, and cold creamy summer soups, and serve with summer squash. They add a dash of color to salads and look pretty on slices of yellow tomato. You can freeze the flowers in ice cubes and use as an unusual garnish for tall drinks.

Crookneck Potato Soup
3 crookneck or yellow summer squash
1 pound 'Yukon Gold' potatoes
4 cups rich chicken stock
2 tablespoons butter
3 tablespoons chopped fresh borage
Salt and white pepper, to taste
1 scallion, thinly sliced, for garnish

Cut the unpeeled squash in 2-inch pieces and place in a large stockpot. Peel the potatoes and cut them in 1-inch cubes. Add them to the pot. Pour in the stock and bring to a boil. Reduce the heat, cover, and simmer until the squash is tender (about 20 minutes). Add the butter, 1 tablespoon of the borage, and salt

the fall. In mild regions sow borage seeds in the fall to germinate the following spring.

Culture
Sow seeds or set out seedlings after all danger of frost has passed. Borage grows in any soil with full sun, or light shade in the South. Do not overwater. Borage often self-sows.

Harvesting
Harvest the leaves just before the first flowers open. They must be young and fresh. Harvest the flowers when they have just opened.

Mince and freeze the leaves, or dry them on screens or in a microwave oven.

and pepper. Remove from the heat. Purée the soup until smooth. Reheat, and stir in the remaining borage. Sprinkle the soup with the scallion slices just before serving.
Serves 4.

SELECTED VARIETIES

Garden catalogs offer the species *Borago officinalis.*

BURNET

Burnet is a ferny perennial 1 to 2 feet tall with pale purple flowers about the size of blackberry blossoms. The plant is especially beautiful after a rain when drops glisten on the leaves.

GROWING BURNET

Burnet is not essential to the great chef's repertoire, but interesting to try. It thrives in containers outdoors as long as the soil remains moist and the plant is fertilized often.

Culture

Plant root divisions in the spring or sow seeds in the fall. Burnet needs neutral pH soil and a minimum of six hours of sun a day. Do not let the plants dry out during droughts.

Harvesting

Cut burnet leaves to the base of the stem; new leaves will follow. The plant remains green all winter, even into Zone 3, so it can be harvested all year around.

COOKING WITH BURNET

The ferny burnet leaves impart a cucumber flavor. Add minced burnet to leafy salads, to dips, to sandwiches instead of lettuce, to chicken dishes, and to sauces for cold chicken. It adds flavor when sprinkled generously over hot pasta

Burnet

sauces. Add to spicy Indian and Thai curries to cool their fire. Mince fresh young leaves into vegetable soups, cream cheeses, and soft butters, or float the leaves in iced drinks. Burnet tea is made by steeping the dried, ground root.

Burnet Salad Dressing

This dressing is suitable for any lettuce.

> 3 tablespoons extravirgin olive oil
> 3 tablespoons white wine vinegar
> 1 teaspoon Dijon-style mustard
> ¼ teaspoon sugar
> Salt and freshly ground black
>   pepper, to taste
> 3 tablespoons finely chopped
>   burnet leaves
> Fresh burnet leaves, for garnish

Combine the oil, vinegar, mustard, sugar, salt, and pepper in a small bowl. Add the burnet. Before serving, whisk the dressing, and garnish with a few fresh burnet leaves.
Makes ½ cup.

SELECTED VARIETIES

Garden catalogs offer the species *Poterium sanguisorba.*

CARAWAY

An aromatic Eurasian herb, caraway is a member of the parsley family. It has finely divided leaves and clusters of small white, pinkish, or greenish flowers. Its fruit, widely used as a seasoning, is seedlike in form, hence the term *caraway seed*. Caraway is used in medicine as well as cuisine.

GROWING CARAWAY

Caraway is a biennial that self-sows generously and so appears to be perennial. The first year caraway produces carrotlike leaves that grow to a height of 8 to 15 inches. The second year the plants reach to 2 feet, forming sturdy shoots topped in spring by flowers and later by seeds. Caraway has a taproot and does not transplant well.

Caraway

Culture

It is easiest to start with a few well-grown seedlings. If you have patience, sow seeds in the garden anytime between April and July. Where winters are mild, sow seeds in early fall.

Harvesting

The seeds are ready to harvest when they begin to turn brown. Snip the seed clusters into paper bags and hang to dry in an airy, warm, dark place.

COOKING WITH CARAWAY

The dark crescent-shaped seeds of the caraway plant are an important ingredient in German and Austrian cakes, pastries, and breads. They are also the main ingredient in the German liqueur called kümmel.

Caraway seeds are added to sauerkraut, cheese dishes, apple pies and apple sauce, brussels sprouts, pickles, and goulash. Some people chew caraway seeds to freshen their breath and aid digestion.

Crush caraway seeds to release their flavor and sprinkle them over rye bread, cheese rarebits, spreads, and dips, as well as over pork, sparcribs, coleslaw, kale, potato salad, cabbage, turnips, and beets.

Every part of the caraway plant is edible, including the mature roots, which are sometimes prepared and cooked like carrots.

Braised Red Cabbage

This is delicious and healthy served alongside simply prepared pork chops or German sausages.

    2 tablespoons vegetable oil
    2 cups chopped onions
    1 large red cabbage, cored, finely
        slivered
    3 tart green apples, peeled, cored,
        cut in thick slices
    1 cup golden raisins
    ¾ cup dry red wine
    ¾ cup red wine vinegar
    3 tablespoons packed dark brown
        sugar
    2 teaspoons caraway seeds
    1 teaspoon dried thyme leaves
    ½ teaspoon salt
    ½ teaspoon freshly ground black
        pepper

Heat the oil in a deep skillet. Add the onions and cook about 10 minutes. Add the remaining ingredients and toss to mix well. Cover and cook over medium heat about an hour, stirring occasionally. If it seems too dry, add a little water. Taste for seasoning and adjust salt and pepper. Serve hot.

Serves 8.

SELECTED VARIETIES

Garden catalogs offer the species *Carum carvi.*

CHERVIL

A member of the carrot family, chervil is an attractive plant and a favorite of gourmet cooks. Sow a patch of chervil if you have space and enjoy experimenting with new flavors. Chervil succeeds in containers outdoors.

GROWING CHERVIL

The plant is an annual whose ferny foliage resembles parsley but is flatter. Branches are ready for harvest six to eight weeks after sowing and last about six weeks. Chervil grows 1 to 2 feet tall and in summer bears dainty white flowers in umbrellalike clusters. Where the garden is too shady for parsley, try chervil as a substitute. It thrives under a tall shrub. Chervil has a long taproot and transplants poorly: If you start seedlings indoors, sow the seeds in individual peat pots.

Culture

Chervil needs moist soil and some shade, but does not tolerate extreme heat. In mild climates sow seeds in late fall. In cool regions sow seeds in early spring or plant seedlings in somewhat acid soil. Pick the flowering stems before they bloom.

Harvesting

In most regions chervil is a grown as a spring green. At the end of the season, harvest the remaining foliage, chop finely, and freeze.

COOKING WITH CHERVIL

The piquant flavor of chervil is a mix of parsley and sweet anise. Like parsley, chervil complements other flavors while imparting its own distinctive taste. In Italy chervil is used in egg dishes and salads, especially those including

Chervil

sauce thickens. Remove from the heat and stir in the cheese. Beat in the egg yolks one at a time, then the seasoning and chervil.

Beat the egg whites until they form stiff peaks but are not dry, then fold them into the cheese mixture. Pour into a 6-cup soufflé dish and bake until well-risen and golden brown (about 30 minutes).
Serves 4.

SELECTED CULTIVARS

Garden catalogs offer the flat-leaf species *Anthriscus cerefolium.*

Curly Chervil Also sold as French parsley, has a similar flavor to *A. cerefolium.*

Winter Chervil Slow bolting and vigorous.

CHIVES, GARLIC CHIVES

The chive plant is attractive and small enough to tuck in anywhere—a rock garden, a window box, a planter or pot, or a flower border. The flowers look like little lavender pom-poms in early summer. They look pretty growing with thyme, sage, burnet, winter savory, yarrow, and lavender cotton. Once established in fertile ground, chives return year after year.

GROWING CHIVES

Chives produce stiffly upright grassy tufts, 10 to 12 inches high, from a small onionlike bulb. Three to six chive plants will be enough.

Garlic chives grow in spreading clusters from bulbs set out in late fall or early spring. In late summer the plants bear fragrant white flowers with a green midriff that attract bees and are lovely in the flower garden. Plant six garlic-chive bulbs in the herb garden for their orna-

sorrel. A quarter cup of minced chervil is in good proportion for a leafy green salad for four.

Sprinkle minced chervil liberally over soups and stews. The French use it in place of parsley, in court bouillons for salmon, sauces for trout, new potatoes, spinach, asparagus, snap beans, Vichyssoise, *potage bonne femme* and other creamy soups, cold fish, and chicken salads. It once was eaten as a green, boiled or raw, and is still a popular spring tonic.

Chervil Soufflé
　3 tablespoons butter
　4 tablespoons all-purpose flour
　1 cup milk
　¾ cup white cheddar cheese, grated
　4 eggs, separated
　Salt and white pepper, to taste
　1 tablespoon chopped chervil leaves

Preheat oven to 375° F. Melt the butter in a saucepan, add the flour, and cook 1 minute. Remove from the heat and slowly stir in the milk. Return to the heat and bring to a boil, stirring constantly, until the

mental value and for the fun of try-
ing a new onion flavor.

Culture

In early spring set out chive plants
in well-drained, rich, slightly
acid soil. Maintain moisture during
droughts. Fertilize in early spring
and monthly during the growing
season. Keep the flowers snipped
out to prevent the formation of seed
heads, which slows the growth of
foliage.

In midautumn plant garlic-chive
bulbs in well-drained soil, 3 to
4 inches deep and 8 to 10 inches
apart. Divide them annually.

Harvesting

Harvest chive leaves at will, but
never strip the plant completely.
With scissors, cut the leaves off
about ½ inch above the soil line.

COOKING WITH CHIVES

Chives are deep green, onion-
flavored grasslike leaves that are
minced and used to flavor and garnish salads, cream soups, stews,
vegetables—anything improved by
a touch of mild onion and a bright
bit of green. Chives are indispensable for topping cream soups such
as Vichyssoise, omelets and scram-
bled eggs, baked or boiled potatoes,
and fish. A tablespoonful does wonders for sliced tomatoes, cottage
and cream cheeses, sour cream,
vinaigrettes, and mayonnaise. The
dryish, lilac-colored flower heads
that appear in late spring and early
summer are edible and make pretty
garnishes.

Garlic chives or Chinese chives
are closely related to ordinary
chives but are taller and flat-
leaved. The flavor has a hint of
garlic and is preferred in eastern
cuisines. Use in the same dishes
as ordinary chives.

Chives

Vichyssoise

    2 tablespoons butter
    1 very small onion, minced
    5 large leeks, white part only,
       cleaned, thinly sliced
    3 cups peeled, diced potatoes
    2 quarts chicken broth
    1 cup half-and-half or whole milk
    Salt, to taste
    ½ cup minced chives or garlic
       chives

Melt the butter and sauté the onion,
leeks, and potatoes until the leeks
wilt. Add the broth and boil gently
until the potatoes are very tender.
Purée to make a smooth, creamy
soup. Season with salt to taste, add
the half-and-half or milk, and chill.
Serve topped with chives.
Serves 6 to 8.

SELECTED VARIETIES

Garden catalogs offer only the
species, *Allium schoenoprasum.*

A few catalogs offer garlic chives,
A. tuberosum, usually in the flower
section. Garden centers often carry
the bulbs.

CILANTRO/ CHINESE PARSLEY/ CORIANDER

To aficionados of Mexican, Asian, and Latin American cuisines, cilantro is an essential herb for the kitchen garden. Sow a patch of cilantro in the herb garden and use the thinnings as an early crop. At the end of the growing season, allow a few plants to develop seed, and harvest the seeds for coriander.

GROWING CILANTRO

Cilantro/coriander is a fast-growing annual 12 to 24 inches tall that tolerates a lot of cold and is slow to bolt in summer heat. The leaves are oval with lacy edges like flat-leaf parsley. The small flowers grow in parasol-shaped clusters. Cilantro grows well in pots.

Culture

Sow seeds where the plants are to grow. Cilantro succeeds in full or partial sun, in light, well-drained neutral soil. Make several sowings two to three weeks apart, starting in early spring. Where winters are mild, sow seeds in fall for a late crop. In good conditions the plant self-sows and tolerates some drought.

Harvesting

For cilantro leaf, use thinnings; then, as the plants fill out, pick leaves as needed.

Cilantro doesn't dry well but it keeps fresh for a week or so in the refrigerator. Do not rinse cilantro before storing, as it tends to rot. Store in a vegetable bag in the crisper. If the leaves dry, soak them for a few minutes in cool water before using.

Cilantro

When the seeds turn tan-brown, pull up the entire plant. Allow the seeds to ripen, then dry on screens and store in sealed jars.

COOKING WITH CILANTRO

The dark pungent green leaf called cilantro, fresh coriander, or Chinese parsley, and the tan aromatic seed known as coriander develop from the same plant. The leaf looks like pale, flat-leaf Italian parsley. The flavor has overtones of parsley, citrus, and nuts, plus an earthy pungency unlike anything else.

Cilantro is the *culantro* sold in Puerto Rican markets. The fresh leaf is used as flavoring and garnish in Mexican and Latin American cuisines, in salads, soups, salsas, guacamole, and other specialties. It is indispensable if you wish to reproduce Chinese, Thai, and Indian recipes.

Tomato Salsa

    2 tablespoons olive oil
    1 medium onion, minced
    1 clove garlic, minced
    1 medium green tomato, chopped
    2 large ripe tomatoes, peeled,
        seeded, chopped
    ¼ teaspoon sugar
    2 serrano chiles, chopped
    Salt and freshly ground black
        pepper, to taste
    1 tablespoon minced cilantro

In a medium saucepan over medium-high heat, heat the oil and sauté the onion and garlic until limp (about 3 to 4 minutes). Add the green tomato and sauté 2 minutes. Add the ripe tomatoes, sugar, and chiles and cook until the sauce thickens a little. Add salt and pepper. Stir in the cilantro and sauté 2 minutes more. Serve hot over meat, fish, rice, or pasta.
Makes 2 cups.

COOKING WITH CORIANDER

The dried seed known as coriander has a sweet lemon flavor with a hint of sage. Ground and combined with cardamom, cumin, and turmeric, coriander flavors mild curries. It is important in chili and in many Spanish recipes. Add to pilafs, sauerkraut, cheese, bread, meat and chicken marinades, sausages, and tomato sauces. In the Far East, the dried seeds are chewed as an after-dinner breath freshener.

Ground coriander flavors cookies, cakes, pastries, lentil and pea soup, coffee, gingerbread, Danish pastry, Swedish coffee cake, and rich egg custards.

Garam Masala

This spicy mixture is used in many Indian dishes and is delicious on rice and in potato salad.

    2 tablespoons ground cumin
    1 tablespoon ground cardamom
    ½ tablespoon ground coriander
    ½ tablespoon ground cinnamon
    1 teaspoon ground cloves
    1 tablespoon freshly ground black
        pepper

Combine spices; bottle, cork tightly, and store in a cool, dark place.
Makes ¼ cup.

SELECTED CULTIVARS

Garden catalogs offer two types of *Coriandrum sativum*. For leaves to use fresh, choose seeds labeled *cilantro*, *santo cilantro*, and *cilantro* 'Slow Bolt'. These strains are slow to produce flowers and best for leaf production.

To harvest seeds, choose cultivars offered as coriander. These flower quickly, making seeds available more quickly.

DILL

Dill is a cool-weather annual, 2 to 4 feet tall, and ready to harvest from seed in about two months. In high heat it bolts, that is, it puts up umbrella-shaped flowers and begins to deteriorate. Strong, healthy plants that make it through summer heat will ripen seed in late summer and early fall. Dill's feathery fronds are beautiful in flowering borders, lovely surrounded by petunias and geraniums.

GROWING DILL

Start seeds indoors six to eight weeks before the last frost. Plant them in individual peat pots: Dill does not transplant easily.

A half-dozen plants will meet your needs. When they begin to flower, allow a few to set seed for later harvest. If the climate permits, make a second sowing in late spring to have fresh dill for fall and to harvest for drying.

Dill, especially the dwarf cultivars, does well in containers outdoors until heat comes. Keep the soil moist.

Culture

In early spring sow seeds thickly where the plants are to grow, and repeat in 10 days to keep young dill coming. Dill needs rich, light, acid soil, full sun (partial in the warm South), and sustained moisture. Keep the flower heads picked until the end of the season, then allow a few to set seed.

Harvesting

With scissors, harvest sprigs high on the plant. Do not rinse dill weed—it tends to rot.

Sealed in vegetable bags, dill keeps for a few days in the crisper. Dill leaves dry rapidly on screens and can then be chopped and stored for winter. To retain its beautiful deep green, keep dill weed away from bright light.

Dill

COOKING WITH DILL

The soft foliage and seeds of dill have a parsley-carrot-lemon-anise flavor. The ferny leaves, called dill weed, are finer than sweet anise or fennel, which they resemble. The foliage and seeds are common flavorings in the cuisines of northern and central Europe, Russia, and Scandinavia. Fresh dill and dill seed are added to soups and preserves, and to cooking water and sauces for potatoes, snap beans, and salads. Dill is an important ingredient in pickle recipes. The fresh leaves enhance poached salmon, eggs, leafy salads, cucumber relishes, steamed cauliflower and carrots, slaws, sauerkraut, and tomato juice.

Dill seeds resemble caraway seeds, and there is a hint of caraway in the flavor.

Baz's Zucchini With Dill and Lemon

    6 zucchini, about 6 inches long,
        very thinly sliced
    2 teaspoons extravirgin olive oil
    1 tablespoon fresh lemon juice
    1 teaspoon fresh dill weed
    Light sprinkle of salt and white
        pepper
    2 tablespoons very finely grated
        Parmesan cheese

Heat the olive oil in a large skillet over medium-high heat. Drop in the sliced zucchini and toss as in a stir-fry. This is best done with 2 utensils. Cook only 2 to 3 minutes. Sprinkle the lemon juice over the top, along with the salt, pepper, and dill weed. Toss again. Serve at once with a light dusting of finely grated Parmesan cheese.
    Serves 4.

SELECTED CULTIVARS

Bouquet 60 days, late blooming; compact, bushy plant grows 18 to 30 inches tall, large leaves, recommended for use fresh.

Fernleaf 60 days, 18-inch dwarf, lovely blue-green color, good choice for containers, All-America Selection 1992.

Mammoth 60 days, 4 feet tall, lovely aroma, recommended for pickling.

Long Island Mammoth 60 days, vigorous plant, matures 6- to 9-inch flower umbels, produces seed quickly.

Dukat 60 days, European clumping strain, related to the 4-foot 'Mammoth', delicate aroma, sweet, foliage abounds before it sends up huge 10-inch seed heads, also offered as 'Tetra-dill'.

EPAZOTE

Also known as "wormseed" for its anthelmintic properties (its ability to dispel parasitic worms from the intestines), epazote has long been used for both culinary and medicinal purposes. In a unique cross of the two, it is used today in many bean dishes to counter their gastrointestinal effects.

GROWING EPAZOTE

Epazote needs hot weather. It grows to 2 to 4 feet tall, and as the season advances produces spikes of inconspicuous yellow-green flowers. The leaves are 3 inches long. Once established, epazote self-sows readily, so it is wise to confine the plant to containers.

Culture

Epazote grows easily and quickly from seed in full sun and poor soil so long as it has heat. Sow seeds thickly on a wide band and thin to stand 6 inches apart when temperatures reach 60° to 70° F.

**Top: Epazote
Bottom: Fennel**

Harvesting

A little epazote goes a long way: It tastes best picked young and used immediately.

COOKING WITH EPAZOTE

Epazote, Mexican tea, is a pungent leaf used widely in bean cookery, tortilla dishes, and in the cuisines of central and southern Mexico. It has light-to-medium green leaves and a very strong citrus-camphor-parsley flavor. Garlic, bay, cumin, and hot peppers frequently accompany epazote in recipes. Because it is commonly held to be an antiflatulent, it is recommended especially for use in bean dishes. Add 1 teaspoon of dried epazote, or 2 teaspoons of fresh leaves, to each 2 cups of simmering beans. Epazote is also cooked with corn, mushrooms, and seafood. In Spain it is known as *pazote* and is steeped for tea. Dried, it is packaged as Jerusalem oak pazote or, more common, in Mexican markets as *Epazote de comer.*

Quesadillas con epazote

This ordinary and simple everyday filling is delicious. Mexicans like to use some strips of *queso de Oaxaca*, a white stringy cheese, a strip of roasted and peeled poblano chile, salt, and some fresh epazote leaves. These ingredients are often not available, but there are adequate substitutions at hand. Canned, peeled green chiles serve well, and Muenster cheese melts readily and is creamy. If fresh epazote cannot be found, soak a few leaves of the dried herb to use in its place.

SELECTED VARIETIES

Garden catalogs offer the species *Chenopodium ambrosioides.*

FENNEL/ SWEET FENNEL

Sweet fennel is not the chef's most essential source of the licorice-lemon-pine flavor, but it is useful, and the foliage is lovely in the herb or flower garden, especially combined with sage, tansy, fox-glove, rue, and southernwood. Sweet fennel has another great asset—it is host to the black and chartreuse caterpillar of the beautiful black swallowtail butterfly.

GROWING FENNEL

A biennial, or perennial, sweet fennel is usually grown as an annual. The tall straight stems are hollow and in rich soil develop a bluish green color. The plant itself is stunning and over the summer reaches a height of 3 to 5 feet. The bronze fennels impart a flavor softer than green fennel. Use both leaves and seeds for flavoring. In regions where winters are mild, the seeds are generally sown in late summer for an early-spring harvest. Fennel grows well in very large planters.

Culture

Sow seeds outdoors in midspring in full sun and well-drained soil with a pH above 6.0. They germinate at temperatures of 65° to 70° F. Thin the plants to stand 10 to 12 inches apart. Maintain soil moisture, and cut the plants back from the top if they become unkempt.

Harvesting

The harvest is ready just as the flowers open. Do not rinse the foliage, as it tends to rot. Seal in vegetable bags and store in the crisper.

Fennel leaves dry rapidly on screens and can then be chopped and bottled.

Harvest and dry seeds as they ripen and turn brown.

COOKING WITH FENNEL

The foliage of sweet fennel has a mild anise-licorice flavor that includes hints of lemon and pine. The green or bronze-purple leaves are finer and softer than dill. Chopped fresh, use sweet fennel as garnish and flavoring for any dish that is enhanced by dill or parsley. Add 1 tablespoon of minced fennel leaf per 4 servings to sauces, soups, salads, or dough.

Fennel is especially good with seafood, meat loaf, pasta sauces, tomatoes, soups, and salads made with macaroni and potato. Use the seeds in court bouillons for fish recipes with a Mediterranean accent. Crush seeds into lentil soups and tomato sauce for spaghetti.

The yellow flowers resemble Queen-Anne's-lace and produce large gray-green seeds with a strong, sweet, slightly anise flavor. Use fennel seeds in cheeses, savory casseroles, meat and vegetable dishes, apple dishes, rye bread, breadsticks, and in Italian and Greek breads and sweet cakes.

Fish Soup Provençale

This is light and delicate, a lovely soup laced with both the subtle flavor of fennel seeds and the sparkle of crunchy fresh fennel.

4 cups fish stock
2 cups peeled, coarsely chopped plum tomatoes, with their juice
2 tablespoons tomato paste
1 tablespoon freshly ground fennel seeds
3 cloves garlic, minced
¼ teaspoon saffron threads, crumbled
1 cup julienned fresh fennel bulb
½ teaspoon salt
Freshly ground black pepper, to taste
4 slices garlic-seasoned toast

In a large saucepan, combine the stock, tomatoes, tomato paste, fennel seeds, garlic, and saffron. Bring to a boil, then lower the heat and simmer, uncovered, for 30 minutes.

Strain the soup, pressing the solids against the strainer to extract all the liquid. Return the liquid to the pan and stir in the fresh fennel. Simmer 2 to 3 minutes, just until the fennel is crisp-tender. Season with salt and pepper. Place a garlic crouton in each bowl before ladling in the soup.

Serves 4.

SELECTED CULTIVARS

Cultivars sold as sweet fennel are green and likely to have the best leaf flavor and seed production. Two fennel cultivars interest the chef: sweet fennel (*Foeniculum vulgare*), the herb grown for its flavorful leaves and seeds, and Florence fennel (sweet anise, *fenouille, finoccio*), the vegetable grown primarily for its bulbous base—*F. vulgare azoricum,* also known as dulce.

Red Leaf Bronze or copper sweet fennel, beautiful plants with lacy bronze foliage or bronze purple-green foliage.

Smokey A bronze fennel.

GARLIC

Long touted for its medicinal powers as well as culinary magic, garlic is grown extensively throughout the world. It has been credited with clearing the blood, aiding digestion, repelling vampires, and curing everything from consumption to baldness. In the kitchen, it is indispensable, although too much can easily overwhelm more delicate flavors.

There are three types of garlic for the home garden: softneck, elephant, and stiffneck.

Softneck The garlic heads of the softneck cultivars are composed of several large cloves on the outside and many small cloves inside. The necks are soft at maturity and easy to braid. This type has the strongest flavor and keeps well.

Elephant This type of garlic is available in many garden catalogs. It is a softneck type with cloves twice the size and much milder than regular garlic. In rich soil, the bulbs grow to ½ pound. It is not very hardy; mulch heavily before winter. Braided elephant garlic makes a handsome rope.

Garlic drying

Stiffneck The bulbs of this type of garlic have four to six large outer cloves, none inside, and are white on the outside and dark red inside. The flavor is milder and the cloves easier to peel than softneck types. These plants send up scapes that form clusters of bulblets. Pinch these off or the main bulbs will be smaller. Use the fresh-cut bulblets in cooking.

GROWING GARLIC

Garlic's bulblike "heads" are composed of several silkily sheathed cloves. When planted, each grows a new garlic plant. The leaves are hollow tubes, like those of onions. Planted in late fall, it grows roots during the winter, sends up onion-like stems in cool spring weather, and forms bulbs when the temperature turns hot and the days are long.

This is not an herb for the flower garden—it belongs in a traditional row-crop garden, and only if you have lots of space to spare. It will grow in pots and containers only if it is kept well fed and watered and in full sun.

Culture

To prepare for a garlic crop, work sand, compost, and a slow-release organic fertilizer into soil in a sunny, well-drained area. If you live in the North, set out garlic in early spring. Elsewhere, plant garlic in fall. Break the heads into cloves; the largest cloves produce the largest bulbs. Plant the cloves root side down, 1½ to 2 inches deep and 4 to 6 inches apart. Roots begin to grow before real cold comes, but there is little or no top growth. Garlic is cold hardy. Mulch to prevent late-winter heaving.

When the garlic tops are 6 to 8 inches high, side-dress the rows with compost or a complete fertilizer low in nitrogen.

Garlic being harvested

Harvesting

Garlic is mature in midsummer when the tops turn yellow and begin to flop over. Push all the tops over and leave them another week or so. With a pitchfork carefully dig the bulbs and spread them to dry in the sun for a few days.

Tie or braid the garlic tops in loose bunches and hang them in a cool, dry place.

COOKING WITH GARLIC

A species of onion, garlic (*Allium sativum*), adds a sweet, rich, mellow flavor when cooked in sauces, casseroles, and soups. It is often combined with onion and other herbs and spices. Used in cuisines virtually the world over, garlic is added, most often with onions, to the hot oil or fat as the first step in preparing soups, curries, stews, and stir-fries.

The flavor of raw garlic is biting, strong, pungent, and, to some people, offensive. But when a discreet amount is mashed into salad dressings, dips, and cheeses, or roasted and smeared over herbed breads, it gives body to the concoction and adds a savory flavor nothing else can provide. The flavor of roasted garlic or garlic cooked in a soup or baked with chicken is nutty, sweet, and mellow.

Roasted Garlic Oil

2 large, plump heads garlic
1 pint bottle of high-quality olive oil, plus 1 tablespoon
8-inch-square aluminum foil

Slice off the tips and set the garlic on the foil. Drizzle the tablespoon of oil over and replace the tops. Seal both heads in the foil. Bake 1½ hours at 250° F. Open the foil, discard the tips, and, with a knife tip, scoop out the softened garlic pulp from each clove and put into the oil. Cap the bottle, shake gently, and refrigerate for 3 or 4 days. Bring to room temperature, remove the garlic, and bottle the oil for sauces, dressings, and cooking.
Makes 1 pint.

SELECTED CULTIVARS

New York White (Polish White)
Softneck type with white skin and a purple flush, disease resistant, productive, and winter hardy in the North and East.

German Extra Hardy Stiffneck garlic, extremely hardy and vigorous.

GINGER

The knotty rootstock of a tropical plant, ginger is a pungent, aromatic rhizome used both for culinary and medicinal purposes. On the bamboolike stems of the plant grow clusters of white flowers streaked with purple. Originally from India, ginger was introduced into Japan, the West Indies, South America, and West Africa. In addition to flavoring food, it is used medicinally: internally for stomachache, externally for pains.

GROWING GINGER

The plant develops from the bulbous root, or rhizome, and grows to 3 feet. It produces narrow leaves about 1 inch wide and up to 12 inches long. The yellow-green flowers grow in dense cone-shaped, 3-inch spikes.

Ginger thrives only in the mildest regions with a very long growing season. Protect it from high winds and low temperatures.

Culture

Plant the roots in full sun in rich, moist soil with good drainage. Set the rhizomes at a slant with the sprout ends up. In about 10 days, bamboolike stems and leaves appear. In six to nine months, the roots begin to grow and become ready for harvest.

Harvesting

As ginger matures it sends up sprouts in the soil—like an iris rhizome. Dig down to bare the root, and if there is tender new growth at the end of the rhizome, break it off to use for cooking. Leave the rest.

Fresh ginger root keeps for weeks in the refrigerator when sealed in plastic wrap.

COOKING WITH GINGER

This aromatic root from the Far East looks like a silky skinned iris rhizome. The flavor is peppery and fruity. Colonial Americans ground it to make ginger snaps, gingerbread men, spice cakes, pumpkin pie, mincemeat, chutneys, ketchup, and curry powder. Candied or crystallized, ginger is a favorite *digestif.* Minced slices of ginger pickled in syrup—"Canton ginger"—are added to fruit compotes, sweet potatoes, and ripe garden tomatoes. Jamaicans used ginger to invent one of the most popular soft drinks of all time—ginger ale.

Shaved marinated ginger is one of the garnishes served with sushi and sashimi. A tablespoon of chopped ginger brightens the flavor of casseroles, soups, squash, hamburger dishes, and mayonnaise. Add fresh, minced ginger to the steamer or cooking water for fish and seafood. A teaspoon of grated ginger root enlivens mashed ripe mangos, compotes of very ripe peaches, fruit dishes, and sweet cherry pies.

Ginger Chicken

1½-inch piece fresh ginger, peeled, sliced
4 cloves garlic
¼ cup rice wine
¼ cup soy sauce *or* mushroom soy sauce
½ teaspoon sugar
6 large chicken legs, skin on

Make a marinade by processing the ginger, garlic, rice wine, soy sauce, and sugar. Marinate the chicken in the mixture, covered, at room temperature 1 to 2 hours. Arrange the chicken, skin side down, on an aluminum foil–lined baking pan. Reserve the marinade. Heat oven to 400° F. Bake chicken 20 minutes. Turn the pieces, baste with pan juices and a little more marinade, then bake another 10 minutes. Spoon the remaining marinade over the chicken and bake 15 minutes more.
Serves 6.

Ginger

SELECTED VARIETIES

Zingiber mioga is offered in the *Deep Diversity Seed Catalog* from Seeds of Change (see page 307). It is described as a moderately hardy rhizomatous ginger whose flower buds and rhizome are traditional Japanese food.

Among the most delicious of all gingers are those the Thai call *ka.* Also known as *galangal* and *laos,* this is an exotic relative of ordinary ginger. It has a mouth-watering flowery aroma and is occasionally found at Asian markets.

LAVENDER

This herb's sweet, extraordinarily long-lasting fragrance has made it a favorite herb for scent. Gourmet cooks also use the flower buds, fresh or dried, for flavoring. The taste is flowery with hints of fiery mint, anise, and rosemary. It is one of the herbs that makes *herbes de Provence* so distinctive.

Make a place for three or four lavender bushes in the herb or flower garden. Lavender is a small, beautiful flowering shrub: Plant it in knot gardens, rock gardens, and especially with roses. It grows slowly to 2½ feet.

GROWING LAVENDER

The plant is a sprawling little perennial evergreen 2 to 4 feet tall with needlelike, gray-green leaves. In late spring stems shoot up bearing small, tightly packed tubular florets which, according to species and cultivar, range from deep purple and blue to lavender, pink, white, and gray-blue.

The seeds are very slow to germinate, so plan to set out seedlings from a garden center. If you insist on starting from seed, catalogs offer specially treated seeds.

Lavender grows well in large planters and survives winters outdoors as far north as Zone 5. It

'Munstead' lavender

thrives in a big tub but is not suited to indoor growing.

Culture

In early spring, or early fall in the South, set out seedlings in full sun in sandy, well-drained, dryish soil with a pH above 6.0. It grows well on a slope. In hot regions lavender tolerates some noon shade. Prune 1 to 2 inches from branch tips in early spring to encourage new growth. Lavender often reblooms if you harvest the first flowers.

Harvesting

For keeping or using right away, harvest stems just before the buds begin to open. Hang in loose bunches to air-dry, then strip away the buds and store them in sealed containers. The stems are fragrant—use them to scent linens.

COOKING WITH LAVENDER

Add fresh and dried lavender buds to herb butters, savory sauces, and grilled fish and steaks. A teaspoon of lavender buds, fresh or dried, adds a hint of sweet mint and rosemary to stews, soups, and marinades for game. Use fresh buds in cucumber dishes, salad dressings, and soups, or to make aromatic sugar, fresh fruit salads, breads, and mint jellies. A lovely lavender ice cream is made in the south of France, and bees there produce a luscious lavender honey.

A sprinkling of fully opened fresh lavender florets makes a very pretty garnish and gives a fresh, minty bite to yogurt, cookies, ice cream, and cakes. Skewer soft sweets and raspberries on stripped lavender stems and serve as an accompaniment to coffee. A spoonful of lavender buds sealed in a jar of sugar for a few days makes a lovely sweetener for custards or a cup of tea.

Herbes de Provence

This mix of dried herbs is popular in southern France, where many of its ingredients grow wild. In Provence gift shops, it is often sold in small cloth sacks to tourists.

1 tablespoon dried marjoram
1 tablespoon dried oregano
1 tablespoon dried savory
1 tablespoon dried minced rosemary
1 tablespoon dried thyme
1 tablespoon dried lavender buds
1 tablespoon dried fennel

Mix well and store in an airtight jar. Add 1 teaspoon to salad dressings, steamed vegetables, meat sauces, casseroles, or fish before grilling.

Makes almost ½ cup.

SELECTED CULTIVARS

The best lavender for flavor is the hardy English type, *Lavandula angustifolia angustifolia.* It also is known as *L. vera,* true lavender, and *L. officinalis.* The following three are excellent cultivars.

Hidcote Very gray foliage, 12 inches tall, deep purple flowers, handsome in containers.

Munstead Old-fashioned favorite, 12 inches tall, gray foliage sets off tall, dark lavender spikes, attracts bees and butterflies.

Lavender Lady Hardy 8- to 10-inch dwarf, flowers from spring-sown seeds, gray-green foliage bears loose cluster of soft lavender flowers in late summer, good size for containers and edging.

L. stoechas Beautiful purple-pink French or Spanish cultivar, makes a pretty pot and basket plant.

L. multifida Also called annual lavender—an oregano-scented plant with dissected leaves.

LEMON BALM

The fragrance of lemon balm is a welcome addition to any garden. Allowed to sprawl over a walk and crushed underfoot, it scents the air with a refreshing aroma. One or two plants attract pollinating bees and provide all the branches and leaves you can use in cooking and bouquets.

GROWING LEMON BALM

Lemon balm is a garden perennial hardy through winters in Zones 4 to 8. The plant grows to 12 to 24 inches, and masses of tender young shoots appear in spring. In summer it is topped by sprays or tufts of very small, dainty white florets. A quick-growing member of the mint family, lemon balm naturalizes readily. Like mint, it pops up all around the original clump and nearby as well. Lemon balm succeeds in large planters and tubs.

Lemon balm

Culture

Set out root divisions in early spring in well-drained, neutral soil. They need six hours of sun daily.

Harvesting

Harvest leaves and young stems of lemon balm from the time the plant starts to grow in early spring until growth stops in late summer.

Dry small leaves on screens or in a microwave oven. Bottle and cap.

COOKING WITH LEMON BALM

Minced lemon balm leaves are used for fish sauces and as garnish for poached cold salmon with mayonnaise. They give a mild citrus tang to green salads and are minced and sprinkled sparingly over fruit salads. Lemon balm flavors the poaching liquid for peaches and nectarines. The leaves are steeped to make fragrant teas and are frozen in ice cubes to add to cool juices and summer drinks. Young stems of lemon balm are used as swizzle sticks for water, iced tea, and fruit drinks. The leaves are floated in finger bowls. Rubbed between the palms, they impart a fresh scent to the skin and the surrounding air.

Air-dry leafy branches for winter arrangements. Use the dried leaves in potpourri.

Lemon Balm Lemonade

    6 cups boiling water
    3 cups loosely packed lemon
       balm leaves
    ½ to 1 cup lemon juice, optional
    3 tablespoons corn syrup
    Ice
    6 thin lemon slices, for garnish
    6 stem sprigs lemon balm, for
       garnish

Pour the boiling water over the leaves and let stand until cooled. Strain and discard the leaves. Stir the lemon juice into the solution if you wish a strong lemon flavor. Add the corn syrup and stir well. Pour into tall glasses filled with ice, and garnish with lemon slices and sprigs of lemon balm.

Serves 6.

SELECTED VARIETIES

Garden catalogs offer the species *Melissa officinalis.*

LEMONGRASS

A tropical grass (*Cymbopogon citratus*) native to southern India and Sri Lanka, lemongrass grows in tall, dense yellow-green clumps. It is predominant in Thai cuisine and yields an aromatic oil used as flavoring and in perfumery.

GROWING LEMONGRASS

In Florida and other mild climates, lemongrass is a handsome perennial quickly reaching a height of 3 to 6 feet. In colder regions lemongrass can be grown in pots that are brought indoors for the winter.

Culture

Cut back the leaves of fresh young shoots of lemongrass to 2 inches. Plant the spears in a deep pot filled with sandy loam with a neutral pH: Set the shoot so 2 inches of the leaves are standing above the soil line. Keep the plant in a warm, sunny window and maintain the soil moisture. In a few weeks, with luck, a fountain of leaves will spring up and grow on through the season. If the climate is tropical or subtropical, plant the roots outdoors in spring where they get at least six hours of sunlight a day.

Harvesting

When old leaves droop and are not revived by additional water, strip them away. Cut fresh young shoots

Lemongrass

about 2 inches above the soil surface and use for cooking.

Spread chopped fresh lemongrass on screens to dry for about 10 days, then bottle and cap.

COOKING WITH LEMONGRASS

The individual stalks of lemongrass are round and tough. Peel to the tender core and chop for a flowery lemon flavor in stews, rice, sweets, and tea. In India it is often coupled with turmeric in gentle curries; in Asian cuisines it is used with garlic, ginger, cilantro, and fish sauce. A tablespoon of minced lemongrass boiled for a few minutes in the water for basmati rice or quinoa, then strained out, adds a taste of flowery lemon.

Grilled Swordfish With Lemongrass

    1 cup orange juice
    1 bunch green onions, tops
        removed, minced
    1 tablespoon minced garlic
    4 teaspoons minced fresh
        lemongrass
    3 tablespoons tomato ketchup
    ⅓ cup honey mustard
    1 tablespoon minced fresh thyme
    1 cup balsamic vinegar
    1½ to 2 pounds swordfish steaks
    Salt and freshly ground black
        pepper, to taste

Heat a grill to medium-high. In a small saucepan, simmer the orange juice, onions, and garlic until reduced by half (about 6 minutes). Stir in the lemongrass, ketchup, honey mustard, thyme, and vinegar and cook, stirring, until thickened. Season the swordfish with salt and pepper. Spread the sauce over the swordfish on both sides. Wrap the steaks in aluminum foil and grill 5 minutes on each side. Serve hot.

Serves 3 to 4.

SELECTED VARIETIES

The species is *Cymbopogon citratus.* It is not carried by most of the familiar mail-order garden catalogs. To obtain plants for the garden, purchase very fresh stalks from an Asian market.

MARJORAM/ OREGANO

An old-world perennial aromatic herb of the mint family, marjoram was used extensively in ancient Greece and Rome, although its reputation for spreading happiness probably dates back to the Middle Ages, when it was used abundantly in cooking because of its disinfecting and preserving powers. Native to North America, Europe, and Asia, marjoram is cultivated for flavoring and for origanum oil, used in perfumed soaps. Its uses are both external and internal, particularly as an aid in digestion.

Sweet marjoram and oregano belong to the genus *Origanum.* Sweet marjoram, a tender perennial grown as an annual, is the species *O. majorana.* The closely related perennial European wild marjoram, *O. vulgare,* is the herb usually sold as oregano. Like their near-relatives the mints, marjoram and oregano are attractive low-growing leafy herbs important enough to be given space in the smallest herb collection. They make handsome filler plants in flower borders.

GROWING MARJORAM AND OREGANO

The plants are 8 to 12 inches tall and produce small oval leaves. The clumps sprawl and in summer bear panicles of tiny, faintly scented, edible, whitish, pink, or lavender florets. Oregano grows more readily from seed than marjoram. In very rich soil, these plants lose their pungency.

The creeping dwarf form called *O. compacta nana* is about 2 inches high and may belong to this group. In the Pacific Northwest, it is grown as an annual. Pinch out the tops when the plants are 2 inches tall to encourage side growth.

O. heracleoticum (O. hirtum), pot marjoram or winter sweet marjoram, is low growing, white flowered, and not invasive. It is one of several species sold as "true Greek oregano." The flavor is hot and spicy, richer than Italian oregano, and the leaves are smaller and more tender. Generally acknowledged as having the weakest flavor of the three most common culinary marjorams, it has the saving grace of being the easiest and most reliable to grow and is an important ingredient of a bouquet garni.

Oregano is a good basket plant outdoors and can be grown indoors in full sun.

Culture

Sow the seeds, or set out seedlings, in late spring after the soil warms. Both herbs succeed in full or partial sun in well-drained soil. Keep the flower spikes pinched out and maintain moisture until the plants are established. Cut back in mid-spring. Marjoram and oregano are durable and drought tolerant once established.

Harvesting

Tie a few of the longest stems to stakes to create a supply of leaves that will not need rinsing. As the flower buds begin to break, harvest the leaves.

Dry oregano leaves on screens, or air-dry whole branches. Try twining long strands of oregano around a circle of rosemary to make a wreath, and air-dry.

COOKING WITH MARJORAM AND OREGANO

Marjoram and oregano are cousins and both are ubiquitous Mediterranean herbs often combined with onions, bay, thyme, basil, and garlic. Marjoram is best used fresh, whereas the more pungent oregano is better dried.

Marjoram has a balsamlike aroma and a warm, peppery bite with hints of thyme and mint. Add it to leafy salads, sliced tomatoes, cucumbers, eggs, cheese, sausage and beans dishes, and herb breads. Use with other herbs for seasoning chicken, turkey, and veal.

Oregano has a bold, peppery bite and much of it is retained in the dried leaves. Use dried oregano in pizza sauces and other intensely flavored, tomato-based Italian, Provençal, Mexican, and Greek recipes. Fresh or dried, oregano is a fundamental flavor in ratatouille, zucchini, and eggplant dishes; it also enhances roasted and grilled meats.

Branches of oregano give a piquant aroma to fresh bouquets. Include the dried leaves in floral potpourri.

Marjoram

Focaccia With Tapénade and Oregano

Tapénade is a salty mixture of pungent black olives, anchovies, capers, garlic, lemon rind, and parsley, available in gourmet stores and some supermarkets.

- ¼ cup extravirgin olive oil
- ½ cup tapénade
- ½ cup peeled, seeded, diced tomato
- ½ cup roasted red bell pepper, slivered
- ⅓ cup sliced black olives
- 1 tablespoon minced fresh oregano
- 2 *focaccia* shells (10 inches each)

Heat the grill to medium-high. Stir the oil into the tapénade, then fold in the tomato, peppers, olives, and oregano. Spread the topping over the shells and grill, uncovered, 4 to 5 inches above the fire until the bottom is browned. Serve at once. *Serves 8.*

SELECTED CULTIVARS

Garden catalogs offer both sweet marjoram (formerly listed as *Marjorana hortensis*) and oregano.

Kent Beauty Ornamental oregano grown for summer bloom, short spikes of pale pink flowers backed by dark pink bracts, leaves may be used in cooking.

MINT

At least two dozen mint species grow in home herb gardens. The green, sometimes hairy, leaves release a sweet, piney scent when brushed against, rubbed between the palms, or chopped for cooking. When they bloom in summer, the fuzzy flower spikes—purple, white, pink, mauve, or lilac—are edible.

You will find use for a half-dozen mint plants. Plant seedlings or root divisions of your favorite types. Harvest branches at the end of the

Spearmint

season for bouquets and drying. Keep the cultivars true by dividing the roots every year. Mints are cold hardy and easily propagated by root division almost anytime.

GROWING MINT

Most mints are hardy perennials between 12 and 36 inches tall. Some have rounded hairy leaves, and others have tiny pointed leaves. There are variegated mints, mints veined chocolate-purple, and some with dark red stems. The stems are square. All mints are fast growing and invasive. They belong in a wild corner of the garden or confined to a container.

Mints thrive in containers, which they soon fill. Most overwinter in tubs or planters that are 14 inches across or larger. They do not survive very long indoors, even under grow lights.

Culture

Plant root divisions in early spring, or in late summer where winters are mild. All mints flourish in full sun or bright shade in moist, well-drained soil that is slightly acid. Fertilize occasionally, and water during droughts.

Harvesting

The sprawling mints get muddied during rainstorms: Stake a few branches to have clean leaves available for cooking.

Dry mint leaves on screens or in a microwave oven. Or air-dry branches, then strip the leaves. Bottle and cap.

COOKING WITH MINT

Mint is an important herb in Middle Eastern and Indian cuisine. Use mint in juleps, minced into vinaigrettes, and jellied as a sprightly sauce for lamb. The tiny tip leaves of small-leaved cultivars make edible garnishes for desserts, soups, fruit salads, yogurt, and anything chocolate. Mint flavors liquors such as crème de menthe. The dried leaves are used to make digestive teas and are added to potpourri.

Tabbouleh

    1 heaping cup bulgur
    1 cup cold water
    ½ cup fresh lemon juice
    ½ cup extravirgin olive oil
    1 cup chopped fresh Italian
      parsley
    1 cup chopped fresh mint leaves
    ½ cup minced red onion
    3 cloves garlic, minced
    ½ teaspoon salt
    1 teaspoon freshly ground black
      pepper
    4 plum tomatoes, seeded and
      diced
    1 large cucumber, peeled,
      seeded, and diced
    Mint leaves, for garnish

Combine the bulgur, water, lemon juice, and half the oil in a large mixing bowl. Mix well and set aside for 30 minutes. Then fluff the mixture with a fork and add the parsley, mint, onion, garlic, salt, pepper, and remaining oil. Mix well. Add the tomatoes and cucumber and toss again. Taste, and adjust the seasonings if desired. Let stand again for 30 minutes to develop the flavor. Garnish with additional mint sprigs or leaves.
Serves 6. Keeps well.

SELECTED CULTIVARS

Spearmint (*Mentha spicata*) The best all-around culinary mint; if you have space for only one, choose this; grows 10 to 24 inches high; small, dainty, pointed leaves; fine, sweet flavor.

Pineapple Mint (*M. suaveolens variegata*) Pretty little leaves splashed with cream; tips of young shoots smell of pineapple.

Apple Mint (*M. suaveolens*) Grows 2 to 3 feet tall, has rounded leaves with a velvety texture, sweet apple scent, great in bouquets.

Peppermint (*M. × piperita*) Excellent dried in herbal teas and potpourri.

Bergamot Mint, Orange Bergamot, or Lemon Mint (*M. × piperita citrata*) The herb that flavors Earl Grey tea; tender plant, not reliably hardy north of Zone 8.

PARSLEY

There are three main types of parsley: the curly or mossy upright cultivars are the most beautiful; the sprawling flat-leaf Italian cultivars are very flavorful; and the turnip-rooted parsleys are planted for their edible root as well as for their pungent leaves.

GROWING PARSLEY

Parsley is a low-growing plant composed of many succulent stems topped by ferny, rich green leaves. It is a biennial that survives winter, provides a lavish spring crop, then bolts and deteriorates.

A half-dozen parsley plants will supply your needs. They are a handsome edging in the herb garden or flower bed. Parsley thrives in containers and is beautiful in a window box with red or hot-pink geraniums. Fertilize at every watering with a houseplant fertilizer.

Culture

In early spring set out two sturdy seedlings for the first crop. Surround these with parsley seeds sown ½ inch deep, 2 to 3 seeds per inch. Parsley thrives in moist, well-worked fertile soil, but usually needs at least three weeks to germinate. The following spring, about the time the original plants bolt, sow more seeds.

'Moss Curled' parsley

Where fall is long, set out parsley plants in late August.

Harvesting

Break off individual stems at the base as needed. Rinse the foliage in many changes of cold water. Drain and store in the crisper in a closed container lined with a paper towel.

For long-term storage, harvest branches, discard the stems, and rinse very well. Drain and spread out to dry completely. Mince in a food processor and freeze.

COOKING WITH PARSLEY

Parsley has a pungent aroma and an earthy flavor that complements other flavors. Finely minced parsley gives hints of lemon as well as of carrot and celery, which belong to the same plant family.

Parsley is the primary green herb and favorite garnish in French and international cuisines. It is one of the fines herbes, along with chervil, tarragon, and sometimes chives, and goes into every stock pot as part of the bouquet garni—three stalks of parsley, one of thyme, and a bay leaf. Some cooks use marjoram, and in Provence a strip of dried orange zest is added.

Lemon and parsley are the classic flavorings and garnishes for fish and seafood. Minced parsley and garlic do wonders for cold, diced beets, frog legs, chicken wings, and escargots. Minced fresh parsley adds a crisp freshness to leafy salads, new potatoes, stuffings, dressings, sauces, casseroles, soups, fish dishes, and sautéed meats.

Because it is rich in chlorophyll, fresh parsley kills odors and is used as a breath freshener.

Green Rice

2 tablespoons butter
2 large cloves garlic, minced
¼ cup minced fresh parsley
3 cups hot, freshly cooked rice

Melt the butter in a large saucepan and, while it is frothing, drop in the garlic. Stir-fry 1 minute, then add the parsley and stir-fry 1 minute more. Add the rice to the butter/herb mixture and toss until the green is evenly distributed.

Serves 6.

SELECTED CULTIVARS

Moss Curled (Double Curled) Dark green, very curly leaves, great as garnish and minced.

Champion Moss Curled Greenhouse plant, excellent in borders and pots.

Clivi Neat, prolific, dwarf of the moss type, ideal for window boxes and containers.

Krausa Dutch moss curled variety, great flavor.

Triple Curled Thickly ruffled, excellent for garnish.

Forest Green Curled variety, recommended for the Northwest.

Moss Curled Forest Green Bears strong clusters of curled leaves on short stems.

Frisca Curly New Dutch introduction, extracurly leaves, withstands bad weather, resists mildew.

Darki Dark green moss curled type; tolerates wet, windy weather; mild, sweet flavor.

Pagoda Triple curled frilly leaves, 10 to 12 inches tall, beautiful.

Italian or Flat Parsley Strong-flavored flat-leaf cultivar, preferred in Mediterranean dishes and for drying.

Single-Leaf Italian Parsley
Broadleaf, recommended for pesto sauce, soups, stews, and drying.

Italian Flat Dark Green Flat, flavorful, glossy green leaves on upright stems.

Catalogno Very strong flavor.

Gigante d'Italia (Italian Heirloom) and Giant Italian Deep green cultivars from northern Italy, 3 feet tall, mellow full flavor, excellent fresh or dried.

Omega and Bartowich Long Root cultivars grown for the fall, winter, or spring harvest, white 7- to 8-inch roots, nutty flavor; roots are used raw in salads or cooked in soups and stews and stored like carrots, can overwinter in the garden under mulch.

ROSEMARY

The distinctive flavor of rosemary earns it a place in any small herb collection. Plant near windows and garden seats with heathers, lavender, rue, savory, and oregano, and it perfumes the air. Where winters are mild, it grows into a sizable bush or tall ground cover planted along driveways, near parking areas, and walks.

GROWING ROSEMARY

A cold-tender Mediterranean subshrub, rosemary has evergreen needles that are glossy, usually dark green with white undersides, and sometimes yellow striped. The plant looks a little like a rigid heather, 2 to 4 feet tall, with blue, white, or pink florets along the stems. Rosemary seeds need nights at a constant 75° F to germinate, and even then germination is slow and uncertain. Three months after you give up, seeds sometimes will sprout.

In the cool North, grow rosemary as a pot plant, outdoors in summer and indoors in winter on a bright, cool sill. A seedling purchased in fall will live all winter in a sunny window. It will need watering almost daily.

Culture

Set out a young plant in midspring. In full sun in well-drained, neutral, sandy, dryish soil, it quickly grows into a handsome little shrub. Once established, rosemary withstands considerable heat and drought.

Harvesting

Pick tender tip sprigs to encourage the plant to bush out. Strip the leaves from the stems and then chop or give the leaves a whirl in a food processor.

North of Zone 7 when frosts threaten, strip rosemary of its youngest branches, dry them on screens, then strip the leaves and bottle them. Or hang and air-dry the branches, then strip off the leaves and bottle.

COOKING WITH ROSEMARY

Rosemary leaves are stiff little needles with a hot, sweet, piney flavor that hints of nutmeg and is indispensable in Mediterranean cuisine. Use minced fresh rosemary in marinades and when steaming and braising vegetables. Toss a handful onto the coals of the barbecue grill. Half a teaspoon of chopped fresh rosemary gives a wonderful lift to roasted or sautéed potatoes, fruit salads, stewed rhubarb, and sliced oranges. Add a tablespoon of minced fresh rosemary to creamy polentas, spoon breads, and biscuits.

Use dried rosemary in cooking and in potpourri, or tie branches into a circle to make a fragrant base for an herb wreath.

Chicken Stuffed With Rosemary
1 large handful fresh rosemary stems
1 whole lemon, pierced 6 times
1 4- to 5-pound roasting chicken
1 tablespoon grainy Dijon-style mustard
Salt and freshly ground black pepper, to taste
1 teaspoon freshly ground coriander
1 cup hot chicken broth
½ cup cream
12 sprigs rosemary florets, for garnish

Preheat oven to 375° F. Wash the chicken and pat it dry. Stuff the rosemary and lemon into the cavity of the chicken and tie the legs. Place the bird in a roasting pan and rub the mustard over the skin and season with salt, pepper, and coriander. Bake 1 hour. Pour the hot chicken broth over the chicken and bake 30 minutes at 350° F. Remove the chicken to a heated serving platter and empty the cavity. Stir the cream into the pan drippings and pour into a sauceboat. Serve the chicken garnished with rosemary florets.
Serves 6.

SELECTED CULTIVARS

Most vegetable catalogs offer only the species *Rosmarinus officinalis*. But many attractive forms are listed among ornamentals in garden catalogs.

Beneden Blue (*R. officinalis angustifolia*) Handsome blue flowers; 'Prostratus' for Zone 8 and southern California; roots readily; low-growing ground cover, in winter it is veiled with ethereal light blue blooms.

De Forest Bright leaves and blue flowers.

Kenneth Prostrate and Huntington Carpet Superior forms.

Golden Prostratus Variegated.

Tuscan Blue Upright, bright green leaves and violet blue flowers.

Majorca Pink and Pinkie Pink flowers.

Rosemary

SAGE

Several colorful sages have good flavor. One or two culinary cultivars and an ornamental variety will enhance your garden and provide for both fresh and dried use.

GROWING SAGE

The sages are velvety, gray-leaved relatives of the mints. The best sage for flavoring is *Salvia officinalis*, a little perennial shrub about 24 inches high. It tends to sprawl and bears violet, blue, or white flower spikes in summer. It is hardy as far north as Zone 4 with some protection.

'Tricolor' sage

Sage succeeds in containers and is attractive in a planter filled with herbs. On its own, culinary sage is not a particularly attractive pot plant. It does poorly indoors.

Culture

In early spring sow seeds, or set out root divisions or seedlings, in neutral, well-drained, fairly fertile soil. Sages rot in wet soil, especially the culinary cultivars. Sage set in full sun gives the best performance, though some protection from the noon sun is helpful in the hottest climates. The sages are drought tolerant but flourish when watered during prolonged dry spells. Pinch back taller plants to keep them trim. Some sages need staking to keep the leaves clean enough for use in cooking.

Harvesting

Pick tender tip sprigs anytime. They keep for a week or more stored in a vegetable bag in the crisper.

Sprigs of sage dry well in a microwave oven, on screens, or tucked into a wreath.

COOKING WITH SAGE

Culinary sage has a strong, sharp flavor that mingles pine, camphor, and citrus. Chopped, fresh sage is combined with parsley to flavor tomatoes and leafy salads. Minced fresh sage is added to sauces for pastas, pork chops, chicken, and vegetables. In cooking, the raw leaves impart a potent flavor that grows stronger the longer it cooks. Sage is an essential ingredient in saltimbocca, a traditional Italian dish combining prosciutto and veal.

Dried, ground sage is used with fatty meats, especially pork and sausage, and in bread stuffings for turkey, duck, and goose.

Sage Butter Sauce

3 tablespoons butter
2 tablespoons minced shallots
3 tablespoons all-purpose flour
2 to 3 tablespoons chopped
   fresh sage
2½ cups hot chicken broth
¼ cup half-and-half *or*
   whole milk
Salt and pepper, to taste
4 tablespoons freshly grated
   Parmesan cheese

Over medium heat sauté the shallots in the butter until golden. Reduce the heat to medium-low and stir in the flour, then the sage. All at once, pour the broth over the roux, and whisk and cook until the sauce is thickened and smooth (about 5 minutes). Stir in the cream, bring the sauce back to a simmer, and turn off the heat. Season with salt and pepper.

Serve on rice, pasta, grilled chicken breasts, or pork chops. When you serve the sauce, sprinkle a tablespoon of Parmesan cheese over each portion.
Serves 4.

SELECTED CULTIVARS

Catalogs offer garden sage *Salvia officinalis.*

S. clevelandii Blue sage, a handsome gray plant, sometimes used instead of garden sage in warm California.

S. officinalis Tricolor Ornamental with rosy, pink, gray, cream, and purple leaves, 6 to 10 inches high.

Icterina Beautiful gray leaves, variegated gold, less hardy than the species, milder flavor.

S. elegans Pineapple-scented variety, attractive scarlet flowers in fall, used for flavoring.

SHALLOTS

The shallot is a type of multiplier onion. As the heads ripen, they divide into separable parts. Use the large heads for cooking and plant smaller ones for next year's crop. Leave some to overwinter in the ground, and harvest larger heads the second year.

GROWING SHALLOTS

Like the other members of the onion family, shallots are perennials native to the northern hemisphere. They are grown as annuals because you harvest the bulb. Tufts of tall, grasslike leaves shoot up directly from the bulb. They are hollow, like chive leaves, and are called "scapes."

Shallots are gourmet items, rather costly in the markets, and hard to find in some regions. Just ¼ pound of shallot sets—or plump fresh shallots from the grocer, are enough to plant a 25-foot row. This yields enough to supply a chef for the coming year.

Culture

Some garden centers and many garden catalogs sell shallot sets, or "planting heads," which you divide into individual bulbs for planting. Plant the bulbs in early fall where winters are mild; in cold regions plant in early spring as soon as the ground can be worked.

Shallots thrive in well-drained, sandy loam that has been fertilized with compost or a slow-release organic fertilizer. They need full sun. Set the root ends in the soil so the tops are covered by about 1 inch of soil. Space the sets about 6 inches apart. Each set divides and multiplies 6 to 10 times. The longer the sets have to grow and mature, the larger the harvest. Save the really small shallots for kitchen use, or sow them for a quick harvest of green onions.

Harvesting

When they are ready for harvest, the tops of shallots soften and fall over. Push the tops all the way over and leave them in the garden for several days more. Then pull up or lift the plants with a spading fork. Leave them to cure for a few days on the soil before gathering the harvest.

Clean and store the bulbs in a cool, dry place. Save the smallest for planting the following season.

Shallots

COOKING WITH SHALLOTS

The shallot looks like a large garlic clove or a small onion encased in a stiff brown or red-brown skin. The taste is similar to both onion and garlic, finer than either, and prized by gourmets. Shallots are more delicate than onions for flavoring sauces, especially fish sauces and those made with white wine.

Pasta and Prosciutto

12 ounces rotini, cooked, drained
⅓ cup sun-dried tomatoes marinated in oil, minced; reserve 2 tablespoons of the oil
1 large ripe tomato, peeled, seeded, diced
¼ pound prosciutto, shredded
¼ cup minced shallots
1 teaspoon minced garlic
½ cup chopped fresh basil leaves
½ cup chopped fresh parsley
½ cup dry white wine
Salt and freshly ground black pepper, to taste
½ cup crumbled feta cheese

Toss the hot rotini in a large serving bowl with the sun-dried and the ripe tomato. Over medium-high heat in a large heavy skillet, heat 2 tablespoons of the sun-dried tomato oil and brown the prosciutto in it. Stir in the shallots, garlic, basil, parsley, and wine. Simmer until reduced by one third (about 5 minutes). Pour over the rotini/tomato mixture and toss until well combined. Season with salt and pepper. Top with feta cheese and serve at room temperature.
Serves 6.

SELECTED CULTIVARS

French Shallot Sets divide during the growing season to provide clusters of six or more, rosy flesh.

Atlas Similar to 'French Shallot', but outer skin is brown-red, flesh is pinkish; very early to mature, easy to grow from seed.

Golden Gourmet Matures early, keeps well.

Red Shallot Very early, high yield, divides naturally into many individual bulblets.

Atlantic Yellow, high yield, mild flavored, easy to grow.

Creation Yellow outer wrapping, white flesh, grows easily from seed, slow to mature, good keeper.

SAVORY (SUMMER/WINTER)

Summer and winter savory, or calamint, are attractive, rather similar plants with tiny, narrow dark green leaves. In summer the glossy foliage sparkles with spikes of dainty, widely spaced pink, lavender, or white flowers.

Summer savory, *Satureja hortensis,* is an annual 12 to 18 inches high. The flavor of the leaves is milder and superior to winter savory, though the plant is less attractive.

Winter savory, *S. montana,* survives winters as far north as Zone 4. It is a low, woody decorative little evergreen attractive in nooks and crannies, in borders, and as edging. Young potted plants from the nursery sometimes live through winter indoors in a sunny window.

GROWING SAVORY

One of each savory—summer and winter—provides a plentiful supply for using fresh and for drying.

Winter savory

Winter savory is pretty planted with bush hyssop, germander, boxwood, bayberry, and miniature roses. The savories thrive in summer in large pots and small planters.

Culture

Plant in early spring in partial or full sun and maintain moisture around the roots until the plants are well established. The savories prefer well-drained, rocky, lime soil and tolerate considerable drought.

For summer savory, sow seeds or, better yet, set out seedlings. Summer savory thrives in light soil that includes lots of humus. It often self-sows.

For winter savory, plant rooted cuttings or seedlings. The plant needs well-drained soil and with-stands more drought than summer savory. Prune heavily in early spring and lightly after flowering.

Harvesting

Pick savory sprigs at will and use with discretion. In mild regions it stays green all winter and may be harvested anytime.

Fresh leaves of both summer and winter savory dry well in a micro-wave oven.

COOKING WITH SAVORY

Savory is a low-growing, very aro-matic herb. The fragrance is vari-ously described as peppery, spicy, piney, thymelike, resinous, or re-sembling camphored honey.

Add fresh minced savory leaves to soups, casseroles, sauces, and salads. A tablespoon of minced fresh summer savory enhances steamed cabbage, broccoli, cauli-flower, and bean dishes.

Dried savory is used to flavor liqueurs and vinegars, soups, stews, salami, sausages, poultry, fish, bean dishes, eggs, cheese soufflés, and avocado dips.

Savory Couscous

    3 cups chicken broth
    1½ cups raw couscous
    1 small bay leaf
    1 tablespoon Roasted Garlic Oil
      (see page 160)
    3 cups chopped kale
    ¼ cup water
    1 tablespoon ground dried savory
    1 teaspoon balsamic vinegar
    Salt and freshly ground black
      pepper, to taste
    ½ cup crumbled chèvre cheese

In a saucepan over high heat, bring the broth to a rapid boil with the couscous and bay leaf. Cover and remove from heat. In a large saucepan over medium-high, heat the oil, then drop in the kale and sauté 3 minutes. Add the water and the savory; cover, and cook until the water has evaporated (about 3 minutes). Sprinkle the vinegar over the kale. In a large serving bowl, toss the kale and the couscous to-gether. Season with salt and pepper and top with the chèvre cheese.

Serves 6.

SELECTED VARIETIES

Most herb catalogs offer summer savory seeds. Winter savory is available from herb nurseries as the species and in a dwarf (*S. montana* 'Nana') and a creeping (*S. m.* 'Procumbens') form.

TARRAGON

Although tarragon is not a very impressive plant, it belongs in every gourmet's herb garden. The long, slim leaves impart a delicate-ly sweet, anise and camphor flavor, but finding a really good tarragon is not easy. Plant seedlings whose flavor you have tasted. True French tarragon is reproduced from cut-tings. When you find one with a fine flavor, never let it die out!

GROWING TARRAGON

Tarragon is a raggedy or sprawling, not-very-hardy perennial, 12 to 24 inches tall. The stems are woody, and the light green, very narrow leaves sometimes grow to 6 inches long. Small, tightly curled whitish green flowers appear in summer once the plant is well established.

Tarragon thrives in containers so long as moisture is sustained and the soil is well drained.

Culture

Set out seedlings in early spring in moderately fertile, very well drained neutral soil. Tarragon does best in full sun, partial sun in the hot South. The plant is fairly tolerant of heat and drought. Prune often to promote growth of tender branches.

Harvesting

Harvest tarragon leaves all season long as needed. The leaves are thin and dry well, either on a screen or in a microwave oven. Or you can air-dry the branches, then strip the leaves. Crumble the dried leaves, bottle, and cap.

COOKING WITH TARRAGON

A favorite herb in French cooking, tarragon is one of the plants used in the fines herbes combinations that form the basis of many traditional stocks and broths. It is used in classic recipes for Green Goddess dressing and béarnaise sauce.

Add a tablespoon of fresh or dried tarragon to flavor salad dressings and sauces, stuffing for chicken, basting sauces for capons, and to enhance delicately flavored fish. Tarragon is used with carrots, veal, and lamb. It is minced into marinades for sliced mushrooms, and used in dips, appetizers, and salads. Tarragon vinegar, widely used in mild vinaigrettes, is made by steeping minced fresh tarragon in hot vinegar. Snip a young, slender branch and add it to the bottle when the vinegar has cooled. Tips of tarragon sprigs are sometimes offered as after-dinner breath fresheners.

The dried leaves scent potpourri and *eaux de toilette*.

French tarragon

Spinach and Mushroom Salad

2 small cloves garlic
½ teaspoon salt
Freshly ground black pepper, to taste
¼ cup light olive oil, plus 1 tablespoon
1 tablespoon lemon juice
1 tablespoon balsamic vinegar
¼ teaspoon creamy French mustard
1 tablespoon minced fresh tarragon
½ pound button mushrooms, stemmed
½ pound small spinach leaves, washed, patted dry
¼ head iceberg lettuce, torn
½ cup croutons

Slice the garlic into a wooden salad bowl, sprinkle with salt, and mash the two together with a wooden spoon. Add a grating of pepper and whisk in the ¼ cup olive oil, lemon juice, vinegar, mustard, and tarragon. Slice the mushrooms and toss with the dressing. Top with the spinach, then with the iceberg lettuce, and chill until ready to serve.

Just before serving, heat the reserved 1 tablespoon of oil in a skillet over high heat, and sauté the croutons, tossing them constantly for 3 minutes. Toss the salad, then top with the croutons.

Serves 4 to 6.

Thyme (*Thymus vulgaris*)

SELECTED VARIETIES

Catalogs and garden centers offer the species *Artemisia dracunculus*, French tarragon. Russian tarragon is greener and less aromatic than the French type. The plants are larger and have pale green leaves.

THYME

Thyme is an aromatic, shrubby plant of the mint family. There are innumerable thyme cultivars, many of them ornamental. Common thyme, used as a seasoning, is an erect plant with grayish branches. It is cultivated mainly in Spain and France. Forgiving plants, most thymes grow readily among stepping stones and cascade over garden walls and rock gardens.

GROWING THYME

Thyme is a perennial related to mint. Culinary cultivars are evergreen with trailing branches 6 to 10 inches high. Tough and often fast spreading, they bear fuzzy clusters of florets in early summer in white, lilac, or pale pink. The flavor of thyme is best when it is grown in full sun and poor, well-drained soil.

Two or three culinary thymes will meet your needs. They grow almost everywhere, even in rock walls and hanging baskets.

Culture

In early spring set out seedlings in full sun in very well drained ordinary soil. Partial sun is suitable in the South. Thyme tolerates considerable drought and abuse. The stems of old thyme plants eventually get dry and wiry—shear these back mercilessly in early spring.

Harvesting

Pick tip sprigs anytime to use fresh. Strip the leaves from the stems, or chop stems and leaves.

Thyme leaves dry quickly on screens or in a microwave oven. Stems of thyme retain their color and flavor when wound into a wreath of twined rosemary branches interspersed with sprigs of sage. You can also air-dry long stems, then strip the leaves.

COOKING WITH THYME

The thymes are small prostrate plants with tiny dark green leaves that have a sharp, clean, intense flavor rather like a strong, earthy mint. They are valued for their flavor and because they combine well with other herbs. Coupled with bay leaf, parsley, and onion, thyme is used in stuffings for fowl, pork, and lamb. It is used in salad dressings, soups, stews, and in Creole dishes and gumbos. Thyme is also an ingredient in a bouquet garni. It joins saffron in bouillabaisse, and flavors New England chowders, boiled onions, carrots, and beets. Parisians sprinkle thyme on steaks for broiling. It can be brewed into a pleasing herbal tea.

Pasta and Thyme
    8 ounces tricolored rotini,
      cooked, drained
    4 cups tiny broccoli florets
    4 tablespoons basil olive oil
    4 teaspoons tarragon vinegar
    1 cup chicken broth
    ½ cup minced chives
    1 tablespoon minced fresh thyme
    ½ cup slivered roasted red bell
      peppers
    Salt and freshly ground black
      pepper, to taste
    ¼ pound chèvre cheese
    Sprigs of fresh thyme, for garnish

Steam the broccoli 6 to 8 minutes until al dente. Combine the oil, vinegar, broth, chives, and thyme to make a dressing. Pour the hot rotini into a large bowl and toss with the dressing. Add the broccoli and peppers to the herbed pasta and toss. Season with salt and pepper. Crumble the chèvre over the pasta and toss again. Garnish with thyme sprigs and chill before serving.
    Serves 6.

SELECTED CULTIVARS

The best thymes for the chef are *Thymus vulgaris* and its cultivars. Both English and French cultivars belong to this species. The flavor is sweeter than other thymes, but plants are not reliably winter hardy. French thyme often is called "summer thyme."

Wedgewood English Excellent taller form.

Orange Balsam Hints of orange in its flavor.

German Thyme or Winter Thyme Good for drying, strongly flavored, hardy, the thyme recommended for the Pacific Northwest.

T. × citriodorus Hardy, distinct scent of lemon or orange.

T. herba-barona Crushed leaves impart the aroma of caraway.

Creeping Thymes Grows 3 to 5 inches high, tiny lavender flower spikes, not as aromatic as common thyme but can be used for cooking, grows well among stepping stones.

Mother-of-Thyme Creeping, 4 inches high, strong flavor.

Lanuginosus Dainty, mat-forming creeper, ½ inch high, bears pink-white flowers in the leaf axils.

Mayfair and Pink Chintz Similar to 'Lanuginosus'.

Argenteus Silver-variegated.

Aureus Gold-variegated leaves, not fine flavored but can be used in cooking, very decorative.

LEAFY GREENS

Greens, such as the kale shown here, pack more vitamins for the calorie than almost any other food. Besides their nutritional punch, they are tasty and flexible culinary ingredients. Use them raw, cooked, even as a thickener.

Growing leafy greens is surprisingly rewarding. They arc easy to tend, and they add flavor, variation, and outstanding nutrition to meals.

Although fruits and vegetables in general offer high doses of vitamins A and C as well as a host of other vitamins and minerals, greens pack a lot of nutrition in their relatively few calories. For instance, there are a mere 10 calories in a heaping cup of watercress and fewer than 65 in a 1-pound bunch of mustard greens. Spinach contains immense amounts of vitamin A—16,000 milligrams per cup. Considerable amounts of calcium can be found in kale, mustard and collard greens, and bok choy. Most greens are high in potassium—465 milligrams in each cup of arugula, cress, and mustard greens; and in the same amount they deliver 125 milligrams of calcium. It should not be forgotten, however, that most greens are also high in sodium. Abundantly nutritious and easy to grow, greens are a sensible and tasty addition to any home garden.

The greens start easily from seed. Where winter is brief, they succeed as spring and fall crops if you start the seeds two to three weeks before planting time. When they have four or five true leaves, transplant seedlings so the soil level is up to the first leaves. Between cool seasons, rows that hosted greens become available for snap beans and other heat-tolerant midseason vegetables.

These greens stand some shade and thrive at temperatures between 65° and 80° F. Many bolt when the weather gets hot. Keep the soil cooler and delay bolting by applying mulch.

The greens related to cabbage grow best in soil between pH 6.5 and 7.5. Work 10–10–10 fertilizer into the row at the rate of 2½ to 4

NUTRITIONAL ELEMENTS

Arugula, 1 ounce

Calories	8
Vitamin A	2,850 mg
Vitamin C	15 mg
Calcium	27 mg

pounds per 100 square feet. Fertile soil needs only 1 to 2 pounds.

If you want lots of thinnings for the salad bowl, sow the seeds of the leafy greens thickly over a wide band. Then as you thin the rows, pick the little leaves for cooking.

Use leafy greens soon after harvesting. To keep them fresh and crisp, harvest them into a bucket of cool water. Rinse crinkly leaved greens in several changes of water to remove soil caught in the creases. Remove from water, drain, and store immediately in the refrigerator. Most leafy greens stay fresh for a few days to a week sealed in vegetable bags in the crisper.

ARUGULA

Arugula is an elegant, crisp, dark-leaved salad green popularized by gourmet chefs. Its pungent aroma and spicy flavor are as unique as cilantro and closely associated with Italian and French menus. The leaf resembles a skinny, deeply in-dented dandelion leaf, and the tiny green-white florets that develop when it bolts are edible.

A dozen arugula plants are ample for most households. Fit them into a few square feet in the front of a flower bed or in the vegetable garden in early spring and again in midautumn. Where winters are mild, a second sowing can be harvested throughout much of the cold season.

GROWING ARUGULA

Arugula is an attractive little plant 6 to 8 inches tall. It thrives in cool weather and provides both early-spring and early-fall harvests, ready in five to six weeks. Where cool weather lingers, sow seeds in succession for a lasting supply. Arugula goes to seed quickly in hot weather. Arugula thrives in pots, window boxes, and planters.

Arugula

Culture

In early spring as soon as the ground can be worked, sow seeds ¼ inch deep, 6 to 8 inches apart, or sprinkle thickly and evenly over the bed and tamp firmly. Maintain soil moisture.

When the weather begins to cool in summer, sow a second crop for fall harvests.

Harvesting

Just before using, pinch off young, bright green leaves 2 to 3 inches long. Or cut off the bunch at ground level. Compost any spoiled leaves.

Rinsed, sealed in a vegetable bag, and stored in the crisper, arugula stays fresh several days.

COOKING WITH ARUGULA

A few leaves of arugula seasoned with a mild vinaigrette make an ample salad for one. Most often, arugula is combined with milder greens. It is surprisingly delicious with fruit—especially watermelon, grapes, and apples—and sauced with a light vinaigrette.

Arugula also is used as an herb— to flavor pizza, for instance. The leaves are often sautéed in olive oil and served at room temperature.

Sweet and Sour Arugula Salad

  6 cups seeded watermelon
    chunks
  3 cups shredded arugula
  ⅔ cup slivered red bell pepper
  ¼ cup slivered red onion
  2 tablespoons light olive oil
  1 tablespoon raspberry vinegar
  1 tablespoon water
  1 clove garlic
  ¼ teaspoon sugar
  Salt and freshly ground pepper,
    to taste

In a salad bowl, combine the watermelon, arugula, bell pepper, and onion. Chill. Blend or process the oil, vinegar, water, garlic, and sugar. Season with salt and pepper. Toss the salad with the dressing and serve chilled.
  Serves 6.

SELECTED CULTIVARS

French Arugula 43 days, refined variety, widely available.

Sylvetta 50 days, small, holds well without bolting.

Italian Wild Rustic Arugula 55 days, small, pungent, slow to bolt.

CELERIAC

Celeriac, also known as celery root, is a dwarfish form of celery with dark green leaves and a knobby, edible root. It was bred for the edible root, which imparts a celery flavor to soups and stews. Like celery, it likes rich soil, cool weather, and lots of water, but it is easier to grow well. If the climate prevents you from growing high-quality celery, try celeriac.

GROWING CELERIAC

Set out seeds in early spring in rich soil and keep moist; it matures in about four months. Where the growing season is short, start seeds indoors 10 to 12 weeks before the last frost.

You can plant a half-dozen among your herbs or flowers.

Culture

As soon as the ground warms, plant seedlings 6 inches apart. Or drop seeds in watered holes or in furrows 2 inches deep in fine, rich, neutral soil (pH 7.0); cover with ¼ inch of soil and tamp. When the seedlings are 2 inches high, thin to 6 inches apart. After thinning, sprinkle a little 4-8-4 fertilizer around each plant. As the plants

NUTRITIONAL
ELEMENTS
Celeriac, 2 roots
Calories 14
Vitamin C 2 mg
Calcium 12 mg

grow, rake soil up 2 inches against the bases—returning to the original soil level.

Harvesting

The roots are best for eating when they are just 2 inches around—about half the mature size. Pull up the plant by its top, clean off the side roots, twist off the tops, and rinse well. Peel just before using.

Unpeeled roots keep for weeks in a vegetable bag in the refrigerator. For long-term storage, keep the roots in moist sand in a cool place. Or cut back the tops of the plants, mound soil around the bases, and harvest before the ground freezes hard.

COOKING WITH CELERIAC

Celeriac is a nutty, celery-flavored vegetable that does everything celery does except provide edible leaves, and it's easier to grow. Peeled, sliced, and steamed, celeriac is a delicious hearty vegetable. Raw young roots, grated and flavored with a piquant sauce, make a delightful first course. Sauced with a mild lemon vinaigrette, grated celeriac makes an interesting relish for grilled meats. Chopped or thinly sliced, it adds crunch and flavor to salads. Sliced celeriac adds the flavor of celery to soups, stews, casseroles, and mashed potatoes.

Celeriac Appetizer

2 medium celeriac roots, peeled
2 tablespoons lemon juice
Salt, to taste
½ cup mayonnaise
3 tablespoons Dijon-style mustard
1 to 2 tablespoons tarragon
   vinegar
2 large ripe tomatoes, peeled
6 hard-cooked eggs, chilled
Minced chervil *or* parsley

Shred or grate the celeriac and toss it with the lemon juice and salt.

Chill. Combine the mayonnaise, mustard, and vinegar. Chill.

Just before serving, slice the tomatoes in 12 thin rounds and arrange on 6 salad plates. Shell and slice the eggs in rounds and place the slices around the tomatoes. Toss the celeriac with the mayonnaise mixture and spoon over the tomatoes. Garnish with chervil or parsley.

Serves 6.

SELECTED CULTIVARS

Diamant 110 days, flavorful and keeps well.

Brilliant 110 days, European strain, harvest roots at 3 to 4 inches, widely available.

Large (Giant) Smooth Prague 120 days, Danish import.

CHARD

Also known as Swiss chard, white beet, seakale beet, or strawberry spinach, chard is a member of the beet family. The spinachlike leaves of standard chard cultivars have creamy white stalks and veining. The cultivar called 'Ruby' or 'Rhubarb' chard has crimson central stalks and veining, and looks like beautiful beet greens or young rhubarb. The flavors are similar. Chard is widely cultivated in France and is prominent in French and Italian cuisine.

GROWING CHARD

Chard is an appealing plant 2 to 2½ feet tall and a lot like a young rhubarb, especially the red varieties. It is a cool-season crop that stands some shade and moderate summer heat. In the North, sow seeds in the open garden about two weeks after the ground can be worked. In the South, plant chard in late summer or early fall and harvest all winter.

Harvest begins about two months after planting. The large outer leaves and fleshy stalks can be cut as the plant grows, so one planting is harvested over many months. Even if you cut off the entire plant 1 or 2 inches above the crown, new leaves grow.

Chard thrives in an open spot in the vegetable garden and in rich, neutral, well-drained soil. It is attractive enough be grown as an edging to flowers or herbs and does very well there too.

Culture

Sow the seeds thickly ½ inch deep. Thin seedlings, or set out transplants, so the plants stand 4 to 8 inches apart.

Harvesting

Harvest thinnings and very young leaves for salads. At any time pick leaves from the outside of the plants at the base. Harvest mature leaves for cooking when they reach 7 to 9 inches long. Take a few leaves from each plant: Do not strip a plant if you want it to keep producing well.

Rinsed, drained, and sealed in a vegetable bag, chard keeps at least a week in the crisper.

COOKING WITH CHARD

To the chef, chard is two or three vegetables. Torn from the stalks and braised, the leafy parts taste like a robust beet green. The stalks are excellent steamed or braised like celery and served with a garlic-and-lemon butter sauce. The stalks and greens, chopped together in 2- to 3-inch pieces and braised, have a tasty, more intense flavor. If the stalks are tough, as they tend to be late in the season, separate them from the greens, chop, and sauté

'Rhubarb' chard

for 5 to 10 minutes before adding the greens to the pot.

However it is cooked, hot chard is delicious: salted and dressed with butter, with a squeeze of lemon and Parmesan cheese, or with olive oil and vinegar. It also is very good served at room temperature with a vinaigrette. In northern Europe, chard leaves are steamed and stuffed with a variety of meaty fillings, then braised in broth, similar to recipes for stuffed cabbage leaves.

NUTRITIONAL ELEMENTS
Chard, cooked, ¼ cup
Calories   18
Vitamin A   6,000 mg
Vitamin C   16 mg
Calcium   73 mg

Chard With Vinaigrette

The flavor of roasted garlic adds a richness to this dish, but you can substitute plain olive oil.

    3 tablespoons Roasted Garlic Oil
      (see page 160)
    1 clove garlic, sliced
    6 cups young chard in 2- to 3-
      inch pieces, rinsed and still wet
    ½ cup water
    Salt and freshly ground pepper,
      to taste
    Vinaigrette, to taste

In a wok over high heat, heat the oil and sauté the garlic 1 minute. Drop in the wet chard and stir-fry 5 minutes. Add ½ cup of water, cover the wok, turn the heat to medium-low, and braise until the stalks are tender and no water remains (about 10 to 12 minutes). Check often and add water if the wok runs dry before the chard stems are tender. Season with salt and pepper and toss with vinaigrette. Serve at room temperature.

Serves 6.

SELECTED CULTIVARS

Argentata 55 days, Italian heirloom, silvery white midribs, sweet.

Paros 55 days, creamy white chard from France, with mild sweet leaves.

Fordhook Giant 58 to 60 days, long-established creamy white variety, thick stalks, crinkly dark green leaves, heat tolerant.

Rhubarb Chard (Ruby Chard) 60 days, beautiful, crimson-ribbed cultivar, produces over a long period when harvested regularly.

Swiss Chard of Geneva 60 days, very large ribs, celerylike stalks, withstands severe winters.

CHINESE CABBAGE, CHINESE MUSTARD

These delicious and versatile greens are related to cabbage. They grow in several shapes and flavors and are known by a confusion of common names. Chinese cabbage, celery cabbage, and pe-tsai are names given to the Pekinensis group, *Brassica rapa.*

Vegetables of the closely related Chinense group are listed in catalogs under names such as Chinese mustard, celery mustard, pak-choi, and sometimes spinach mustard and Chinese spinach. Pac choi, pak choi, pok choi, and bok choy are all variations of the name pak-choi. Mustard greens, which are different from Chinese mustard, are described on page 200. They are cultivars of *Brassica juncea* and are spicier.

Chinese cabbage, or celery cabbage, is cabbage flavored and comes in head-forming (napa), semiheading, and loose-leaf cultivars. Another group of greens called Chinese cabbage—and also called Oriental greens, Chinese mustard, and Chinese spinach—forms open rosettes of dark green, spoon-shaped leaves, and these have a more robust, spinach-cabbage-turnip flavor.

GROWING CHINESE CABBAGE

These are cool-weather plants that bolt when heat comes. Where summers are cool and the growing season short, grow one crop of an early variety. Usually transplants, started four to six weeks before the early-spring planting season, are set out. Loose-leaf types can be picked in 47 to 55 days; heading types mature in approximately 45 to 85 days.

'Tah Tsai' Chinese cabbage

Sow the seeds in individual peat pots, and plant—pots and all. In warm regions Chinese cabbage is usually planted in August or early September for fall and early-winter harvest. Try a new variety every season. They are tastier than cabbage and mature more quickly—ideal for the small home garden.

The open-rosette types belong in a garden row or along the edge of a salad garden.

For soil, fertilizer, and water requirements of these cabbage-related vegetables, see page 261.

Culture

Sow seeds sparsely ½ inch deep, and thin seedlings to 18 inches apart. Maintain soil moisture until the seedlings are sturdy. If the maturing crop seems puny at half-season, apply a side dressing of straight nitrogen fertilizer.

Harvesting

Use thinnings for salads. Harvest the side leaves of more-open forms as needed. Harvest the heading forms when mature: Pull up the entire plant and compost the tough outer leaves.

NUTRITIONAL ELEMENTS
Chinese cabbage, cooked, ½ cup
Calories 8
Vitamin A 130 mg
Vitamin C 26 mg
Calcium 26 mg

Rinsed, drained, and sealed in a vegetable bag, these greens keep at least a week in the crisper.

COOKING WITH CHINESE CABBAGE

All these greens are excellent stir-fried, braised, or steamed. The thinnings and young side leaves are outstanding in mesclun salad mixes. Mixed with fresh pineapple or carrots, the heading types make excellent coleslaw. Semiheading forms stuffed with seasoned minced chicken or pork make good cabbage rolls. Cultivars with thick, succulent stalks are used in Asian soups and sukiyakis and are stir-fried with ginger; they are also used raw in salads. Steamed and lightly buttered, they are especially good with duck or roast pork.

When selecting cultivars, investigate the edible flowering forms for a beautiful as well as service-able garden.

Wilted Chinese Cabbage
4 large stalks Chinese cabbage
½ small cucumber
2 small summer squash
2 tablespoons raspberry vinegar
2 tablespoons soy sauce
1 teaspoon sugar
1 tablespoon walnut oil *or* corn oil
Sesame oil
Zucchini *or* nasturtium blossoms, for garnish

Chop the cabbage. Slice the cucumber and squash in narrow rounds. In a small bowl, blend the vinegar, soy sauce, and sugar to make a dressing.

Heat wok to medium-high, swirl in the tablespoon of oil, and add the cabbage. Stir-fry until wilted (about 3 to 5 minutes). Add the cucumber then the squash, stir-frying 1 minute after each addition. Remove to a serving dish and toss with the dressing. Serve cold or at room temperature, sprinkled with a few drops of sesame oil and garnished with zucchini or nasturtium blossoms, if you wish.
Serves 4.

SELECTED CULTIVARS

Tah Tsai (Tatsoi) Far Eastern, large flat rosette of sweet, spoon-shaped leaves, described as a spinach mustard.

Joi Choi F1 Far Eastern, wonderfully mild.

Pac Choi 50 days, loose-leaf, thick, rounded, sweet-tasting green leaves, celerylike stalks, cultivars have either long petioles (stems) or short petioles, may be grown from early spring to late fall.

Orient Express 43 days, very early heading type, 8 to 9 inches tall, inner leaves well branched, crisp, peppery, heat tolerant.

Michihili Jade Pagoda Hybrid 60 to 70 days, semiheading, about 6 by 12 inches, bright green, well-packed creamy yellow hearts, vigorous, hardy, slow to bolt, disease resistant, grows best in mild climates.

Two Seasons Hybrid 62 days, large oval heads, 7 by 10 inches, tight crinkled leaves, succulent midribs, resists bolting, may be grown for spring or fall harvest.

Napa 70 days, big, light green, barrel-shaped heading type, slow to bolt, mature heads weigh as much as 6 to 9 pounds.

Wong Bok 85 days, late variety; forms firm, blocky, cannon-ball-shaped heads, may weigh 10 pounds at maturity; light green leaves, suitable for fall or winter planting in mild regions.

COLLARDS

Collards are a species of nonheading cabbage that grow in a large rosette of crisp, coarse, blue-green leaves. Their flavor is similar to that of kale and other leafy cole crops. They are a traditional vegetable of the Deep South, but thrive almost everywhere. Like other leafy crops, they are extremely prolific; one to three full-grown plants in a home garden supply enough collards for a family.

GROWING COLLARDS

Unlike their close relative kale, collards withstand considerable heat. They also tolerate more cold than cabbage; they're hardy to 15° F. In the cool North, collards transplants are set out in July and August and harvested two months later. A little frost sweetens the flavor. In mild regions start collards in February or March and they mature before the hot weather. In the South, in all but the coldest regions, plant collards in spring and again in fall.

Grow collards in their own row in the vegetable garden. For the soil, fertilizer, and water requirements of this cabbage-related green, see page 261.

Culture

Sow seeds ¼ inch deep. For large heads, thin seedlings to 10 to 15 inches apart; for bunchy plants with easy-to-harvest side leaves, thin plants to 5 to 7 inches apart.

Harvesting

Harvest seedlings, then young side leaves, and finally the mature heads, as needed. The flavor is best when collards are used soon after harvesting.

Rinsed, drained, and sealed in a vegetable bag, collards keep up to a week in the crisper.

COOKING WITH COLLARDS

The flavor of collards is somewhere between the spicy bite of mustard greens and the earthy taste of cabbage. Compost the tough stems. If the midrib is very coarse, tear off the greens and compost the midrib. Otherwise, chop in 2- to 3-inch pieces and cook the whole leaf. Simmer young collards until tender (12 to 15 minutes). Overcooking spoils the flavor. In the South, salt pork is added to the cooking water, and the "pot likker" that remains is served with hot corn bread.

Collard greens go well with fried chicken, panfried fish, and fried green tomatoes and add flavor to southern-style pea soup. Cooked collard greens can be topped with a dab of butter and grated cheese and broiled.

NUTRITIONAL ELEMENTS

Collards, cooked, ½ cup

Calories	29
Vitamin A	7,000 mg
Vitamin C	46 mg
Calcium	152 mg

'Hicrop' collards

NUTRITIONAL ELEMENTS

Cress, 1 ounce

Calories	8
Vitamin A	3,000 mg
Vitamin C	15 mg
Calcium	27 mg

Bacon-Flavored Collards

Although higher in saturated fat than foods cooked with vegetable oils, this version is a traditional and well-loved recipe in many parts of the American South. The flavor is so rich it's worth an occasional splurge.

  3 tablespoons bacon fat
  6 cups chopped collard greens, rinsed and wet
  ½ cup water
  Salt and freshly ground pepper, to taste
  1 cup crumbled bacon bits
  6 large, fresh corn muffins

Follow the instructions for cooking chard on page 188, but use bacon fat instead of oil, and top with crumbled bacon bits. Serve with hot corn muffins.
  Serves 6.

SELECTED CULTIVARS

Georgia Blue Stem 70 to 80 days, clusters of soft blue-green leaves, 24 and 30 inches tall, recommended for the hot South.

Hicrop 75 days, hybrid with a mild, sweet flavor, good texture, slow to bolt in hot weather.

Vates 75 days, low-growing, compact strain with thick, broad leaves, overwinters well.

Champion 75 days, slow-bolting 'Vates' selection, short stemmed, thick leaves, can stand a lot of winter cold.

BOLTING

Bolting is the rapid formation of a seed stalk. Biennials, spring-sown salad greens, and leafy cool-season crops that have overwintered bolt as spring moves into summer and temperatures exceed 50° F. A 2- to 3-inch mulch cover helps keep the soil cool and may delay bolting.

CRESS

Curly cress, also called pepper-grass, is a small, low-growing, quick-to-mature cool-season annual. It thrives in the short days of early- and mid-spring and in late summer or early fall. Curly cress looks well anywhere—at the edge of a flower bed, in a corner of the herb garden, and in window boxes. The plant called upland cress, broadleaf cress, winter cress, or Belle Isle cress is a small, hardy perennial or biennial that provides spicy greens in fall, winter, and early spring.

GROWING CRESS

Curly cress germinates so quickly that harvests begin in two weeks. It bolts with heat, leaving space for another green. It succeeds in partial shade. Where cool growing weather lingers, sow seeds in succession for a lasting supply.

Plant upland cress in late summer, though early-spring crops are possible. From seed, harvest is ready in about 50 days.

Culture

Sow seeds for either type of cress in early spring as soon as the ground can be worked, or in late summer. Plant seeds ¼ inch deep, or spread over the soil thickly and tamp firmly. Keep the soil damp. Harvest seedlings for mesclun salad mixes, leaving plants 2 to 3 inches apart.

Harvesting

As the plants mature, harvest young leaves just before using. Compost spoiled leaves.

Rinsed and drained, cress stays fresh for several days in a vegetable bag in the crisper.

COOKING WITH CRESS

The two types of garden cress are both sharply flavored and attractive enough to take the place of water-cress as a garnish. Curly cress is both spicy and pretty; upland cress has a milder flavor and a flatter, plainer leaf.

The cresses are delicious in salads of mixed greens, in cream cheese sandwiches and dips, in appetizers such as mushrooms marinated in tarragon vinegar, and with crab in a light mayonnaise-and-yogurt dressing. The bright green leaves are used as garnish for omelets, grilled meats, creamy casseroles, steamed vegetables, and cold pastas and to add a touch of color to any dish.

**Cress and Romaine
With Feta Cheese**
    1 bunch cress, rinsed, patted
      dry, chilled
    1 heart of romaine, in 1-inch
      slices
    2 tablespoons Roasted Garlic Oil
      (see page 160)
    1 tablespoon raspberry vinegar
    1 tablespoon water
    1 clove minced garlic
    Salt and freshly ground pepper,
      to taste
    ½ cup crumbled feta cheese
    10 red currant tomatoes

Toss the cress and the romaine together. Blend the oil, vinegar, water, and garlic. Season with salt and pepper. Pour over the greens. Sprinkle the cheese over the greens. Garnish with tiny tomatoes. Chill. Toss well before serving.
    Serves 6.

SELECTED CULTIVARS

Cresson or Curly Cress 12 days, French variety with curly leaves, peppery tang.

Reform Broadleaf 12 days, Dutch variety with sword-shaped leaves.

Cressida 12 days, European broadleaf, frilly leaves.

Upland Cress 50 days, widely available.

'Upland' cress

Dandelion

DANDELION

Wild dandelion greens may be harvested from fields and are especially good when lush growth crowds the leaves, blanching the heart. Cultivated dandelions form the same leafy rosettes, but the leaves are thicker and milder. The flavor is best in early spring.

GROWING DANDELIONS

If you love bitter greens, half a row will not seem like too many plants, particularly if you blanch them. Plant dandelions in the vegetable garden well away from the flower beds. The leaves are ready for picking in 70 to 95 days from sowing.

The plant has a long taproot and returns year after year unless completely uprooted. Dandelions will go wild, and neighbors sometimes object to them in a cultivated garden. Do not let the flowers go to seed.

Culture

In early spring or midsummer, sow seeds thickly over a wide band, and thin so plants stand 6 to 8 inches apart. Dandelions thrive in rich, heavy soil. To blanch the leaves, two or three days before harvesting tie the long outer leaves together at the top, or cover the centers with a plate to flatten them and keep out the light.

Harvesting

In early spring, harvest the tender inner leaves and buds for salads. Rinse in many changes of water, composting dark, broken, and imperfect leaves.

Seal in a vegetable bag and store in the crisper. Dandelion greens stay fresh several days.

COOKING WITH DANDELION GREENS

The tender springtime leaves of the dreaded dandelion are a delicious salad green. Picked small and young, the greens are strongly flavored, pleasingly bitter, and delicious dressed with a hearty vinaigrette flavored with garlic or onion. As the greens mature, they are better sautéed in Roasted Garlic Oil (see page 160) or bacon drippings and topped with bits of crisp bacon. They are tasty combined with pasta, roasted pimientos, black olives, and feta cheese. The Dutch serve the older leaves wilted and sauced with bacon fat or butter.

Dandelion and Lettuce Salad

3 cups lettuce thinnings
3 cups dandelion greens
4 green onions, trimmed to 3 inches, minced
2 large cloves garlic, minced
½ red bell pepper, chopped
¼ pound Jarlsburg™ cheese, diced
3 tablespoons light olive oil
3 tablespoons tarragon vinegar
Salt and freshly ground pepper, to taste
½ cup croutons

Wash, dry, and crisp the lettuce and the greens and chop very coarsely. Combine the onions, garlic, bell pepper, and cheese. Blend the oil and vinegar, season with salt and pepper, and pour over the greens. Toss, top with the pepper mixture, and garnish with croutons. Toss well before serving.

Serves 6 to 8.

SELECTED CULTIVARS

Montmagny 75 days, refined French selection, tastes like mild chicory, the root also is eaten.

Pissenlit Improved 90 days, French, makes a bushy mound of leaves, resembles curly endive.

Improved Thick-Leaved 95 days, widely distributed.

ESCAROLE AND ENDIVE (CHICORY)

Escarole, curly endive, and the brilliant little scarlet-purple globe called radicchio are all forms of chicory. To make names even more confusing, the blanched torpedo-shaped vegetable called Belgian endive is the forced and blanched root of either escarole or curly endive. Escarole has wide, twisted, flattened leaves and forms a loose head. Curly endive produces a rosette of very deeply cut and curly leaves. Both are blanched toward the center.

GROWING ESCAROLE AND ENDIVE

Escarole and curly endive are cool-season annuals moderately tolerant of light frost. Seeds are sown in the garden in very early spring or in late summer. Some cultivars are sweeter after the first frost. Harvest begins six weeks to three months from seed, depending on the variety. Early cultivars of escarole and curly endive compete for spring garden space with other fast-growing greens. In a small garden, they often are reserved for late-summer sowing and fall and winter harvests.

Culture

Sow seeds closely in drills or furrows ¼ to ½ inch deep. When they are 1 inch high, thin to 8 to 10 inches apart. Crowding helps to blanch the centers.

To heighten the natural blanching of the centers, two or three days before harvesting, cover and weight the centers with a plate.

Harvesting

Cut off the plants at the soil line. Harvest them young and before the heat comes: Allowed to stand, they grow big and become bitter.

Escarole keeps for several days rinsed, drained, sealed in a vegetable bag, and stored in the crisper. In fall, harvest with the roots on and store in a cool, dark place to blanch.

COOKING WITH ESCAROLE AND ENDIVE

Broadleaf escarole and curly leaved endive are forms of the plant Europeans call chicory. They are crisp, pleasingly bitter, and used in salads

NUTRITIONAL ELEMENTS

Chicory greens, 10–12 small leaves

Calories	7
Vitamin A	3,000 mg
Vitamin C	7 mg
Calcium	25 mg

and for garnish. Like dandelion greens, escarole and endive are best when served dressed with a strong vinaigrette that includes lots of garlic or onion. The lacy golden inner leaves of endive are used in commercial mesclun salad mixes.

Escarole and curly endive are also braised, steamed, stir-fried, or wilted, and served at room temperature with a vinaigrette. Escarole is sometimes used as a soup green.

Chicory Salad

This is a version of the classic French *salade frisée*, which is very popular in the bistros of Paris.

    1 shallot, peeled, minced
    1 tablespoon Dijon-style mustard
    5 teaspoons red wine vinegar
    4 tablespoons extravirgin olive oil
    Salt and freshly ground pepper,
      to taste
    4 ounces thickly sliced bacon, cut
      in ½-inch pieces
    ½ cup French bread croutons
    4 cups torn chicory leaves, rinsed
      and patted dry

Combine the shallot, mustard, and vinegar in a small bowl. Add the olive oil slowly, whisking constantly. Add the salt and pepper.

Sauté the bacon in a small skillet over medium heat until it is well browned (about 5 minutes). Remove the bacon and set aside. In the fat remaining in the pan, sauté the croutons, stirring constantly, until hot and golden.

Remove the skillet from the heat and carefully and quickly add the dressing. Stir well. Place the chicory in a salad bowl and toss at once with the hot dressing, bacon, and croutons. Serve immediately.
Serves 2 or 3.

SELECTED CULTIVARS

Escarole

Nuvol 55 days, large, heavy, wavy-edged leaves; full, self-blanching heart, good for spring planting, slow to bolt.

Sinco 80 days, cool-season cultivar for spring and fall harvesting, very big heads, creamy hearts, overwinters in mild climates.

Batavian Full-Hearted 90 days, wavy, dark green leaves, well-blanched heart, withstands cold at end of season; plant closely to increase blanching.

Endive

Neos (Chicory Frisée) 45 days, extra-frilly, compact, somewhat upright, self-blanching, resists bottom rot, recommended for midspring and early-fall crops.

President 80 days, deeply cut and frilled dark green leaves, creamy core, hardy.

Salad King 90 to 100 days, 2-foot heads, white-ribbed leaves, resists bolting, tolerates early frost, widely available.

'Batavian Full-Hearted' escarole

KALE

Kale is a nonheading species of cabbage. It forms a bouquet, or cluster, of curly leaves that are deep green tinted blue, gray-blue, or purple. The most popular variety is a tightly curled blue-green type. Different and interesting are cultivars of red Russian kale: As the weather cools, these develop a strong purple cast.

GROWING KALE

Kale is the most cold hardy of the leafy greens and is a favorite fall crop in warm regions. It bolts quickly in heat, so set out seedlings started four to six weeks before planting time if you want to harvest a spring crop.

For a fall and winter crop, sow seeds in mid-July or August; harvests begin in October. The flavor is improved by frost. In temperate regions kale is a reliable source of greens from late fall through spring. During winter there is little growth, but it resumes in late winter or very early spring. Harvests continue until the plants bolt and go to seed in mid- or late spring. The edible flowers taste a little like broccoli. Allowed to go to seed, kale self-sows in the cool, moist Northwest.

Many kale cultivars are handsome plants. Toward the end of summer, try 6 to 12 seedlings edging the flower border, herb bed, or salad garden, or in large planters. If you enjoy it, make room for more in the open garden next year. For soil, fertilizer, and water requirements, see page 183.

Culture

Sow seeds thickly ½ inch deep over a wide band. Thin plants to 2 feet apart. Set out transplants in rows, 18 to 24 inches apart. Mulch to control weeds. Kale that has overwintered in the row starts to grow again in late winter or early spring. When growth begins, scratch in a side dressing of compost or fertilizer.

Harvesting

Harvest thinnings and young side leaves as needed. Or cut off mature plants at the base and compost the outer leaves.

Rinsed, drained, and sealed in a vegetable bag, kale keeps at least a week in the crisper.

COOKING WITH KALE

This blue-green leaf is a nutritional bonanza laced with the rich flavor of cabbage and broccoli but in a delicious class of its own. It has been a major source of vitamins and iron in the winter diet of northern Europeans since the dawn of history.

Thinnings and baby kale leaves are excellent in salads. Chopped, tender young leaves are delicious stir-fried, or braised and served with butter. When the leaves are older, only the leafy parts are used for greens; the midribs can be used in soups or stews. Kale and potatoes are a fine combination, and kale is also very good braised with smoked ham, salt pork, fatback,

COLE GREENS

Some of the best-tasting leafy greens are species and cultivars of the genus *Brassica*. Plants in this genus are called cole crops and include the familiar cabbage-related vegetables such as broccoli, brussels sprouts, cauliflower, and kohlrabi. Also included in this group are Chinese cabbage, Chinese mustard, collards, kale, and mustard. The greens of this last group are especially delicious. All cole crops are healthier if planted where they neither follow nor precede each other in the garden.

NUTRITIONAL ELEMENTS

Kale, cooked, ¼ cup

Calories	28
Vitamin A	6,000 mg
Vitamin C	62 mg
Calcium	179 mg

or bacon. Chopped kale adds a hearty flavor to bean soups and sausage dishes.

Kale With Balsamic Vinegar

    6 cups chopped kale, rinsed
    3 tablespoons olive oil
    ½ to 1 cup water
    1 tablespoon butter
    1 tablespoon balsamic vinegar
    Salt, to taste

In a wok over medium-high, heat the oil and drop in the wet kale. Stir-fry until the kale turns a rich green and begins to wilt (3 to 4 minutes). Add ½ cup water, cover, reduce the heat to medium-low, and braise, stirring frequently until no water remains (12 to 15 minutes). Check the water often, and if it evaporates before the greens are cooked, add a little more. Remove from the stove and allow to finish cooking in its own heat. Season with butter, balsamic vinegar, and salt. Serve at room temperature.

Serves 4 to 6.

SELECTED CULTIVARS

Red Russian (Ragged Jack) 48 days, 2 to 3 feet tall, wavy blue-green leaves, veins turn deep purple-red in cold weather.

Siberian 50 days, frilly dark green leaves; sweet, succulent stalk, forms a rosette 24 inches in diameter at maturity, slow to bolt in April.

Westland Winter 50 to 60 days, Scotch kale, 2 feet tall, deeply curled and frilled leaves, new leaves form a yellow rosette.

Dwarf Blue Curled Scotch Vates 55 days, widely planted, low, compact, spreading, curled leaves.

Lacinato 62 days, heirloom Italian variety; thick, crinkled, strappy, dark blue-green leaves, mild flavor.

Dwarf Siberian 65 days, 12 to 15 inches tall, large, coarse, blue-green leaves, frilled edges.

'Dwarf Blue Curled Scotch Vates' kale

MACHE/ CORN SALAD

Mâche, also called corn salad or *feldsalat,* is a low-growing European herb. It is a common wild plant in much of Europe and Asia and has been cultivated for hundreds of years. In England, the word *corn* means grain. Mâche grows wild in fields of grain, and was often collected there for salads, hence, its English name. Like most greens, it tastes best if grown rapidly in cool weather.

GROWING MACHE

Mâche is a cool-season annual. The oval or spoon-shaped leaves grow in attractive rosettes that become rounded mounds. From seed—depending on the variety—you can begin harvesting in 45 to 80 days. Mâche can also be set out early as a seedling. Cultivars planted in spring will bolt and die in high heat. Where fall is long and winters are mild, seeds of cold-hardy cultivars are sown in successive plantings beginning in late summer. Harvest begins in midfall and continues through the following spring. Mâche survives mild winters as far north as Zone 7.

Mâche is pretty enough to fit anywhere. It can edge the flower bed, be the early-spring crop in a window box or planter, and it thrives in a cool greenhouse.

Culture

As soon as the ground can be worked, sow seeds ¼ inch deep, either in rows or 6 to 8 inches apart or sprinkle thickly and evenly over the bed. Keep the soil damp.

Harvesting

Pinch off individual sprigs at the base, rinse gently in cold water, and drain. Or cut off the whole plant, or a section of the plant, at the base and break into sprigs.

Unrinsed mâche sprigs keep a few days sealed in a vegetable bag and stored in the crisper.

COOKING WITH MACHE

Mâche is appreciated for its mild nutty flavor and buttery texture. It is served alone as a leafy green and in salads and mesclun mixes, generally with a mild vinaigrette. A handful of the 4- to 5-inch leaves is enough to make a salad for one. It combines well with other ingredients—chopped apples and nuts, hard-cooked eggs, slivered dried apricots, and with diced cooked beets, garlic, and walnut oil.

Spring Salad With Mâche

2 cups mâche leaves
1 cup curly endive sprigs
1 cup red oak leaf *or* other lettuce thinnings
½ cup chopped arugula
¼ cup minced chervil *or* parsley
3 tablespoons olive oil
1 tablespoon raspberry vinegar
1 tablespoon water
1 heaping teaspoon creamy Dijon-style mustard
1 small garlic clove, minced
Salt and freshly ground pepper, to taste

Rinse and drain all the greens and place them in a salad bowl. Top with chervil or parsley and chill briefly. Blend the oil, vinegar, water, mustard, garlic, and salt and pepper to taste. Pour the dressing over the greens. Toss before serving.
Serves 6.

SELECTED CULTIVARS

Gayla 70 to 80 days, good spring and excellent fall and winter variety, vigorous, cold tolerant.

NUTRITIONAL ELEMENTS
Mâche raw, 3½ ounces
Calories 21

Verte de Cambrai 50 to 80 days, small-seeded variety, bears 3- to 4-inch rounded leaves, recommended for cold regions.

Vit 50 days, good for spring and fall planting, long leaves form a dense mound, mildew tolerant.

MUSTARD GREENS

This loose-heading cabbage relative, *Brassica juncea,* is a cousin of Chinese cabbage or Chinese mustard. It has a finer leaf and a sharper, more piquant flavor than Chinese mustard, with a hint of Dijon-style mustard. There are many cultivars, some green, some red, each with a slightly different flavor, leaf shape, and texture.

GROWING MUSTARD GREENS

Mustard greens grow well in cool weather, withstand some frost, and bolt when days grow long in spring. Plant the spring crop as soon as the soil can be worked. To get mustard greens off to a fast start, dig and fertilize the planting row the preceding fall. Then start seeds three weeks before planting time in a hotbed, a cold frame, or indoors. A fast grower in fertile soil, mustard greens can be ready 35 to 55 days from seed. From transplants, you can harvest side leaves in 25 days. In mild regions there is time for a fall crop to mature from seeds sown in late summer.

'Red Giant' mustard greens

Both the green and the red (purple, really) mustard greens are attractive plants about 1 foot tall. They generally grow in their own row in the vegetable garden, but to test your enthusiasm for the flavor, first try 6 to 12 plants in a flower bed or herb garden.

For the soil, fertilizer, and water requirements of this cabbage-related vegetable, see page 261.

Culture
Sow seeds thickly ½ inch deep over a wide band and thin to 4 to 8 inches apart.

Harvesting
Use seedlings in mesclun mixes. Harvest outside leaves for salads and cooking when they reach 3 to 4 inches long. Mustard is best fresh from the garden before it matures. When the weather begins to warm, cut off the plant at the root and plant something else in its place.

Sealed in a vegetable bag, mustard greens keep well in the crisper for two or three days. Rinse just before using.

COOKING WITH MUSTARD GREENS

Some cooks grow mustard greens for the lively flavor that the thinnings and young leaves bring to mesclun salad mixes. Use the young leaves in piquant salads with baby beet greens, minced onion, and chopped hard-cooked eggs.

Cook mature mustard greens in the same manner as collards and kale—stir-fry, braise, or simmer with salt pork. They cook tender in 10 to 12 minutes. In the South they are added to pork dishes the last 15 minutes of cooking. Mustard greens are also excellent sautéed in a little olive oil with minced garlic, then salted and piled onto hot, crusty French bread or corn bread

and served with pork chops, sausages, fried chicken, or fish. Onions, garlic, lemon juice, and ham go well with mustard greens.

Greens and Poached Eggs
6 cups torn mustard greens, rinse well, discard stalks
2 cups boiling water
3 tablespoons butter
Salt and freshly ground pepper, to taste
12 poached eggs
6 English muffins, split, toasted
Paprika
12 pieces crisp bacon

Cover the greens with rapidly boiling water and simmer until tender (12 to 15 minutes). Drain well, chop, and drain again. Return the greens to the pot. Return the pot to the heat and shake to dry the remaining moisture. Flavor with butter, salt, and pepper. Keep warm.

When the eggs are poached, arrange 2 muffin halves on each plate and top each with mustard greens, a poached egg, and a dash of paprika. Crumble the bacon over the eggs and serve at once.
Serves 6.

SELECTED CULTIVARS

Southern Giant Curled 35 to 50 days, a favorite, upright, bright green leaves with very curly edges, slow to bolt, All-America Selection.

Osaka Purple 40 days, from Japan, 12 to 14 inches tall, handsome, mild, purple-tinged green leaves with white veins.

Red Giant 45 days, 16 to 18 inches tall, decorative red-bronze leaves with purple-red veins, noticeable flavor of Dijon mustard.

Green Wave 55 days, long standing, finely frilled, dark green, slow to grow, slow to bolt, raw leaves have strong mustard flavor.

NUTRITIONAL ELEMENTS
Mustard greens, cooked, ½ cup
Calories   23
Vitamin A   5,800 mg
Vitamin C   48 mg
Calcium   138 mg

RADICCHIO

Radicchio is costly in stores, so this is a gourmet item worth cultivating. Radicchio is a type of chicory, and it needs a long, cool season and a place of its own in the vegetable garden to develop well. A dozen plants supply a family with young radicchio for mesclun mixes and a later harvest of mature heads.

GROWING RADICCHIO

Seeds are sown in the garden in early to midspring in the North, and when summer begins to cool in the South. Older cultivars of radicchio must be cut back to produce the tight little heads favored: Choose newer cultivars. Heads of spring-planted radicchio are ready to harvest in early fall in 60 to 110 days; heads of fall-planted radicchio are ready to harvest in the winter or early spring.

Culture

Sow seeds ¼ inch deep. Thin the plants to 8 to 10 inches apart.

Harvesting

Slice the heads from the roots and remove and compost the spoiled outer leaves.

Sealed in a vegetable bag, radicchio keeps for several weeks in the crisper.

COOKING WITH RADICCHIO

Radicchio looks like a refined, pretty little red cabbage about the size of a softball. It is not technically a "leafy green" because of its color, but it fits within this group of leafy vegetables. The flavor is tart and peppery. It is a delicious and colorful ingredient in salads and is indispensable in mesclun mixes. Separated, the cupped leaves make

'Guilio' radicchio

beautiful vessels for crab salad, potato salad, and other mild-flavored foods. Serve radicchio as a salad course combined with other ingredients, especially mandarin orange segments, grapefruit, walnuts, and pine nuts.

Rice With Spicy Greens
This is a perfect side dish with pork or chicken.

  2½ cups water
  1 cup long-grain rice
  1 tablespoon butter
  1 tablespoon olive oil
  2 cloves garlic, minced
  1½ cups coarsely chopped
      arugula
  1 cup coarsely chopped water-
      cress leaves
  2 tablespoons chopped flat-leaf
      parsley
  1½ cups julienned radicchio
  Salt and freshly ground pepper,
      to taste

Bring the water to a boil in a saucepan. Add the rice, lower the heat, cover, and simmer 20 minutes.

Heat the butter and oil in a large skillet. Add the garlic, arugula, and watercress. Cook, stirring constantly, until the greens are slightly wilted. Add the cooked rice along with the parsley, radicchio, and salt and pepper. Stir to blend thoroughly and serve at once.
Serves 4 to 6.

SELECTED CULTIVARS

Alto 60 days, plant any season, slow to bolt.

Chioggia Red Preco No. 1 60 days, early, large, purple-red heads.

Medusa 65 days, medium-sized, dark red round heads.

Augusto 70 days, plant late summer to harvest in fall, frost tolerant.

Giulio 80 to 90 days, Dutch strain, beautiful garnet-colored heads, small, solid, resists bolting.

Red Verona 85 to 100 days, firm, apple-sized bright red heads.

Palla Rossa Special 85 days, medium-early, plant in summer for fall harvest.

Palla Rossa Tardiva 85 days, very large crimson heads, plant in summer for fall harvest, slow to bolt.

Rossana 90 days, beautiful cultivar, heat tolerant.

Marina 110 days, sow in spring for heads by midfall.

SPINACH
This is not a crop to experiment with—it takes a whole packet of spinach seeds to get a meaningful harvest. In early spring, as soon as the ground can be worked, plant any variety. After April, plant one of the slow-bolting or long-standing cultivars, 'Mazurka', for instance. For fall and winter harvests, choose cultivars advertised as disease resistant, such as 'Bloomsdale' and 'Tyee'. For the cook in a hurry, the most satisfactory spinach cultivars are those with smooth leaves: The cultivars that have puckered, or savoyed, leaves are tasty, but their crevices provide hiding places for grit, so they need lots of rinsing.

Between the spring and the fall spinach seasons, harvest crops of the spinachlike greens called New Zealand spinach (*Tetragonia tetragonioides*), and Malabar or Indian spinach, *Basella rubra*. Both can withstand heat and produce in partial shade. New Zealand spinach is a drought-tolerant, low-growing plant. Malabar or Indian spinach is a vinelike plant that needs a 3-foot support. These seeds are slow to germinate: Start them indoors

SPINACH DISEASE RESISTANCE
B   Blight
DM   Downy mildew
M   Mosaic

NUTRITIONAL ELEMENTS

Spinach, cooked, ½ cup

Calories	21
Vitamin A	8,000 mg
Vitamin C	25 mg
Calcium	83 mg

in individual peat pots and set out the seedlings after the last spring frost. They develop more rapidly if you harvest some leaves as the plants are growing.

GROWING SPINACH

True spinach is a cool-weather plant that consists of low-growing rosettes of dark green leaves. It's an in-and-out crop to plant in a garden row. From seed, spinach matures in six to seven weeks, leaving space to plant midsummer vegetables. The first spinach crop has to go in early because it bolts when the days grow long and the weather warms. For a long season of harvests, sow seeds every two weeks from early spring until six weeks before daytime temperatures reach 75° F. Where winters are mild, plant spinach from October to March. Spinach thrives in well-drained, neutral soil with an abundant supply of nitrogen and sustained moisture. Let two years pass before replanting spinach in a row in which it was the former crop.

Culture

Sow seeds ½ inch deep and 1 inch apart over a wide band; thin to 3 to 4 inches apart. Weed early and often. When the spinach plants are thinned and the weeds are under control, mulch lightly. When the plants are established, scratch in a side dressing of blood meal or some other high-nitrogen fertilizer.

Harvesting

Pick spinach leaves when the plants are 6 to 8 inches tall. Harvest individual outer leaves or cut off the whole plant. If there are signs the plants are bolting, harvest the entire crop.

Rinsed, drained, and sealed in a vegetable bag, spinach keeps at least a week in the crisper. Even when frozen, fresh spinach maintains a lot of the original color, flavor and nutritional value.

COOKING WITH SPINACH

Fresh spinach has a beautiful bright green leaf and an elegant flavor. It is also very high in vitamins A and B_2 and is rich in iron, calcium, and protein.

Spinach should never be cooked for more than a few minutes—just enough to thoroughly wilt it and dry the cooking water. The rinse water clinging to it is enough for cooking it. Dressed with a light vinaigrette and served at room temperature, garden-fresh spinach is a delicacy. Braised two to four minutes and seasoned with freshly grated nutmeg, it is a superb accompaniment for steaks, lamb chops, grilled pork, meaty casseroles, and savory omelets. For brunch, try lightly buttered spinach seasoned with nutmeg on toast and topped with poached eggs. Spinach soufflé and spinach soup are other specialties.

Spinach thinnings and baby leaves are excellent additions to mesclun mixes. Young or mature, the leaves add richness to salads. Topped by mushrooms marinated in tarragon vinegar and blue-cheese dressing, raw spinach makes an excellent appetizer or first-course salad.

Creamy Spinach Soup

4 tablespoons butter
¼ cup flour
5 cups hot beef bouillon
6 cups packed spinach
2 cups whole milk
Salt and freshly ground pepper, to taste
Pinch ground nutmeg
1 tablespoon chopped sorrel, for garnish

In a large saucepan over low heat, melt the butter and stir in the flour to make a smooth paste. Pour in the hot broth all at once and whisk until the sauce thickens and becomes smooth. Simmer 2 minutes. Stir in the spinach, cover, and simmer until the spinach is tender and deep green (about 5 minutes). Stir in the milk and heat. Season with salt, pepper, and nutmeg. Serve hot. Garnish with sorrel, if you wish.

Serves 6.

SELECTED CULTIVARS

Spring Spinach

Nordic 39 days, smooth-leaved Dutch variety, for cool and warm seasons, slow to bolt. (DM)

Vienna 40 days, deeply savoyed, early hybrid, thick leaves, slow to bolt. (B, DM)

Virginia Blight Resistant Savoy 40 days, slow to bolt.

Italian Summer 40 days, high yield, savoyed, slow to bolt.

Space F1 41 days, smooth, spoon-shaped leaves, very productive, heat tolerant.

Giant Nobel 40 to 48 days, smooth, thick leaves, excellent flavor, slow to bolt.

Melody 42 days, semisavoyed, slow to bolt, All-America Selection. (DM, M)

Tyee F1 45 days, semisavoyed, upright leaves, slow to bolt. (DM)

Mazurka F1 45 days, smooth thick leaves, slow to bolt.

Bloomsdale Savoy 48 to 50 days, savoyed, hardy in mild regions, slow to bolt.

'Melody' spinach

Long-Standing Spinach

Wolter 40 days, Dutch, adapted for fall, winter, and early spring crops in the South and West. (DM)

Hybrid No. 7 42 days, recommended for fall and winter. (B, DM)

Virginia Savoy 42 days, recommended for fall and winter.

Winter Bloomsdale 46 days, recommended for cold mountain regions and for fall and winter planting.

Ace Japanese Spinach F1 Upright plant; smooth, long stalks, good for spring and fall planting in moderate climates. (DM)

SQUASHES, PUMPKINS, AND GOURDS

Pumpkin and winter squash, such as these 'Blue Ballet' and 'Red Kuri' Hubbard squash, are powerful sources of beta carotene, an important anti-oxidant.

Even a small garden has space for a couple of squashes. Both summer and winter types are rewarding crops. Summer cultivars are light, refreshing, low calorie, high in vitamin A, and amazingly productive. The richly flavored yellow, orange, and red winter squashes provide lots of vitamin A and phytochemicals. And you cannot celebrate Halloween and Thanksgiving without pumpkins.

Squashes are sprawling, heat-loving plants. Sown in the garden after the weather has warmed, the seeds germinate rapidly. Sow seeds 1½ to 2 inches deep in damp soil and do not water again until the seedlings appear: They do best when they emerge in a fairly dry environment. Where spring is late or cold and wet, start seeds in individual peat pots three to four weeks before planting weather.

The summer squashes, including zucchini, are large, upright plants that produce early and continue until fall if you keep the young fruit picked. Winter squash, pumpkins, and gourds are vining plants. They mature only a few fruit each and are harvested in fall, after the rinds ripen and harden.

Heavy feeders, the squashes thrive in soil rich in humus and fertilized at the rate of 1 pound of 5–10–10 for each 25 feet of row. A midseason side dressing of fertilizer or compost helps. Squashes withstand some drought, but for abundant production they need sustained moisture.

These plants belong to the gourd, or cucurbit, family, which includes cucumbers and melons. Keep them far apart in the garden or they will cross-pollinate. Do not plant these where other squashes, cucumbers, or melons were the preceding crop.

SQUASH (SUMMER)

There are four basic types of summer squash: straightneck yellow squash, which is straight and tapering; crookneck yellow squash, which has a tapered body and a curved neck; round green-white scallop, or patty pan, squash, which is shaped like a flying saucer with scalloped edges; and the various zucchini, which are mostly green skinned, straight, and cylindrical, but sometimes are round and sometimes yellow.

GROWING SUMMER SQUASH

Summer squash reaches picking size from seed in six or seven weeks. If everything else in the garden goes wrong, these plants will come through, especially zucchini. They are succulent, bushy plants that tend to take over the space allotted to them and often produce more than you counted on. Summer squash needs a space about 4 feet by 2 feet. Four plants are likely to produce enough for a family. Two types of zucchini and one each of yellow summer squash and the scallop patty pan squash, will provide the chef with a large, interesting array.

Culture
See previous page.

Harvesting
Summer squash must be harvested almost daily. The flavor is best when harvested so young that the seeds have barely developed. If squash matures enough that skin starts to toughen, the seeds too become large and tough. Zucchini is considered mature at 5 to 8 inches long; straightneck and crookneck types are best picked at just 4 to 5 inches. Left on the plant, zucchini becomes enormous. Pick the scalloped patty pans when they are 3 to 4 inches across.

Summer squash keeps well for at least a week sealed in a vegetable bag right after picking and stored in the crisper.

Squash does not freeze well, but use an overabundance to prepare ratatouille, or add to tomato sauce for spaghetti, which can be frozen.

COOKING WITH SUMMER SQUASH

One of the garden's special treats is summer squash 2½ to 3 inches long, steamed, and seasoned with freshly grated Parmesan cheese and very little salt and butter. Fresh summer squash picked at 5 to 6 inches long has skin so tender it is easily pierced by a fingernail, so it is not peeled. The easy way to prepare summer squash is to halve and cook it until it is translucent and tender. Steamed, it cooks in 15 to 20 minutes; grilled, it is ready in 8 to 10 minutes; sliced in thin rounds and sautéed in Roasted Garlic Oil (see page 160), it cooks in 6 to 8 minutes.

Zucchini is excellent stir-fried in walnut oil with slivered onions and seasoned with soy sauce, a bit of sugar, salt, and pepper. Yellow summer squash is elegant sliced thinly and braised in butter, then simmered in a little whole milk seasoned with nutmeg, salt, and pepper. Patty pan squash is delicious baked under any of the pasta sauces. All the summer squashes go well with tomatoes, basil, parsley, oregano, thyme, and other Mediterranean herbs.

Raw summer squash adds crunch and color to salads. Use thick slices of raw zucchini for tempura, in ratatouille, and with crudités. 'Ronde de Nice' zucchini, harvested when it is 1 inch long and sautéed whole, makes a tasty and interesting presentation.

When a zucchini grows beyond medium-large (some invariably do), halve it, stuff the halves, bake them, and serve with or without a sauce. In Provence, big squash are sliced in 1-inch rounds, seasoned, floured, and panfried with garlic in olive oil.

Nan Hubbard's Baked Summer Squash

6 very young summer squash
Roasted Garlic Oil (see page 160)
Garlic salt
2 tablespoons freshly grated
 Parmesan cheese
Freshly ground black pepper,
 to taste

Trim the stem ends of the squash, slice them in half lengthwise, and sprinkle the cut sides with garlic salt. Arrange the halves, cut side up, in a glass baking dish and drizzle with Roasted Garlic Oil. Cover the plate with plastic wrap and place it in the microwave oven. Bake on high for 5 minutes. Remove from the oven, uncover the squash, and sprinkle with Parmesan cheese. Cover loosely, and return to the microwave oven for 2 minutes more on high. Season with pepper to taste.
Serves 6.

SELECTED CULTIVARS

Straightneck Squash

Sundrops 50 days, compact bush, bears creamy yellow miniature oval squash, 2 inches across, All-America Selection.

Early Prolific Straightneck 52 days, big bush, bears cylindrical light yellow fruit, best picked under 6 inches, All-America Selection.

'Yellow Crookneck' squash

Crookneck Squash

Valley Gold 45 days, F1 hybrid, butter yellow fruit, matures to yellow-orange.

Dixie 51 days, smooth, bright yellow fruit, 4 to 6 inches long, medium to small bush.

Yellow Crookneck 58 days, bears late but yields consistently once producing, excellent flavor.

Scallop/Patty Pan Squash

Yellow Bush 49 days, disk-shaped fruit, scalloped edges, miniature-sized for small spaces.

Peter Pan 50 days, 2½ to 3 inches, light green, medium-sized, All-America Selection.

'Peter Pan' scallop squash

Greyzini 47 days, light green, gray mottling, high yield, compact plant, All-America Selection.

Chefini 48 days, early producer, medium-green fruit, All-America Selection.

Vegetable Marrow 49 to 56 days, British variety, with 8-inch light-green fruit.

Aristocrat 50 days, very dark green, smooth, cylindrical, 7½ to 8 inches long, compact plant, All-America Selection.

Gold Rush 52 days, flavorful, deep gold, 7 to 8 inches long, kelly green stems, small plant, All-America Selection.

Blackjack 53 days, very dark green, 6½ to 7½ inches long, on a compact plant.

Sun Drops 55 days, 3- to 4-inch fruit, oval, yellow, compact plant, All-America Selection.

Cocozelle 55 days, Italian strain, vining, green striped lighter green.

Zucchetta Rampicante 58 days, Italian vining heirloom, pale lime green, curved S-shape, 12 to 15 inches, can be trained up a trellis.

Scallopini 50 days, scalloped, dark green, very productive, medium-sized, All-America Selection.

Sunburst 53 to 60 days, bright golden yellow, green at the edges, lightly scalloped, very compact, All-America Selection.

Early White Bush (White Patty Pan) 60 days, 7 inches across, pale green rind.

Zucchini

Golden Dawn 11 45 days, long, thin, dark golden fruit, on a compact plant.

SQUASH (WINTER)

There are six popular winter squashes: Acorn squash is an accordion-pleated green ball the size of a small grapefruit. Banana squash is very large and long with smooth skin. Butternut squash has tan or buff-colored skin and is shaped like a fat-bottomed vase; its texture is more mealy than that of a pumpkin. Hubbard is a very large squash that is round to oval, ribbed, and bumpy. Spaghetti squash looks like an off-white smooth-skinned melon. Turban squash is definable by its shape, which makes it unmistakable.

GROWING WINTER SQUASH

There are bushlike strains of winter squash, ready in 65 to 85 days, but vining cultivars, ready in up to 120 days, are more common. Small vining winter squash develop on 6- to 8-foot runners and need about 3 by 6 feet of space; large vining types need 3 by 10 feet all around. They are sown in hills, or groups, 4 to 6 seeds to a hill. Before the seedlings start vining, thin to 2 to 3 plants per hill.

Small-fruited cultivars are easily trained upward, which makes them a good choice for a small garden. They also do well grown at the edge of the garden with their runners trained out over the lawn. Long-standing winter squash can be set out in rows left empty as the leafy greens fade before the heat, or where spring bulbs once flowered. Their foliage will shade the soil and benefit the bulbs by providing them with a cool, dryish summer. Large cultivars can be grown at the base of corn or pole beans.

Whereas summer squash are early and prolific bearers, winter squash produce just a few fruits per plant. For a small family, a half-dozen plants of two cultivars is a good beginning—butternut and spaghetti squash are most popular. For the gourmet cook, 'Black Forest' might be more interesting.

Culture

With winter squash, encouraging rapid growth in the young plants is important because they need time to fully mature. The earlier the fruit sets, the longer it has to mature in the field, and the better it will taste. So the soil should be well supplied with organic matter, watered enough to maintain moisture, and side-dressed with fertilizer or compost once or twice during the season.

Squash produce both male and female flowers. The stem of the female flower is slightly thickened below the ovary, which develops into the fruit. The petals of the male flowers drop off. Some growers pinch off the male flowers so that all the plant's strength goes into ripening the fruit.

For the best winter squash, in early September pinch off all the new female flowers and little squash as they appear. This helps the vines to ripen the fruit that is already maturing, and the result is large fruit and better flavor. Some growers recommend removing the

Female zucchini blossoms, such as this one, have small fruit at their base. Male blossoms have only stalks.

211

NUTRITIONAL ELEMENTS

Winter squash, baked, ½ cup

Calories	63
Vitamin A	4,200 mg
Vitamin C	13 mg
Calcium	28 mg

foliage shading fruits as they approach maturity. Long runners may be cut off after some fruit has set so long as enough leaves remain to nourish the plant.

Harvesting

Winter squash is ready for harvesting when the stems become dry and brittle. When ripe, most green cultivars show some brown or bronze coloring. Cut the stems about an inch or two from the vine.

Let the fruit cure in the garden for 10 days, covered at night if there's a chance of frost. If it rains, cure the squash indoors in a warm room for four or five days.

Winter squash keeps for many weeks stored at 50° to 60° F in a dry, airy place.

COOKING WITH WINTER SQUASH

Winter squashes deserve to be better appreciated. More flavorful than their summer cousins, they are as simple to prepare as potatoes. Butternut, and others with bright orange or red flesh, are as delicious as yams and sweet potatoes and they supply a large amount of vitamin A. Spaghetti squash is a healthy delight. Bake or simmer about an hour, split, prod a little with a fork, and you have a delicious mass of pale gold strands that are an excellent low-calorie side dish.

Halve, seed, and scrape winter squash to remove the fibers lining the seed cavity. Bake thick-skinned types such as acorn squash in their rind. Peel the thin-skinned squash, such as butternuts, before steaming or braising. They are all excellent mashed, lightly buttered, and flavored with crumbled bacon, nutmeg, cinnamon, or citrus juices. Brush with Roasted Garlic Oil (see page 160) and grill. Stuff with

sausage, hashed ham or chicken, crabmeat, fish, mushrooms, hash browns, or other vegetables and bake. Bake with butter, and sauce with applesauce or crushed pineapple thickened with cornstarch. Winter squashes make wonderful rich and hearty soups and vegetable stews. They provide substantial body to vegetarian chili and curries.

Used in recipes calling for pumpkin, butternut and some of the more mealy winter squashes make excellent pies, breads, and muffins.

Honey-Baked Winter Squash

3 small acorn or butternut
    squash, halved, seeded
½ lemon
2 tablespoons butter
Salt and freshly ground black
    pepper, to taste
2 tablespoons honey
1 tablespoon minced fresh
    oregano *or* parsley, for garnish

Preheat oven to 375° F. Place the squash, cut side up, in an ovenproof dish. Squeeze lemon juice over them, dot with butter, season with salt and pepper, and drizzle with honey. Bake until very tender (1 to 1½ hours). Garnish with a pinch of oregano or parsley.
Serves 6.

SELECTED CULTIVARS

Acorn Squash

Cream of the Crop 65 days, bushy hybrid, beautiful 5- to 6-inch fruit, cream-colored rind, golden flesh, All-America Selection.

Table King 75 days, bush type, bears 5- to 6-inch dark green, glossy fruit with golden flesh, good keeper, All-America Selection.

Snow White 80 days, compact plant, heavy clusters of 6 to 10 fruit, skin is white, flesh is buttery white with a mellow flavor.

Table Queen 90 days, semibush, dark green rind, orange-yellow flesh, excellent flavor.

Delicata 97 days, compact plant, 8-inch fruit, creamy green striped with darker green, flesh is orange and sweet.

Banana Squash

Pink Banana Jumbo 105 days, 75-pound fruit are cylinders with rounded ends, rind is grayish green turning bright pink at maturity, flesh is orange and sweet.

Blue Banana 120 days, huge fruit, smooth gray rind and yellow flesh.

Butternut Squash

Early Butternut 80 days, productive semibush hybrid, tan rind and orange flesh, All-America Selection.

Waltham Butternut 85 to 90 days, 8- to 10-inch fruit, light tan skin, dark orange flesh.

Butterbush 75 days, small fruit weighing less than 2 pounds, reddish-orange rind and flesh, compact bush can be grown in a tub, ideal for the small garden.

Hubbard Squash

Mountaineer 90 days, cold tolerant, small variety for short-season gardens.

Black Forest 95 days, medium-small squash, flat and round, dark green skin, exceptionally tasty deep orange flesh, plants average four or five fruit.

Golden Hubbard 102 to 105 days, slightly warted orange rind with tan stripes and deep orange flesh, 9 to 11 inches in diameter, up to 10 pounds.

'Buttercup' turban squash

Green Hubbard 115 days, heirloom variety, very dark green warted skin, excellent rich golden yellow flesh, 13 to 15 inches, 12 to 14 pounds.

Blue Hubbard 120 days, New England strain, large, long fruit, 40 to 50 pounds, rind is blue-gray, orange flesh.

Spaghetti Squash

Vegetable Spaghetti 90 to 100 days, spreading vine, 10- by 8-inch oval fruit, 1½ to 3 pounds, tan rind, interior strands pale gold.

Tivoli F1 100 days, compact bush, profusion of 3- to 5-pound cream-colored fruit, All-America Selection.

213

Turban Squash

Sweet Mama 85 days, short vine recommended for small gardens, large fruit, dark gray-green skin, deep gold sweet flesh, All-America Selection.

Buttercup 105 days, small plant, 4½- to 6½-inch fruit, striped and mottled dark green rind, sweet and tasty orange flesh.

Turk's Turban 105 days, fruit striped with bright orange or red, edible squash often listed with ornamental gourds.

'Gold Rush' zucchini

PUMPKIN

A pumpkin is a bright orange winter squash that grows on a vine running along the ground. Like winter squash, plant pumpkins in spring and harvest late in the fall after the rind hardens. Most cultivars produce 3 to 12 fruit per vine.

GROWING PUMPKINS

Pumpkins come in many sizes. The small and miniature sizes range from under 1 pound to 4 pounds and mature from seeds in 85 to 105 days. Standard sizes range from 5 to 25 pounds and are mature in 90 to 160 days. The giants weigh from 50 to several hundred pounds and mature in 110 to 120 days.

For a small family, a couple of standard-sized pumpkins and a few ornamental miniatures trained up a trellis are enough. Small vining pumpkin plants need about 3 by 6 feet of space; large vining types need 3 by 10 feet all around. Giant pumpkins take up to 70 square feet of space.

In the traditional row garden, pumpkins often grow at the base of corn or at the edge of the garden so the runners can spread out.

Culture

Sow pumpkin seeds in hills 1½ to 2 inches deep, 4 to 6 seeds to a hill. Thin to two to three seedlings per hill before the plants start vining.

Treat pumpkins much like winter squash: Encourage rapid growth in young plants, especially the large sizes, which need time to mature. The earlier the fruit sets, the larger the harvest. As large pumpkins mature, set them on scrap lumber to keep the bottoms from rotting.

To obtain maximum size in giant pumpkins, allow each vine 70 square feet to roam, and remove all but 1 pumpkin from each vine.

Provide side dressings of fertilizer at regular intervals during the growing season.

Harvesting

Harvest pumpkins in the fall when the rind hardens, the foliage starts to die, and the stems get dry and brittle.

Cut the stems 1 to 3 inches from the vine, longer for bigger pumpkins, shorter for smaller ones. Let the fruit cure in the row for 10 days in the sun. If frost is due, cover the pumpkins at night. If rain threatens, cure them indoors in a warm room for four or five days. They keep for many weeks stored at 50° to 60° F in a dry, airy place.

COOKING WITH PUMPKIN

The pumpkin is the quintessential Halloween symbol, the main ingredient in everyone's favorite Thanksgiving pie, and a great source of vitamin A. It's also a flavorful squash, excellent steamed or baked until tender, and dressed with lemon and butter or with honey and salt and pepper. Cubes

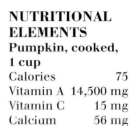

NUTRITIONAL ELEMENTS
Pumpkin, cooked, 1 cup

Calories	75
Vitamin A	14,500 mg
Vitamin C	15 mg
Calcium	56 mg

'Atlantic Giant' (front) and 'Autumn Gold' pumpkins

of pumpkin are delightful steamed, baked, or simmered, then mashed with brown sugar and butter, and seasoned with a little orange or lemon juice.

Miniature pumpkins are used largely as ornaments, but they are tasty seeded, steamed, and stuffed with hot crabmeat, steamed miniature carrots, and any number of other savory mixes. They also make a novel vessel for individual servings of soup.

'Baby Bear' pumpkin

Giant pumpkins are the largest vegetable. These cultivars are selected for their potential size, and though fun and ornamental, they are not famous for flavor.

Pumpkin seeds make a nutritious snack: Roast them following the recipe for Roasted Sunflower Seeds on page 285.

Pumpkin Bread

2 cups all-purpose flour
1 teaspoon salt
1 teaspoon baking soda
1 teaspoon baking powder
½ teaspoon ground cinnamon
½ teaspoon ground dried ginger
½ teaspoon freshly grated nutmeg
4 eggs
2 cups sugar
2 cups mashed, baked, or
   steamed pumpkin flesh
1½ cups melted butter
1 cup chopped pecans

Preheat oven to 350° F. Sift the flour, salt, baking soda, baking powder, cinnamon, ginger, and nutmeg together three times.

Beat the eggs until thick and gradually beat in the sugar. Fold the pumpkin into the eggs, then fold in the melted butter. Stir in the dry ingredients, then the nuts. Pour into 2 buttered loaf pans. Bake 1 hour or until a toothpick inserted into the center of each loaf comes out clean.
Makes 2 loaves.

SELECTED CULTIVARS

Small and Miniature Pumpkins

Small Sugar 85 to 115 days, takes little space, small, slightly squat, 8 to 10 inches, 5 to 9 pounds, recommended for pies, prefect for carving.

Jack Be Little 90 days, classic little bright orange pumpkin, 2 inches high, 3 inches around.

Baby Boo 90 days, like 'Jack Be Little' but smaller, creamy white, grows well on vertical supports.

Northern Bush 90 days, bright orange, 6 inches, good in pies, recommended for cool and unreliable climates.

Baby Bear 105 days, bright orange, 5 to 6 inches, 3½ to 4 inches high, 1½ to 2½ pounds, with minimal ribs.

Standard Pumpkins

Seneca Harvest Moon F1 90 days, round, 6 to 14 inches, 8 to 12 pounds, vigorous, prolific, recommended for short seasons.

Frosty 90 days, compact bush, early, bright orange, 10 inches, 15 to 20 pounds, fine-grained flesh, used for pies.

Autumn Gold 90 days, early variety, 7 to 10 pounds, glossy golden orange, recommended for jack-o'-lanterns, All-America Selection.

Jack-O-Lite 90 days, classic 12- to 15-pound jack-o'-lantern cultivar, good for carving and baking.

Spirit 100 days, compact semi-bush, smooth, symmetrical, 12 inches, well-formed handle, great for carving, tasty thick orange flesh, All-America Selection.

Trick or Treat F1 105 days, tall pumpkins, 12 pounds, great jack-o'-lanterns, savory seeds.

Jack O' Lantern 110 days, 8 by 8 inches, smooth, clear orange rind, great for carving.

Connecticut Field 110 days, 15 to 18 pounds, bright orange, variety of sizes and shapes.

Triple Treat 110 days, 9 inches across, 8 pounds, recommended for carving, pies, and seeds.

Lumina 115 days, 10 inches, 10 to 12 pounds, white, insides bright orange, tasty.

Rouge Vif d'Etampes 130 to 160 days, Cinderella's pumpkin, 8 inches high, 15 inches wide, 5 to 40 pounds, deep ridges, glowing mahogany-orange fading to creamy inside the ridges.

Giant Pumpkins

Big Moon 110 days, can weigh more than 200 pounds, good pie pumpkin.

Atlantic Giant 115 days, easily 50 to 100 pounds, the World Pumpkin Confederation expects this seed to produce the first 1,000-pound pumpkin (an 800-pound pumpkin recorded).

Prizewinner 120 days, 80 to 100 pounds, classic shape and color, great for carving.

GOURDS

Squashes classed as "gourds" are ornamental hard-shelled cultivars of *Cucurbita* and *Lagenaria*. For the most part, they are bitter and inedible. There are exceptions to the inedible rule, and these are picked young while the skin is still tender. Among the edible gourds are the "bitter gourds" or "bitter melons," popular in China, Japan, India, and the Philippines. Chinese chefs stuff bitter gourds and also chop them and add them to soups and stir-fries. Some West Coast growers market Asian cultivars developed in Hong Kong and Thailand.

GROWING GOURDS

Most of the gourds grown in the home garden are vining plants. Like winter squash, you plant in spring and harvest in fall after the rinds harden into shells.

Gourds are appealing crops because they provide lots of ornamental material. Youngsters especially enjoy turning them into bottles, dippers, and birdhouses.

Gourds are easy to place. Train smaller cultivars on trellises or along fence tops. Plant larger forms at the edge of the vegetable garden and allow the runners to grow over the grass. Many seed companies offer packets of mixed cultivars, and these provide the best return on the time and space invested.

Culture

Encourage rapid growth in young plants so they have time to mature fully, just like winter squash. The soil needs plenty of organic matter. Maintain even moisture on the plants and side-dress with fertilizer or compost once or twice during the season.

Harvesting

Harvest gourds when the stems are dry and brittle. Cut them about an inch or two from the vine and cure the fruit for 10 days, leaving it in the garden and covering it at night if there is a chance of frost. If rain is expected, cure gourds indoors for four or five days in a warm room.

SELECTED CULTIVARS

Edible Gourds

Bitter Gourd (Taiwan Large) 100 days, green skin, thick white flesh, top-quality cooking gourd.

Calabash 110 days, medium-long, light green, bat-shaped fruit, 3 to 4 inches across, 15 inches long, young fruit used in stir-fries and soups; round calabash cultivars are available; also listed as decorative.

Italian Edible 100 days, 4 to 5 inches long, 2 to 3 inches wide, tapering toward the stem end, edible at a young stage.

Wax Gourd (Winter Melon) 110 days, round, 15 to 20 pounds.

'Large Bottle' gourds

Fuzzy Gourd (Little Winter Melon) 100 days, hairy fruit, pick for cooking when 4 to 6 inches long.

Cucuzzi 120 days, Italian, sizable edible fruit to 3 feet or more, harvested at 8 pounds, eat like zucchini.

Small Decorative Gourds

Pear Bi-Colored 100 days, pear shaped, about 3 inches long, 1½ inches in diameter at the base, lower half green with yellow stripes, upper half yellow or buff colored.

Small Spoon 100 days, orange and green fruit; long, slender, curving necks above an oval bulb.

Small Orange 100 days, round fruit, 2½ to 3 inches in diameter with a hard, smooth, bright orange exterior.

Yellow Warted 100 days, round or slightly flattened, about 2 to 3 inches in diameter, yellow, hard, warted.

Large Decorative Gourds

Luffa (Vegetable Sponge, Dishcloth, or Rag Gourd) 90 to 120 days, 12 to 18 inches long, 3 or 4 inches around, tapered toward one end, green to gray-green at maturity; skinned, the interior resembles a sponge.

Calabash 110 days, 5 inches in diameter, 12 to 15 inches long, short curved neck at the stem end, tan and smooth shell, cut off stem end to make a water dipper or birdhouse.

Long-Handled Dipper 110 days, slender neck 16 inches or longer, dipper bulb 6 to 8 inches across, smooth and tan.

Crown of Thorns 110 days, 'Shenot' strain, looks something like an acorn squash but has

'Long-Handled Dipper' gourds

10 small projections jutting up from the blossom end, colorfully striped white, orange yellow, and shades of green.

Bird House 120 days, 4 to 5 inches in diameter, tapers sharply toward the stem end, shell is tan and smooth, makes a neat birdhouse.

Large Bottle Gourd 120 days, shaped like a bottle, 10 inches around, 12 to 15 inches long, neck flares out into a smaller bulb, used in some cultures for carrying water, makes great birdhouse.

MELONS

Most watermelons, such as these 'Crimson Sweet' melons, need weeks of long hot nights to become as sweet as they can. Some varieties have been developed for northern regions, but watermelons are best in the Deep South.

The flavor of melons ripened on the vine is unbeatable. Muskmelons especially, both the orange- and the green-fleshed cultivars, are worth every inch of garden space you give them. Nutritionally, they provide vitamins A and C and the important phytochemicals.

There are two main types of muskmelon: cantaloupes and winter melons. Honeydews, casabas, and Crenshaws are winter melons. Watermelon is a different species and needs more heat and space, but its other growing requirements are quite similar.

Sow melon seeds in the garden after temperatures reach 70° to 80° F. To get a head start, sow seeds in a hotbed, a cold frame, or indoors three to four weeks before the outdoor planting date and transplant when seedlings have four leaves and/or tendrils.

Melon vines often reach 10 feet across. Semibush cultivars are smaller. Prepare planting hills 4 to 6 feet apart. Allow 6 to 12 feet between hills for large melons. Sow the seeds ½ inch deep, in hills (groups) of four to six, and thin to the best two or three seedlings.

Work 1 pound of 5-10-10 fertilizer into each 30 feet of row, and dig a spadeful of compost or dried manure into each hill. When the runners are 1 foot long, scratch a handful of fertilizer into the soil about 8 inches from each plant. When the first young melons set, side-dress once more.

Water new melon plants well, but avoid wetting the foliage. As melons mature, hold back on water to improve the flavor.

Choose disease-, wilt-, and mosaic-resistant strains. Do not plant melons where another variety of melon or member of the gourd or cucurbit group was the previous crop.

221

MUSKMELON DISEASE RESISTANCE

F   Fusarium race 1

PM Powdery mildew

'Jenny Lind' cantaloupe

MUSKMELON

The cantaloupe vines are the first to produce ripe fruit, usually in two to three months from seed. Most cultivars have netted, tan-colored rinds and most, but not all, are orange fleshed.

Casaba and Crenshaw melons mature after the honeydews in late summer. Some cultivars need 110 days to mature their fruit. The rind of the casaba is somewhat wrinkled and bright yellow-gold when mature. Its flesh is sweet, juicy, and white-green with hint of melon-pink in the flesh just below the seeds. The Crenshaw has salmon-pink flesh and a dark green rind that turns yellow at maturity.

GROWING MUSKMELON

Winter melons ripen in 80 to 95 days from seed. The rind of the honeydew is usually (but not always) creamy white and smooth. Most cultivars have sweet, soft, lime-green or green-white flesh, but some are orange fleshed.

Culture

See previous page.

Melons produce both male and female flowers. The stem of the female flower is slightly thickened below the ovary, which develops into the fruit. The petals of the male flowers drop off. Some growers pinch off the male flowers so that all the plant's strength goes into ripening the fruit.

Harvesting

Muskmelon flavor is at its best when the fruit is picked fully ripe. It is ripe for harvesting when the stem breaks cleanly when you lift the fruit. There are other signs, though none considered all that reliable: Sniff the end of an aromatic variety and, if it is ripe, there's a perfumed aroma, a hint of the flavor to come, especially in the delicious 'French Charentais' cantaloupes. Some cultivars become more heavily netted as they ripen. In others the color of the rind changes at maturity. Seed catalogs and packets usually explain the signs of maturity in each variety.

A whole ripe muskmelon keeps well for a few days in the crisper. Not-quite-ripe melon may be left a day or two at room temperature to ripen fully before being stored in the refrigerator. Before refrigerating a cut melon, seal it in plastic wrap or a vegetable bag.

Frozen melon retains its flavor, but the texture changes some. To freeze, remove the rind and cube the sweetest portions, or scoop out

melon balls and freeze them in a sealed container.

COOKING WITH MUSKMELON

The aroma and flavor of the various muskmelons are most delicious when the fruit is served at room temperature. In Europe a wedge of muskmelon is often served as a first course. Cantaloupe is sometimes flavored with a few grains of salt. In Italy cantaloupe is seasoned with fresh pepper or peeled and wrapped in a paper-thin slice of salty prosciutto. In America melon halves or wedges are often served as dessert, filled with vanilla or fruit-flavored ice cream or yogurt, or with sliced strawberries, raspberries, a dollop of mango chutney, or minced candied ginger or mint. Honeydews and the other winter melons are often flavored with a wedge of lime. As an alternative to mango, a firm, slightly underripe cantaloupe makes a fine chutney.

All the muskmelons combine well with other fruits and are delicious in fresh fruit salads.

Cantaloupe and Prosciutto Appetizer

    6 pitted ripe black olives
    6 toothpicks
    6 small diamonds red bell pepper
    1 large ripe cantaloupe
    6 paper-thin slices prosciutto
    Arugula *or* parsley, for garnish

Pierce each olive with a toothpick and then push the toothpick through a piece of red pepper. Slide them halfway up the toothpick. Halve and seed the melon and divide it into 6 slices. Cut off the rind. Wrap a slice of prosciutto around the middle of each melon slice, and fix the overlap with one of the toothpicks. Arrange on a plate and garnish with arugula or parsley.

Serves 6.

Casaba and Ginger

    1 medium-sized ripe casaba
    1 lemon, halved
    1 tablespoon granulated sugar
    6 large pieces candied ginger
    6 large sprigs fresh rosemary,
      for garnish

Halve and seed the melon. Divide each into 3 equal portions. Squeeze a few drops of lemon juice over the melon slices. Combine the sugar and the ginger in a food processor, or mince together by hand. Sprinkle the ginger and sugar over the melon slices and garnish with sprigs of rosemary. Serve at room temperature.

Serves 6.

SELECTED CULTIVARS

Cantaloupes

Minnesota Midget 60 days, compact vine, 4-inch fruit, needs only 3 feet of space, recommended for small gardens.

Extra Early Nutmeg 61 to 63 days, green-fleshed heirloom variety, very sweet, more cold tolerant than most.

Early Hanover 68 to 70 days, globe-shaped fruit, orange flesh, good home-garden variety.

Scoop Hybrid 11 68 to 70 days, salmon-colored flesh, fine aroma, lots of 5½- to 6-inch fruit, high disease resistance.

Sweet Granite 70 days, orange fleshed, 2 to 3½ pounds, succeeds in northern gardens.

Sweet Bush Hybrid 74 days, compact plant, 2 to 4 pounds, netted skins, aromatic, deep orange flesh.

Honey Girl Hybrid 75 days, 2-pound 'French Charentais' type, deep orange flesh, very fine flavor.

NUTRITIONAL ELEMENTS

Cantaloupe, 1 cup

Calories	57
Vitamin A	6,500 mg
Vitamin C	68 mg
Calcium	17 mg

Casaba, 1 cup

Calories	45
Vitamin A	46 mg
Vitamin C	27 mg
Calcium	9 mg

Small melons can be grown on a trellis to conserve space if the weight is supported. One method, shown here, is to use shelves. A sling of flexible fabric, such as old panty hose, tied to the trellis also works.

Savor 78 days, 'French Charentais' type, 2 to 2½ pounds, aromatic, orange flesh, very round, smooth gray-green rind, dark green seams.

Jenny Lind 80 days, highly recommended aromatic heirloom, 1 to 2 pounds, green flesh, 5-foot vines, can be grown on a strong trellis, recommended for cool climates.

Amber Nectar 82 days, 3 to 4 pounds, fine sweet flavor, salmon-colored flesh, netted rind turns golden when ripe, recommended for cooler regions.

Galia Perfume Melon 85 days, import from Israel; sweet, aromatic, honey green flesh; green-gold netted rind, 2 to 3 pounds, good keeper well.

Pulsar F1 85 to 90 days, flavorful, round, 6 pounds, orange flesh, heavily netted rind, disease resistant, tolerates low nighttime temperatures.

Ambrosia 86 days, extra-sweet hybrid, juicy salmon-colored flesh, small seed cavity. (PM)

Iroquois 88 days, 7 inches, sweet, deep orange flesh, heavily netted gray-green rind.

Banana Pink 94 days, up to 16 inches, salmon pink flesh, creamy yellow rind.

Honeydews

Early Dew F1 80 days, 2 to 2½ pounds, lime green flesh, recommended for northern gardens and short seasons. (F)

Casablanca Hybrid 85 days, oval, 4-pound Moroccan type, 6½ to 7½ inches, sweet, juicy, soft white flesh with hint of pink, dark green netting on rind, turns yellow-gold when ripe. (PM)

Venus Hybrid 88 days, 5 to 6 inches, light green, sweet, light netting over smooth rind.

Golden Honeydew 92 days, small honeydew, bright green flesh, keeps well.

Golden Crispy Hybrid 95 days, from Japan, small, oval, bright yellow fruit, 4 to 5 inches long, sweet white flesh, fine aroma.

Limelight Hybrid 96 days, big, luscious, up to 7½ pounds, with green flesh.

Morning Dew 96 days, hybrid, 10- to 12-pound fruit, unusually sweet flavor.

Casabas and Crenshaws

Marygold Casaba 80 to 85 days, vigorous vine, 3 to 4 pounds, white flesh, yellow rind brightens when ready to pick.

Casaba Oasis Hybrid 86 days, rounded, oval; light green to cream-colored flesh; smooth, creamy yellow rind when mature.

Sugarshaw 85 days, early Crenshaw, heart shaped, up to 14 pounds, very sweet, peach orange flesh, rind turns yellow at maturity, recommended for cool regions.

Early Hybrid Crenshaw 90 days, large, oval, up to 14 pounds, thick peach pink flesh, dark green rind ripens to yellowish green, matures early enough to be worth a try in cool regions.

Crenshaw 110 days, salmon pink flesh, dark green, turns yellow at maturity, famous for its distinctive aroma and flavor.

WATERMELON

Because they need more summer heat than cantaloupes, watermelons aren't grown successfully everywhere. But where nights are warm enough, they are a special treat in midsummer. They are native to North Africa, but have been cultivated all over the world for thousands of years.

GROWING WATERMELON

The familiar red watermelon, along with the newer yellow and white cultivars, thrives on heat and is most successful where summer nights are warm. You can grow the 25- to 30-pound sizes in the home garden, but try one of the modest icebox sizes. They taste just as good as the larger melons and some are seedless, a definite improvement.

Culture

See page 221. The large vining cultivars need 3 to 4 feet of space all around.

Harvesting

Knowing when to pick a watermelon is a challenge. Some growers claim that the melon is ripe when the little pig's-tail curl, where the fruit is attached to the vine, turns brown and dries up; but in some cultivars it dries up 7 to 10 days before the fruit is fully ripe. The surest sign of ripeness in most

NUTRITIONAL ELEMENTS
Watermelon, 1 cup

Calories	50
Vitamin A	1,200 mg
Vitamin C	15 mg
Calcium	13 mg

'Sugar Baby' watermelon

'Moon and Stars' watermelon

Ripe sweet melon freezes well: Remove the rind and cube the sweetest portions, or scoop out melon balls and freeze them in a sealed container.

COOKING WITH WATERMELON

Watermelon is a sweet, crisp, refreshing summertime treat, the perfect end to a clam bake, a corn roast, or a picnic. It is easy to grow the little, round icebox watermelons with their tiny seeds and sweet flesh, so delicious chilled and sliced. Watermelons grow in an array of colors: There are reds, yellows, and some cultivars that are almost white.

Peel, seed, and chill chunks of watermelon for a delicious first course. Try some surprising combinations: with pungent greens, especially arugula; with cold white fish sauced with a vinaigrette; in chicken salad spiked with shallots and raspberry vinegar. Sprinkle a little sugar over cubes of watermelon and place in the freezer. After an hour or two, whirl it quickly in a processor and enjoy a wonderfully refreshing sorbet.

If you have time and plenty of watermelon, pickle the rind.

Watermelon Cocktail
    5 cups watermelon balls
    1 cup seedless green grapes, halved
    1 cup freshly squeezed orange juice
    1 teaspoon granulated sugar
    1 tablespoon chopped mint

Combine the melon balls and the grape halves with the orange juice, cover, and chill. Serve in dessert cups, sprinkled with sugar and garnished with chopped mint.
    Serves 6.

cultivars is the color of the rind on the underside. As the melon matures, the rind on the ground turns from pale tan to yellow or rich gold. Also, the rind of ripe watermelons becomes dull.

A whole ripe melon keeps in the refrigerator about one week. Leave a not-quite-ripe watermelon to ripen a day or two at room temperature before storing in the refrigerator. Seal cut melon in plastic wrap or a vegetable bag before refrigerating.

SELECTED CULTIVARS

Sugar Baby 68 to 86 days, small, round, 7 to 8 inches, 8 to 12 pounds, medium red, sweet, small seeds, green rind turns almost black when ripe.

Northern Sweet 68 to 75 days, nearly round, red-orange flesh, dark green rind, recommended for shorter growing seasons.

Golden Crown 70 days, 4 to 5 pounds, sweet red-pink flesh, small dark brown seeds, pale green rind turns to bright golden yellow when mature, recommended for the Northeast and Midwest, All-America Selection.

Yellow Doll F1 78 days, round, 6 to 7 inches, yellow flesh, rind light green with dark green stripes, smaller than average vines.

Bush Baby II Hybrid 80 days, round, 10 pounds, bright red flesh, dwarf bushes suitable for the small garden.

New Orchid F1 80 days, sweet, bright orange flesh, medium sized, dark green skin striped with lighter green.

Sugar Bush 80 days, 6 to 8 pounds, scarlet flesh, medium-green rind, darker veining, ideal for small garden, 3- to 3½-foot-long vines need only 6 square feet.

Yellow Baby 80 days, 9 to 12 pounds, sweet, yellow-fleshed version of 'Sugar Baby', almost seedless.

Crimson Sweet 80 to 97 days, 15 to 25 pounds, very sweet, dark red flesh, rind striped with dark green, semiearly variety suited only to warm regions.

Moon and Stars 85 days, heirloom, 10 to 15 pounds, sweet pink-red flesh, dark green rind, leaves spotted yellow.

Black Diamond 90 days, round, very large, green rind, flavorful red flesh.

Carolina Cross 100 days, giant, grows to 200 pounds if summer is hot and long, exhibition melon.

'Carolina Cross' watermelons at a competition

BEANS, PEAS, AND OTHER LEGUMES

Pole beans can grow to 8 feet high. Train them up poles arranged in teepee fashion, as here, or vertically. Use rough poles—the beans climb by wrapping around the poles, and can slip down smooth poles and end up in a heap at the bottom.

Legumes are delicious and easy to grow, but to harvest substantial quantities you must give each variety a full garden row and plant crops in succession.

Nutritionally, legumes are important sources of protein, amino acids, and fiber, and a good substitute for starchy vegetables. The nutrients in shell beans are credited with dramatically lowering cholesterol. They are a rich natural source of the B complex vitamins, calcium, iron, and other minerals.

Peas are the early crop. Plant as soon as the ground can be worked, and they start maturing 8 to 10 weeks later. When heat comes, the season is over.

Snap beans, also known as green beans or string beans, are a summer crop. Sown after the soil has warmed, they mature seven to eight weeks later and continue producing for four weeks. They are the young pods of bean plants.

Shell beans are the mature seeds of cultivars bred for shelling. Sow the seeds a little later than snap beans, and they begin to produce late in the season.

Legumes have an unusual characteristic. Soil bacteria natural to the roots of legumes extract nitrogen from the air, making it available to the plant. To enhance the harvest, dust with pea and bean inoculant just before sowing bean or pea seeds. The inoculant contains the dormant bacteria and is available in most places where pea and bean seeds are sold.

Beans and peas need little extra fertilizing. Hoe around the plants to chop off weeds and let in air.

Buy disease-resistant cultivars, and stay out of the garden when the foliage is wet to avoid spreading diseases.

SNAP BEANS

Bush cultivars of snap beans are less demanding than pole cultivars. Pole cultivars are a little different in their requirements: They take more heat and drought than the bush varieties.

GROWING SNAP BEANS

Planted in midspring, with warm weather bush cultivars are ready for harvest in about 50 to 60 days. Individual plants produce for three to four weeks. A succession of plantings every two weeks provides the family with beans all summer.

Plant pole cultivars after the weather warms and provide strings for them to climb on. They begin to produce in about two months and continue for another two months, so only one sowing is necessary.

Culture

Sow bean seeds 1 inch deep (1½ inches in sandy soil), four to six seeds per foot. Thin the seedlings of standard bush beans to stand 3 to 4 inches apart; allow an inch or so more space for the cultivars with flat pods.

Plant pole beans in hills, four to five seeds per group, 2 to 3 feet apart. Support for most cultivars should be about 6 feet high, but not so high that it makes harvesting difficult. Eight to 10 hills supplies the average family.

Harvesting

Pick pods of snap beans, wax or golden beans, and purple beans before the beans inside get big. This means snap beans at 4 or so inches, wax beans at 5 to 6 inches, and purple beans at 6 inches.

After rain or overhead watering, wait until the plants dry out before weeding or harvesting. When they are in full production, snap beans need to be picked clean of maturing beans every day or two to keep the plants producing.

Before cooking, snap off the pointed tips and the stem ends. If the beans are thicker than a pencil, French-cut them (slice from top to bottom through the center, not the seam). Catalogs and kitchen shops sell tools that make this quick and easy.

Beans are best when just picked, but stored in a vegetable bag in the crisper they stay fresh for at least a week. When frost threatens the bean crop, pick all the beans, sort them into batches of similar sizes, steam-blanch, and freeze.

'Blue Lake Bush' beans

COOKING WITH SNAP BEANS

When you break off the end of a mature bean pod, a "string" pulls free along the seam. Modern cultivars have a minimum of string and retain their snap for many days. They're called snap beans because you know they are fresh if they snap in two when you bend them. Beans harvested early do not snap—they bend.

Once you've tasted baby beans—beans picked when they are 4 to 5 inches long—you will not have trouble remembering to keep the plants picked. Baby beans are a genuine taste treat.

Pick standard cultivars when they are 5½ to 6 inches long, round, dark green, and tender. Beans thicker than a pencil are best French-cut before cooking.

Classic toppings for cooked snap beans are sautéed almond slivers, sautéed mushrooms, and minced fresh parsley. Cut up snap beans and stir-fry them with a little sausage meat and onion. They are a delicious accompaniment to grilled meats and fish, and combine well with other vegetables. Small red potatoes steamed with cut snap beans and a few slivers of onion is delicious.

There are many cultivars of snap beans. French "filet" cultivars produce slender beans ⅛ to ¼ inch thick and 6 to 7 inches long. These are as delicious as the tiniest standard snap beans. It takes a lot of beans to make a serving, but the flavor is fabulous.

Snap beans come in a variety of colors. Golden wax beans are sweet and mealy and taste great simmered in milk and seasoned with a pinch of nutmeg. Purple and purple-striped beans turn green when cooked but are colorful used raw in salads. Use them in recipes in place of green or wax beans.

Broad, flat, green snap beans, called Italian beans, have a distinctive flavor. Prepare and serve them like regular snap beans, but cook a few minutes longer and include their rudimentary seeds.

'Kentucky Wonder' is the best known of the superlong snap beans. These grow to 9 inches and retain their tenderness and flavor. Use in hors d'oeuvres and crudité platters and in recipes calling for string beans.

Snap Beans With Dill and Butter

1 to 2 cups water
½ teaspoon salt
1 large sprig fresh dill *or* ½ teaspoon dried dill weed or seed
4 cups 4- to 5-inch snap beans, stemmed
2 tablespoons butter

Pour the water into a saucepan and fit the pan with a steamer insert. Bring the water to a boil over high heat. Place the beans in the steamer and sprinkle with salt and dill. Cover and steam until they are just tender (8 to 10 minutes), depending on the age and thickness of the beans. Place the beans in a heated bowl, add the butter, and stir gently until it is melted.
Serves 4.

Sautéed Spinach and Wax Beans

1 tablespoon plus 1 teaspoon butter
½ cup chicken broth
1 pound wax beans, cut diagonally in 2-inch pieces
1½ cups fresh spinach leaves
1 tablespoon chopped parsley
Generous pinch cayenne pepper
¼ teaspoon grated nutmeg
Salt and freshly ground pepper, to taste

Melt the tablespoon of butter in a saucepan over medium heat. Add the broth and bring to a boil. Add

NUTRITIONAL ELEMENTS

Snap beans, cooked, ½ cup

Calories	15
Vitamin A	325 mg
Vitamin C	7 mg
Calcium	31 mg

Wax beans, cooked, ½ cup

Calories	22
Vitamin C	13 mg
Calcium	50 mg

the beans, cover, and cook until they are barely tender (about 8 minutes). Uncover and continue cooking until the liquid is reduced by half.

Add the spinach and parsley to the beans and cook, tossing constantly to wilt the spinach (about 3 minutes). If the mixture seems very juicy, continue to cook until it is fairly dry. Stir in the 1 teaspoon of butter, the cayenne, nutmeg, and salt and pepper to taste.

Serves 4.

SELECTED CULTIVARS

Bush Snap Beans

Earliserve 48 days, early, high-quality flavor.

Contender 49 days, slim dark green, resistant to disease and tolerant of adverse weather.

Tenderpod 50 days, thick, cylindrical deep green, All-America Selection.

Provider 50 days, 5 to 5½ inches, compact plants, recommended for the cold North.

Green Crop 51 days, long lasting, flat, dark green, 'Kentucky Wonder' type, All-America Selection.

Topcrop 52 days, slender, medium green, reliable favorite, high yield, All-America Selection.

Roma II (Bush Romano) 53 days, flat Italian type, green, bush form of pole 'Romano'.

Jumbo 55 days, flat Italian type, extra-long, related to 'Romano' and 'Kentucky Wonder'.

Blue Lake Bush 57 days, 6 inches, mature simultaneously, great for canning and freezing.

Left: 'Royal Burgundy' beans
Right: 'Romano' pole beans

Jade 60 days, round, straight, excellent flavor.

Dwarf Bees 65 days, scarlet runner type, attractive scarlet blossoms, long, flat multipurpose; use fresh, shelled, or dried; produces all summer until frost.

Bush Wax Beans

Burpee's Brittle Wax 52 days, 7 inch, golden, high yield.

Goldcrop 54 days, shiny, yellow, easy to pick, very resistant to diseases, All-America Selection.

Dorabel 57 to 60 days, French, slender, fleshy, bright yellow, recommended for flavor.

Wax Romano 59 days, flat Italian type, broad.

Dragon's Tongue 57 days, Dutch, long, flat, creamy yellow with thin purple stripes, excellent flavor, prolific.

Purple Snap Beans

Royal Burgundy 51 days, round, 6-inch pods in clusters, yields well even under cool conditions, produces an abundance of lavender flowers.

Sequoia 60 days, flat Italian type, beautiful, 4 to 5 inches, stringless, prolific, purple skins turn bright green when cooked, good short-season variety.

French Filet Beans

Decibel 58 to 60 days, very narrow, 7 and 8 inches, excellent flavor.

Fin des Bagnols 45 to 55 days, heirloom, good green color, exceptional flavor.

Maxibel 50 days, long, slender, firm texture, good flavor.

Pole Snap Beans

Blue Lake 60 days, medium-green pods, white beans, good shelled, high yield, extended harvest.

Kentucky Blue 60 days, round, straight, very productive, recommended for the small garden, All-America Selection.

Romano (Italian Pole Bean) 60 days, wide, flat, excellent distinctive flavor.

Kentucky Wonder 65 days, thick, oval, 9 inches, use as fresh snap beans or shell for drying, most widely grown pole bean for home gardens.

Pole Wax Bean

Goldmarie 45 days, flat Italian type, 8 to 10 inches, golden.

'Goldmarie' pole wax bean

SHELL BEANS

There are dozens of cultivars of shelling beans and they vary in the length of time needed to produce a crop. Sow fava beans as soon as you can work the soil in the spring, and sow all other shell beans after the soil warms. The length of the growing season determines which cultivars you can try.

Cowpeas Also known as black-eyed peas and southern peas, botanically, they are beans; they are planted and cultivated like shell beans. Use young pods like snap beans, and cook the shelled peas fresh or dry them for later use.

Fava Beans The broad fava beans develop blocky seeds rather like lima beans. Frost tolerant, they offer gardeners limited by high altitudes or short growing seasons the opportunity to harvest shell beans. Picked when the seeds are pea-sized or smaller, they can be used as snap beans, but they are usually grown to maturity and used as shell beans. For fresh shell beans, pick the pods just as they begin to plump out. For dry beans, harvest broad beans just as the pods turn dark.

Chickpeas Also known as garbanzo beans or grams, these round, nutty little legumes develop in pods. They thrive in hot, dry climates. Harvest the short, chunky pods when young and use fresh as snap beans, or allow to mature and shell for fresh use or for drying. Harvest them when the pods begin to split.

Lima Beans Limas have a nutty flavor and buttery texture, whether fresh shelled or dried. They are not easy to shell, but if you press firmly on the pod seam with your thumb, the beans usually pop out. There are small- and large-seeded cultivars. The small-seeded cultivars are called baby limas or butter beans; all baby limas are bush beans. Large limas are available in bush and pole types. Harvest lima beans as soon as the pods are well filled but while still bright and fresh in appearance.

Scarlet Runner Bean For the gardener experimenting with shell beans for the first time, one of the most appealing is the gorgeous scarlet runner bean. The plants bear clusters of beautiful, big red flowers followed by large beans. Harvest the beans young and use as snap beans, or harvest later and use as shell beans. For drying, harvest the beans even later still. The large black-and-red beans inside are strong flavored. In the Southwest, the shell beans are used in chili recipes. If you have room only for one bean, try this. It flourishes even in a container.

Scarlet runner beans

Yard-Long/Asparagus Beans

These plants are very productive and tasty. Harvest pods young before they change color and use as snap beans, or allow the pods to mature and harvest for fresh or dried beans.

GROWING SHELL BEANS

Cowpeas require 65 to 80 days to mature from seed.

Fava beans are picked 85 to 90 days after sowing the seeds.

Chickpeas require 105 days to mature from seed. The bush-type plants are 1 to 2 feet high and require a long growing season.

Lima beans are ready in 60 to 70 days from seed; lima pole types are ready in 85 to 90 days from seed. Lima beans grow in the same way as snap beans except they are spaced 8 inches apart and need a longer, hotter growing season. Very hot days sometimes interfere with production.

Scarlet runner beans are ready in 60 to 70 days from seed. The plant grows rapidly to 10, sometimes 20 feet, a dense yet delicate vine with pods 6 to 12 inches long. Culture is the same as for snap beans, but give scarlet runners more space.

Yard-long or asparagus beans are ready in 65 to 60 days from seed. Their unusual length, 15 to 20 inches, makes them fascinating to grow. The pods look like very long snap beans, but the plant actually is a vining variety of the cowpea. It is a vigorous climber that must be trained to a wire or trellis.

Culture

With the exception of fava beans, plant shell beans after the soil warms. Sow the seeds ½ to 1 inch deep, five to eight seeds per foot of row. Thin to 3 to 4 inches apart. To encourage productivity, apply a side dressing of 5–10–10 fertilizer (1 pound per 33 feet of row) after the plants are up.

To grow fava beans in cool regions, plant in spring after the last frost. In mild-winter areas, plant in the fall for a spring crop. The plants grow 3 to 5 feet high, and most cultivars benefit from a support.

Harvesting

Harvest shell beans for use as snap beans anytime before the pods start to swell. Harvest shell beans for use as fresh shell beans when the outline of mature beans forms inside the pod. Harvest for drying when the beans separate from the pods and the pods start to split.

Fresh-shelled shell beans sealed in a vegetable bag and stored in the crisper stay tender for several days to a week. Steam-blanched and then frozen, fresh shell beans retain their flavor.

To dry shell beans, spread them in a single layer over a screen and leave them in a hot, dry place for a week or two, until they are completely dry.

COOKING WITH SHELL BEANS

Young shell beans look like snap beans. When very young most cultivars, including scarlet runner beans and yard-long or asparagus beans, can be harvested and used in the same ways as snap beans. The main crop is the bean seed that swells in the pod as the season advances. Shelled, the beans can be used fresh or they can be dried and stored in an air-tight container.

Nutritionally, beans are a bonanza. They include important B complex vitamins, calcium, iron, protein, carbohydrates, and fiber. They are a valuable substitute for starches, and vegetarian cooks combine beans with grains to form high-protein meat substitutes.

NUTRITIONAL ELEMENTS
Shell beans, cooked, ½ cup
Calories — 95
Calcium — 50 mg

Simmer fresh shell beans until tender (about 20 to 45 minutes) and season with spices from cumin to exotic mixtures such as *Garam Masala* (see page 153). Beans are excellent flavored with ham, salt pork or bacon, or the drippings from lamb or beef.

Dried beans must be soaked then simmered until tender, a matter of several hours. Dried beans are included in soups and stews all over the world. They are fundamental to Mexican and Latin American cuisines. Italians combine small white shell beans with sausages and pasta. The French cook them with lots of garlic. Chilled and marinated in a spicy sauce, shell beans such as chickpeas and dark red beans are excellent in salads and hors d'oeuvres. They are also delicious mashed with butter or served like fresh shell beans and limas in the drippings from a savory roast.

'King of the Garden' lima beans

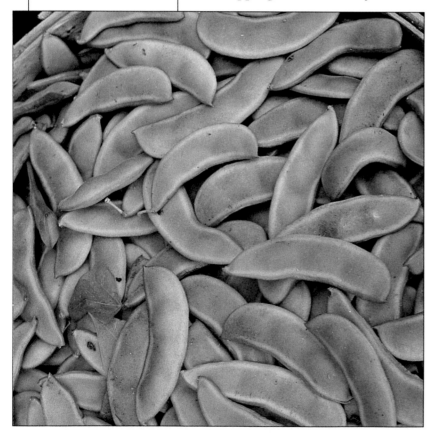

Many colorful shell bean varieties have given rise to some famous dishes. The 'Black Turtle' cultivar is used in black bean soup and in many Caribbean and Central and South American recipes. Pinto beans are the basis of Mexican *frijoles refritos.* Red kidney beans are used in chili. Lima beans combined with corn make succotash, a classic Southern dish. Cooks in the Middle East make hummus, an appetizer of chickpeas, garlic, lemon juice, and sesame paste. Native Americans used many colorful cultivars now classed as heirlooms and available only from specific suppliers.

Four Bean Salad

¼ cup olive oil
¼ cup raspberry vinegar
1 teaspoon brown sugar
½ teaspoon salt
1 large clove garlic
1 cup each of lima beans, dark red kidney beans, chickpeas, and pink *or* pinto beans, cooked, chilled (4 cups total)
½ red onion, sliced in very thin rounds
½ cup minced fresh parsley
1 head romaine, pale inner portion *or* 1 small Boston lettuce

In a blender or food processor, blend the oil, vinegar, brown sugar, salt, and garlic to make a vinaigrette. Combine the beans, onion, and parsley in a large salad bowl and toss with the vinaigrette. Tear the lettuce into bite-sized pieces and cover the beans with it. Cover and chill for at least 1 hour. Before serving, toss the beans with the lettuce.
Serves 4 to 6.

SELECTED CULTIVARS

Cowpeas

Pinkeye Purple Hull 78 days, most popular cowpea, young peas are white with a small pink eye.

Favas and Broad Beans

Jumbo (Nintoku Giant) 70 days, short fat pods, very large seeds, high yield.

Windsor 75 days, flat, meaty beans, long pods, 2- to 3-foot plants.

Long Podded Fava 83 to 90 days, English broad bean, 7-inch pods containing five or six big beans.

Chickpeas

Black Kabouli 100 days, black-seeded pods, 2-foot plant, withstands extreme drought.

Lima Beans

Henderson Bush 65 days, small-seeded variety, white beans.

Jackson Wonder 65 days, small-seeded, bush variety, beige beans marked in purple, extremely heat and drought tolerant.

Florida Butter (Calico) 90 days, beige beans splashed with purple, recommended for Florida and very hot regions.

King of the Garden 88 days, good climber, large, flat beans, four to five seeds per pod.

Prize Taker 90 days, largest pole lima bean.

Scarlet Runner Beans

Scarlet Emperor 75 to 120 days, heirloom, used ceremonially in the Southwest and Mexico; fat, slightly fuzzy pods, scarlet flowers, green beans with seeds mottled black and purple, used to make bean jewelry.

Red Knight 70 days, showy scarlet flowers, big 10- to 12-inch pods, 8- to 12-foot vines, handsome screening for the home garden.

Yard-Long/Asparagus Beans

Orient Wonder 60 days, early asparagus bean, 15- to 20-inch pods, deep green, stringless, sweet, 9- to 12-foot vines, very productive.

Asparagus Bean Yard-long, 50 days, very long pods, flavor best when picked under 18 inches, needs strong support.

Colorful Shell Beans and Peas

Flageolet Chevrier Vert 75 days, French heirloom, used to make cassoulet, compact 14-inch bushes, bears prolifically.

California Blackeye 75 days, large, smooth-skinned, flavorful shelling peas, white with black spots, vigorous vine.

Pinto U 111 85 to 91 days, beans have deep pink speckles on a tall vining plant.

Black Turtle (Midnight) 104 days, small black bean, tall plants.

GARDEN PEAS

Called "English peas" in produce markets and "garden peas" elsewhere to distinguish them from edible-pod peas, snap peas, cowpeas, and the other "peas," this vegetable is the real "pea." The seed is soft and sweet, but the pod is tough and inedible. They are a popular crop with children, who love to hunt for ripe peas among the vines and eat them raw.

GROWING GARDEN PEAS

The various pea cultivars mature crops in 65 to 85 days. There are extra-early, early, midseason, and late peas. In cool regions the planting holes for garden peas are often

NUTRITIONAL ELEMENTS

Peas, cooked, ⅔ cup

Calories	71
Vitamin A	540 mg
Vitamin C	20 mg
Calcium	23 mg

'Super Sugar Mel' snap peas

dug in the fall in a sunny, protected spot and supplied with a shovelful of sand to lighten the soil and help it to warm early. This allows the gardener to sow seeds in late winter or early spring, even before the soil has lost its chill.

Sow a succession of cultivars from late winter to midspring to provide harvests from spring through early summer. Peas stop producing when the temperature exceeds 70° F. Late in the season, a little shade helps. In warm regions sow peas in fall, winter, and very early spring.

Culture

Sow the seeds 2 inches deep. See also page 229.

The low-growing bush cultivars do not require staking and are the easiest to handle. Plant them in rows 18 to 24 inches apart. The climbers are more productive but must be trained on chicken wire or a string or trellis. The most effi-

cient support is chicken wire strung between two rows of peas. The lazy way is to train pea vines over branches pruned from nearby brambles and trees.

Harvesting

Garden peas are sweetest picked just as the pods swell and round out but before the peas make a hard, bumpy outline on the pod. Harvest sugar peas and sugar snap peas just as the seeds begin to form but while the pod is still flat.

To shell peas, turn the pod upside down so the rounded tip is uppermost in your hand and press the rounded tip: The pod will break open along the seam. Turn the pod in your hand and run your thumb down it to pop the peas loose.

To prepare sugar peas and sugar snap peas, snap off the tip of both ends and discard the string (if there is one).

Immediately seal just-picked peas in a vegetable bag and store in the crisper. Do not shell them until shortly before cooking time.

Steam-blanched and then frozen, the various peas retain much of their flavor but lose their texture.

COOKING WITH GARDEN PEAS

Called *petits pois* in France, English peas in the South, and just plain garden peas everywhere else, this is the first shell bean crop of the year. The flavor is incomparable when the peas are picked very young. Shelled, they are used raw for garnish and in salads. Cooked, they are excellent with fish and meats. They are also delicious braised in a little water until just tender and then flavored with a dash of brown sugar and a dab of butter. Peas and pearl onions, peas and celery, and peas and carrots are classic combinations.

Closely related but quite different are sugar peas, also known as snow peas. These are short, wide, flat pea pods harvested when the peas inside are very immature. The sweet, crisp pods are a staple of Asian cuisines, delicious stir-fried and seasoned with soy sauce. Raw and chopped, they add crisp texture and flavor to salads; steamed briefly, they are a delicious, colorful ingredient in vegetable platters.

A close relative of the sugar pea is the chunky sugar snap pea, sometimes just called the snap pea. These are remarkably sweet when picked about 2½ inches long. They can be steamed or used in stir-fries, but they taste best fresh—as part of an hors d'oeuvres plate, with crudités, and in salads.

Peas With Lettuce and Mint

2 tablespoons butter
¼ cup water
4 cups shelled young peas
1 thin slice small onion
1 teaspoon brown sugar
¼ teaspoon salt
Freshly ground pepper, to taste
1 tablespoon minced fresh mint
1 Boston lettuce, rinsed, separated into leaves

In a heavy saucepan over medium heat, melt the butter. Add water and bring to a boil. Add the peas and onion slice, and season with sugar, salt, pepper, and mint. Cover with lettuce leaves. Cover the saucepan, reduce the heat, and simmer until the peas are tender and no water remains (about 4 minutes). Serve hot, including some lettuce with each portion.
Serves 6.

SELECTED CULTIVARS

Garden Peas

Knight 56 days, 24-inch vine, 4-inch pods, high disease resistance.

Alaska 56 days, 3-foot vine, needs support, one of the earliest, popular, hardy, prolific, lower in sugar than many, good for canning, bears 2½-inch pods with six to eight peas.

Little Marvel 63 days, early 18 inch vine, needs no staking, very sweet 3-inch pods with eight peas.

Montana Marvel 64 days, 18-inch vine, adapted to cool climates, 3½-inch pods with eight to nine peas.

Green Arrow 66 days, 30-inch vine, longtime favorite, productive, dwarf shelling pea.

Wando 67 days, 30-inch plant, very heat and cold tolerant, good variety for planting late, 3-inch pods with seven to eight peas.

Sugar Peas/Snow Peas

Dwarf Gray Sugar 63 days, 2½-foot vine, may not need staking, light green pods to 3 inches long.

Oregon Sugar Pod II 68 days, productive 2-foot vine, 4-inch pods, usually two per cluster, resistant to virus, wilt, and powdery mildew.

Chinese Snow 65 days, 9-foot vine with purple flowers, sweet, flat, crunchy pods.

Sugar Snap Peas

Sugar Bon 56 days, compact 2-foot vine, sweet 3-inch pods, resistant to powdery mildew.

Sugar Ann 56 days, extra early, 18- to 30-inch vine, needs no staking.

Super Sugar Mel 68 days, high-yielding 3-foot vine, 4-inch pods.

Sugar Snap 70 days, vigorous 6-foot vine, crunchy 3-inch pods, wilt resistant, All-America Selection.

Sugar Daddy 74 days, compact 2½-foot vine, crispy, stringless pods.

ROOT CROPS, PEANUTS, AND POTATOES

Root crops include most of the starchy vegetables, those that make the backbones of our meals. They provide a wealth of nutrition along with the starch, and their starch is in a complex form, which digests slowly and is considered the best source of energy.

If you like to store lots of vegetables for winter, grow root crops. Plain and simple beets, carrots, parsnips, potatoes, sweet potatoes, turnips, and their yellow cousins the rutabagas have a lot to offer. Of course, they are very good fresh. Beets, turnips, and rutabagas provide delicious, vitamin-rich greens and calcium. Eating a raw carrot from the garden row is a real treat. Baby potatoes and the silky, colorful fingerling potato cultivars are as delightful to the palate as to the eye. Peanuts are legumes, not root crops, but they mature underground and are therefore included with this group.

Root crops require a garden row and are generally grown from seeds planted spring or fall, or both. They do best in light or sandy soil with lots of organic matter. Apply a low-nitrogen fertilizer (such as 5–10–10) at the rate of about 3 pounds per 30-foot row.

A root crop needs weeding early and often. Vegetable seedlings are easy to distinguish from weed seedlings, but because they germinate so close together weeds must be pulled by hand.

Harvest root crops growing in light soil by pulling or digging them up. In heavy clay soil they must be dug. Potatoes and peanuts are always dug, never pulled.

The root vegetables keep well for several months layered in damp sand at temperatures of 33° to 40° F. Sealed in vegetable bags and stored in the crisper, they stay firm for at least a week, often longer. Remove the greens before storing root crops.

BEETS

This sweetest and most colorful of the root crops originated in the Mediterranean region in classical times, but as a leafy vegetable rather than a root crop. Large-rooted varieties didn't become popular until the 1800s. Red varieties "bleed" into other foods, dyeing them red. If you prefer not to have a red stew but want to include beets, select a white or yellow variety.

GROWING BEETS

Beets are low-growing leafy plants with round or elongated roots. They grow during the cool seasons and are out of the garden row in about two months.

Two beet crops are possible. Sow seeds for the spring crop as soon as the soil has lost its winter chill and harvest before the weather warms. (Left in the ground, beets become large and woody.) In temperate regions sow a second beet crop in mid-July and harvest when the weather cools in early autumn. Farther south, plant the second crop in August; in Florida, plant in late September. In Zones 9 and 10, beets can overwinter in the ground but must be harvested by March; once they start to flower, they become fibrous.

A beet seed is actually a fruit containing clusters of seeds—so beet seeds germinate in clumps. To allow each beet root the space it

'Detroit Dark Red' beets

needs to develop well, it is essential to thin the seedlings. Seed cultivars advertised as "monogerm" (single seeded) germinate an individual beet rather than a clump. Plant these more sparsely and don't thin.

Provide deeply dug, well-drained soil and work lots of compost or dried manure into the row.

Culture

As soon as the soil begins to warm, sow the seeds ½ inch deep and cover loosely with soil. When the seedlings are 1 to 2 inches high, weed diligently. Thin to 2 to 4 inches apart and mulch lightly.

Harvesting

Beet thinnings and the young side leaves are excellent in spring salads. You can take as much as one third of a beet plant's leaves without harming the root crop. Beet roots are at their best when harvested at 2 to 3 inches around.

Before storing beets, cut off the greens, leaving just an inch or two. Save the greens. Rinse the roots and leaves in several changes of water until there is no sand left in the sink after the water drains. Drain and then store leaves and roots in separate vegetable bags, because the leaves deteriorate before the roots. The roots keep two to three weeks in the crisper.

COOKING WITH BEETS

When you grow your own beets, you get two vegetables in one: the beet and its leaves. Steamed briefly, beet greens are sometimes preferable to spinach. Fresh young beets have a rich, earthy flavor and they are as sweet as fresh corn on the cob. The color is magnificent—a deep ruby red that brightens the dinner plate and excites the appetite. Hot beets and cold pickled beets are delicious with flavorful meats—steaks, grilled pork chops, and roast turkey. Cook, chill, dice, and toss with minced parsley, garlic, and olive oil for an elegant appetizer to serve with crusty bread. They are also tasty in salads. Simmer with beef broth and spike with sugar and white vinegar to make borscht. Boiled until tender, then skinned, beets can be served in many ways: whole or sliced with a little salt; chopped and topped with sour cream; or diced and dressed with fresh dill in a vinaigrette.

The red beet's brilliant color is both an asset and a drawback. It tends to leave a pink stain on white utensils and it colors ingredients next to it in a salad. If you leave an inch or two of the leaf stems on

'Chioggia' beets

NUTRITIONAL ELEMENTS

Beets, cooked, ½ cup

Calories	27
Vitamin C	5 mg
Calcium	12 mg

Beet greens, cooked, ½ cup

Calories	18
Vitamin A	5,100 mg
Vitamin C	30 mg
Calcium	99 mg

'Burpee's Goldenbeet' beets

beets when cooking them whole, the color won't bleed. There are golden and cream white beets with fair flavor, and these do not bleed.

Steamed Crispy Beets

    4 medium beets
    Olive oil
    Garlic salt
    4 teaspoons butter
    1 tablespoon minced fresh
      parsley

Cut the beet leaves off at the top of the beet and reserve them to cook as greens. Peel the beets, rinse in cold running water, and slice them in half. Arrange the halves on a steam rack, brush with olive oil, and sprinkle with garlic salt. Cover and steam for 20 minutes. Serve hot, with butter and parsley.
    Serves 4.

SELECTED CULTIVARS

Red Ace 53 days, globe-shaped hybrid, smooth dark red flesh.

Chioggia 55 days, attractive, rings of pink and white inside, appealing flavor.

Burpee's Goldenbeet 55 days, sweet, golden yellow, fine flavor, excellent greens.

Crosby's Egyptian 56 days, flattened globe-shaped root, glossy and delicious greens, sweet smooth flavor.

Albina Vereduna 58 days, large, very sweet white flesh.

Green Top Bunching 58 days, round, blood red, delicious bright green foliage.

Detroit Dark Red 60 days, dark rich color, neat globe shape, some strains resistant to downy mildew.

Lutz Green Leaf (Winter Keeper) 80 days, large, shaped like a top, dark red flesh with lighter zones, delicious glossy green foliage has pink midribs, good choice for fall crop and for storing.

CARROTS

Carrots are available in several forms. The most popular are the long, tapered 'Imperator' types; the shorter, chunkier 'Danvers' varieties; the still shorter and blunt-ended 'Nantes'; the shorter yet and both tapered and ball 'Chantenay'; and the ball types, the shortest of all standard carrots. The miniature, or fingerling, carrots mature at only 3 to 4 inches and are charming but considered difficult to grow.

Carrots are classed by length because success with them has everything to do with the quality and depth of the soil. They need loose, light soil, deeply dug and well stocked with organic matter. A raised bed is ideal. Cultivars that develop long tapered roots need loose, sandy soil worked to a depth of 6 to 10 inches with lots of organic matter. If the soil is heavy or rough, shorter carrots are a better choice. In less-than-ideal conditions, the little ball-shaped 'Planet' types are the easiest. They do well in a cold frame or container.

GROWING CARROTS

A row of just-germinated carrots is often full of fresh-sprouted weeds. You must hand-pick the weeds without disturbing the tiny carrot ferns or they will drown in weeds.

In the North, sow carrot seeds three weeks before the last expected frost. Carrot seeds take one to three weeks to germinate. A succession of sowings every two to three weeks produces carrots all season long. The harvest of young carrots begins about two months after sowing, and the crops mature in 70 to 90 days. Where fall is long and mild, plant a second crop in late summer and harvest until the ground freezes. In the Southwest, plant carrots February through August and harvest almost all year long.

Planting carrots in soil with fresh manure may result in hairy, split, or forked roots. Manure should be aged for a month or two in the soil. Just before sowing carrot seeds, rake the bed smooth and remove all rocks, even small ones.

Culture

Sow about four seeds per inch over a broad bed. Cover with ½ inch of vermiculite rather than soil. This improves germination and marks the row. Maintain the soil moisture through germination and early growth and keep the bed weed free.

When the carrot greens are 2 inches high, thin them to 2 to 3 inches apart. Cover the soil around the tops with a light mulch to keep out weeds.

Harvesting

When carrots reach pulling size, the orange shoulder usually pushes up through the soil. To harvest, grasp the foliage near the top of the root and tug gently. If the bed is dry, moisten it first to make pulling easier. If the carrots are still hard to pull, use a spading fork to gently loosen the surrounding soil.

Remove the greens and rinse the carrots thoroughly before using.

Young carrots keep for two weeks or longer sealed in a vegetable bag in the crisper. To keep winter carrots, remove the tops and layer the roots in damp sand or peat in a cool place.

'Imperator' carrots

**'Thumbelina'
carrots**

COOKING WITH CARROTS

If carrots had no virtue other than their sunny color, they would still be welcome at the table. But they have much more to offer: They are high in beta carotene, which is a precursor of vitamin A, and in vitamins B, C, D, E, and K. Carrots are delicious raw and crispy cold as an appetizer and in salads, or cooked in orange juice. They are also delicious cooked Chinese style—roll cut, stir-fried, and seasoned with a hint of sugar and soy sauce.

There is not a great difference in flavor among carrot cultivars, but the flavor does vary according to the season: Spring carrots have a fresh, light, dry flavor whereas long-standing winter carrots have a rich, sweet, mellow taste. Delicately flavored spring carrots go well with savory meats, chicken, peas, beans, and other vegetables. They are an essential ingredient in casseroles such as *blanquette de veau* and *boeuf bourguignonne.* In *cordon bleu* cooking, carrots are used in stocks and sauces for seafood, casseroles, and soups.

Flavorful winter carrots are delicious diced and cooked with cubed potatoes and turnips or rutabagas. They can be baked, or roasted, or simmered and sprinkled with lemon juice and salt. Shredded winter carrots make a great slaw and give texture and moisture to muffins and sweets such as spicy carrot cake.

Carrot and Grape Slaw
⅔ cup sweet seedless green grapes
2 cups coarsely grated raw
   carrots
Mayonnaise, to taste
½ small onion
¼ cup orange juice
Pinch of salt, to taste

Halve the grapes. Moisten the carrots with mayonnaise to taste. Grate the onion over the carrots. Toss with the orange juice and grapes. Salt to taste. Chill two hours.
Serves 4.

SELECTED CULTIVARS

Long (8 to 10 Inches)

A Plus 71 days, exceptionally flavorful, deep orange, recommended for its vitamin A.

Gold Pak 76 days, 8 to 9 inches, particularly deep color.

Imperator 75 days, 8 to 9 inches, standard market carrot.

Medium (6 to 8 Inches)

Napoli F1 60 days, 7 to 8 inches, 'Nantes' type, earliest long carrot, excellent flavor.

Danvers Half Long 70 days, 6 to 7 inches, 1½ inches wide, almost perfectly cylindrical, performs well in heavier soil.

Royal Chantenay 70 days, 6 to 7 inches, slightly tapered, improved strain of 'Red-Cored Chantenay', keeps well in the row.

Touchon 75 days, French import, 8 inches, slim and fine textured, practically coreless, recommended for juicing.

Short (3 to 6 Inches)

Thumbelina 56 to 65 days, nearly round, smooth skin, fine flavor, recommended for rocky soil, All-America Selection.

Parmex 75 days, nearly round, sweet, grows well in shallow or rocky soil.

Fingerling/Miniature (3 to 4 Inches)

Baby Spike 52 days, excellent color and flavor.

Little Finger 55 to 60 days, baby carrot for canning, pickling, or eating fresh.

Minicor 55 to 60 days, good flavor.

'Royal Chantenay' carrots

PARSNIPS

This root crop is a favorite for the sweet, distinctive flavor it adds to winter stews. The flavor of parsnips marries well with squash and other winter vegetables, adding a hearty touch to cold-weather fare. Native to the Mediterranean region, parsnips have been cultivated since antiquity.

GROWING PARSNIPS

Parsnips are like large, coarse, cream-colored carrots—8 to 24 inches long and 2 to 3 inches wide at the top—and are grown in much the same manner as carrots. In the North, plant as soon as the ground can be worked. Cold tolerant, they can be harvested from late fall

NUTRITIONAL ELEMENTS

Parsnips, cooked, ½ cup

Calories	66
Vitamin C	10 mg
Calcium	45 mg

'Cobham Improved Marrow' parsnips

through winter (mulch the ground to keep it from freezing) and until late spring. Parsnips are sweeter after frosts because their starch converts to sugar in near-freezing temperatures.

Parsnip roots develop best in soil that has been worked to a depth of 18 to 24 inches and is well supplied with compost. Avoid manure and other high-nitrogen fertilizers.

Parsnips grown from seeds produce 12- to 18-inch-long white to cream-colored roots in 100 to 120 days. Parsnip seeds cannot be stored from one year to the next.

Culture

Parsnip seeds tend to germinate poorly, especially in dry climates, so it is important to sow them in damp soil and to maintain the humidity. Sow seeds ½ inch deep and press them into the soil—they are very lightweight. Sow heavily because the germination rate is low, and thin to 4 inches apart after they are 1 inch high. Keep the parsnip row weed free as the seeds germinate, and fertilize once or twice during the growing season.

Harvesting

Begin the harvest after the first frost. Grasp the foliage near the top of the root and tug gently. Parsnips can overwinter in the row and be harvested at will. To keep the ground from freezing, apply a thick mulch of hay. Before new growth begins in spring, dig up the remaining crop.

Before using, remove the greens and rinse the roots thoroughly. The tips often are stringy, so discard them. Peel the roots and quarter the thick lower portion before cooking.

Parsnips keep for two or three weeks sealed in a vegetable bag in the crisper. Remove the tops before storing.

COOKING WITH PARSNIPS

Parsnips are a root crop of cream-colored tapering roots with a flavor that has a hint of lemon but is sweeter than a carrot. The texture is mealy like that of a yam. Parsnips enrich hearty beef casseroles and vegetable soups. They are delicious roasted in the pan with beef or pork. An excellent addition to a platter of steamed vegetables, they are also very good alone flavored with lemon or orange. Cooked mashed parsnips are shaped into round cakes and sautéed. They can be puréed by themselves or with mashed potatoes for a contemporary accompaniment to grilled or roasted meats.

Honey-Orange Parsnips

8 parsnips, peeled, quartered
lengthwise
2 teaspoons grated orange rind
½ cup orange juice
¼ cup honey
¼ teaspoon salt
2 tablespoons butter

Preheat oven to 350° F. Steam the parsnips until barely tender (about 10 minutes). Combine the honey with the orange rind and orange juice and stir to dissolve. Layer the parsnips in a small buttered baking dish and sprinkle each layer with a little salt and the orange-juice mixture. Dot the top with the butter. Bake until completely tender (10 to 15 minutes).
Serves 5.

SELECTED CULTIVARS

Hollow Crown 100 to 130 days, 12 inches, improved variety, smooth, mild, sweet, nutty flavor.

Harris Model 100 to 110 days, early variety, smooth, white, recommended for flavor.

Lander 120 days, long, slender, and smooth, very sweet, recommended for high tolerance to canker.

Cobham Improved Marrow 120 days, English variety, smooth, tapered roots, high sugar content.

PEANUTS

Peanuts are seeds inside a shell. Plant peanuts shelled or unshelled—just be sure the thin brown skin that covers the seed is intact or the seed will not germinate.

The way peanuts develop is unique. Clusters of yellow, pealike flowers appear four to six weeks after planting. There are two types of flower on each plant: One is fertile and the other is not. After pollination, the fertile flowers head down on their stalks and burrow into the ground in the area above the roots. There, the ovary ripens and becomes a peanut. Each plant produces 40 to 60 peanut pods.

GROWING PEANUTS

Peanut plants are leafy and about 20 inches tall. Plant the seeds in the garden when night temperatures stay above 50° F. They need four to five months of growing weather to mature a crop. The plants withstand light frosts in spring or fall, so they grow even in cold regions if started indoors in large peat pots.

'Jumbo Virginia' peanuts

NUTRITIONAL ELEMENTS

Peanuts, raw with skin, 1 ounce

Calories	152
Vitamin C	traces
Calcium	18 mg

When the soil warms to 60° to 70° F, it is time to set out the seedlings. In the South, plant peanuts in the garden about the time the last frost is expected.

Peanuts grow best in light, sandy soil. Avoid manure and high-nitrogen fertilizers.

Culture

Plant the seeds 1 inch deep in the North, 2 inches deep in the South, three seeds per hill 5 inches apart. Space the hills 2 to 3 feet apart. When the plants are about 12 inches tall, hill the soil up around the plants and cover with a mulch of straw.

Harvesting

Begin harvesting when the leaves turn yellow or when frost kills the plants. Dig or pull up the plants, shake off the earth, and hang them in an airy place for several weeks until the leaves are dry. Harvest the pods and store the peanuts in an airtight container.

Before shelling and using peanuts as a snack or in most recipes, you must roast them. Heat them in their shells for 20 minutes at 350° F. Store shelled, roasted peanuts in an airtight container.

COOKING WITH PEANUTS

Peanuts are a classic sandwich filler and midnight munch, and the heart of peanut butter cookies and peanut butter soup. Chopped, they add nutritional crunch to grilled chicken, fish, and bland vegetables. They are used in Thai sauces and are scattered over a variety of Chinese stir-fry dishes. Children love making their own peanut butter from home-grown nuts and are fascinated by the plants' unusual production method. Peanuts are very high in fat, potassium, and phosphorus.

In the South peanuts are often harvested immature and cooked and served with peas or shell beans. The flavor of the immature nut is similar to both beans and peas.

Peanut Sauce With Crudités

1 tablespoon vegetable oil
1 clove garlic, minced
3 green onions, trimmed to 3 inches and minced
2 medium red bell peppers, seeded and shredded
1 teaspoon sugar
2 tablespoons curry powder
1 cup coconut milk *or* half-and-half
½ cup peanut butter *or* ground roasted peanuts
½ teaspoon cayenne *or* hot-pepper flakes
Sugar and salt, to taste
6 cups mixed raw vegetables

Heat a wok to medium (350° F) and swirl in the oil. Stir in the garlic and cook 1 minute. Add the onions, sautéing 1 minute more. Add the peppers and stir-fry 1 minute more. Season with sugar and curry powder, then stir in the coconut milk. Bring to a boil. Reduce the heat to simmer and mix in the peanut butter and the cayenne. Stir until the sauce is as thick as mayonnaise. Season with a few grains of sugar and salt. Serve warm as a dipping sauce with the raw vegetables.

Makes about 2½ cups.

SELECTED CULTIVARS

Spanish Peanut Improved 110 days, early maturing, large crop, big, sweet.

Tennessee Red 120 days, long-shelled, three or four nuts per pod, red skinned.

Jumbo Virginia 120 days, very productive, one to two large nuts per pod.

POTATOES

Potatoes grow from "eye-sets"—cut-up pieces of potato that have sprouted eyes. To test your interest in growing potatoes, leave a few potatoes to age and sprout eyes, then cut them up and plant the sprouted pieces. For a real potato crop, buy eye-sets or seed potatoes from a reliable source that advertises disease-free cultivars. Some seed catalogs specializing in potatoes sell tiny seed potatoes they call minitubers. Minitubers are produced by tissue culture and are free of the problems that often plague potatoes started from eye-sets.

To taste what you have never tasted before, try colorful cultivars or some of the attractive fingerling potatoes. To have lots of new potatoes to harvest, plant a high-yielding variety of one of the four standard potatoes. New potatoes are just baby spuds harvested early, when they reach 1½ to 2½ inches around.

The four basic potato types are russets, long whites, round whites, and round reds. The russets have a floury texture when cooked and are ideal for baking, mashing, and for thickening soups and chowders. Long whites are oval with light tan skin, somewhat less starchy than the russets, and recommended for boiling and panfrying. The tan-skinned and red-skinned round whites keep their shape and taste best roasted and in potato salad.

GROWING POTATOES

Potatoes are the underground tubers of leafy, sprawling plants that thrive in cool regions. They are

POTATO DISEASE RESISTANCE

LB   Late blight
S   Scab

'Katahdin' (left) and 'Red Pontiac' potatoes

**NUTRITIONAL
ELEMENTS**
**Potato, cooked,
1 medium**
Calories   76
Vitamin C   20 mg
Calcium   7 mg

most successful where summers cool off as the crop is maturing. Plant potatoes as soon as the soil can be worked in spring, and they mature in 90 to 120 days. They thrive in light, sandy, acidic soil, pH 4.8 to 5.4, with sustained moisture. Three to 4 pounds of seed potatoes will plant a 30-foot row and yield ½ to ¾ bushel of mature potatoes.

Culture
Cut up the seed potatoes several days before planting time. Make sure each piece has at least 1½ to 2 square inches of potato and includes at least one fresh-looking, strongly growing eye. Cure the pieces for two or three days in a cool environment, 50° to 65° F. Some growers recommend dipping the cut pieces in a commercial fungicide to prevent rot.

Plant the seed potatoes eyes up, cut sides down, 2 to 3 inches deep in heavy soil (4 to 6 inches deep in light soil), and 12 inches apart.

Cover this with 2 to 3 inches of mulch. The potatoes sprout in two to three weeks and grow quickly until the foliage becomes a living mulch. If that is not enough to keep weeds down, add mulch. When plants are 5 to 6 inches high, hill up the soil around the stems and scratch a handful of compost or 5-10-10 fertilizer into the soil beside each plant.

Keep the soil moist, especially in the early weeks. If new leaves turn bluish at the tips, the crop needs watering even if the soil is damp.

Harvesting
New potatoes are ready to harvest about two weeks after the plants flower. Find them by scratching around in the soil under a plant. Take a few new potatoes from each plant, and leave the rest to mature.

Potatoes are mature when the vines yellow and die back. Leave them in their hills for about two weeks after the vines have died

'All Blue' potatoes

252

down. Early cultivars may be left in the ground for as long as several weeks if the weather is dry and cool. The late cultivars can stay in the row three to four weeks after the tops have died down. Before digging the potato crop, loosen the soil with a spading fork.

New potatoes are not good keepers: Store them in vegetable bags in the crisper. Cure mature potatoes by storing them in the dark for a week at 70° F. After that they keep for several months stored 35° to 40° F.

COOKING WITH POTATOES

Potatoes have a flavor potential that is rarely maximized. They also supply minerals—especially potassium—and a fair amount of vitamin C at a modest cost in calories.

The little "new" potatoes and the shiny 2½-inch fingerlings steamed in their skins, lightly crusted with salt, and served with a dab of cold butter are as sweet a vegetable as anyone could wish for.

The world's most prevalent starchy vegetable is available in exotic colors—from golden yellow and orange to purple and deep pink. The vegetable's color is

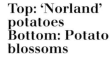

Top: 'Norland' potatoes
Bottom: Potato blossoms

affected by the mineral content in the soil—the higher the mineral content, the more intense the color. Steamed purple potatoes topped with slivers of roasted red pepper are jewel-like on the plate.

Steamed Baby Potatoes and Feta

16 1½- to 2-inch potatoes in their skins
1 large red bell pepper, seeded, cut in 6 strips
¼ cup extravirgin olive oil
¼ cup balsamic vinegar
1 teaspoon fresh thyme
2 tablespoons minced fresh basil
Salt and freshly ground black pepper, to taste
Pinch of sugar
½ cup peeled, seeded, diced tomato
12 black olives, sliced, optional
1 cup crumbled feta cheese
10 to 12 large basil leaves, for garnish

Steam the potatoes and the pepper strips 20 minutes. Combine the oil, vinegar, thyme, basil, salt, pepper, and sugar; stir in the tomato and the olives. Arrange the steamed potatoes in a serving dish, top with the pepper strips, and toss with the dressing. Sprinkle feta cheese over the vegetables and garnish the plate with basil leaves.
Serves 4.

SELECTED CULTIVARS

Early (90 to 110 Days)

Caribe Blue skin, white flesh, large, excellent flavor, very productive.

Red Sun Early, 1 to 1½ inches, bright red skin, delicious as new potatoes.

Norland Very early, red, medium-sized, oblong, widely adapted, favored by home gardeners. (S)

Midseason (100 to 120 Days)

All Blue Indigo blue skin, mealy, round, medium-sized, flesh turns soft purple-blue when cooked, excellent flavor, gorgeous color.

Blossom Smooth pink skin, pink flesh, oblong, one of the prettiest.

Lavender Lavender skin and flesh, deep eyes.

Yukon Gold Yellow flesh, fine yellow skin, oval-round.

Yellow Finn Buttery yellow flesh, smooth-skin, rounded, medium-sized, excellent for boiling or baking.

Late (110 to 140 Days)

Giant Peanut Fingerlings Firm buttery flesh, tan skin, look like fat 3- to 4-inch-long peanuts, hint of chestnut in the flavor.

Russian Banana Yellow skin, light yellow flesh, banana-shaped fingerling, excellent flavor. (LB, S)

Butte Russet-skinned hybrid, very similar to its grandparent 'Russet Burbank', high in protein and vitamin C, improved yield. (LB, S)

Katahdin White-skinned, large, round to oblong, widely adapted, excellent for baking.

Kennebec White-skinned, block shaped, excellent eating quality, one of the best for baking, frying, and hash browns, stores moderately well. (LB, S)

Red Pontiac Red-skinned, oval, may become too big with abundant rainfall, fair table quality, used for boiling, very good keeper, succeeds in heavy soil.

SWEET POTATOES

Sweet potatoes and yams need more summer heat than any other vegetable in the home garden. The plants are leafy vines that bear attractive flowers like those of their relative the morning glory. They mature only where they have 90 to 120 days of summer growing weather. Plant sweet potatoes and yams in full sun after the soil temperature reaches 50° F—a light frost will kill the leaves.

The vines start from leafy slips called root sprouts, a variation on the sprouted eye-sets that give ordinary potatoes their start. Supermarket tubers often are treated to prevent sprouting. But if yours have sprouted, preparing them for planting is an interesting project to share with youngsters.

GROWING SWEET POTATOES

Set the sprouted potatoes, whole, in a box of moist sand or sawdust and keep them at 75° to 80° F while the sprouts become leafy shoots 6 to 9 inches long. Pull the shoots, roots and all, from the potatoes, cut off and discard the bottom inch, and plant the shoots. Another method is to cut the potatoes in pieces; each piece must include a leafed-out sprout and as much of the root as possible. Plant these pieces.

For a guaranteed crop, buy disease-free slips from a reliable garden center or catalog: 12 plants fill 18 feet of row. In the North, cover the row with black plastic to warm the soil. If the soil is heavy and slow to drain, make a raised row 6 to 12 inches high by working in compost and sand. Two weeks before planting, work in ½ to 1 pound of 5–10–10 fertilizer. From an 18-foot row, you will harvest 14 to 16 pounds of potatoes.

Culture

Set the plants 9 to 12 inches apart. Do not let the soil dry out. Check the longer vines as they develop and pull them loose if they start to root. The rooted nodes form small tubers that drain the energy from the parent plant. Two weeks before harvest time, allow the row to dry out.

Harvesting

Begin the harvest when the leaves show some yellow. Harvesting does not become urgent until frost threatens, but if frost touches the vines, dig the tubers. Let them dry in the row for two to three hours.

Sweet potato plants

NUTRITIONAL ELEMENTS
Sweet potato, baked, ½ cup
Calories   47
Vitamin A   2,700 mg
Vitamin C   7 mg
Calcium   14 mg

'Centennial' sweet potatoes

Cure sweet potatoes at 85° to 90° F for 10 to 14 days. Store them in an airy place at 55° F. They keep two to six months. Sweet potatoes get sweeter as their starches turn to sugar.

COOKING WITH SWEET POTATOES

The northern version of the sweet potato is pale yellow and moderately sweet. The dark orange, rather moist, distinctly sweet vegetable called a yam is the southern sweet potato. Real yams are a different plant altogether, a starchy root grown in the tropics.

Sweet potatoes and yams are used interchangeably in recipes, but the sweet potato is drier. Sweet potatoes and yams can be baked in their skins or steamed. Try them baked with orange juice, raisins or cur-

rants, or with a topping of crushed pineapple. Some cooks add marshmallows. Sweet potatoes and yams are perfect with smoked ham, pork, lamb, and turkey. They serve very well as a substitute for pumpkin in pies, cakes, breads, and muffins.

Sweet Potatoes and Cranberries
  4 large sweet potatoes or yams, peeled, halved lengthwise
  Salt and freshly ground black pepper, to taste
  2 cups fresh cranberries, coarsely chopped
  ½ cup all-purpose flour
  ½ cup firmly packed light brown sugar
  ½ cup rolled oats
  Grated zest of 1 large orange
  4 tablespoons cold butter
  1 tablespoon chopped cashews *or* other nuts

Preheat oven to 350° F. Steam the tubers 15 minutes until almost tender. Arrange in a buttered casserole. Season with salt and pepper. Sprinkle the cranberries over the tubers. Mix the flour, brown sugar, oats, nuts, and orange zest; cut the butter into this mixture. Spoon the flour mixture over the tubers and cranberries. Bake 20 minutes.
Serves 4 to 6.

SELECTED CULTIVARS

Vardaman 90 days, gold skin, deep orange flesh, bush type, recommended for small gardens.

Georgia Jet 90 days, red skin, deep orange flesh, large, suited to the Northeast.

Centennial 95 days, orange inside and out, high yield, recommended for short growing seasons.

Porto Rico 125 days, copper-colored skin, reddish flesh, recommended for baking, short-vined, for small gardens.

TURNIPS AND RUTABAGAS

Like other cabbage relatives, turnips and rutabagas are cool-weather crops, improved by a light frost as they mature. This makes them good candidates for late-summer planting. Sow seeds as soon as the ground can be worked in spring. Where summers are hot and winters mild, fall and winter crops do best.

GROWING TURNIPS AND RUTABAGAS

Turnips, which have rough, hairy leaves, need only 30 days to produce greens mature enough to harvest. The roots mature in 45 to 82 days. Sow spring crops three weeks before the last frost date. They are harvested before the temperature reaches 75° F. Plant fall crops in midsummer, two months before the first frost date. Turnips need well-drained, deeply dug soil.

The leaves of rutabagas are smooth and waxy. The roots need 80 to 95 days to mature. They are best planted as fall crops. In the northern tier, plant the seeds mid-July and harvest in late October. In the South, sow in late summer for fall and winter harvest. They thrive in medium-heavy soil.

Culture

Broadcast turnip seeds thickly about ¼ inch deep for spring crops, ½ inch deep for fall crops. Pick the thinnings until the plants stand 3 to 4 inches apart.

Sow rutabaga seeds ½ inch apart, ½ inch deep, and cover the seeds with fine compost to ensure germination. As they grow, thin the seedlings to about 8 inches apart.

Weed diligently, then mulch between the maturing tops. Keep turnips and rutabagas well watered.

Harvesting

To use turnip and rutabaga thinnings in salads, harvest the young side leaves, taking care not to damage the growing tips. Never strip a plant of the majority of its leaves. The plants produce new greens and the roots continue to grow. To harvest the roots, loosen the soil with a spading fork and gently pull them up by their tops.

Harvest turnips as the roots reach 2 to 3 inches. Allowed to grow larger, turnips become pithy.

Harvest baby rutabagas at 3 to 4 inches. Harvest the main crop after the first touch of frost, as this improves the flavor. A heavy frost can cause damage.

'Early Purple-Top Milan' turnip

Rinsed and sealed in a vegetable bag, the greens stay fresh for three to seven days.

To store the roots, cut off the tops, leaving an inch or so of stem, and store, unwashed, in a cool, dark place.

Cover rutabagas left in the ground for storage with a thick layer of straw or hay mulch to keep the ground from freezing hard. Or pull all the roots in mid- to late October, cut off the tops to 1 inch, shake off the soil, and store in a cool cellar or storage pit.

'York' rutabaga

COOKING WITH TURNIPS AND RUTABAGAS

These closely related vegetables are from the cabbage group, the *Brassica* species. Most turnips have crisp, watery white flesh, and most rutabagas have dense yellow flesh; however, some turnips are yellow and some rutabagas are white. To confuse things further, rutabagas are known in Canada as turnips and in some regions of the United States as Swedish turnips. Nutritionally, rutabagas are superior to turnips: They have more vitamin A, potassium, and other nutrients. They are also sweeter and larger and keep well for months.

Baby turnips, 1 to 2 inches in diameter, are crisp and peppery, excellent served as a crudité with a mustard dip or sliced into salads. Mature turnips are delicious roasted with beef or lamb, or steamed or mashed. Scalloped and fried turnips are classic accompaniments for pork and game. They add flavor to casseroles, soups, and stir-fries.

Peeled and steamed, rutabagas have a stronger, richer flavor than turnips and are wonderful additions to broiled dinners, casseroles, and soups. Mashed rutabagas are a good choice to serve with roast duck and turkey. Diced and boiled gently for 20 minutes with diced potatoes and carrots, they make a sweet, earthy mélange that is great with steak.

Some gardeners grow turnips as much for the greens as for the roots; some turnip cultivars have been bred for the greens. 'Seven Top' and 'Shogoin' are examples. The tops of both vegetables have a spicy flavor and are cooked and used like mustard greens (see page 201). They are a good source of vitamins A and C. Turnip and rutabaga thinnings add spice to salads, and the tender young leaves are excellent cooked with mustard and chard.

Turnip and Carrot Mélange
2 cups peeled, diced white turnips
2 cups diced carrots
Cold water
2 tablespoons butter
2 teaspoons lemon juice
Salt, to taste
1 tablespoon minced fresh dill *or* fennel, for garnish

Barely cover the turnips and carrots with cold water. Cover, bring to a boil over high heat, then reduce heat and simmer until just tender (10 to 15 minutes). Drain the vegetables and return them to the pan. Shake them over the heat to dry the remaining moisture. Toss with the butter and the lemon juice, then season with salt to taste. Serve garnished with the minced herb.
Serves 6.

Rutabagas Baz
This is a simply prepared medley of sautéed winter vegetables that can take the place of potatoes on the dinner plate. It has everything to be desired in a vegetable dish— bright color, succulent texture, and great flavor. Leftovers are also delicious cold.

2 turnips (about 4 ounces each), peeled
2 medium carrots, scraped
2 rutabagas (about 4 ounces each), peeled
2 medium 3- to 4 inch-long broccoli stems
1 tablespoon butter
2 tablespoons olive oil
2 large shallots, peeled and minced
Salt and freshly ground black pepper, to taste

Cut the root vegetables and broccoli in julienne strips and blanch until barely tender. Drain well. Heat the butter and olive oil in a large skillet or wok until they sizzle. Add the shallots. Stir-fry them 1 minute, then add the vegetables. Sauté, tossing to mix well and cook evenly. Add salt and pepper to taste, toss again, and serve hot.
Serves 6.

SELECTED CULTIVARS

Turnips

Market Express 30 days, Japanese, white, pick at 1 inch.

Red Milan 35 days, round, reddish tops, white bases, butter flavored, pick very young.

Tokyo Cross Hybrid 35 days, 2-inch pure white roots grow large without becoming pithy, All-America Selection.

Early Purple-Top Milan 45 days, flattened 3- to 4-inch roots.

Seven Top 45 days, grown for greens only, planted for winter greens in South.

Golden Ball 45 to 65 days, yellow flesh, round, keeps well.

White Egg (Snowball) 49 to 63 days, solid white, fine-grained 2-inch roots.

Purple-Top White Globe 58 days, standard variety for roots, nearly round, smooth, bright purple tops, creamy white bases.

Rutabagas

Laurentian 77 to 80 days, smooth roots, purple tops, yellow bases, yellow-orange flesh, popular, a good keeper.

American Purple Top Yellow 88 days, an old-timer, purple above, light yellow below, flesh is yellow and mild.

York 95 days, pale yellow flesh, sweet, from New Brunswick.

NUTRITIONAL ELEMENTS
Turnip, cooked, ⅔ cup
Calories 23
Vitamin C 22 mg
Calcium 35 mg

Rutabaga, cooked, ½ cup
Calories 35
Vitamin A 550 mg
Vitamin C 26 mg
Calcium 59 mg

BROCCOLI, CABBAGE, AND RELATIVES

Here's a lovely patch of 'Red Acre' cabbage, one of the attractive red cabbages. To keep the bright color in cooked red cabbage, add some acid in the form of vinegar, lemon juice, or tart apples.

The cole vegetables are the nutritionists' darlings—broccoli in particular, but also brussels sprouts, cabbage, cauliflower, and kohlrabi. The flavor is delicious and they keep well. All except kohlrabi develop on tall, sturdy, succulent central stalks that need space. Kohlrabi is an oddly shaped vegetable—like a flying saucer sprouting leaves.

Cabbage relatives thrive in temperatures between 65° and 80° F, tolerate temperatures as low as 20° F, and mature in cool weather. Plant and harvest them in spring, or start them as seedlings in summer and harvest in mid- to late fall, or winter.

In the open garden, sow seeds 1 inch apart and cover with ½ to 1 inch of soil; or set out transplants started six to eight weeks early. Plant seedlings in soil up to the bottom of the first leaves. Garden centers sell seedlings. Choose those whose stems are no thicker than a pencil; large transplants bolt when exposed for two to three weeks to temperatures below 50° F.

The cole group does best in soil with a pH between 6.5 and 7.5. They are heavy feeders with shallow root systems, and to develop well they need sustained watering and regular fertilizing with 10–10–10. In rainy areas and in sandy soil, apply a midseason side dressing of 2 pounds straight nitrogen fertilizer per 20 feet of row (blood meal, for instance). Mulch is beneficial.

The coles are subject to diseases. Do not precede or follow one cabbage relative with another in the same garden location.

Leafy cole crops, such as collards, kale, and Chinese cabbage are grouped with the leafy greens in the chapter beginning on page 183.

BROCCOLI

Broccoli is among the most nutritious vegetables, and its florets are one of the most elegant. The little "trees" tempt many children into eating their vegetables, especially if they can be dipped in a cheese sauce. The stems of broccoli, although not as attractive as the florets, are even tastier. Do not neglect them.

GROWING BROCCOLI

The flower heads of immature buds develop at the top of sturdy stems—24 to 26 inches in the tallest cultivars, 20 inches in compact forms. If the central head is harvested before it reaches its full size and before the buds open, side shoots grow out and provide harvests for an additional month.

The most challenging aspect of growing broccoli is choosing the right planting date. Broccoli requires two to three months to mature from seed. Planted too late in spring, the plants will bolt. If young transplants are exposed to too much cold or get too dry, they may flower prematurely. In moderate climates both spring and fall crops are possible. For the spring crop, start seeds indoors in a sterile growing medium five to seven weeks before the last frost date. Set out the seedlings two to three weeks before the last anticipated frost in spring.

For the fall crop, sow seeds 10 to 12 weeks before the first anticipated frost. Where winters are mild, broccoli planted in fall provides a long winter harvest.

Culture

Before planting, work ¼ to ½ cup of a complete slow-release fertilizer into the soil under each transplant. Set transplants in the soil up to their bottom leaves, and mulch to keep the ground cool. Seeds should be planted ½ inch deep. Set transplants, or thin seedlings, to stand 18 inches apart. Overwintering plants benefit from a side dressing in February of ¼ cup organic fertilizer given to each plant.

Harvesting

Harvest the central head when it is about two thirds of its potential size and while the buds are still very tight. This encourages the production of side shoots. Harvest side shoots as they mature, leaving in place the base of the shoots and a couple of leaves to continue production. If the weather heats up, harvest the heads quickly or they will deteriorate.

'Premium Crop' broccoli

Immediately after picking seal broccoli in a vegetable bag in the crisper. It will stay fresh for at least 10 days. Cut in florets, it keeps almost as well as it does stored as a full head.

COOKING WITH BROCCOLI

Broccoli, which looks like dark green cauliflower, tastes similar to cauliflower and kale. It is rich in vitamins A, B, and C as well as iron and calcium. In recent years broccoli has soared in popularity, especially since researchers at the Johns Hopkins School of Medicine credited it, most notably the 'Saga' cultivar, with inducing enzymes that detoxify carcinogens.

Cut in ½-inch florets and steamed five to seven minutes, broccoli is a fine salad ingredient and garnish. But be forewarned: Overcooked broccoli turns yellow-green and smells strongly of cabbage. Broccoli is excellent dressed with minced oregano or a dash of nutmeg. It makes a delicate quiche, a fine soufflé, a tasty soup, and is a splendid addition to a stir-fry. It is a colorful appetizer with any vinaigrette. Served with a bit of salt or Parmesan cheese, it is a delicious vegetable accompaniment to everything but fish.

The leaves and the stems contain valuable nutrients and should not be wasted. Peeled, ½-inch pieces of broccoli stem cook almost as rapidly as the florets. Broccoli florets and their leaves are also good raw in salads.

If you like broccoli greens, plant 'Salad Raab', one of several cultivars harvested for the tender greens and small 1¼-inch florets. A dozen plants will supply the average family.

Broccoli in Vinaigrette

1 large broccoli, cut in ½-inch florets
1 tablespoon chopped roasted red bell pepper
1 teaspoon minced garlic
⅓ cup olive oil
1 tablespoon minced shallot
1 tablespoon water
1 tablespoon balsamic vinegar
½ tablespoon minced oregano
½ tablespoon minced parsley
1 teaspoon minced thyme
Salt and freshly ground pepper, to taste

Steam the broccoli florets until tender but still bright green (about 5 minutes). Drain, transfer to a serving dish, and chill.

In a small saucepan over medium heat, sauté the red pepper and garlic in the oil for 2 to 3 minutes. Add the shallot and sauté 1 minute more. Stir in the water, vinegar, oregano, parsley, and thyme and simmer until the herbs turn bright green (about 1 minute). Toss the broccoli in the hot vinaigrette, season with salt and pepper, and serve.
Serves 4.

SELECTED CULTIVARS

Salad Raab 50 to 60 days from seed, grown for the tender greens and small 1¼-inch florets, sharp, sweet flavor.

Early Dividend F1 43 days from transplants, earliest head-forming broccoli, loose heads, 4 to 5 inches, plenty of large side shoots.

Early Emerald Hybrid 50 days from transplants, early, rich blue-green heads, 5 to 6 inches, produces over a long period.

Green Comet 55 days from transplants, firm dark green heads, good producer of side shoots, All-America Selection.

NUTRITIONAL ELEMENTS
Broccoli, cooked, ⅔ cup
Calories 26
Vitamin A 2,500 mg
Vitamin C 90 mg
Calcium 88 mg

Premium Crop 58 days from transplants, very large blue-green heads, fine texture, excellent quality, good side-shoot production.

Sprinter F1 60 days from transplants, recommended for mountain areas.

Waltham 29 75 days from seed, low growing, compact, larger central head, survives hot weather well, recommended for Florida.

Southern Comet 80 days from seed, early, 4- to 6-inch heads, many side shoots.

Romanesco Minaret 85 days from seed, unusual chartreuse heads, shaped like the top of a conch shell.

'Romanesco
Minaret' broccoli

BRUSSELS SPROUTS

Brussels sprouts develop in the axils of the leaves of tall, very sturdy stalks. These hardy vegetables will survive the winter in Zones 8 and 9 and persist deep into fall or winter in most climates. When harvest is almost over and the stems are picked clean, the leafy tops look like small palm trees, an anomaly in the winter landscape, especially when capped with snow.

GROWING BRUSSELS SPROUTS

One of the most cold hardy of the cabbage group, brussels sprouts need 80 to 115 days to mature crops from seed, 75 to 95 days from transplants. Some long-standing cultivars take 160 to 200 days to mature. For an earlier harvest, set out transplants.

In most regions of the U.S., it is best to start brussels sprouts indoors four to six weeks early and set out after June 1. The first sprouts begin to swell in late summer and are ready to harvest in the fall after the weather cools. Cool temperatures during sprouting make for attractive, compact sprouts. The flavor of some cultivars is improved by frost. In warm regions plant brussels sprouts in late summer for winter and spring harvests.

Plant brussels sprouts in a row or two in the vegetable garden. A dozen plants is enough for the average family.

Culture

The culture of brussels sprouts is similar to that of broccoli and cabbage. Set transplants to stand 24 inches apart. Provide a monthly side dressing of balanced fertilizer high in nitrogen.

Where winter comes early, hasten maturity by pinching out the tops of the plants as they reach 15 to 20 inches tall: Sprouts should be about ½ to ¾ inch in diameter at that point. When you pinch the tops, the sprouts mature in a couple of weeks, but the harvest is smaller than if you allow the tops to grow and produce more sprouts.

Harvesting

The sprouts at the bottom of the stalk mature first. When they're big enough to touch each other, it is time to harvest. Break off the leaves below the lowest sprouts, then snap off the sprouts. As you harvest the lower sprouts, those above continue to develop and mature, extending the harvest by many weeks. When all the sprouts are gathered, use the tender leaves at the top of the plant as greens.

If severe frosts threaten while the stalks are loaded with sprouts, cut off the stalk and store it whole in a cool, dry place: You can harvest sprouts from storage for the next several weeks.

Sprouts keep well a week or more sealed in a vegetable bag immediately after picking and stored in the crisper.

COOKING WITH BRUSSELS SPROUTS

Brussels sprouts look and taste like tiny cabbages 1½ to 2 inches in diameter. They taste best steamed until tender—7 to 14 minutes, depending on variety and size—and dressed with lemon juice or a vinaigrette. Sprouts are also served au gratin, in cheese sauces, and with hollandaise sauce. They combine well with new potatoes and are an excellent accompaniment to roasted and grilled meats, broiled steak, pork roast, and sausages.

Brussels Sprouts With Parmesan

24 to 36 young brussels sprouts
1 teaspoon salt
2 to 3 tablespoons butter, in thin pats
⅓ cup freshly grated Parmesan cheese
Salt and freshly ground pepper, to taste
1 tablespoon minced fresh marjoram *or* dill, for garnish

Rinse the sprouts and remove and discard the tough outer leaves. In a large saucepan, bring to a rapid boil enough salted water to just cover the sprouts. Add the sprouts. Cook, uncovered, until the sprouts are tender but still somewhat green (10 to 12 minutes). Drain, return to

NUTRITIONAL ELEMENTS
Brussels sprouts, cooked, 6 to 8 medium
Calories 36
Vitamin A 520 mg
Vitamin C 87 mg
Calcium 32 mg

'Prince Marvel' brussels sprouts

the pot, and shake over low heat to dry remaining moisture. Distribute the butter and Parmesan cheese over the sprouts and toss gently until the butter is melted. Season with salt and pepper and garnish with the marjoram or dill.

Serves 4 to 6.

SELECTED CULTIVARS

Prince Marvel F1 76 to 85 days from transplants, small, hard, superior flavor.

Catskill Strain (Long Island Improved) 90 days from transplants, 20-inch plant, firm, tightly packed, 1¼ to 1½ inches.

Jade Cross E Hybrid 90 to 95 days from transplants, an improved 'Jade Cross', vigorous, heavy yield, larger sprouts, produces well in both summer and fall.

'Ruby Ball' cabbage

CABBAGE

This productive and tasty vegetable has been overcooked for generations. Treat it as the sweet and delicate food it is by steaming it gently for just a few minutes to soften it slightly, then enjoy its light flavor with a touch of flavored vinegar. When boiled into submission, as has been the habit in the past, some of the complex flavoring compounds in cabbage break down into sulfates, which give cabbage its strong smell and flavor. When not overcooked, however, the "smell of boiled cabbage" is nonexistent.

GROWING CABBAGE

Cabbages develop at the top of sturdy stalks. Grow them as transplants or sow directly in the soil. They develop best in cool, moist conditions. There are early and late cultivars. For an early crop, start seeds in late winter five to seven weeks before the garden is ready for planting. Harvesting begins 65 to 95 days later. In most areas the early cultivars are planted as transplants March through June. Set out the slow-growing and late-maturing cultivars as seedlings 10 to 12 weeks before the first frost date. The heads form when the weather cools. In the South grow cabbage all year around except summer.

Fertile soil grows the best cabbages. Work 1½ to 2 cups of 5-10-10 fertilizer into the soil around each planting hole. Water consistently so they develop quickly—they need 1½ inches of water weekly.

Timing is important with cabbages. In warm weather heads of early cultivars split soon after they fill out. Harvest promptly and plant only what you can use. The slow-growing cultivars mature late in the summer, and during autumn hold in the row much longer.

Cabbages belong in a row of their own in the vegetable garden. One to two dozen plants meets the needs of the average family.

Culture

Plant cabbage seeds ½ inch deep, five seeds per foot. Set transplants, and thin seedlings, 18 inches apart for compact cabbage cultivars, 24 inches apart for larger types. Mulch is helpful.

Harvesting

Harvest heads when they are firm and shiny. Cut just under the head, leaving some basal leaves to support the growth of the small lateral heads that follow.

Stored at just above freezing, fall cabbage keeps for up to six months; early types last one to two months.

COOKING WITH CABBAGE

Gardeners can choose among three types of cabbages. There is the familiar smooth white-green type; the beautiful, tightly packed, crimson-maroon red cabbage; or the crinkle-leaved ornamental savoy. All three go well with pork dishes, ham, rice, and potatoes.

Tender young green cabbage fresh from the garden, cut in narrow wedges and steamed or braised 6 to 10 minutes, is delicate and delicious when flavored with lemon, dill, or a light cheese sauce. Green cabbage is preferred for coleslaw, sauerkraut, corned beef, soups, egg rolls, and stir-fries.

Red cabbage adds flavor and color to salads and slaws. When cooking it, include tart apples or lemon juice in the water to help maintain the color. Use the ornamental leaves of the savoy cabbage in salads and to line food platters; the savoy also makes the finest cabbage salads.

Green Cabbage Chowder

1 tablespoon butter
1 small onion, minced
2 quarts water
1 small bay leaf
1 teaspoon fresh thyme
1 large sprig parsley, minced
2 large baking potatoes, peeled, diced
2 carrots, peeled, diced
2 stalks celery and leaves, chopped
1 small green cabbage, shredded
1 cup half-and-half *or* whole milk
Salt and freshly ground pepper, to taste
1 tablespoon minced parsley, for garnish

In a large stockpot over medium heat, melt the butter and sauté the onion until translucent (about 5 minutes). Add the water, bay leaf, thyme, and parsley and bring to a boil. Stir in the potatoes, carrots,

NUTRITIONAL ELEMENTS

Green cabbage, cooked, ¾ cup

Calories	20
Vitamin A	130 mg
Vitamin C	33 mg
Calcium	44 mg

Red cabbage, cooked, ¾ cup

Calories	31
Vitamin A	40 mg
Vitamin C	61 mg
Calcium	42 mg

'Savoy Ace' cabbage

and celery. Cover and return to a boil. Reduce the heat, cover, and simmer until the broth begins to thicken a little (about 45 minutes). Add the cabbage and simmer 20 to 30 minutes more. Stir in the half-and-half and heat through. Season with salt and pepper. Serve hot, garnished with parsley.

Serves 6 to 8.

Swiss Red Cabbage Slaw

  1 medium red cabbage, trimmed, shredded
  1 cup finely chopped celery
  ¼ pound Swiss cheese, cut in thin strips
  1 clove garlic, minced
  4 anchovy filets
  1 tablespoon lemon juice
  1 teaspoon Dijon-style mustard
  1½ teaspoons white wine vinegar
  5 tablespoons olive oil
  Freshly ground black pepper, to taste

Combine the cabbage, celery, and cheese in a large bowl. In a small bowl mash the garlic and anchovies to a smooth paste. Stir in the lemon juice, mustard, vinegar, and oil and blend well. Pour the sauce over the vegetables and cheese and mix well. Add the pepper to taste. Chill.

Serves 4 to 6.

SELECTED CULTIVARS

Green-Leaved Cabbage

Resistant Golden Acre (Derby Day) 58 to 64 days, early, round, firm, medium green.

Charmant F1 66 days, dense, stands weeks without splitting.

Early Jersey Wakefield 63 days, small to medium, conical, sweet, mild flavor.

Golden Cross 40 days from transplants, a hybrid for small gardens, tight, sweet, golden yellow.

Stonehead F1 60 to 70 days, extremely solid, blue-green leaves,

'Stonehead' cabbage

holds well in the garden, All-America Selection.

Grenadier 65 days, early Dutch hybrid, good flavor, crack resistant, holds well in the garden.

Copenhagen Market 66 to 72 days, vigorous, round, medium-sized heads.

Early Flat Dutch 85 days, large, flattened, medium green, split resistant.

Danish Ballhead 100 to 105 days, late season, solid, medium-sized, stores well.

Late Flat Dutch 100 days, vigorous, large, flat, medium green.

Red Cabbage

Ruby Ball F1 68 days from transplants, early, small, round, holds well, All-America Selection.

Lasso Red 70 to 80 days, forms bright red heads that keep well in the field.

Red Acre 76 days, compact, solid, deep red.

Savoy Cabbage

Salarite 48 days from transplants, early, round, glossy green with compact heads.

Savoy Ace F1 78 days, semi-globed, firm, finely wrinkled leaves, medium-to-large plant, All-America Selection.

Promosa Baby Savoy 60 days, Dutch hybrid, small, 4 to 5 inches, withstands heat, has blue-green crinkled leaves.

Savoy King Hybrid 90 days, high yield, semiglobed, deep green.

Savoy Chieftain 88 days, with densely curled blue-green leaves, large and firm.

CAULIFLOWER

An elegant and sophisticated vegetable in the kitchen, cauliflower's delicate white color, interesting shape, and light flavor add interest and brightness to vegetable dishes. In the garden, it's a bit of a prima donna, demanding just the right conditions and timing to make the best heads.

Although we are used to thinking of cauliflower as white or creamy white, it is also available in purple and purple-and-green shades. Try these unusual varieties. They are a little easier to grow than the white varieties because they don't need blanching. Although they look a little like broccoli, their flavor is still that of cauliflower.

GROWING CAULIFLOWER

Like cabbage, cauliflower tops a sturdy succulent stalk and needs cool weather to mature perfectly. It reacts poorly to extremes of temperature, both hot and cold. Cauliflower is usually set out as a transplant. Sow seeds in a hotbed, a cold frame, or indoors five to seven weeks before the average date of the last frost. Transplants need about 60 days of cool weather to mature heads. In most of the country, two crops are possible—a spring crop and a fall crop. In mild regions cauliflower overwinters and provides spring crops from seeds sown between mid-July and late August.

To do well cauliflower cultivars need to grow rapidly, especially early cultivars, and they must never go dry. Cauliflower grows best in fertile soil with a pH of 6.5 to 7.5. Work ¼ to ½ cup 10–10–10 fertilizer into each planting hole before setting out the transplant, and apply

NUTRITIONAL ELEMENTS

Cauliflower, cooked, 1 cup

Calories	22
Vitamin C	55 mg
Calcium	21 mg

monthly side dressings of a high-nitrogen fertilizer.

Catalog descriptions of cultivars that "self-wrap" refer to the custom of blanching the heads: The leaves of self-wrap cultivars curl up over the curd and help keep it white. What the plant does not do, the gardener must do. To have creamy white cauliflower rather than slightly yellow heads, when the curd starts to form, tie up the inner leaves or break them over the curd so they lie flat on the flower. Sprinkle the blanching heads with water if the weather turns hot, and look inside now and then to make sure pests are not eating them.

Culture

See page 261.

Harvesting

When the head is mature, the florets begin to separate a little, so you know it is time to cut the head from the stalk. Catalogs refer to

the curd as getting "ricey": This is a grainy look that replaces the creamy look of early maturity. At the ricey stage, the cauliflower flavor is still optimum but the vegetable is not as attractive as before.

Cauliflower stored immediately after harvesting in a vegetable bag keeps for two to three weeks. Cut cauliflower florets stay fresh for about one week.

COOKING WITH CAULIFLOWER

Cauliflower is broccoli's creamy cousin, a tightly packed flower head, called the curd, rich in iron and vitamins A, B, and C. It grows to maturity inside handsome blue-green cabbagelike leaves. The curd in some cultivars is tinted lavender-purple, and there are green-headed cultivars as well; both lose their color when cooked.

Its crispy texture makes cauliflower a favorite for crudité plat-

'Snow Crown' cauliflower

ters. Raw or cooked, cold cauliflower tastes good in salads and with vinaigrettes.

Half-inch florets of cauliflower steamed, poached, or stir-fried five to seven minutes have a delicate flavor that goes well with light cheese sauces, most herbs, or a dash of mace. Cauliflower is excellent served au gratin or puréed, and it makes a fine soufflé. Cauliflower complements pork, sausages, steaks, or any other strongly flavored meat.

Cauliflower is a welcome and tasty addition to the home garden. A dozen or two plants will supply the average family.

Cauliflower and Shrimp Salad

Serve this attractive salad with crusty French bread and herb butter as a luncheon main course.

    1 teaspoon salt
    1 bay leaf
    1 teaspoon fresh thyme
    1 large onion, sliced
    1 medium cauliflower, cut in
        ½-inch florets
    ½ cup oil-and-vinegar dressing
    6 to 8 leaves of leafy red lettuce
    1 pound small raw shrimp,
        shelled
    ½ cup light mayonnaise
    1 heaping teaspoon grainy Dijon-
        style mustard
    1 teaspoon strained lemon juice
    Salt and freshly ground pepper,
        to taste

Bring to a boil in a saucepan about a quart of water containing the salt, bay leaf, thyme, and onion. Add the cauliflower, cover, and simmer until tender (about 5 minutes). Remove the cauliflower with a fine-mesh strainer, drain, and transfer the florets to a bowl. Toss with the oil-and-vinegar dressing. Line a serving bowl with the lettuce leaves and transfer the cauliflower to the bowl.

Return the water to a boil and drop in the shrimp. After the water boils again, cook the shrimp 3 minutes, then drain. Combine the mayonnaise, mustard, and lemon juice in a mixing bowl and season with salt and pepper. Toss the shrimp in the mayonnaise mixture, then pour them over the cauliflower. Serve at room temperature.

Serves 6.

SELECTED CULTIVARS

Caulibroc Hybrid 62 days, combination of cauliflower and broccoli, lime green curd, flavor resembles broccoli.

Snow King 45 to 48 days, extra-early, All-America Selection.

Snow Crown 50 to 53 days, hybrid, deep, rounded, pure white, withstands adverse conditions, All-America Selection.

Extra Early Snowball 60 days, medium, smooth, white, good for early and late crops.

Violet Queen 55 days, colorful burgundy-violet, pale green after cooking, needs no tying, good side shoots.

Self Blanche 71 days, good wrapper leaves, white curds, recommended for full fall season.

Alert 52 days, for high-altitude gardens.

Early White Hybrid 52 days, very large, round, white, good wrapper leaves.

Elby Hybrid 70 days, self-wraps, easiest cauliflower.

Green Goddess 75 days, medium large, light green.

Purple Head 85 days, deep purple on top, turns green when cooked, does not need blanching, holds well in garden.

KOHLRABI

This strange-looking vegetable is a favorite of children because of its odd shape. Another member of the cabbage family, kohlrabi has been bred for its stem, which fattens into a perfect sphere with leaves emerging like wings from a chubby little cherub. The stem has the taste and cool crispness of a radish, but with less heat. When the weather is warm, pick it while the stem is the size of a baseball for the mildest flavor. In cooler weather, you can let it grow larger.

GROWING KOHLRABI

Plant kohlrabi in the vegetable garden—or try a few seeds here and there among the herbs or flowers just to see what it is like. It can stand a little shade. Like the turnip, kohlrabi is a cool-weather vegetable. It forms a round bulb just above the ground and, including the leaves, reaches 10 to 12 inches.

As soon as the ground can be worked in spring, sow seeds in a succession of plantings over a period of three or four weeks. Begin harvesting in 60 to 70 days. Each sowing is likely to mature over a period of two weeks. Where the growing season is brief, sow kohlrabi seeds four to six weeks early in individual peat pots and transplant. Harvest begins about 40 days later.

Kohlrabi must be harvested before the heat of summer, because if it stands in the row it becomes woody, hot tasting, and bolts. Sow the fall crop over a three- to four-week period in late summer, and it can stay in the garden for many weeks without becoming woody. In mild regions make a succession of sowings through the fall and into the winter.

Kohlrabi is an easy crop to succeed with so long as the soil is fertile. Prepare the soil by working in ¼ to ½ cup 10–10–10 fertilizer for every 5 feet of row.

'Grand Duke' kohlrabi

Culture

Sow seeds about ¼ inch apart in the row, ½ inch deep. Harvest radish-sized kohlrabi to thin the row until the seedlings stand 3 to 4 inches apart. Keep the row weeded.

Harvesting

Harvest spring-planted kohlrabi small, about 2 inches in diameter. Allow fall-grown kohlrabi to grow to 3 or 4 inches; it is not likely to get woody.

Sealed in a vegetable bag, kohlrabi keeps for several weeks in the crisper.

COOKING WITH KOHLRABI

The *kohl* in *kohlrabi* is for *cole*, a name for the cabbage clan; *rab* is for turnip. Kohlrabi looks like a purple-tinged or light green turnip with wings, and it tastes like a crisp, sweet cabbage. Not only the appearance of kohlrabi, but also the flavor and texture are refreshingly different. Kohlrabi contains substantial amounts of potassium. It has long been a staple in northern European home gardens.

If you harvest kohlrabi when it is the size of a radish, you can stir-fry it—leaves, skin, and all. Harvest it under 2½ inches and steam it, skin on, until tender—about 15 to 20 minutes—and flavor it with nutmeg or dill. With slightly larger sizes, peel and grate it for slaw; mix with mayonnaise and Dijon-style mustard, and use as a bed for a fish appetizer; or cut it in sticks for crudités. Kohlrabi also can be mashed, and it tastes good in combination vegetable dishes and casseroles. The leaves make excellent braised greens or can be used in soups.

Kohlrabi in Cream

    6 to 8 small kohlrabi and leaves
    2 cups water
    ½ teaspoon salt
    1 tablespoon butter
    4 tablespoons cream
    Salt and freshly ground black pepper, to taste
    1 tablespoon minced fresh dill, for garnish

Cut off, rinse, and chop the leaves. Rinse, drain, peel, and dice the bulbs. Bring the water to a rapid boil with the salt and drop in the diced bulbs. Cover and simmer until almost tender (5 to 8 minutes). Add the chopped greens and stir until they wilt. Cover, reduce the heat to medium, and cook until no water remains. Toss with the butter and the cream, and season with salt and pepper. Garnish with the minced dill.

Serves 4.

SELECTED CULTIVARS

Grand Duke 45 to 50 days, large, compact, early bearing, crisp, mild, white flesh, All-America Selection.

Kohlpack F1 50 days, light green, tender even when large.

Winner F1 53 days, large, compact, early bearing, light green.

Early White Vienna 55 days, 2-inch bulbs, best-known variety.

Kolibri F1 58 days, medium purple, crisp, white inside, fine flavor, even when mature.

Early Purple Vienna 60 days, later and larger than 'Early White Vienna', greenish white inside, purple outside.

Super Schmeltz 60 days, Swiss, very large, sweet, tender.

NUTRITIONAL ELEMENTS

Kohlrabi, cooked, ⅔ cup

Calories	24
Vitamin C	43 mg
Calcium	33 mg
Potassium	260 mg

TALL VEGETABLES

Sunflowers form a cheerful picture when planted close together. They can also be separated a bit and used as supports for beans or other vining crops—scarlet runner beans are beautiful growing on a sunflower. After you harvest the sunflower head, leave the stalk for the beans.

Introducing the tall ones—corn, popcorn, okra, and sunflowers. They are delicious and nutritious. Birds and children are wildly enthusiastic about sunflower seeds; and though the chef in you may not be, watch a giant sunflower grow to the sky and you may fall in love.

Tall plants needs space. When you plant, be aware that they block the sun from plants behind them. In cool regions the best location is usually at the very end of the garden. But in hot climates, tall plants placed in the last row on the west side provide welcome protection from the scorching afternoon sun.

Snap beans, broccoli, cabbage, kohlrabi, and artichokes benefit from the shade of tall crops. Basil and chives grow best in full sun but tolerate filtered shade. Leafy greens and lettuces for fall harvest sown in midsummer need the shade if temperatures exceed 80° F.

It is a common practice to grow living mulch at the base of the tall vegetables. Squash and pumpkins, which mature late in the season, work well. If you do not interplant the tall vegetables with a leafy crop, mulch to keep the soil cool and the weeds out.

Prepare the soil for tall plants with lots of fertilizer and organic material: They have masses of foliage to develop and maintain. And they grow quickly, so keep the soil well supplied with water during droughts.

CORN

Finding your way through the seed cultivars in garden catalogs is daunting. To understand the catalog offerings, here is what you need to know:

Sweet corn, or "normal sugary" (su), cultivars are the tried-and-true types that are sweet when picked, but convert their sugar to starch within minutes or hours.

Sugar-enhanced (se) cultivars have a modified gene that increases the original levels of sugar and extends the period of peak flavor by slowing the conversion of sugar to starch from minutes to days.

Supersweet, or "extrasweet" (sh2), cultivars have a shrunken gene that raises the original levels of sweetness even further and extends their period of peak flavor even longer. The seed is wrinkled.

There are yellow, white, and bicolored cultivars available in all three categories.

Ornamental or Indian corn seeds produce colorful ears developed

'Silver Queen' corn

from strains grown by Native Americans. Typically, the seeds are mahogany red, gray-blue, dark blue, or a mix of these and other colors. They are used primarily as decorations in autumn. Some of the cultivars are sold as popping corn—but they are not the best popcorn you can grow, and the kernels usually pop white, not the color of the kernel. See Cooking With Popcorn, page 279.

Dent corn is field corn grown to feed animals and to make cornmeal; the kernels are dented.

GROWING CORN

Corn is a leafy plant 6 to 7 feet tall. Corn sown in midspring usually matures two ears per plant in 10 to 12 weeks. The top ear generally ripens first. Corn grows when the weather heats up, and the number of days to harvest is affected by the warmth of the season. In most regions plant a succession of early, midseason, and late cultivars two to three weeks apart, and you can harvest corn from midsummer to early autumn.

All cultivars of corn, including popcorn, grow the same way. Corn is wind pollinated. To ensure pollination, plant corn in the vegetable garden in blocks of four short rows rather than one long one.

Categories of corn cross-pollinate unless they are separated by space or time, creating corn that is a blend of its parents' characteristics. Keep a distance of 250 feet between categories, or space plantings of different categories at least four weeks apart.

Corn germinates poorly in soil that is cooler than 60° F. Sugar-enhanced and supersweet corn must have soil at 65° F or warmer to germinate properly. Where the growing season is short, give the corn a quick start by warming the planting row with sheets of black plastic. When the soil has warmed under the plastic, plant the seeds through x's cut in the plastic.

Another way to get a head start is to plant the corn in a trench 6 to 8 inches deep, cover the seeds with 1 inch of soil, and cover the soil with a sheet of clear plastic. This creates a makeshift greenhouse. When the weather warms and the corn plants are bumping their greenhouse ceiling, slit the plastic and free the plants. Make the slits large enough to allow a plentiful supply of water to reach the soil. Or install a soaker hose under the plastic.

Because they are large, corn plants use up a lot of nutrients in the soil. Work in an inch of chicken manure, or 5–10–10 fertilizer, at the rate of 8 pounds for four 33-foot-long rows. Apply the fertilizer in bands on either side of the seed, 2 inches from the seed and 1 inch deeper than seed level. As the corn reaches 8 inches, repeat the application, and again when the plants are 18 inches tall.

Plant corn at the north end of the garden where it will not block the light needed by shorter vegetables. Interplanting corn with pumpkins, cucumbers, squash, or gourds is traditional: the low-growing vines shade out weeds and keep the corn roots cool.

Culture

Plant corn seeds 1 to 2 inches deep, three to five seeds per foot, in rows 30 inches apart. Thin fast-growing early cultivars to 8 to 10 inches apart; thin midseason and late corn to 12 inches apart. Keep the rows weed free until the corn plants are knee high, or interplant with sprawling vines. Corn is shallow rooted, so if you hoe to get rid of weeds, keep the hoe away from the main stem. Do not remove suckers.

NUTRITIONAL ELEMENTS

Corn, yellow, 4-inch ear

Calories	100
Vitamin C	9 mg
Calcium	3 mg

Popcorn, 1 cup

Calories	54
Calcium	2 mg

Corn needs plenty of water, especially as the tassels form. If the leaves roll up at times other than in noon heat, the plants are not getting enough water.

Harvesting

Corn silk appears about three weeks before the ears mature. When the silk turns brown and dries, pick the ears. If you push hard on a ripe kernel, it spurts milky juice. Pick corn by holding the ear at its base and bend and twist it downward. The trick is to break the ear off close to its base without harming the central stalk.

If you must store the corn rather than eat it at once, leave the husks on and refrigerate immediately after picking. The long-keeping corn cultivars are excellent for several days. Steam-blanched and frozen immediately after picking, corn is excellent.

Harvesting Popcorn Pick popcorn when the stalks turn brown and the kernels are full, glossy, and dry. Husk the ears, then hang them in open-mesh bags in a dry, airy place for several weeks. Test-pop a handful of kernels now and then during the curing period to find out if they are ready for stripping.

When the kernels are thoroughly dry, put on a pair of clean garden gloves and twist the ears as though wringing wet clothes; the kernels will strip off. Store in an airtight jar.

COOKING WITH CORN

It is true that the best-tasting corn is picked after the cooking water has begun to boil. This is because the sugar in corn starts converting to starch the moment it is harvested. The sooner it is cooked, the sweeter the corn. However, since sugar-enhanced and supersweet cultivars became available, the

truism needs to be adapted: It still holds for standard cultivars, but does not necessarily apply to the newer varieties. The sugars in these ears convert much more slowly, and the ears remain fresh tasting days after they reach peak maturity. Nonetheless, regardless of cultivar, the sooner fresh-picked corn is eaten, the better it tastes.

The easiest way to cook corn on the cob is to microwave or steam unshucked ears. They will be done in five to eight minutes, depending on how many ears you cook. Corn tastes as good roasted or grilled in the husk for about 20 minutes. Wet the ears and wrap them in aluminum foil before putting them on a grill. Corn on the cob goes especially well with roasted chicken, baked ham, hamburgers, lobster, fried clams, and soft-shell crab.

Fresh sweet corn is also delicious stripped from the cob and simmered briefly in milk. Succotash is a classic southern dish combining baby lima beans and corn. Corn chowder traditionally includes sautéed salt pork, diced green bell pepper or pimiento, corn kernels, and diced potatoes; corn soufflé is made with puréed creamed corn.

Corn in the Husk

8 ears fresh corn, unshucked
4 tablespoons butter, in 8 pieces
4 slices bread, cut in halves
Salt and freshly ground black pepper, to taste

Remove the coarsest of the outer husks without shucking the corn or removing the silk. Rinse and place in a microwave oven. Cook on high 7 to 8 minutes, then shuck the corn and remove the silk. Arrange the ears on a serving plate. With each ear of corn, serve a pat of butter and a slice of bread to use as a spreader for the butter. Offer salt and pepper.

Serves 8.

COOKING WITH POPCORN

The ears of popping corn are filled with rows of dry, pointed kernels, which are harvested after they have fully matured. Popped in a few tablespoons of hot oil in a covered container set over medium heat, it is a popular and nutritious snack. To keep the kernels from burning, you must shake the pot from the moment it gets hot until the popping stops. Remove the lid as soon as it is done, and pour the popcorn into a large bowl; flavor it with melted butter and salt, or with cumin, chili powder, granulated garlic, lemon pepper, dried vegetable powder—anything that tastes good to you.

To microwave popcorn, place the ears or loose kernels in a paper bag and fold it closed. Place the bag in the microwave oven with the fold side down. Microwave on high until the popping sounds cease.

White hull-less popcorn is favored, but yellow and blue popcorn also pop white.

Molasses Popcorn

    8 cups freshly popped popcorn
    ⅔ cup molasses
    1½ cups sugar
    1 teaspoon vinegar
    ½ cup water
    ¼ to ½ teaspoon salt
    3 tablespoons butter
    3 cups roasted peanuts

In a heavy saucepan, combine the molasses, sugar, vinegar, water, and salt. Stir over low heat until the mixture begins to boil. Cook without stirring until it reaches the hard-ball stage, 270° F on a candy thermometer. Remove the syrup from the heat, stir in the butter, and pour over the popped corn, taking care to coat all the kernels. Add the peanuts and toss until the nuts are distributed evenly throughout the corn. Break the mass into small chunks and allow to cool.
Makes 12 cups.

SELECTED CULTIVARS

Sweet Corn (su)

Early Sunglow 62 days, 4½ feet tall, 6-inch ears, 12 rows of yellow kernels, fast maturing, for areas with cool spring weather.

Seneca Chief 82 days, standard late or main-season hybrid, slender 8-inch ears, 12 to 16 rows of yellow kernels, sweet, tender, one of the most popular for home gardens.

'Honey 'n Pearl' corn

Golden Cross Bantam 85 days, standard hybrid by which all yellow sweet corns are judged, 7½- to 8-inch ears, 10 to 14 rows of yellow kernels, main-crop favorite.

Iochief 89 days, 9-inch ears, 14 to 18 rows of yellow kernels, wind and drought tolerant, All-America Selection.

Golden Jubilee F1 90 to 105 days, extra-large ears 8½ to 9 inches long, 16 to 20 rows of yellow kernels, exceptional flavor for a late-maturing hybrid, tolerates more cold in the soil at planting time than most.

'Strawberry' corn

Silver Queen 92 days, a standard, most widely favored hybrid white corn, 8- to 9-inch ears, 14 to 16 rows of kernels, very sweet (almost too sweet for some), great flavor and tenderness.

Honey & Cream F1 77 days, long-established favorite bicolor, 7- to 8-inch ears, 14 rows of crisp, sweet kernels, successful in cool climates.

Sugar-Enhanced Corn (se)

Precocious F1 65 to 75 days, early but with quality of long-season corn, 7-inch ears, 14 to 16 rows of sweet, buttery yellow kernels.

Sugar Buns F1 70 to 80 days, early, 5 to 5½ feet tall, 7- to 7½-inch ears, 14 rows of tender, creamy, sweet yellow kernels.

Kandy Korn 85 days, extra-sweet, bears 8-inch ears, 16 to 20 rows of yellow kernels, faint red stripes and dark red tips on the husks, retains flavor and tenderness for an extended time; unlike most supersweet hybrids, does not require isolation from other sweet corn.

Platinum Lady 70 days, early, 7½-inch ears, 12 to 14 rows of white kernels.

Sugar Snow F1 70 to 80 days, early, 8-inch ears, 14 full rows of white kernels, for the home garden.

Seneca Dawn F1 75 to 85 days, beautiful bicolor, can stay on the stalk 10 to 14 days after first maturity without ruining the sweet, creamy flavor.

Supersweet Corn (sh2)

Early Xtra-Sweet 70 days, early, 7- to 9-inch ears, 12 to 16 rows of yellow kernels, All-America Selection.

Illini Xtra Sweet 83 days, 8-inch ears, 14 to 18 rows of yellow kernels.

How Sweet It Is 80 days, 8-inch ears, 16 to 18 rows of white kernels, All-America Selection.

Honey 'n Pearl 78 days, 9-inch ears, 16 rows of bicolored kernels, All-America Selection.

Eagle 81 days, midseason, 8- to 9-inch ears, 16 to 22 rows of small bicolored kernels.

Ornamental Corn

Black Aztec 75 days, blue corn of pre-Columbian vintage, eat fresh during the milk stage, most often dried to grind for blue cornmeal.

Chinook 85 to 90 days, beautiful 5- to 6-inch ears, 12 to 14 rows of kernels in colors ranging from dark maroon through tan, with shades of red, bronze, and orange.

Strawberry Corn 105 days, chunky little 3-inch ears, mahogany red kernels, recommended for Christmas ornamentation, also used for popping.

Indian Fingers 110 days, 2½- to 4½-inch ears, small, shiny kernels in mahogany, yellow, red, purple, and orange.

Rainbow Inca 120 days, 8- to 10-inch ears, crosses large, flat, white Peruvian Indian 'Chokelo' cultivars with multicolored southwest Indian corns, eaten fresh as sweet corn, highly ornamental.

Popcorn

Tom Thumb 90 days, early, 3½ to 4 feet tall, 3- to 4-inch ears, for short growing seasons.

Robust 20-82 W 93 days, early, hull-less, crisp, snowy white kernels.

White Cloud F1 95 days, many small ears packed with plump white kernels, vigorous dwarf for short seasons.

Baby Blue 105 days, 5 to 6 feet tall, 3- to 4-inch ears with shiny blue kernels.

Mini Blue 105 to 110 days, two 2- to 4-inch ears, deep colonial blue kernels, handsome dried for use also as an ornamental corn; there is a 'Mini Pink'.

OKRA

Brought to Louisiana by French colonists in the early eighteenth century, okra has long been associated with southern cooking. This hot-weather plant thrives in long, hot summers, but doesn't grow so vigorously in cooler climates. The flowers are very attractive, but the large, coarse nature of the plant keeps it from becoming a favorite edible ornamental. The large leaves have spines that can irritate the skin. If you are sensitive to them, wear gloves and long sleeves when working among the plants.

GROWING OKRA

Okra pods develop on tall plants with flowers like a hibiscus or a single hollyhock. Some cultivars have deep burgundy branches and stems. The tallest cultivars reach between 4 and 7 feet at maturity; dwarfs remain at or under 3 feet.

Like corn, sow okra seeds after the soil warms and temperatures exceed 50° F at night. It needs heat to grow well. The pods begin to mature about eight weeks after planting. Okra thrives in fertile, well-watered soil. Extended cloud cover and cool weather causes some blossoms to drop, but when the sun returns, the plants resume production.

NUTRITIONAL ELEMENTS
Okra, cooked, 8–9 pods

Calories	29
Vitamin A	490 mg
Vitamin C	20 mg
Calcium	92 mg

'Clemson Spineless' okra

Where the growing season is brief, give okra a head start. About four to six weeks before planting time, plant seeds ¼-inch deep in individual peat pots, two or three seeds per 2-inch pot. When the seeds emerge, thin to one seedling per pot. To speed germination, soak seeds for 24 hours before sowing them. Warm the soil by covering it with black plastic. Plant the seedlings in x's cut in the plastic. In warm regions sow seeds for a late crop directly in the garden.

Culture

Transplant seedlings, or sow seeds and thin the seedlings, so the plants stand 8 to 10 inches apart. Keep the soil well watered and weeded until the plants are knee high.

Harvesting

Clip okra pods as they reach 3 to 5 inches to keep the plants producing—and because that is when they taste best. Mature pods are too fibrous. Pick regularly.

Be gentle when harvesting. If the pods break open or are damaged, they will ooze during cooking.

Okra keeps its flavor for a few days sealed in a vegetable bag in the crisper. Dried okra pods can be used in winter arrangements.

COOKING WITH OKRA

A dark green, ridged pod a few inches long, okra is a vegetable popular in the South. Its flavor has found a home in Creole soups called gumbos, and in fish and chicken casseroles. Okra releases a slippery, mucilaginous substance when the stems are cut, and this, along with filé powder, is the thickening agent in Creole cookery. Quick cooking minimizes the gummy potential of okra and preserves the flavor.

Okra is delicious sliced in rounds and fried, steamed whole for about seven minutes, or baked. Dipped in batter or rolled in cornmeal and deep fried, okra is an excellent

accompaniment to grilled meats and fish. Okra combines wonderfully with other vegetables, especially tomatoes, onions, and green bell peppers, as well as with rice. Cooking in metal other than stainless steel causes a chemical reaction which, although harmless, discolors the pods.

Okra, Texas Style

4 cups okra, ends and tips cut off, sliced in rounds ¼ inch thick
¼ cup all-purpose flour
½ teaspoon salt
Freshly ground pepper, to taste
1 egg, lightly beaten
1 tablespoon cold water
1 cup white cornmeal
2 tablespoons olive oil
2 tablespoons butter

Pat the okra dry with paper towels. Combine the flour, salt, and pepper in a bag and shake the okra pieces in the mixture. Beat the egg with the water. Coat the okra with the egg and water mixture, then dredge the pieces in the cornmeal. Spread the okra on paper towels. In a large skillet over medium-high, heat the oil and butter. When the butter is frothing, transfer the okra to the skillet and sauté until golden brown. Drain on a few layers of paper towels.
Serves 6.

SELECTED CULTIVARS

Annie Oakley F1 48 to 55 days, compact, medium height, strong branching, long, slender pods, suited to growing north of the Mason-Dixon line.

Blondy 48 to 55 days, early dwarf, suited to short seasons, All-America Selection.

Perkins Spineless 50 days, semi-dwarf, 3½ feet tall, very tender, almost fiberless.

Red Okra 55 to 65 days, 5 to 6 feet tall, red or bronze-red stems, leaves, and pods when immature.

Clemson Spineless 56 days, midseason, grows to 4 to 5 feet, lots of slightly grooved 7- to 8-inch pods, popular, All-America Selection.

Burgundy 60 to 64 days, 3 to 4 feet tall, burgundy stems, early-maturing red pods retain excellent eating quality even when mature, suitable for cooler regions, All-America Selection.

'Burgundy' okra

**NUTRITIONAL
ELEMENTS**
**Sunflower seeds,
1 ounce**

Calories	157
Vitamin C	14 mg
Calcium	34 mg

**'Sunspot'
sunflower**

SUNFLOWERS

A huge sunflower turning to follow the sun across the sky is a fascinating sight. The flowers are harvested for their seeds. Dried, they feed birds and animals and make nutritious snacks that are a favorite of children.

Any very sunny spot on the patio or in the garden is a fine place for the sunflower crop. Most grow to 6 to 7 feet tall but some soar beyond. A child's garden is an ideal spot for sunflowers. They also grow in any container heavy and deep enough to anchor the stalks as they rise.

GROWING SUNFLOWERS

A half-dozen sunflower plants is plenty for a first experience. Because the stalk of a sunflower goes straight up, the plant needs relatively little space all around.

When it is time to plant corn, it is time to sow sunflower seeds. The flowers bloom in 68 to 110 days, depending on the size of the plant and the variety. The very tall Russian type produces strong stalks with huge flower heads packed with seeds. There are many ornamental sunflowers, but the giant Russians are the best for harvesting.

Culture

Sow seeds 1 inch deep and 6 inches apart. Water thoroughly. Thin the smaller cultivars to 12 inches apart, larger sizes to 18 inches apart. Apply 3 inches of mulch to keep down the weeds. Water the plants regularly.

Harvesting

If you want to keep the seeds from the birds—not every gardener does—cover the flower heads with paper or mesh bags as they begin

to mature. Harvest time is as soon as the seeds start turning brown or when the backs of the flowers begin to yellow. Cut off the heads with about 2 inches of stem attached.

Hang the sunflowers in a dry, hot, well-ventilated place—an attic or a garage works well. When they are completely dry, rub the heads against each other to loosen the seeds, or use a wire brush to scrape them out. Spread the seeds on screens to finish drying.

Store dried seeds in mesh bags until you are ready to roast them.

COOKING WITH SUNFLOWER SEEDS

To prepare the seeds for eating, soak them overnight in salted water, drain, air-dry, then roast in the oven or in a heavy skillet. In the Southwest, sunflower seeds are seasoned with chili powder as they roast. They are also good raw.

Roasted Sunflower Seeds
    2 cups dried sunflower seeds
    2 tablespoons butter
    ½ teaspoon salt

Preheat oven to 200° F. Place the butter in a shallow baking dish and melt it on the stove-top. Scatter the seeds over the melted butter and toss until coated. Roast in the oven until crisp (2 to 3 hours), shaking the pan occasionally. Season lightly with salt. Serve hot, or allow to cool completely and seal in a glass jar with a tight lid.
    Serves 4.

SELECTED CULTIVARS

Sunspot Miniature ornamental, 2-foot stalks, 10-inch nodding heads, seeds for birds and people.

Russian Mammoth 80 to 100 days, 9 to 12 feet tall, plump, thin-shelled, striped seeds.

Sun 891 110 days, 7 feet or more, high-yielding seed-filled heads 8 to 12 inches across.

Tceqa Seeds yield a blue-black dye used by the Hopi to color wool and baskets, edible.

TOMATILLO/ HUSK TOMATO

The names are misleading because the tomatillo and husk tomato do not taste like a tomato. They just look a little like tiny green tomatoes once you remove the outer husk. They are easy plants to grow and very prolific producers. The tomatillo grows to 4 feet whereas

'Indian Strain' tomatillos

the husk tomato and ground cherry are shorter but sprawling.

The tomatillo (*Physalis ixocarpa*) and its close relative the husk tomato (*Physalis peruviana*) are small yellow-green, tomatolike fruit, loosely covered with a thin husk, or skin. When the fruit ripens, the husks first turn gold, then light brown, and the fruit drops to the ground. Another species of husk tomato is the ground cherry (*Physalis pruinosa*), which is also called the strawberry tomato and poha berry. It is about the size of a cherry tomato and grown the same way.

GROWING TOMATILLOS

In hot regions, set out seedlings. Start your own six weeks before the outdoor planting date. Sow seeds ½ inch deep in individual peat pots. Tomatillos mature 90 to 100 days from setting out.

Culture

The plants produce well in marginal soil but not in rich soil. Light applications of compost are enough. After frost has passed, set out seedlings, or sow seeds, three to five seeds to a hill. Maintain soil moisture in the seedbed until the seedlings emerge. When the plants are 4 to 6 inches tall, thin the hills to one or two plants. Mound soil lightly around the base to give support. At 16 inches tall, build up the hills again. Water deeply once a week.

Harvesting

Harvest when the husks turn brown and begin to open, showing the fruit. With time they become seedier, but sweeter for eating fresh. Green cultivars turn yellow; purple cultivars turn deep purple.

Picked while still in the husk, the fruit keeps several weeks in the crisper.

'Toma Verde' tomatillo

COOKING WITH TOMATILLOS

The fruit of the tomatillo and its cousin the husk tomato are crisp, with hints of the flavor of lemon and apple; when fully ripe they are somewhat sweet. The ground cherry is most often used to make a sweet jam. Tomatillos are larger than husk tomatoes and are used in salads and vegetables dishes.

In Mexican cookery many sauces use tomatillos for their bright green color and equally bright taste. Tomatillos are a main ingredient in the ubiquitous salsa, which is made by lightly roasting the green or purple fruit and blending it with jalapeño peppers, onions, cilantro, lime juice, and salt.

Shep Ogden's Salsa

    10 pounds ripe tomatoes
    12 assorted hot peppers: ha-
        banero, anaheim, cayenne,
        jalapeño; stemmed, seeded,
        and chopped
    3 medium onions, chopped
    4 cloves garlic, minced
    6 tomatillos, chopped
    2 tablespoons salt
    ½ cup olive oil
    ½ cup vinegar
    2 tablespoons maple syrup
        or sugar
    1 tablespoon minced basil
    1 tablespoon minced cilantro
    1 tablespoon minced parsley
        or chervil

Toss together the tomatoes, peppers, onion, garlic, tomatillos, and salt. Pour into a colander and leave at room temperature for 2 hours. Drain, transfer to a large pot, and set over medium heat. Stir in the oil, vinegar, maple syrup or sugar, and herbs; simmer, stirring often, until the sauce has thickened and the flavor has developed. Use some of the salsa fresh and pack the re-mainder into hot sterilized jars and process according to proper canning procedures.
Makes 4 quarts.

SELECTED CULTIVARS

Indian Strain 55 days, small, sweet-sour flavor popular in Mexican cuisine, salads, and salad dressing.

Toma Verde (Tomatillo Verde or Green Husk Tomatillo) 60 days, globe-shaped, 2-ounce fruit used for Mexican cuisine and salads.

Purple Tomatillo 80 days, preferred by southwestern gardeners for its color, delicious when ripe.

Yellow Husk Ground Cherry (Golden Tomatillo or Cape Gooseberry) 80 days, sweet, mellow flavor that suits salsa, also tasty fresh.

NUTRITIONAL ELEMENTS
Tomatillos, 1 pound, as harvested

Calories	221
Vitamin A	3,000 mg
Vitamin C	44 mg
Calcium	38 mg

'Toma Verde' tomatillo

A FEW FABULOUS PERENNIALS

Artichokes are thistles; you can see the relationship in the prickles at the ends of the bud scales, and in the large violet flower that develops if you don't pick the bud. In California, where artichokes grow as perennials without special protection, they are sometimes raised for their ornamental value.

Only a few perennials belong in the vegetable garden, but they are all handsome plants and dear to the chef. Artichokes, asparagus, rhubarb, and strawberries are the stuff of gourmet meals. According to botanists, the artichoke is a fruit, as are strawberries—but never mind, they deserve a space. Rounding out this group are chayotes and Jerusalem artichokes, or sunchokes, the tuberous roots of tall, small-flowered sunflowers.

Once you plant a perennial, it comes back year after year. This is a great labor-saver, but perennials do need some maintenance. Crabgrass can make a mess of a young strawberry patch, and asparagus and other perennial ferns also are vulnerable to weeds. A 3-inch mulch helps keep out the weeds, and, if you are wise, you will pull the few that do come through.

Place perennials a safe distance from mowers and rotary-tiller activity because they remain in the same spot year after year. In the hot South, artichokes benefit from a little shade in the late afternoon, and the asparagus patch succeeds near tall deciduous trees because the harvest is over before the leaves are fully out.

Because perennials stay in place and need to be productive for many years, provide generous planting holes well supplied with slowrelease fertilizers and compost or dried manure. Apply an annual mulch to replenish the soil. Fertilize in September and again in early spring just as growth begins. Water when the sky runs dry.

ARTICHOKES

Artichokes are handsome plants that can take the place of shrubs in the herb garden or the perennial border. They also look attractive as edging or as a backdrop in the vegetable garden. Two or three plants satisfy the needs of the average family—a mature plant yields as many as 40 heads.

Artichokes develop at the tops of long stems branching from a shrublike perennial. Left on the plant, the artichokes open into big violet flowers. The harvest season is April and May in mild regions, summer and fall in the North. Where winter temperatures stay above 20° F, the plant is perennial and usually produces for three to five years. It thrives on the mild West Coast.

GROWING ARTICHOKES

In cooler areas artichokes survive moderate winters given a mulch. Cut the plant to the ground before applying the mulch, then cover it with an upside-down bushel basket. In spring, remove the basket and mulch as soon as danger of frost has passed: The plants tend to rot if you don't. The current season's artichokes develop from offshoots of the original plants. In regions where summers are very hot, artichokes benefit from some shade in the afternoon.

Where winters are very severe, grow artichokes as tender perennials. In late fall, dig the roots, store them for the winter in damp sand in a cool place, and replant them the following spring.

Culture

Artichokes are easiest to grow from root divisions. Some catalogs offer seeds. Seeds started four to six weeks early and transplanted to the open garden in May usually produce a crop the first season. It takes 100 days of frost-free sunshine for a transplant to mature a crop.

Plant root divisions in holes, or trenches, 8 inches deep and lined with 1 inch of compost or manure. Or prepare the trench by loosening the bottom 2 inches of soil and mixing in a handful of 10–10–10 fertilizer. For each artichoke plant, prepare a planting hole big enough to handle a medium shrub, and dig in 1 cup of 10–10–10 fertilizer or a shovelful of compost or chicken

Artichoke blossom

manure. Set each plant so the crown is at ground level with 3 to 5 feet of open space all around. Water consistently to promote rapid growth and early fruition.

Where the plants are dormant in winter, fertilize in early spring with 1 cup of 10-10-10 fertilizer for each. In regions where artichokes grow all year, fertilize in the fall. Production stays high if you divide the roots every three to four years: Split a big clump into three or four divisions.

Harvesting

An artichoke is ready to harvest when it is the size of a medium orange—about 4 inches across. Cut about 2 inches of stem with the artichoke. Take the central head first and the side heads as they develop.

Artichokes keep in the crisper for two to three weeks.

COOKING WITH ARTICHOKES

The elegant globe-shaped artichoke is the flower bud of a big, coarse, thistlelike herb that grows to 4½ feet tall and almost as wide. Artichokes have a mild and somewhat earthy flavor. The edible portion of a mature artichoke is the thickened bottom part of the leaf where it attaches to the heart. Dip this end into the condiment of your choice and pull the lower-half of the leaf upside down through your teeth. At the core of the artichoke is a hairy mass called the "choke." Scrape this away to reveal the delicious artichoke heart beneath.

Steam artichokes, or poach them in simmering salted water until tender, and serve them hot with lemon juice, hollandaise sauce, or a ramekin of light mayonnaise. They may be served cold with a piquant vinaigrette.

In Europe, early in the artichoke season, tender baby artichokes are served raw with a sharp vinaigrette. Very young artichokes are also trimmed of their outer leaves, steamed and eaten whole or halved or quartered. These are excellent left to soak in a pungent marinade before being eaten.

Artichokes With Lemon Butter

4 medium-to-large artichokes
½ tablespoon salt
Juice of ½ medium lemon, strained
6 tablespoons cold, lightly salted butter, cut up

Turn the artichokes stem end down and rinse them. Cut the stem end from each so that the artichoke sits flat. Peel the cut-off stem ends to the tender core—this is edible, too. Trim about 1 inch off the top and cut off the thorny tips of the leaves.

Place the artichokes in a saucepan small enough to keep them pressed together and upright. Fill the saucepan with cold water to cover and add the salt and the stems. Cover and bring the water to a rapid boil over high heat. Reduce the heat and simmer the artichokes 45 minutes. Turn off the heat and leave the artichokes in the water 15 to 30 minutes more.

In a small saucepan, simmer the lemon juice until reduced by one fourth. Add the butter all at once and, as it melts, beat it into the lemon juice. Drain the artichokes and serve them in small bowls accompanied by small dipping bowls of lemon butter.
Serves 4.
Note: If you have a pressure cooker, it is possible to steam the artichokes in as little as 10 minutes after reaching optimum pressure. Not only are they ready to eat sooner, but they will never be soggy, and few valuable nutrients are lost because the artichokes are not submerged in boiling water. Although this is a particularly good

NUTRITIONAL ELEMENTS
Artichoke, cooked, 1 large
Calories   44
Vitamin C   8 mg
Calcium   51 mg

**'Green Globe'
artichoke**

ASPARAGUS

Asparagus thrives almost everywhere in the country except the hot Southeast. It is grown commercially where it is cold enough in winter to freeze the top few inches of soil.

A bed started from seed should not be picked until its fourth or fifth year, though some growers say certain cultivars can be picked the second year. Most home gardeners set out two- or, better yet, three-year-old roots. These are harvested the second or third year after planting. An asparagus bed produces for as many as 20 years, and maturing plants produce seedlings which grow up to take the place of the parents. Be sure to plant cultivars specified as rust resistant.

Growers offer male plants that do not produce berries and are thought to have more energy to produce spears.

Cultivars of asparagus that blanch well are called "white asparagus"; these are much appreciated in Europe. Blanched, the spears are pale gold and the tips touched with green. The flavor is dry—not as sweet as green asparagus. Blanch a few spears by mounding the mulch or soil 6 to 8 inches high just as they start to pop up. To harvest, gently poke your finger into the mound, locate the spear, and bend until it snaps off.

Ten plants per family member provide enough for serving fresh and freezing.

way to steam artichokes, a pressure cooker is a healthy and nutritious alternative to boiling and simmering any vegetable that benefits from longer cooking.

SELECTED CULTIVARS

Green Globe Improved Standard artichoke variety, 2½ to 4½ feet tall, green flower buds within 100 days of transplanting, recommended for cooler regions.

Imperial Star Perennial for Zones 8 to 10, elsewhere a hardy annual, 3 to 4 feet, produces artichokes in one season.

GROWING ASPARAGUS

Established plants send up spears rapidly in early- to mid-spring and can be harvested for about six weeks. Then allow the spears to grow up into stalks 4 to 5 feet tall. These develop into beautiful, very fine feathery ferns.

Asparagus needs a bed with several short rows. It can be located anywhere—along a fence, at the back of a perennial border, or at the back of the vegetable garden where it will not interfere with the annual tilling. Asparagus tolerates a little summer shade from deciduous trees. Organic gardeners often interplant asparagus with tomato plants because asparagus beetles dislike the tomato odor.

Culture

Start asparagus 10 to 12 weeks before the last frost is expected, by sowing seeds indoors ¼ inch deep in a sterile growing medium in individual peat pots. Sow one seed to a pot. Transplant the seedlings to the garden after all danger of frost has passed.

Plant asparagus roots in early fall or early spring. If you grow asparagus in sandy loam that warms quickly in spring, the crop comes in early. Plant the roots in trenches 4 feet apart and 10 inches deep. Mix the soil from the trenches with one third its volume of sharp sand; line the floor of the trench with 1 inch of dried cow manure or compost. Cover that with 4 inches of the sandy soil.

Spread the roots and center them 18 inches apart. Cover the roots with 2 inches of soil. As the asparagus spears grow up, add another 2 inches of soil. Continue adding soil every two weeks until the trenches are slightly mounded above the ground. Water generously as the tops develop.

Each year in early spring before the spears appear, work a handful of compost or a tablespoon of 10–10–10 fertilizer into the soil over each plant. Just before spring growth starts, work in 1 tablespoon of sodium nitrate per plant. After the cutting season, rake 1 pound of sodium nitrate into the bed for every 40 plants and apply a 3-inch layer of mulch to conserve moisture and keep down the weeds.

In August, or early spring, transplant to a new row seedlings that volunteer in the asparagus bed. Asparagus ferns often contain diseases that are hard to detect. As a health measure, when the asparagus ferns begin to die down in fall,

'Mary Washington' asparagus

NUTRITIONAL ELEMENTS

Asparagus, cooked, ⅔ cup

Calories	20 to 50*
Vitamin A	900 mg
Vitamin C	26 mg
Calcium	21 mg
B₁	.18 mg
B₂	.20 mg

*Depending on storage

---

trim all the stalks back to 5 inches. Remove the ferns to the garbage and do not compost them.

Harvesting

Both seed- and root-grown asparagus plants need to grow the first year. Do not harvest this year. Harvest lightly the second year from plants started as roots, picking 6- to 8-inch spears for four full weeks as they appear. If you fail to keep these harvested, they shoot up into ferns and production of spears slows.

Do not harvest at all the second year from plants started from seed, although these can be harvested lightly the third year.

To harvest, bend and break 6- to 8-inch spears close to or just under the soil line. When production slows noticeably, stop picking and let the ferns grow out.

To keep harvested asparagus fresh, recut the stems indoors and set them bottom-down in an inch of water in a tall container. Cover with plastic and store in the refrigerator. Or steam-blanch and freeze the spears.

COOKING WITH ASPARAGUS

This elegant vegetable is loaded with B vitamins as well as vitamin C and calcium. Asparagus is delicious steamed until just tender (a little salt helps keep the green color bright). If the spears turn yellow-green, they are overdone.

If the spears are thin, cut them in 2-inch pieces and stir-fry them with mushrooms. Thin raw asparagus cut in 1-inch pieces adds a nice crunch and flavor to spring salads. These slim spears are great crudités. A half-dozen spears, cooked, chilled, topped with vinaigrette, or rolled in thin slices of ham and served with a lemony mayonnaise sauce, makes a great first course.

Asparagus With Sauce Marcel

24 to 36 large asparagus spears
2 teaspoons salt
1 cup mayonnaise
Juice of ½ lemon, strained
2 teaspoons grainy Dijon-style mustard

Rinse the asparagus in a sinkful of cold water. Bend the tough bottom portion of each spear back until it snaps off. Stand the asparagus upright in a steamer with only the stem ends in simmering salted water. Cover snugly. They are done when the stem ends are fork tender (6 to 10 minutes). Lift the spears onto a paper towel and cover with more paper towels until serving.

Using a fork, whip together the mayonnaise, lemon juice, and mustard. Serve the asparagus on heated plates with a ramekin of this Sauce Marcel on the side.

Serves 4 to 6.

SELECTED CULTIVARS

Jersey Giant From Rutgers University, large succulent green spears, mostly male, fine flavor, rust and disease resistant; recommended for Northeast, Midwest, and mid-Atlantic and Great Plains states.

Larac F1 Early European hybrid, blanches well, tolerates some cutting the second year from seed, recommended for flavor.

UC 157 F2 Developed for mild-winter areas including the Northwest, Southwest, and South; high yields of predominantly male spears, some resistance to diseases.

Mary Washington Thick, straight, dark green tinged with purple at the tips, highly resistant to rust, new selections bear earlier and produce larger spears without the purple overcast; 'Waltham Washington' is an improved hybrid with higher resistance to rust.

CHAYOTES

The chayote (pronounced *chy-YOH-tee*) is also known as vegetable pear, mirliton, mango squash, and by many other common names. Exceptionally high in vitamin C, it looks a little like a large green pear or an apple with a cleft and is used like summer squash. It is a tropical vine and a cousin to summer squash and cucumber.

Chayote is an evergreen perennial where winters are frost free, especially in parts of southern California and along the Gulf Coast. After the second year's growth, the large root tubers can be dug and used like potatoes.

GROWING CHAYOTES

In warm regions, plant chayotes in fall or early spring when the soil warms to at least 60° F. Young chayote shoots grow out in spring. Between fruiting seasons, prune back the chayote's large central stem to about 6 feet.

In regions where the ground freezes no more than 1 inch deep, chayote tops die back; but with a 10-inch mulch for winter protection, the root usually survives. In spring the vine revives and rapidly covers a 10- to 15-foot section of fence. With a plentiful supply of water, it produces 30 to 100 fruit per vine in five to six months.

In cool climates, plant chayote after the last frost in spring and grow it as an annual. Provided

Chayote vine

NUTRITIONAL ELEMENTS
Chayote, raw, ½ cup
Calories   30
Vitamin C   2,000 mg
Calcium   15 mg

Chayote fruit

there are five or six months of growing season ahead, the chayote will mature fruit.

Culture
To produce fruit, chayotes must cross-pollinate, which means you need to plant at least two. The large-lobed leaves and quick growth make it a suitable plant for summer screening. It also grows well in big tubs or planters.

Dig a shovelful of dried cow manure into the planting holes and add another shovelful of compost. Space the holes 12 feet apart and provide strong supports. The whole fruit is the seed: Plant the chayote on its side with the broad end down in the earth and a little of the narrow end showing above the soil. Water well and sustain soil moisture. Halfway through the growing season, work a cupful of compost or 10-10-10 fertilizer into the soil around each plant.

Harvesting
Harvest the fruit young, when they are 4 to 6 inches long.

Young fruit sealed in a vegetable bag keeps for at least a week. Older fruit has a heavier skin and keeps even longer in a cool, dry place.

COOKING WITH CHAYOTES

The flavor of chayote is mild and the flesh is crisp. An older chayote with hardened skin should be peeled. A tender young chayote, like tender young squash, has edible skin. Halve it, cutting through the flat inner seed, and steam or microwave the halves, seed included. A chayote can be diced or mashed, or stuffed and baked. Cooked, the chayote has a very delicate taste and needs to be enhanced with seasonings. It may be prepared in the same ways as the summer squashes.

Steamed Chayote
2 large fresh chayotes, halved
2 tablespoons melted butter
Garlic salt, to taste
4 teaspoons freshly grated
  Parmesan cheese
½ teaspoon dried oregano
½ teaspoon dried thyme
Freshly ground black pepper

Halve the chayotes and place them, cut side up, in a steamer. Drizzle the melted butter evenly over them, and season each piece with a little garlic salt and a teaspoon of grated Parmesan cheese. Rub the dried herbs between your fingers and let the bits fall evenly over the chayotes. Cover and steam 20 minutes. Serve the chayotes with a little black pepper.

Serves 4.

SELECTED VARIETIES

A few national garden catalogs offer the species *Sechium edule.*

JERUSALEM ARTICHOKES

The Jerusalem artichoke is also called sun-turner and sunflower. In France the roots are sold as *topi-nambours;* the Italian word is *gira-sole.* The plants are 3 to 6 feet tall, topped by masses of 3- to 4-inch sunflowers. Jerusalem artichokes are perennial, and a stand of them is an asset to almost any sunny corner of the garden, and especially appropriate in a wild garden. The height makes them suitable for use as a divider between landscape areas. Once established, Jerusalem artichokes go on almost forever without much care—in fact, they are hard to get rid of and can become pests. They grow as well in the cold North as in the hot South.

Jerusalem artichoke

Jerusalem artichoke

NUTRITIONAL ELEMENTS

Jerusalem artichoke, raw, 4 small

Calories	7 to 75*
Vitamin C	4 mg
Calcium	14 mg

*Depending on storage

GROWING JERUSALEM ARTICHOKES

Jerusalem artichokes do well where potatoes succeed, and they thrive in sandy, light soil with sustained moisture. But they will grow under almost any conditions as long as they have sun.

Culture

Seed tubers of Jerusalem artichokes, like potatoes, are sold whole. You cut or break them into pieces, each with one or two eyes, and plant them while the cuts are fresh. In cool regions planting time is as soon as the ground can be worked in spring, between April and May. In the South, plant them in the fall.

Plant the fresh-cut pieces of tuber in hills of six. Set them 4 inches deep in holes 12 inches apart. Set the pieces eyes up, cut sides down. When the plants are 5 to 6 inches high, mound the soil around the stems and scratch a handful of compost or 5–10–10 fertilizer into the soil beside each plant.

Harvesting

The harvest usually begins in fall after the tops die down. But the tubers are ready for digging as early as 100 to 105 days after planting. To harvest, cut back the tops of the plants whose tubers you are digging and, with a spading fork, gently lift the tubers. Harvest only what you can use, and dig more as needed. Leave a few tubers in the ground to develop next year.

Rinse the tubers in many changes of water, and scrub with a stiff-bristled brush to remove all the soil. If they are young and fresh looking, leave on the skin. If the tubers are old, peel them.

You can harvest Jerusalem artichokes in late fall and store them in layers of damp sand, but you can also leave them in the ground until you need them.

COOKING WITH JERUSALEM ARTICHOKES

Jerusalem artichokes are not from Jerusalem nor are they related to artichokes. Their slightly nutty flavor is reminiscent of the globe artichoke, but their texture is closer to that of celeriac. These knobby tubers are the roots of a species of small-flowered American sunflower. They have thin, reddish brown skin and creamy white flesh. Calorie counters can use Jerusalem artichokes as a substitute for potatoes.

The tubers are delicious boiled in their skins and lightly salted. Overcooked, they seem a little stringy. Jerusalem artichokes are also good sliced and sautéed or mashed like potatoes. In the South, they are pickled, or sliced thinly and dressed with vinegar, salt, and pepper.

Purée of Jerusalem Artichokes
Here we combine potatoes with the subtle sweet taste of the Jerusalem artichoke and hazelnuts to accent their mild nuttiness. This purée is very good with roasted beef.

    1 pound Jerusalem artichokes,
      peeled
    1 large potato, peeled
    4 tablespoons butter
    ½ medium onion, chopped
    ½ cup toasted hazelnuts, chopped
    2 tablespoons cream
    Grated zest of 1 medium lemon
    ⅛ teaspoon cayenne pepper
    Salt and freshly ground black
      pepper, to taste

Slice the Jerusalem artichokes and potatoes ¼ inch thick. Put them in a pot of enough boiling water just to cover them. Cook just until tender (about 20 minutes). Drain and set aside.

Preheat oven to 350° F. Melt 2 tablespoons of the butter in a skillet and sauté the onions until golden (about 10 minutes). Process the cooked vegetables with the remaining ingredients, except the salt and pepper, until smooth. Season with salt and a generous grinding of black pepper. Transfer to a casserole, smooth the top, and bake just until the top is golden and the mixture is hot (15 to 20 minutes).

Serves 6.

SELECTED CULTIVARS

Stampede 90 to 100 days, extra-early, high yield, large, white tubers, plants flower in July, winter hardy in severe cold.

Nova Scotia Redskin 90 to 100 days, attractive purple skin, creamy white interior, excellent flavor.

RHUBARB

Rhubarb is a handsome perennial with a cluster of thick 20-inch crimson or crimson-green edible stalks topped by big bold arrow-shaped green leaves. Never eat the leaves—they contain toxic levels of oxalic acid. Rhubarb, especially the very red varieties, is attractive enough to be used as a bold foliage accent in the perennial border. It also makes a handsome low divider and it thrives in a large tub.

GROWING RHUBARB

To succeed, rhubarb needs a spring that is long and cool and a winter with a period when the ground freezes for several inches down. If you plant rhubarb in the vegetable garden, position it at the side or the back, out of the way.

Rhubarb

Harvest in midspring when the plants are growing vigorously. Once the weather warms and growth slows, the harvest is over. The plants then send up majestic panicles of dainty white florets which should be cut off so the plant puts its strength into growth for next year's supply of rhubarb stalks.

Three to four plants supply the average household generously. Rhubarb is productive for four to six years.

Culture

As soon as the ground can be worked in early spring, plant one-year-old crowns, or root divisions, with one to three buds, or eyes. Harvest begins the second season. You can start rhubarb from seed in a cold frame, but success is difficult.

Prepare a planting hole about 2 feet deep with 3 to 5 feet all around. Mix a shovelful of compost or dried cow manure into the soil taken from the hole, and another into the soil at the bottom of the hole. Refill the hole to within 4 inches of the top. Set the crown of the plant in the center and fill the hole with water. When it has drained, cover the crown with soil and tamp gently. Water again, then mulch to keep down weeds.

Fertilize each rhubarb plant in spring with a spadeful of dried manure, or with 1 cup of 5–8–7 or 5–10–5 fertilizer. Divide rhubarb when the stalks become thin and the plant appears crowded. Dig up the roots in spring when the tips of the stalks are beginning to show, and divide so that each piece of the crown has one to three good eyes.

Harvesting

Harvest begins in spring when the thick, fast-growing stalks are coming in rapidly. Twist the stalk and pull gently but firmly to free it from the crown.

Cut the stalks an inch or two below the bottom of the leaf. Compost all portions of the leaf and the rough bit at the bottom of the stalk. Use a potato peeler to peel the coarse skin off tough old stalks.

Do not harvest stalks the first year. The second year, over one to two weeks, pull stems as they reach mature size. From the third year on, harvest stalks for eight weeks or more. Never take more than half the stalks from any one plant.

Rhubarb freezes well. Rinse and cut the stalks in 1- to 2-inch pieces, sprinkle with sugar, cover, and freeze; or stew rhubarb and freeze.

COOKING WITH RHUBARB

Tender young stalks stewed with sugar make one of the world's finest fruit compotes. Stewed rhubarb folded into stiffly whipped cream makes a delicious instant mousse. Combined with strawberries in a pie filling, rhubarb is ambrosial. It also makes a great sauce for pancakes and a wonderful jam.

Rhubarb Country Tart

Pastry
   1¼ cups all-purpose flour
   1 tablespoon sugar
   Generous pinch of salt
   6 tablespoons cold butter, cut
      in pieces
   1 teaspoon grated orange zest
   2 tablespoons ice water

Filling
   5 tablespoons confectioners'
      sugar
   2½ cups 1-inch rhubarb chunks
   Slivered orange zest

Make the pastry shell by combining the flour, sugar, and salt in a mixing bowl. Toss with a fork to blend. Cut in the butter and the zest until the mixture resembles coarse crumbs. Sprinkle the water, 1 tablespoon at a time, over the mixture and toss until it can be gathered into a ball.

Knead it together and flatten it slightly. Wrap in plastic wrap and refrigerate 30 minutes.

Preheat oven to 350° F. Roll out the chilled dough on a lightly floured surface to make an 11-inch circle. Transfer it to a baking sheet. Lightly mark a 9-inch circle in the center. Sprinkle the center area with 3 tablespoons of the confectioners' sugar. Spread the rhubarb evenly over the sugar in the inner circle and sprinkle on the remaining 2 tablespoons sugar and the slivered zest.

Fold the edges of the dough up and over the fruit to cover the outer edges of the circle. Lightly crimp the fullness. If you wish, you may brush the top edge of the tart with milk then lightly sprinkle it with granulated sugar. Bake the tart until the crust is golden and the filling bubbling (about 35 to 45 minutes).

Serves 8.

SELECTED CULTIVARS

Victoria Crimson stalks, green near the leaf, heavy yield, some catalogs also offer rooted plants, good for northern gardens.

Valentine Deep red stalks, retains color when cooked, sweet, good for northern gardens.

McDonald's Bright red stalks, popular in cold-winter areas.

Giant Cherry Red stalks, needs less cold to break dormancy, good where winters are mild.

Rhubarb in a flower bed

STRAWBERRIES

Strawberries are low-growing, pretty little plants whose starry white flowers turn into berries. Plant them in a garden row or in a bed of their own and they quickly send out runners. The runners root new plantlets which, once well established, can be severed from the parent plant and used to start a new row or renew the original bed. Strawberry beds are best renewed every four to six years.

These winter-hardy plants are available in cultivars that produce one crop a year, either early (June-bearing) or midseason, and in ever-bearer cultivars whose main crop ripens in late summer. A new type of everbearer described as "day neutral" produces its largest crop midseason through fall. Two dozen plants of each keeps a family in berries from the first June crop through September's "day neutral" bonanza.

Alpine strawberries, or *fraises des bois*, are small-leaved plants whose tiny flowers are followed by little, pointed, tart-sweet fruit with the taste of wild field berries. Because they don't produce runners, they can be used to edge a perennial border or a sunny herb garden. They produce a few berries all season long, but unless you plant masses of them, you will not be serving them by the bowlful. They are also most commonly sold as seed.

GROWING STRAWBERRIES

In cool regions set out strawberry plants in early spring as soon as the soil can be worked. In warm regions set them out in spring or fall.

Strawberries are usually planted at the edge of the vegetable garden or in a bed of their own. They do best in fertile, light, somewhat acid soil, and poorly where lime has recently been applied. A few weeks before planting, prepare a well-worked row 4 inches wide. Top the soil with 2 inches of compost or dried manure and dig it in to a depth of 4 to 6 inches. Installing a soaker hose under a 2-inch mulch keeps the plants growing early in the season without overwatering.

The first season, keep June bearers picked of all flowers; they will give a lavish first crop the following

'Alexandria' strawberry

year. Pick flowers on everbearers throughout their first appearance in spring and allow them to bloom and set fruit starting in July. Remove blossoms of "day neutral" strawberries until midseason, and they produce through fall. Cut off all runners the first season.

Culture

When planting strawberry plants, there are two firm rules: Do not let the sun touch the roots, and plant the crowns at the exact level at which they were growing before. Never plant strawberries deeply. Make a small hump of soil in the floor of the bed; holding the plant by its central leaves, set it over the hump, the crown level with the soil surface. Spread the roots over the hump and out over the bed and cover them with about 1½ inches of soil. Tamp the soil firmly over the roots and mulch lightly.

About six weeks after planting, strawberry plants send out run-ners. The casual approach is to let them run at will. However, with the years, the growth of the runners can make the bed so broad and dense that fruit production drops and problems develop. An easy solution is to cut the bed back to 12 to 18 inches by mowing away the plants on the sides. Mulch the cut-back areas with straw and train the new runners from the original bed to grow over the straw. They will be a source of berries the following year, and will form the new bed.

The more formal approach to runners is to cut them off until the bed has been producing for three years. The fourth year allow them to grow and root, and transplant the following spring to start a new bed. The spring after that, the new bed will be in full production, and you can dig up the original bed.

In winter as the temperature drops toward 20° F, cover straw-berry plants with a 6-inch straw mulch. After the ground freezes hard, pile on a foot more of straw. In early spring remove the uppermost layer of mulch, leaving the straw that has matted down to make a clean bed for the berries to rest on. The custom of mulching strawberries with straw is what gave them their name.

Birds do get at bright red berries! The only effective solution is a physical barrier—a covering of nylon mesh, screening, cheesecloth, or a floating row cover.

Harvesting

If the berries ripen on mulch or clean straw, the fruit never has to be rinsed and it is better tasting for it. Ripe strawberries are perfect for only a day or so—keep the beds picked. Harvest berries into glass or plastic containers, not metal.

Strawberries remain in good condition a day or two sealed in a vegetable bag and stored in the crisper. Bring them back to room temperature before serving.

Strawberries freeze well. Hull the berries, transfer to plastic containers, and freeze. If the berries must be rinsed clean, drain and air-dry them, then freeze.

COOKING WITH STRAWBERRIES

Strawberries are one of nature's greatest successes. One of the best things about having a vegetable garden is that you can bypass those woody, half-ripe, hollow, tasteless strawberries at the market. Let yours ripen to perfection and eat them warm from the sun.

Strawberries are ideal with their fresh green hulls and stems still attached. They are just as perfect stemmed, sliced, and served over ice cream, frozen yogurt, or shortcake.

NUTRITIONAL ELEMENTS
Strawberries, raw, 1 cup
Calories	45
Vitamin C	85 mg
Calcium	21 mg

'Earliglow' strawberries

group warrants—proportions are immaterial. Very quickly rinse freshly picked strawberries, swishing them in a sweet white wine. Drain at once. Pile them high in a pretty bowl or napkin-lined basket.

Sieve light brown sugar and pile it into a serving bowl. Stir low-fat sour cream to thin it slightly and spoon it into a glass bowl.

To serve, spoon portions onto individual plates. Dip a strawberry into sour cream, then into brown sugar, then pop it into your mouth. Be aware that it is too easy to eat too many.

SELECTED VARIETIES

A few catalogs advertise strawberry plants and some offer seeds as well. For best success buy cultivars suited to your area from a local nursery.

Alpine Strawberries
Most alpine varieties are available as seed. Some nurseries carry them as started plants.

Alexandria 120 days from seed, larger than most alpines, survives considerable neglect.

Baron Solemacher Available as seed, intensely sweet and fragrant fruit.

Charles the Fifth Produces a handful of tiny, intensely flavored berries throughout the season.

Improved Rugens Popular late-season bearer that produces fruit from midsummer till midautumn, neat plant without runners.

Mignonetti 75 days from seed, recommended for hanging baskets, containers, and window boxes.

White Alpine Produces whitish fruit, bears the second year from seeds sown four weeks before the first frost.

When the berries are small, or you have too many, pick them ripe and make strawberry jam or pie. Strawberries also pair well with rhubarb, walnuts, breakfast cereal, and waffles. Blend them with ice, low-fat yogurt, and ripe bananas to make great summer "smoothies."

Glorious Strawberries
For breakfast, brunch, or dessert, this is truly a glorious way to enjoy fresh, sweet strawberries.

Use as many strawberries and accompaniments as the size of your

Standard Strawberries

Annapolis Vigorous and productive over a period of several weeks, Zones 3 to 8, recommended for cooler regions.

Big Red Early-maturing, June-bearing variety, large, tangy red berries with lots of runners with which to renew the bed.

Cardinal Strong midseason producer of large berries that are red all the way through, disease resistant and cold hardy.

Cavendish Winter-hardy berry recommended for cool regions, resists red stele disease.

Dunlap Reliably large yield of smooth scarlet berries that hint at wild berry flavor, insect and disease resistant.

Earliglow Early variety that produces sweet, glossy, red fruit, Zones 4 to 8.

Honeoye Vigorous producer of large, cone-shaped berries, recommended for sweetness.

Jewel Bright red wedge-shaped berries over an unusually long span of weeks, recommended for you-pick farming.

Sparkle Deep red berries in late June, plentiful supply of runners, recommended for cold regions.

Spring Giant Berries up to 3 inches across, requires cross-pollination from another strawberry for best production.

Surecrop Very large sweet berries, disease resistant, Zones 4 to 8.

Everbearing Strawberries

Ever Red Everbearing variety of 'Big Red', vigorous plants produce large berries all season long.

Fort Laramie Large berries with firm flesh, lots of runners, which can be trained to grow up a post, withstands cold and heat.

Ogallala Combines wild strawberry flavor with the productivity associated with standard types, plants begin bearing in May and continue through September, hardy and drought tolerant.

Ostara Prolific bearer of very large berries.

Ozark Beauty Large berries in June and another crop of mid-sized fruit six to eight weeks later, high yield, Zones 4 to 8.

Picnic 120 days from seed, produces a steady supply of mid-sized fruit on bush, compact plants with only a few short runners, recommended for containers and edging.

Selva Heavy producer of sweet, wedge-shaped fruit, very disease resistant.

Shortcake Long glossy fruit is red throughout, the second crop of berries is larger than most everbearers, Zones 4 to 8.

Sweetheart 120 to 122 days from seed, everbearing variety that produces firm, juicy berries from July to fall, needs winter protection in cool regions.

Day Neutral Strawberries

September Sweet Sweet mid-sized fruit on disease-resistant plants, fruiting begins in June with the heaviest crop in September, Zones 4 to 8.

Tristar Large berries are red throughout, heaviest production in the fall, in cool regions winter protection is recommended, Zones 4 to 8.

SOURCE LIST

It's generally best to purchase seeds and other garden material from a local nursery or garden center. However, if a local nursery doesn't carry the varieties you want, here are some mail-order sources. Most carry vegetable, herb, and flower seeds as well as books, tools, and supplies. Those that have a specialty are noted in the comments; those without comments are general-purpose suppliers. All have catalogs; some are free, and others are available for a small fee.

Abundant Life Seed Foundation
Box 772
Port Townsend, WA 98368
206-385-7192
Open-pollinated and heirloom varieties

Bountiful Gardens
18001 Shafer Ranch Road
Willits, CA 95490
707-459-6410
Open-pollinated and heirloom varieties

Burgess Seed & Plant Co.
905 Four Seasons Road
Bloomington, IL 61701
309-663-9551

W. Atlee Burpee Co.
300 Park Avenue
Warminster, PA 18974
800-888-1447 fax: 800-674-4170

The Cook's Garden
Box 535
Londonderry, VT 05148
802-824-3400 fax: 802-824-3027
International, mostly European varieties

Evergreen Y. H. Enterprises
Box 17538
Anahiem, CA 92817
Asian vegetable seed only

Henry Field's Seed & Nursery Co.
415 North Burnett
Shenandoah, IA 51602
605-665-9391 fax: 605-665-2601

Filaree Farms
Route 2, Box 182
Concunully Highway
Okanogan, WA 98840
Garlic only—64 varieties

Fox Hollow Herb & Heirloom Seed Co.
Box 148
McGrann, PA 16236
Heirloom varieties

Garden City Seeds, Inc.
778 Highway 93 North
Hamilton, MT 59840
406-961-4837 fax: 406-961-4877
Vegetables for northern gardens

Gardener's Supply Co.
128 Intervale Road
Burlington, VT 05401
800-863-1700
Supplies for vegetable gardeners, including frost protection supplies

Gleckler's Seedmen
Metamora, OH 43540
Unusual vegetable varieties; huge sizes, strange colors and shapes

The Good Earth Seed Co./ Tsang & Ma
Box 5644
Redwood City, CA 94063
Asian varieties only, mostly Chinese

The Gourmet Gardener
8650 College Boulevard
Overland Park, KS 66210
913-345-0490
International, mostly European varieties

Gurney's Seed & Nursery Co.
110 Capital Street
Yankton, SD 57079
605-665-1671 fax: 605-665-9718

Harris Seeds
60 Saginaw Drive
Box 22960
Rochester, NY 14692-2960
716-442-0100 fax: 716-442-9386

High Altitude Gardens
Box 1048
Hailey, ID 83333
208-788-4363 fax: 208-788-3452
Short-season varieties

Johnny's Selected Seeds
Foss Hill Road
Albion, ME 04910-9731
207-437-4301

J. W. Jung Seed Co.
Foss Hill Road
Albion, ME 04910
800-247-JUNG

Kilgore Seed Co.
1400 West First Street
Sanford, FL 32771
407-323-6630
Varieties for tropical climates

D. Landreth Seed Co.
Box 6246
Baltimore, MD 21230
800-654-2407 fax: 410-244-8633
Heritage varieties

Le Champion Heritage Seeds
Box 1602
Freedom, CA 95019-1602
408-724-5870
Heritage varieties

Le Jardin du Gourmet
Box 75
St. Johnsbury Center, VT 05863-0075
800-659-1446 fax: 802-748-9592
French varieties

Lockhart Seeds
Box 1361
Stockton, CA 95201
209-466-4401
Varieties for western climates

Native Seeds
2509 N. Campbell Avenue #325
Tucson, AZ 85719
*Southwest Native American
varieties only*

Nichols Garden Nursery
1190 North Pacific Highway
Albany, OR 97321
503-928-9280 fax: 503-967-8406

Ontario Seed Co., Ltd.
Box 144
Waterloo, ON N2J 3Z9
Canada
519-886-0557 fax: 519-886-0605

P & P Seed Co.
14050 Gowanda State Road
Collins, NY 14034
716-532-5995
Giant vegetable varieties only

George W. Park Seed Co., Inc.
Kokesbury Road
Greenwood, SC 29647-0001
800-845-3369

The Pepper Gal
Box 23006
Fort Lauderdale, FL 33311
305-537-5540 fax: 305-566-2208
*Hot, sweet, and ornamental
peppers only*

Pinetree Garden Seeds
Box 300
New Gloucester, ME 04260
207-926-3400 fax: 207-926-3886
*Small, inexpensive packets for
small gardens*

Redwood City Seed Co.
Box 361
Redwood City, CA 94064
415-325-7333
Ethnic and imported varieties

**Ripley's Believe It or Not
  Seed Catalog**
521 Riverside Avenue
Westport, CT 06880
203-454-1919

Rocky Mountain Seed Co.
Box 5204
Denver, CO 80217
303-623-6223
Varieties for the West

Ronniger's Seed Potatoes
Star Route
Moyie Springs, ID 83845
*Potatoes only; dozens of modern
and heirloom varieties*

Seeds of Change
Box 15700
Santa Fe, NM 87506-5700
505-438-8080 fax: 505-438-7052
*Organically grown heirloom and
Native American varieties*

Seeds West
Box 27057
Albuquerque, NM 87125-7057
505-242-7474
*Varieties for western climates
and soil*

Shepherd's Garden Seeds
6116 Highway 9
Felton, CA 95018
408-335-6910 fax: 408-335-2080
*International, mostly European
varieties*

R. H. Shumway, Seedsman
Box 1
Graniteville, SC 29829
803-663-9771 fax: 803-663-9772
*Open-pollinated and heirloom
varieties*

Southern Exposure Seed Exchange
Box 170
Earlysville, VA 22936
804-973-4703 fax: 804-973-4703
*Open-pollinated and heirloom
varieties*

Southern Seeds
Box 2091
Melbourne, FL 32902
407-727-3662
Hot-weather varieties

Stokes Seeds
Box 548
Buffalo, NY 14240-0548
716-695-6980 fax: 716-695-9649

Sunrise Enterprises
Box 330058
West Hartford, CT 06133-0058
Asian varieties only, mostly Chinese

Territorial Seed Co.
Box 157
Cottage Grove, OR 97424
541-942-9547 fax: 541-942-9881
*Varieties adapted to the Pacific
Northwest*

Thompson & Morgan
Box 1308
Jackson, NJ 08527
800-274-7333 fax: 908-363-9356

Tomato Growers Supply Co.
Box 2237
Fort Meyers, FL 33902
813-768-1119 fax: 813-768-3476
*Tomatoes and peppers only, special-
izing in tomatoes (220 varieties!)*

Vermont Bean Seed Co.
11 Garden Lane
Bomoseen, VT 05732
802-273-3400
Short-season varieties

Vesey's Seeds, Ltd.
From the United States:
Box 9000
Calais, ME 04619-6102
800-363-7333 fax: 902-566-1620
From Canada:
Box 9000
Charlottetown, PEI C1A 8K6
Short-season varieties

Willhite Seed Co.
Box 23
Poolville, TX 76487
817-599-8656 fax: 817-599-5843
Melons

CLIMATE ZONE MAP

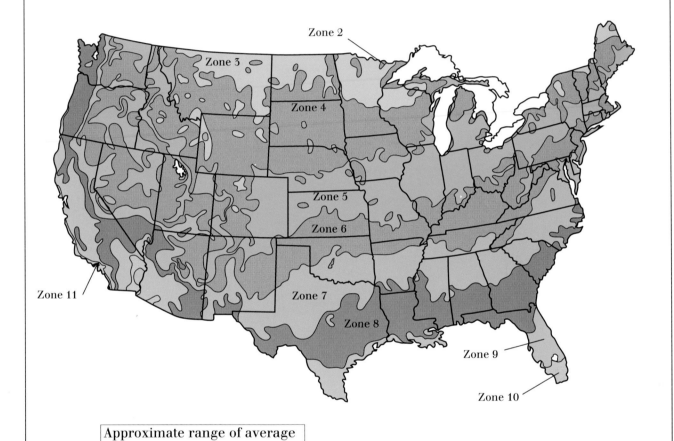

Zone 2
Zone 3
Zone 4
Zone 5
Zone 6
Zone 11
Zone 7
Zone 8
Zone 9
Zone 10

Approximate range of average annual minimum temperature for each zone.	
Zone 1	Below –50° F
Zone 2	–50° F to –40° F
Zone 3	–40° F to –30° F
Zone 4	–30° F to –20° F
Zone 5	–20° F to –10° F
Zone 6	–10° F to 0° F
Zone 7	0° F to 10° F
Zone 8	10° F to 20° F
Zone 9	20° F to 30° F
Zone 10	30° F to 40° F
Zone 11	Above 40° F

Based on the 1990 USDA Climate Zone Map.

Oregano
ornamental, 'Kent
Beauty', 168
see also Marjoram
Origanum
compacta nana
(creeping dwarf
marjoram), 166
O. heracleoticum (pot
marjoram; winter
sweet marjoram),
166
O. hirtum. See
Marjoram, pot
O. majorana (sweet
marjoram), 166
O. vulgare (oregano;
wild marjoram), 166
Ortho Problem Solver,
The, 98
Oven, drying vegetables
in, 86

P

Pak-choi (bok choy; pac
choi; pok choi). *See*
Chinese mustard
Parsley, 170–72
Chinese. *See* Cilantro
cultivars
'Bartowich Long', 172
'Catalogno', 172
'Champion Moss
Curled', 171
'Clivi', 171
'Darki', 171
'Forest Green', 171
'Frisca Curly', 171
'Giant Italian', 172
'Gigante d'Italia'
('Italian
Heirloom'), 172
'Italian Flat Dark
Green', 172
'Italian' ('Flat
Parsley'), 171
'Krausa', 171
'Moss Curled'
('Double Curled'),
170, 171
'Moss Curled Forest
Green', 171
'Omega', 172
'Pagoda', 171
'Single-Leaf Italian
Parsley', 172
'Triple Curled', 171
French. *See* Chervil
Green Rice with, 171
root, 172

Parsnips, 82, 247–49
cultivars
'Cobham Improved
Marrow', *248,* 249
'Harris Model', 249
'Hollow Crown', 249
'Lander', 249
Honey-Orange, 249
Pazote, 156
Pazote, Jerusalem oak.
See Epazote
Pea enation, 62
Peanuts, 249–50
cultivars
'Jumbo Virginia', *249,*
250
'Spanish Peanut
Improved', 250
'Tennessee Red', 250
Sauce, with Crudités,
250
"Peanuts," foam packing,
for containers, 29
Peas
black-eyed. *See*
Cowpeas
garden (English peas),
237–39
cultivars
'Alaska', 239
'Green Arrow', *84,*
239
'Knight', 239
'Little Marvel', 239
'Montana Marvel',
239
'Wando', 239
with Lettuce and
Mint, 239
southern. *See* Cowpeas
sugar snap (snap pea),
239
cultivars
'Sugar Ann', 239
'Sugar Bon', 239
'Sugar Daddy', 239
'Sugar Snap', 239
'Super Sugar Mel',
238, 239
sugar (snow peas), 239
cultivars
'Chinese Snow',
239
'Dwarf Gray
Sugar', 239
'Oregon Sugar Pod
II', 239
Peat moss, 36, 41
Peat pellet, for seeds,
69–70, 75

Peat pots, seeds in,
69–70, 75
Peppergrass. *See* Cress,
curly
Peppers, 120–26
bell, 120–21
cultivars
'Bell Boy', 125
'Big Bertha',
124–25
'Cadice', 124
'Cubanelle', 124
'Golden Cal
Wonder', 125
'Golden Summer',
125, *126*
'Gypsy', 125
'Lilac Belle', 125
'New Ace', 124
'Orange Belle', 125
'Orobelle', 125
'Park's Early
Thickset', 124
'Purple Bell', 126
'Red California
Wonder', 125
'Redskin Hybrid',
124
'Sweet Banana',
125, *125*
'Sweet Chocolate',
125
'Vanguard', 124,
124
'Yolo Wonder', 125
and Tomato Salad,
123
Oven-Roasted, with
Vegetables, Rose-
mary, and Garlic, 124
to roast, 123
seeds, to collect, *89*
see also Chiles;
Pimientos
Perennials, 289
container-grown, 29, 67
planting season for,
66–67
Perlite, 36
Pesticides, use of, 96–97
Pests
integrated manage-
ment of (IPM),
96–103
seeds resistant to, 62
Pe-tsai. *See* Chinese
cabbage
Phosphorus (P), 42, 49
PH reaction, 32, 34–36
to test, *35*

Physalis
ixocarpa (tomatillo),
285–87
P. peruviana (husk
tomato), 285–87
P. pruinosa (ground
cherry), 286
Pimientos, 121
cultivars
'Pimiento Perfection',
126
'Pimiento Select', 126
Pimpinella anisum (anise;
aniseed), 140–41
Pine needles, for
mulch, 36
Planter
redwood, 29
self-watering, 51, 55
Planting, 9
seasons for, 64–68
succession, 20–21
Plants
attracting beneficial
insects (*list*), 97
names of, 59
repelling insects
(*list*), 98
watering established,
50–51
Plastic
for frost protection,
75, 80
as mulch, 41–42
Pockets, seeds in, 75
Poha berry. *See* Ground
cherry
Polymers. *See* gel
Popcorn, 277, 278, 279
cultivars
'Baby Blue', 281
'Mini Blue', 281
'Mini Pink', 281
'Robust 20-82 W', 281
'Tom Thumb', 281
'White Cloud F1', 281
Molasses, 279
Potassium (K)
in soil, 36, 42
vegetables for dietary, 7
Potatoes, 251–54
cultivars
'All Blue', *252,* 254
'Blossom', 254
'Butte', 254
'Caribe', 254
'Giant Peanut
Fingerlings', 254
'Katahdin', *251,* 254
'Kennebec', 254
'Lavender', 254
'Norland', *253,* 254

U.S. MEASURE AND METRIC MEASURE CONVERSION CHART

		Formulas for Exact Measures			Rounded Measures for Quick Reference		
	Symbol	When you know:	Multiply by:	To find:			
Mass (weight)	oz	ounces	28.35	grams	1 oz		= 3 0 g
	lb	pounds	0.45	kilograms	4 oz		= 115 g
	g	grams	0.035	ounces	8 oz		= 225 g
	kg	kilograms	2.2	pounds	16 oz	= 1 lb	= 450 g
					32 oz	= 2 lb	= 900 g
					36 oz	= 2¼ lb	= 1000 g (1 kg)
Volume	pt	pints	0.47	liters	1 c	= 8 oz	= 250 ml
	qt	quarts	0.95	liters	2 c (1 pt)	= 16 oz	= 500 ml
	gal	gallons	3.785	liters	4 c (1 qt)	= 32 oz	= 1 liter
	ml	milliliters	0.034	fluid ounces	4 qt (1 gal)	= 128 oz	= 3¾ liter
Length	in.	inches	2.54	centimeters	⅜ in.		= 1.0 cm
	ft	feet	30.48	centimeters	1 in.		= 2.5 cm
	yd	yards	0.9144	meters	2 in.		= 5.0 cm
	mi	miles	1.609	kilometers	2½ in.		= 6.5 cm
	km	kilometers	0.621	miles	12 in. (1 ft)		= 30.0 cm
	m	meters	1.094	yards	1 yd		= 90.0 cm
	cm	centimeters	0.39	inches	100 ft		= 30.0 m
					1 mi		= 1.6 km
Temperature	° F	Fahrenheit	⅝ (after subtracting 32)	Celsius	32° F		= 0° C
	° C	Celsius	⅘ (then add 32)	Fahrenheit	212° F		= 100° C
Area	in.²	square inches	6.452	square centimeters	1 in.²		= 6.5 cm²
	ft²	square feet	929.0	square centimeters	1 ft²		= 930 cm²
	yd²	square yards	8361.0	square centimeters	1 yd²		= 8360 cm²
	a.	acres	0.4047	hectares	1 a.		= 4050 m²